Barcelona

"All you've got to do is decide to go
and the hardest part is over.

So go!"

TONY WHEELER, COFOUNDER – LONELY PLANET

D0036830

THIS EDITION WRITTEN AND RESEARCHED BY
Regis St Louis, Sally Davies

Contents

(left) **La Sagrada Família p121** Witness Gaudí's unfinished masterpiece.

(above) **Park Güell p152** Explore vibrant mosaics.

(right) **Markets p32** Enjoy an array of fresh produce.

Gràcia & Park Güell (p150)

Camp Nou, Pedralbes & La Zona Alta (p162)

Barceloneta & the Waterfront (p105)

La Sagrada Família & L'Eixample (p119)

La Ribera (p88)

La Rambla & Barri Gòtic (p52)

El Raval (p75)

Montjuïc, Poble Sec & Sant Antoni (p173)

Welcome to Barcelona

Barcelona is an enchanting seaside city with boundless culture, fabled architecture, and a world-class drinking and dining scene.

A Moveable Feast

The masters of molecular gastronomy – Albert Adrià, Carles Abellan et al – are part of the long and celebrated tradition of Catalan cooking. Simple, flavourful ingredients – seafood, *jamón* (cured ham), market-fresh produce – are transformed into remarkable delicacies and then served in captivating settings. Feast on hearty, rich paella at an outdoor table overlooking the sea or step back to the 1920s at an elegant art nouveau-filled dining room. Barcelona's wide-ranging palate adds further complexity: Basque-style tapas bars, Galician seafood taverns, avant-garde Japanese restaurants and sinful chocolate shops are all essential parts of the culinary landscape.

Architecture of the Ages

Barcelona's architectural treasures span 2000-plus years. Towering temple columns, ancient city walls and subterranean stone corridors provide a window into Roman-era Barcino. Fast forward a thousand years to the Middle Ages by taking a stroll through the shadowy lanes of the Gothic quarter, past tranquil plazas and soaring 14th-century cathedrals. In other parts of town bloom the sculptural masterpieces of Modernisme, a mix of ingenious and whimsical creations by Gaudí and his Catalan architectural contemporaries.

Under the Iberian Sun

The deep blue Mediterranean beckons. Sun-drenched beaches make a fine backdrop to a jog, bike ride or long leisurely stroll along the seaside – followed by a refreshing dip. Looming behind the city, the rolling forest-covered Collserola Hills provide a scenic setting for hiking, mountain biking or just admiring the view. Closer to the city centre, hilltop Montjuïc offers endless exploring amid botanic and sculpture gardens, an old castle and first-rate museums with panoramic views at every turn.

Twenty-Four Hour Party People

The night holds limitless possibilities in Barcelona. Start with sunset drinks from a panoramic terrace or dig your heels in the sand at a rustic beachside *chiringuito*. As darkness falls, live music transforms the city: the rapid-fire rhythms of flamenco, brassy jazz spilling out of basements, and hands-in-the-air indie-rock at vintage concert halls. Towards midnight the bars fill. Take your pick from old-school taverns adorned with 19th-century murals, plush lounges in lamp-lit medieval chambers or boisterous cava bars. If you're still standing at 3am, hit the clubs and explore Barcelona's unabashed wild side.

Why I Love Barcelona

By Regis St Louis, Writer

I love the sea, and taking an early-morning jog along the Mediterranean is my favourite way to start the day. I'm also a bit of a history nerd, and relish strolling the cobblestone lanes of the Gothic quarter, thinking about the people in past centuries who walked these streets. Then there's the food and drink – the first-rate tapas bars, the abundant and inexpensive wine, the superb and reasonably priced multicourse lunches. Add Catalan creativity (Modernisme, Miró, Dalí), bohemian bars and stunning nearby getaways and you have, quite simply, one of the world's most captivating cities.

For more about our writers, see p288.

Barcelona's
Top 10

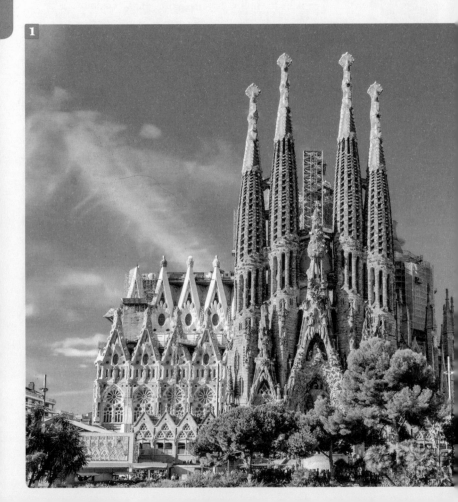

La Sagrada Família *(p121)*

1 One of Barcelona's icons, the Modernista masterpiece remains a work in progress more than 90 years after the death of its creator, Antoni Gaudí. Fanciful and profound, inspired by nature and barely restrained by the Gothic style, Barcelona's quirky temple soars skyward with a playful majesty. Stepping through its sculpted portals is like walking into a fairy tale, where a forest of columns branch towards the ceiling and light shimmers through brilliant stained-glass windows. Rich with beautifully wrought detail and packed with symbols, the basilica invites hours of contemplation.

👁 *La Sagrada Família & L'Eixample*

New Catalan Cuisine *(p31)*

2 Barcelona's most celebrated chefs blend traditional Catalan recipes with new cooking techniques to create deliciously inventive masterpieces. Leading the way are Albert Adrià, the molecular gastronomy whiz behind a growing empire of restaurants, and Carles Abellan, who elevated the humble tapas to high art in restaurants such as Tapas 24 (p124). The result: Barcelona has become one of the world's great culinary destinations. No matter where you go in the city, you won't be far from a memorable meal. And the critics agree: the city has two dozen Michelin-starred restaurants.

FERRAN AND ALBERT ADRIÀ'S TAPAS BAR, TICKETS (P184)

🍴 *Eating*

ALEPIYEGOROV/GETTY IMAGES ©

RANDOLPH IMAGES/ALAMY STOCK PHOTO ©

Museu Picasso (p90)

3 For a portrait of the artist as a young man, head to the Museu Picasso, which showcases perhaps the world's best collection of the master's early work. Picasso lived in Barcelona between the ages of 15 and 23, and elements of the city undoubtedly influenced his work, from the colourful but simply painted frescoes hanging in the Museu Nacional d'Art de Catalunya to the imaginative *trencadís*-style mosaics (pre-Cubist some say) of Gaudí. The museum's setting – inside five contiguous medieval mansions – adds to the appeal. *LAS MENINAS* ROOM

⊙ *La Ribera*

Modernista Architecture (p142)

4 Few cities are defined by their architecture to quite the same extent as Barcelona. The weird and wonderful undulations of Antoni Gaudí's creations are echoed in countless Modernista flights of fancy across the city. Visiting these masterpieces is like entering a fairy tale. You'll find shimmering mosaics, wild details (in stained glass, iron, ceramic) and sculptural elements that reference nature, mythology and medieval days. Gateway to these astonishing architectural works is L'Eixample, which was a blank canvas for some of Spain's finest buildings in the late 19th and early 20th centuries. PARK GÜELL (P152)

⊙ *Antoni Gaudí & Modernisme*

Magical Montjuïc (p173)

5 When the temperature rises, head up the hill of Montjuïc for fresh air and breathtaking views over the city, best enjoyed from the dizzy heights of one of its cable cars. At any time of year it makes for a great day out, with endless parkland, themed gardens and museums to suit every taste, whether your fire is lit by sport, art or ancient remains. If you have kids in tow, meanwhile, the kitsch wonderland of the Poble Espanyol is a must.

⊙ *Montjuïc, Poble Sec & Sant Antoni*

Mercat de la Boqueria (p77)

6 This temple of temptation is one of Europe's greatest permanent produce fairs. Restaurant chefs, homemakers, office workers and tourists all stroll amid the seemingly endless bounty of glistening fruits and vegetables, gleaming fish counters, dangling rolls of smoked meats, pyramids of pungent cheeses, barrels full of olives and marinated peppers, and chocolate truffles and other sweets. In the back, a handful of popular tapas bars serve up delectable morsels. There's always a line, but it's well worth the wait.

✖ *El Raval*

La Catedral (p58)

7 A masterpiece of Catalan Gothic architecture, La Catedral is rightly one of the first stops on any visit to the Ciutat Vella (Old City). You can wander wide-eyed through the shadow-filled interior, with a dozen well-concealed chapels, an eerie crypt and a curious garden-style cloister that's home to 13 geese (which are deeply connected with the mythology of Barcelona's co-patron saint, Santa Eulàlia). Outside, there's always entertainment afoot, from *sardana* dancing on weekends to periodic processions and open-air markets, and street musicians are never far from the scene.

◉ *La Rambla & Barri Gòtic*

Strolling La Rambla *(p54)*

8 Sure it's the most touristy spot in town. But you can't come to Barcelona and not take the 1.2km stroll down the famous pedestrian boulevard that stretches towards the sea. It's pure sensory overload – with a parade of people amid open-air cafes, fragrant flower stands, a much-overlooked mosaic by Miró and the rather surreal human sculptures. Key venues line both sides of the street, including the elegant Gran Teatre del Liceu, the sprawling Mercat de la Boqueria and several major galleries.

◉ *La Rambla & Barri Gòtic*

Nightlife in Sant Antoni *(p184)*

9 Barcelona is a city known for reinvention, but none of its neighbourhoods has seen a regeneration as dramatic as that of the unremarkable grid of streets around the splendid old Mercat Sant Antoni. It started with the tentative opening of a couple of hip cafes on Carrer del Parlament, but over the last couple of years this has bloomed into a lively strip of bars and restaurants, with an influx of hipster pleasure-seekers and entrepreneurs, and this in turn has kick-started a slew of openings in surrounding streets. BAR CALDERS (P184)

🍷 *Montjuïc, Poble Sec & Sant Antoni*

Camp Nou *(p164)*

10 For the sports-minded, little can compete with the spectacle of a match at FC Barcelona's massive football stadium. With a loyal fan base and an incredibly gifted team led by the likes of Lionel Messi, Camp Nou always hosts a good show – even if you can't make it to a game, it's still worth visiting. The 'Camp Nou Experience' is an interactive museum and stadium tour that takes you through the locker rooms and out onto the pitch, hallowed ground for many Catalans.

⚽ *Camp Nou, Pedralbes & La Zona Alta*

What's New

Craft Makers

At long last, microbreweries have arrived in Barcelona, bringing an abundance of craft beer bars in their wake. You're never far from a unique IPA, no matter where you roam.

The New Wave Stay

One of Barcelona's best new boutique hotels has opened recently, and its focus isn't on luxury. The Hotel Brummell is about soul, creativity and connecting with the neighbourhood treasures in Poble Sec. (p206)

Architecture After Hours

There's a new way to experience the Modernista masterpiece of La Pedrera: on an evening tour with a surreal audiovisual show on the rooftop, followed by Champagne in the courtyard. (p128)

The Epicentre of Design

After years in the works, the Museu del Disseny de Barcelona has opened, with four floors of beautifully lit exhibits covering graphic design, textiles, fashion and ceramics. The museum also stages thought-provoking temporary shows. (p110)

Surfing with a Paddle

The increasingly popular sport for beach goers is gliding along on a stand-up paddle board (SUP). Outfitters in Barceloneta hire out gear, and you can take a lesson if you've never tried.

The Meat-Free Revolution

Vegetarians and mindful eaters need not give Barcelona a pass when planning their next holiday. The city has seen an explosion of healthy animal-free eateries in recent years (and even vegan clothing shops). (p159)

Sant Antoni on the Rise

If you're looking for the newest creative spaces (cafes, eateries, clothing boutiques), head to Sant Antoni, the hipster epicentre of Barcelona.

Poblenou Renaissance

This formerly industrial 'hood is on the make, with new galleries, colourful shops and restaurants forming the intersection for the creative tech and design folk who are increasingly moving here.

Hiroshima, Mon Amour

Barcelona continues to be an arts innovator. Spaces like Hiroshima, which opened in 2015, offer a wide-ranging repertoire of cutting-edge dance, music and multidisciplinary works. (p186)

Adrià's Culinary Kingdom

Famed chef Albert Adrià now runs five celebrated restaurants (including Tickets), all within strolling distance of one another in Sant Antoni. A sixth, Enigma, opens in late 2016. (www.elbarriadria.com; p184)

Foodie Focus

Some of the most talked-about restaurants in the city aren't the old-guard Michelin-starred places, but unique, artfully designed spaces in Poble Sec, where non-celebrity chefs are creating extraordinary dishes.

For more recommendations and reviews, see **lonelyplanet. com/spain/barcelona**

Need to Know

For more information, see Survival Guide (p231)

Currency
Euro (€)

Languages
Spanish, Catalan

Visas
Generally not required for stays of up to 90 days per 180 days (visas are not required at all for members of EU or Schengen countries). Some nationalities need a Schengen visa.

Money
ATMs are widely available (La Rambla has many). Credit cards are accepted in most hotels, shops and restaurants.

Mobile Phones
Local SIM cards can be used in unlocked European and Australian phones. Other phones must be set to roaming.

Time
Central European Time (GMT/ UTC plus one hour)

Tourist Information
Oficina d'Informació de Turisme de Barcelona (☑93 285 38 34; www.barcelonaturisme.com; Plaça de Catalunya 17; ⊙9.30am-9.30pm; ⓂCatalunya) provides maps; sights information; tours; concert and events tickets; and last-minute accommodation.

Daily Costs

Budget: Less than €60
➡ Dorm bed: €17–28
➡ Set lunch: from €10
➡ Bicycle hire per hour: €5

Midrange: €60–200
➡ Standard double room: €80–140
➡ Two-course dinner with wine for two: €50
➡ Walking and guided tours: €15–25

Top End: More than €200
➡ Double room in boutique and luxury hotels: €200 and up
➡ Multicourse meal at top restaurants per person: €80
➡ Concert tickets to Palau de la Música Catalana: around €50

Advance Planning

Three months before Book accommodation and reserve a table at a top restaurant.

One month before Check out reviews for theatre and live music and book tickets.

One week before Browse the latest nightlife listings, art exhibitions and other events to attend while in town. Reserve spa visits and organised tours.

A few days before Check the forecast on weather.com.

Useful Websites
➡ **Barcelona** (www.bcn.cat) Town hall's official site with plenty of links.
➡ **Barcelona Turisme** (www.barcelonaturisme.com) City's official tourism website.
➡ **Lonely Planet** (www.lonelyplanet.com) Destination information, hotel bookings, traveller forum and more.
➡ **BCN Mes** (www.bcnmes.com) Trilingal monthly mag of culture, food, art and more.
➡ **Spotted by Locals** (www.spottedbylocals.com) Insider tips.

WHEN TO GO

Summer (July and August) is peak tourist season, when crowds swarm the city. For pleasant weather come in late spring (May).

°C/°F **Temp**
Rainfall Inches/mm

Arriving in Barcelona

El Prat airport Frequent *aero-búses* make the 35-minute run into town (€5.90) from 6am to 1am. Taxis cost around €25.

Estació Sants Long-distance trains arrive at this big station near the centre of town, which is linked by metro to other parts of the city.

Estació del Nord Barcelona's long-haul bus station is located in L'Eixample, about 1.5km northeast of Plaça de Catalunya, and is a short walk from several metro stations.

Girona-Costa Brava airport The 'Barcelona Bus' operated by Sagalés (one way/return €16/25, 90 minutes) is timed with Ryanair flights and goes direct to Barcelona's Estació del Nord.

Reus airport Buses operated by Hispano-Igualadina (one way/return €16/25, 90 minutes) are timed with Ryanair flights and go direct to Barcelona's Estació Sants.

For much more on **arrival** see p232

Getting Around

Barcelona has abundant options for getting around town. The excellent metro can get you most places, with buses and trams filling in the gaps. Taxis are the best option late at night.

➡ **Metro** The most convenient option. Runs 5am to midnight Sunday to Thursday, till 2am on Friday and 24 hours on Saturday. Targeta T-10 (10-ride passes; €10.30) are the best value; otherwise, it's €2.15 per ride.

➡ **Bus** A hop-on, hop-off Bus Turístic (p237), from Plaça de Catalunya, is handy for those wanting to see the city's highlights in one or two days.

➡ **Taxi** You can hail taxis on the street (try La Rambla, Via Laietana, Plaça de Catalunya and Passeig de Gràcia) or at taxi stands.

➡ **On foot** To explore the old city, all you need is a good pair of walking shoes.

For much more on **getting around** see p233

Sleeping

Barcelona has a wide range of sleeping options, from inexpensive hostels hidden in the old quarter to luxury hotels overlooking the waterfront. The small-scale B&B-style apartment rentals scattered around the city are a good-value choice. Wherever you stay it's wise to book well ahead. If you plan to travel around holidays such as Christmas, New Year's eve and Easter, or in summer, reserve a room three or four months ahead of time.

Useful Websites

➡ **Lonely Planet** (www.lonelyplanet.com) Neighbourhood profiles, plus extensive listings of hotels, hostels, guesthouses and apartments.

➡ **Oh Barcelona** (www.oh-barcelona.com) Hotel and apartment listings, plus tips on deciding where to stay.

➡ **Barcelona Bed and Breakfasts** (www.barcelonabedandbreakfasts.com) Listings of low-key, oft-overlooked lodging options.

For much more on **sleeping** see p198

First Time Barcelona

For more information, see Survival Guide (p231)

Checklist

➡ Check all airline flight prices before booking a ticket.

➡ Find out if you can use your phone in Spain and ask about roaming charges.

➡ Book your first nights accommodation to ensure an easy start to your stay.

➡ Check the calendar to figure out which festivals to attend or avoid.

➡ Organise travel insurance.

What to Pack

➡ Passport and/or national ID card (EU citizens)

➡ Driving licence

➡ Phrasebook

➡ Money belt

➡ Mobile phone (and charger)

➡ Earplugs for noisy weekend nights

➡ Walking shoes

➡ Reading material (try page-turners by Carlos Ruiz Zafón or Manuel Vázquez Montalbán)

➡ Rain jacket or umbrella

Top Tips for Your Trip

➡ Plan your visiting times to avoid the worst of the crowds. Go early in the morning or late in the day for the top Gaudí sites and the Museu Picasso.

➡ When possible, book tickets online. This will allow you to bypass the queues.

➡ Be mindful of siesta time (generally 1pm to 4pm). Plan your shopping for mornings or early evenings.

➡ Travel smart; keep valuables tucked away and out of sight. Pickpocketing is a concern in busy, touristy areas.

➡ Save time and money on public transport by purchasing 10-ride passes (10-Targeta), which can be used on the metro, buses and funicular.

➡ Take advantage of multi-course lunch specials. These are offered by many restaurants, and are often great value.

What to Wear

In Barcelona just about anything goes, and you'll rarely feel uncomfortable because of what you're wearing. That said, Catalans are fairly fashion conscious and well dressed. Most folks dress smart casual, with something perhaps a bit dressier if going somewhere special for the evening.

If you're planning on clubbing, bring something stylish (T-shirts, sandals or sneakers are no-go). Meanwhile, La Catedral advertises a policy of no admittance to those in sleeveless tops and shorts. The rule isn't always enforced, but it's best not to take the risk.

Be Forewarned

➡ Violent crime is rare in Barcelona, but petty crime (bag-snatching, pickpocketing) is a major problem.

➡ You're at your most vulnerable when dragging around luggage to or from your hotel; make sure you know your route before arriving.

➡ Be mindful of your belongings, particularly in crowded areas.

Money

ATMs are widespread and most allow you to use international debit or credit cards to withdraw money in euros. Remember that there is usually a charge (around 1.5% to 2%) on ATM cash withdrawals abroad.

Credit cards are widely accepted throughout Spain, although there may be a minimum purchase requirement of €5 or €10.

When paying with a credit card, a photo ID is often required, even for chip cards where you're required to enter your PIN (for US travellers without chip cards, just indicate that you'll give a signature).

For more information, see p238.

Taxes & Refunds

Value-added tax (VAT) is a 21% sales tax levied on most goods and services. For restaurants and hotels it's 10%. Most restaurants include VAT in their prices; it's usually included in hotel-room prices, too, but be sure to ask when booking.

Tipping

➡ **Restaurants** Catalans typically leave 5% or less at restaurants. Leave more for exceptionally good service.

➡ **Taxis** Optional, but most locals round up to the nearest euro.

➡ **Bars** It's rare to leave a tip in bars, though a bit of small change is always appreciated.

Plaça Reial (p62)

Etiquette

Barcelona is fairly relaxed with it comes to etiquette. A few basics to remember:

➡ **Greetings** Catalans, like other Spaniards, usually greet friends and strangers alike with a kiss on both cheeks, although two males rarely do this. Foreigners may be excused.

➡ **Eating & Drinking** Waiters won't expect you to thank them every time they bring you something, but in more casual restaurants and bars they will expect you to keep your cutlery between courses.

➡ **Visiting Churches** It is considered disrespectful to visit churches as a tourist during Mass and other worship services. Taking photos at such times is a definite no-no.

➡ **Escalators** Always stand on the right to let people pass, especially when using the metro.

Language

English is widely spoken in Barcelona. Even Catalans with only a few English words are generally happy to try them out. Learning a little Spanish before you come will greatly enhance your experience, not least in your ability to converse with locals. Even better if you can learn some Catalan.

English signage is available at most museums (though not all). Many restaurants have English-language menus, though simpler places may have them only in Spanish and Catalan.

Top Itineraries

Day One

La Rambla & Barri Gòtic (p52)

 On day one spend the morning exploring the narrow medieval lanes of the Barri Gòtic. Have a peek inside **La Catedral** – not missing its geese-filled cloister – and stroll through the picturesque squares of **Plaça de Sant Josep Oriol** and **Plaça Reial**. Discover Barcelona's ancient roots in the fascinating **Museu d'Història de Barcelona**. Before lunch have a wander down La Rambla to take in the passing people parade.

> **Lunch** The beautifully designed Federal (p68) whips up delicious fare.

La Ribera (p88)

In the afternoon, wander over to La Ribera, which is packed with architectural treasures. Have a look inside the majestic **Basílica de Santa Maria del Mar**. At the **Museu Picasso**, beautifully set inside conjoined medieval mansions, you can spend a few hours taking in the early works of one of the great artists of the 20th century.

> **Dinner** Sample tapas with global accents at creative El Atril (p98).

La Ribera (p88)

Before having a late dinner (as is the custom in Spain), catch a show inside the **Palau de la Música Catalana**, one of the great Modernista masterpieces of Barcelona. Afterwards end the night with tropically infused libations at candlelit **Rubí**.

Day Two

L'Eixample (p119)

On day two start with a morning visit to **La Sagrada Família**, Gaudí's wondrous work in progress. It's worth paying a little extra for a guided tour (or audioguide) for a deeper understanding of Barcelona's most famous sight.

> **Lunch** Celebrated Disfrutar (p132) produces an imaginative Catalan feast.

L'Eixample (p119)

After lunch, explore more of the great Modernista buildings by taking a stroll down L'Eixample's **Passeig de Gràcia**. Have a look at the three most famous buildings that make up the **Manzana de la Discordia**. Then visit one of Gaudí's house museums on the street – either **Casa Batlló** or **La Pedrera** further up the avenue.

> **Dinner** Enjoy excellent wines and tasty sharing plates at Viblioteca (p157).

Camp Nou, Pedralbes & La Zona Alta (p162)

In the evening catch a football match at **Camp Nou**, the home of the top-ranked FC Barcelona. Amid the roar of the crowds, prepare for a serious adrenaline rush, especially if Barça is playing arch-rival Real Madrid. Afterwards explore lesser-known gems in the area, like the plaza-side **El Maravillas** (great for tapas and drinks) or **Bangkok Cafe**, serving Barcelona's best Thai dishes.

Day Three

Barceloneta, Port Oímpic & the Waterfront (p105)

 On your third day in Barcelona it's time to take in the lovely Mediterranean. Start the morning with a stroll, jog or a bike ride along the waterfront. Beach-facing restaurants and cafes provide refreshment along the way.

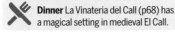 **Lunch** Go early to snag a table at tiny La Cova Fumada (p111).

Barceloneta, Port Olímpic & the Waterfront (p105)

Stroll through Barceloneta, stopping for a peek inside the **Mercat de la Barceloneta** and for pastries at **Baluard**. Afterwards visit the **Museu d'Història de Catalunya** and peel back the centuries on an interactive journey into Catalan history.

Dinner La Vinateria del Call (p68) has a magical setting in medieval El Call.

La Rambla & Barri Gòtic (p52)

At night catch a live band inside the Gothic quarter. **Harlem Jazz Club** and **Jamboree** are good bets for jazz and world music. If you still have energy, check out a few bars more off the beaten track, like **L'Ascensor**, a cosy drinking den with nicely mixed cocktails and a more grown-up crowd than other parts of Barri Gòtic.

Day Four

Montjuïc (p173)

 Start the day with a scenic cable-car ride up to Montjuïc, followed by a stroll past flower and sculpture gardens to the **Museu Nacional d'Art de Catalunya (MNAC)**. Take in the magnificent Romanesque frescos, vivid Gothic paintings and works by 17th-century Spanish masters.

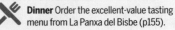 **Lunch** Pepa Tomate (p156) is a neighbourhood charmer on a peaceful square.

Gràcia (p150)

After getting a taste of Montjuïc, hop on the metro up to Gràcia and wander through its enchanting village-like streets. Cafes, bookshops and vintage shops all make for some worthwhile exploring. The bars surrounding its plazas come to life around sundown.

Dinner Order the excellent-value tasting menu from La Panxa del Bisbe (p155).

El Raval (p75)

Take in the bohemian side of Barcelona in El Raval. Browse record shops and vintage stores, check out a live band at the **Jazz Sí Club**, or watch an indie feature at the **Filmoteca de Catalunya**. Finish the night over a few housemade vermouths at **La Confitería**, or at dance favourite **Moog** for something livelier.

If You Like...

Markets

Els Encants Vells Sprawling flea market with plenty of treasures and trash on the edge of Poblenou. (p117)

Mercat de la Boqueria One of Europe's largest food markets, with tempting delicacies, plus tapas bars at the back. (p77)

Mercat de Sant Antoni A massive but largely tourist-free food market that also hosts a flea market on Sunday. (p186)

Mercat de Santa Caterina La Ribera's bountiful food market, with its wavy roof and archaeological fragments from the 1400s. (p95)

Mercadillo de la Plaça de Sant Josep Colourful collection of artworks sold by local artists on weekends in the Plaça de Sant Josep Oriol. (p62)

Port Antic Tiny weekend antiques market on the waterfront, at the foot of La Rambla. (p117)

Feria de Artesanía del Palau de Mar This waterfront market is a fine nautical place to browse for handicrafts and souvenirs. (p117)

Parks & Gardens

Parc de la Ciutadella Pretty landscaped grounds with dramatic fountain, curious artwork, the Catalan parliament building and a zoo. (p94)

Park Güell Green wonderland with fine views over the city, and surreal sculptural architecture courtesy of Gaudí. (p152)

CORNFIELD/SHUTTERSTOCK ©

Museu Nacional d'Art de Catalunya (MNAC; p175)

Top: Closing ceremony of Festes de la Mercè (p24)

Bottom: Pride Barcelona celebrations

around the city. It usually runs in late May or early June.

June

Tourist numbers are well on the rise as Barcelona plunges into summer. Live music festivals and open-air events give the month a festive air.

✷ Festival Pedralbes

This summertime fest (www.festivalpedralbes. com) takes place in lovely gardens and stages big-name performers (Pet Shop Boys, Carla Bruni, Kool & the Gang) from mid-June to early July.

☆ Festival Piknic Electronik

Every Sunday from late June through September, you can enjoy a day of electronic music (barcelona. piknicelectronik.com/en) at an outdoor space on Montjuïc. It attracts a mix of young families and party people.

✷ La Revetlla de Sant Joan

On 23 June locals hit the streets or hold parties at home to celebrate the Revetlla de Sant Joan (St John's Night), which involves drinking, dancing, bonfires and fireworks. In Spanish, it's called 'Verbenas de Sant Joan'.

✷ Pride Barcelona

The Barcelona Gay Pride festival (www.pridebarcelona.org) is a week of celebrations held late June or early July with a crammed program of culture and concerts, along with the traditional Gay Pride march on Sunday.

☆ Sónar

Usually in mid-June, Sónar (www.sonar.es) is Barcelona's massive celebration of electronic music, with DJs, exhibitions, sound labs, record fairs and urban art. Locations change each year.

July

Prices are high and it's peak tourist season, but it's a lively time to be in the city with sun-filled beach days, open-air dining and outdoor concerts.

Festival del Grec

The major cultural event of the summer is a month-long fest (grec.bcn.cat) with dozens of theatre, dance and music performances held around town, including at the Teatre Grec amphitheatre on Montjuïc, from which the festival takes its name.

August

The heat index soars; barcelonins leave the city in droves for summer holidays, as huge numbers of tourists arrive. It's a great time to hit the beach.

Festa Major de Gràcia

Locals compete for the most elaborately decorated street in this popular week-long Gràcia festival (www.festamajordegracia.cat) held around 15 August. The fest also features free outdoor concerts, street fairs and other events.

Festes de Sant Roc

For four days in mid-August, Plaça Nova in the Barri Gòtic becomes the scene of parades, the *correfoc* (fire runs), a market, traditional music and magic shows for kids.

September

After a month off, barcelonins return to work, although several major festivals provide ample amusement. Temperatures stay warm in September.

Festa Major de Sants

The district of Sants hosts a five-day fest (www.festa-majordesants.net) with concerts, outdoor dance parties, *correfocs* (fire runs) and elaborately decorated streets.

Diada Nacional de Catalunya

Catalonia's national day curiously commemorates Barcelona's surrender on 11 September 1714 to the Bourbon monarchy of Spain, at the conclusion of the War of the Spanish Succession.

Festes de la Mercè

Barcelona's co-patron saint is celebrated with fervour in this massive five-day fest (merce.bcn.cat). The city stages sporting events, free concerts, dance performances, human towers of *castellers,* parades of *gegants* and a *correfoc* (fire run).

Festa Major de la Barceloneta

This big September celebration in Barcelona honours the local patron saint, Sant Miquel, on 29 September. It lasts about a week and involves plenty of dancing and drinking, especially on the beach.

October

While northern Europe shivers, Barcelona enjoys mild October temperatures and sunny days. With the disappearance of the summer crowds and lower accommodation prices, this is an excellent month to visit.

Mercat de Mercats

The 'market of markets' is a celebration of Catalan cooking and those wonderfully locally sourced ingredients that have made Barcelona such a foodie destination. Over one weekend in October, this food fair features great foods, wines and workshops. Held in front of La Catedral.

November

Cooler days and nights arrive, along with occasional days of rain. For beating the crowds (and higher summer prices), though, it's an excellent month to visit.

Fira de Santa Llúcia

Held from late November to Christmas, this holiday market (en.firadesantallucia.cat) has hundreds of stalls selling all manner of Christmas decorations and gifts – including the infamous Catalan Nativity scene character, the *caganer* (the crapper).

With Kids

Barcelona is great for older kids and teens – the Mediterranean attitude means they are included in many seemingly adult activities, like eating late meals at bars or restaurants. Babies will love the welcoming Mediterranean culture, and toddlers will be showered with attention.

Aquàrium (p108)

Dining Out With Kids

Barcelona – and Spain in general – is super-friendly when it comes to eating with children. Locals take their kids out all the time and don't worry too much about keeping them up late, so going out to eat or to sip a beer on a terrace on a summer evening needn't mean leaving children with minders – and they're bound to strike up a friendship or two.

Spanish kids tend to eat the Mediterranean offerings enjoyed by their parents, but many restaurants have children's menus that serve up burgers, pizzas, tomato-sauce pasta and the like. Good local – and child-proof – options commonly found on tapas menus are the *tortilla de patatas* (potato omelette) or *croquetas de jamón* (croquettes with ham).

Best Kid-Friendly Eateries

La Nena

Fantastic for chocolate and all manner of sweet things, this cafe (p155) has a play area, and toys and books in a corner.

Bar del Convent

With a safe, traffic-free terrace to play in, and a raft of games and toys indoors, del Convent (p101) is a great all-weather option.

NEED TO KNOW

➡ **Babysitting** Get a babysitter at Tender Loving Canguros (www.tlcanguros.com) or **5 Serveis** (☎93 412 56 76; www.5serveis.com; Carrer de Pelai 50; ⓂCatalunya).

➡ **Supplies** Nappies (diapers), dummies, creams and formula can be bought at any of the city's many pharmacies.

➡ **Metro** Barcelona's metro is accessible and great for families with pushchairs. Be mindful of pickpockets.

➡ **Accessibility** The narrow streets of the Ciutat Vella, with their unpredictable traffic and cobbled streets, are less buggy-friendly than the rest of Barcelona.

Filferro

Sit outside this tapas and snack bar (p111) while junior busies about in the adjacent playground.

Pepa Tomate

With crayons provided and a tiny playground near the plaza-side tables, this fun tapas joint (p156) is a winner.

Best Parks & Open Spaces

Parc de la Ciutadella

This park (p94) has a zoo, a pond and a playground that gets a bunch of fun toys out after 4pm.

Parc d'Atraccions

This fabulous funfair (p168) on top of Tibidabo is excellent for adrenaline-loving kids and grown-ups.

Parc de la Creueta del Coll

An excellent park (p166) for its splashing pool, swings and snack bar.

Font Màgica

The light show (p178) is guaranteed to make the little ones shout 'Again!'

Parc de Collserola

A huge park (p168) in the hills that's attractive for its trails and picnic spots.

Best Kid-Friendly Museums

CosmoCaixa

A great science museum (p167) whose interactive displays fascinate kids of all ages.

MIBA

The Museum of Inventions and Ideas (p61) is great for toddlers and older kids thanks to its fun, interactive displays.

Museu de la Xocolata

This museum (p97) is all about chocolate – need we say more? Don't miss the chocolate model-making sessions for kids.

Zoo de Barcelona

You'll find all the animals you can think of in this relatively small zoo (p95), from yawning hippos, to spluttering elephants and frowning gorillas.

L'Aquàrium

This a fantastic aquarium (p108), one of Europe's largest. Seeing sharks gliding overhead is bound to be a lasting memory.

Poble Espanyol

Kids and parents can enjoy going through a mini Spain (p179) together; there are also special kid-oriented games and quests.

Best Ways to See the City

By Bike

Barcelona has tonnes of bike tours and outlets that hire out bicycles with little trolleys in the front for transporting the little ones, including **Trixi** (☑699 984726; www.trixi.com/barcelona; Plaça dels Traginers 4; 30min/1hr/2hr/4hr tour €18/30/50/85; ⊘9am-8pm Mar-Nov; ⓂJaume I).

On Segway

Parents and older kids can scoot around town with **Segway Fun** (☑670 484000; www.barcelonasegwayfun.com; Carrer del Sotstinent Navarro 26 meeting point; tours €45-55; ⓂJaume I).

By Bus

Barcelona's bus tours (p237) are great for older kids – hop on, climb up to the open top floor and see the views.

By Cable Car

Travel to Montjuïc from Barceloneta beach through the air. The Transbordador Aeri (p179) is bound to be loved by all ages.

Best Shopping

Papabubble

Watch candy being made the old-fashioned way at this inviting shop (p74).

Tintin Shop

A plethora of Tintin-related items make for gorgeous gifts in this Gràcia space (p160).

El Rei de la Màgia

A cabinet of curiosity for all budding magicians (p103).

Like a Local

Whether you're a frequent visitor or a first-timer, taking a local approach when it comes to eating, drinking and other amusements offers a rewarding way to experience the city. You'll find Catalans much more open if you try to blend in as much as you can (and learn a few words of Catalan).

tart a night out with predinner tapas

MATTEO COLOMBO/GETTY IMAGES ©

When to Dine

In Barcelona, and elsewhere in Spain, meal times run late. Most restaurants don't open for dinner until 8.30pm or 9pm and close at midnight or 1am; peak dining time is around 10pm. Locals commonly have lunch between 1pm and 4pm. This is then followed by a nice long siesta (a loll on the beach or a park is a fine choice when the weather is pleasant). Locals aren't big on breakfast – a croissant and a *cortado* (espresso with milk) is a typical way to start the day.

Water & Wine

Lunch or dinner, wine is always a fine idea, according to most *barcelonins*. Luckily, many restaurants offer *menú del día* (menu of the day, or fixed price) lunches that include a glass of red or white. If you become a regular, waiters may give you complimentary refills or even leave the bottle. If drinking water, note that no one drinks it straight from the tap (taste it and you'll know why). Order *agua mineral*, either *con gas* (bubbly) or *sin gas* (still).

Tapas

When hunger pains arrive in the afternoon or early evening, locals head out for a predinner tapa. This means heading to the local favourite for a bite of anchovies, sausage, squid, wild mushrooms or dozens of other tempting morsels. Wine, *cava* and beer all make fine accompaniments.

Many tapas spots are lively stand-around-the-bar affairs; Bormuth (p97) and Vaso de Oro (p112) are great places to start. When it's time for a change of scenery, *barcelonins* might make their way to dinner or just head to another tapas bar.

Local Meal Spots

La Rambla is fine for a stroll, but no local would eat there. The same holds for Carrer Ferran and other tourist-packed streets in Barri Gòtic. The Gòtic does, however, have some local-favoured gems, particularly on the narrow lanes of the east side – such as Onofre (p69) and Cafè de l'Acadèmia (p68). For a more authentic neighbourhood

NEED TO KNOW

➡ **Miniguide** (miniguide.es) Culture, food, nightlife, fashion and more; published 10 times a year.

➡ **Barcelona Cultura** (barcelona-cultura.bcn.cat) Upcoming cultural fare, including concerts, exhibitions and festivals.

➡ **Spotted by Locals** (www.spottedbylocals.com/barcelona) Reviews of favourite spots – restaurants, bars, cinemas, galleries and more, written by local residents/expats.

➡ **Barça Central** (barcacentral.com) The latest about FC Barcelona.

➡ **In & Out Barcelona** (www.inandoutbarcelona.net) New restaurants, bars, cafes, shops and clubs with lovely photos – in Spanish.

dining experience, browse the streets of El Born, Barceloneta, El Raval and Gràcia.

Weekends

Many *barcelonins* head out of town on the weekends. That could mean skiing in the Pyrenees in winter, or heading up the Costa Brava in summer. Those that stick around might check out flea markets or produce markets, head to the beach or have an outing in the park. The parks are liveliest on weekends, when local musicians, picnickers, pop-up markets and playing children add to the city's relaxed air. Culture-craving locals might hit an art opening (openings at CCCB (p79) and MACBA (p78) are good fun) see a rep film – Filmoteca de Catalunya (p85) has intriguing fare – or catch a concert, at Jazz Sí Club (p85) or Sala Apolo (p186), perhaps.

The Sunday Feast

Sunday is typically the most peaceful day for Catalans, and a fine occasion for gathering with family or friends over a big meal. Lunch is the main event, and many restaurants prepare Sunday-only specials. Lots of places close on Sunday nights too, so it's worth lingering over a long multicourse meal. A rich paella in Barceloneta – try Barraca (p112) or Can

Ros (p112) – followed by a long leisurely stroll along the waterfront is always a hit.

Festivals & Other Events

One of the best ways to mingle with locals is during one of the city's big festivals. In summer, Música als Parcs features 30 or so open-air concerts at a dozen parks in Barcelona, and free concerts are held at venues around the city. Stop in at a tourist office for the latest schedule. Other great open-air concerts in summer include Festival Piknic Electronik and Festival Pedralbes.

Local Listings

If you can read some Spanish (Castilian), browse the latest art openings, film screenings, concerts and other events in the *Guia del Ocio* (www.guiadelocio.com), *Time Out Barcelona* (www.timeout.cat) or daily papers like *La Vanguardia* (www.lavanguardia.com) and *El Periodico* (www.elperiodico.com). Friday papers list the weekend's events (most with pull-out supplements), and are often worth a read even if your Spanish is limited.

Football

FC Barcelona plays a prominent role in the city's imagination. Heading to a match at Camp Nou (p172) from September to May is the best way to catch a bit of Barcelona fever, but watching it on screen at a tavern can be just as much fun depending on the crowd. For the most fervent fan base, head to Barceloneta, El Raval, Gràcia or Sarrià, where you'll find lively spots to catch a game. The daily journal *Marca* (www.marca.com) gives the latest on sporting news.

Tickets can be bought at www.fcbarcelona.com or FC Botiga (p74).

Sardana

The traditional Catalan folk dance *sardana* still attracts a small local following. On weekends aficionados gather in front of La Catedral for group dancing to a live 10-piece band. The action happens at 6pm on Saturday and noon on Sunday and lasts about an hour.

For Free

With planning Barcelona can be a surprisingly affordable place to travel. Many museums offer free days, and some of the best ways to experience the city don't cost a cent – hanging out on the beach, exploring fascinating neighbourhoods, and drinking in the views from hilltop heights.

Walking Tours

Numerous companies offer pay-what-you-wish walking tours. These typically take in the Barri Gòtic or the Modernista sites of L'Eixample. Recommended outfitters include the following:

Discover Walks (www.discoverwalks.com)

Feel Free Tours (www.feelfreetours.com)

Orange Donut Tours (www.orangedonut tours.com)

Runner Bean Tours (www.runnerbeantours.com)

Travel Bound (www.travelbar.com)

Festivals & Other Events

Barcelona has loads of free festivals and events, including the **Festes de la Mercè** (www.bcn.cat/merce; ☺Sept) and the **Festes de Santa Eulàlia** (www.bcn.cat/santaeulalia; ☺Feb). From June to August, the city hosts Música als Parcs (Music in the Parks), a series of open-air concerts held in different parks and green spaces around the city. Over 40 different concerts feature classical, blues and jazz groups. Popular venues include Parc de la Ciutadella, Parc de Joan Miró (Carrer de Tarragona, Sant Antoni) and Parc Turó (Avenida de Pau Casals 19, Sant Gervasi). Stop in at the tourist office or go online (www.bcn.cat) for a schedule.

Sights

Entry to some sights is free on occasion, most commonly on the first Sunday of the month, while quite a few attractions are free from 3pm to 8pm on Sundays (see reviews for more details). Others are always free. The following are most likely to attract your attention.

Free

➡ Centre de la Imatge (p55)
➡ Centre d'Art Santa Mònica (p55)
➡ Basílica de Santa Maria del Mar (p92)
➡ Estadi Olímpic Lluís Companys (p179)
➡ Palau del Lloctinent (p60)
➡ Temple Romà d'August (p64)
➡ Antic Hospital de la Santa Creu (p79)
➡ Font Màgica (p178)
➡ Jardins de Mossèn Cinto de Verdaguer (p180)
➡ Cementiri del Poblenou (p110)
➡ Universitat de Barcelona (p128)

Occasionally Free

➡ Museu d'Història de Catalunya (p108)
➡ Museu Nacional d'Art de Catalunya (p175)
➡ Museu Picasso (p90)
➡ La Catedral (p58)
➡ Museu Frederic Marès (p63)
➡ Castell de Montjuïc (p178)
➡ Museu-Monestir de Pedralbes (p165)
➡ Jardins del Laberint d'Horta (p170)
➡ Museu de la Música (p110)
➡ Museu d'Història de Barcelona (p61)
➡ Museu Marítim (p107)
➡ Ajuntament (p60)

Tapas at Quimet i Quimet (p182)

Eating

Barcelona has a celebrated food scene fuelled by a combination of world-class chefs, imaginative recipes and magnificent ingredients fresh from farms and the sea. Catalan culinary masterminds like Ferran Adrià and Carles Abellan have become international icons, reinventing the world of haute cuisine, while classic old-world Catalan recipes continue to earn accolades in dining rooms and tapas bars across the city.

New Catalan Cuisine

Avant-garde chefs have made Catalonia famous throughout the world for their food laboratories, their commitment to food as art and their crazy riffs on the themes of traditional local cooking.

Here the notion of gourmet cuisine is deconstructed as chefs transform liquids and solid foods into foams, create 'ice cream' of classic ingredients by means of liquid nitrogen, freeze-dry foods to make concentrated powders and employ spherification to create unusual and artful morsels. This alchemical cookery is known as molecular gastronomy, and invention is the keystone of this technique.

Diners may encounter olive oil 'caviar', 'snow' made of gazpacho with anchovies, jellified Parmesan turned into spaghetti, and countless other concoctions.

The dining rooms themselves also offer a reconfiguration of the five-star dining experience. Restaurateurs generally aim to create warm and buzzing spaces, with artful design flourishes, and without the stuffiness and formality typically associated with high-end dining.

Top Chefs

Albert Adrià, brother of Ferran of El Bulli fame, has brought culinary fame to Barcelona with his growing culinary empire of restaurants. Tickets (p184) is a delectable showcase of whimsy and imagination, with deconstructed tapas dishes like liquid olives, 'air baguettes' (made with Iberian ham) and fairy-floss-covered trees with edible dark chocolate 'soil'.

Other great chefs continue to redefine contemporary cuisine. The Michelin-starred chef Carles Abellan, creator of Suculent (p80), Tapas 24 (p132) and other restaurants, playfully reinterprets traditional tapas with dishes like the *melón con jamón,* a millefeuille of layered caramelised Iberian ham and thinly sliced melon.

Another star of the Catalan cooking scene is Jordi Vilà, who continues to wow diners at Alkímia (p184) with reinvented Catalan classics. Other major players on the Catalan dining scene are Jordi Artal at Cinc Sentits (p132), Xavier Pellicer at Barraca (p112), Jordi Cruz at ABaC (p169) and the trio of Mateu Casañas, Oriol Castro and Eduard Xatruch at Disfrutar (p132).

NEED TO KNOW

Price Ranges

In our listings, we've used the following price codes to represent the cost of a main course:

€ less than €10

€€ €10 to €20

€€€ over €20

Opening Hours

Most restaurants open from 1pm to 4pm and from 8.30pm to midnight.

Reservations

At midrange restaurants and simpler taverns you can usually turn up without booking ahead. At high-end restaurants, especially for dinner, it is safer to make a booking. Thursday to Saturday nights are especially busy.

Tipping

A service charge is rarely included in the bill. Catalans and other Spaniards are not overwhelming tippers. If you are particularly happy, 5% on top is generally fine.

Menú de Degustación

At high-end restaurants you can occasionally opt for a *menú de degustación,* a tasting menu involving samples of different dishes. This can be a great way to get a broader view of what the restaurant does and has the advantage of coming at a fixed price.

Tapas Bars

Tapas, those bite-sized morsels of joy, are an essential pillar of Barcelona's culinary scene. As with all elements of Catalan cuisine, the breadth of choice when it comes to tapas is extraordinary. Tapas bars are found all across the city. Most open earlier than restaurants – typically around 7pm – making them a good predinner (or instead-of-dinner) option. Some open from lunch and stay open without break through late-evening closing time.

As per the 'bar' designation, these places are less formal than restaurants, and drinking is an essential component of the experience.

TOP TAPAS PLATES

If you opt for *tapes*/tapas, it is handy to recognise some of the common items:

➡ **bombes/bombas** meat and potato croquettes

➡ **boquerons/boquerones** white anchovies in vinegar – delicious and tangy

➡ **carxofes/alcachofas** artichokes

➡ **gambes/gambas** prawns, either done *al all/al ajillo* (with garlic), or *a la plantxa/plancha* (grilled)

➡ **navalles/navajas** razor clams

➡ **patates braves/patatas bravas** potato chunks bathed in a slightly spicy tomato sauce, sometimes mixed with mayonnaise

➡ **pop a feira/pulpo a la gallega** tender boiled octopus with paprika

➡ **truita de patates/tortilla de patatas** potato-filled omelette; one with vegetables is a *tortilla de verduras*

➡ **xampinyons/champiñones** mushrooms

Classic Catalan Cuisine

Traditional Catalan recipes showcase the great produce of the Mediterranean: fish, prawns, cuttlefish, clams, pork, rabbit, game, first-rate olive oil, peppers and loads of garlic. Classic dishes also feature unusual pairings (seafood with meat, fruit with fowl) such as cuttlefish with chickpeas, cured pork with caviar, rabbit with prawns, or goose with pears.

Great Catalan restaurants can be found in nearly every neighbourhood around town. The settings can be a huge part of the appeal, with candlelit medieval chambers in the Ciutat Vella and Modernista design in L'Eixample setting the stage for a memorable feast. Although there are plenty of high-end places in this city, foodie-minded *barcelonins* aren't averse to eating at humbler, less elegant places – which sometimes cook up the best meals.

Catalan Specialities

STARTERS

➡ **Calçots amb romesco** Sweet and juicy spring onions cooked up on a barbecue

➡ **Escalivada** Red peppers and aubergines, grilled, cooled, peeled, sliced and served with an olive oil, salt and garlic dressing

MAIN COURSES

➡ **Arròs a la cassola/arroz a la catalana** Catalan paella, cooked without saffron

➡ **Arròs negre** Rice cooked in black cuttlefish ink

➡ **Bacallà a la llauna** Salted cod baked in tomato, garlic, parsley, paprika and wine

➡ **Botifarra amb mongetes** Pork sausage with fried white beans

➡ **Cargols/Caracoles** Snails, often stewed with *conill/conejo* (rabbit) and chilli

➡ **Fideuà** Similar to paella but with vermicelli noodles as the base. Often accompanied by *allioli* (pounded garlic with olive oil), which you can mix in as you wish

DESSERTS

➡ **Crema catalana** A cream custard with a crisp burnt-sugar coating

➡ **Mel i mató** Honey and fresh cream cheese

Market Shopping

Barcelona has some fantastic food markets. Foodies will enjoy the sounds, smells and most importantly tastes of the Mercat de la Boqueria (p77). This is probably Spain's biggest and best market, and it's conveniently located right off La Rambla. Here you can find temptations of all sorts – plump fruits and veggies, fresh-squeezed juices, artisanal cheeses, smoked meats, seafood and pastries. The best feature: an array of tapas bars and food stalls where you can sample amazingly fresh ingredients cooked to perfection. Some other great market options:

➡ Mercat de Sant Antoni (p186)

➡ Mercat de Santa Caterina (p95)

➡ Mercat del Ninot (Map p274)

➡ Mercat de la Llibertat (p154)

➡ Mercat de l'Abaceria Central (p161)

Lonely Planet's Top Choices

Disfrutar (p132) A new and avant-garde addition that has rapidly become Barcelona's most talked-about restaurant.

Cinc Sentits (p132) Tasting menus that showcase the best of Catalan cooking.

Tickets (p184) The celebrated restaurant of Albert Adrià, showcasing Barcelona's best *nueva cocina española*.

Tapas 24 (p132) Carles Abellan creates some of Barcelona's best tapas.

Cal Pep (p99) One of Barcelona's most famous tapas spots serves imaginative and mouthwatering dishes.

Restaurant 7 Portes (p113) An elegant spot that's famed for its delectable paella.

Best by Budget

€

La Cova Fumada (p111) Barceloneta hole-in-the-wall with excellent small plates.

Bormuth (p97) Tasty tapas in an old-city setting.

€€

Suculent (p80) Carles Abellan's bistro serves excellent Catalan cooking.

Casa Delfín (p98) Delicious Mediterranean fare in an atmospheric setting.

€€€

Disfrutar (p132) Expect the unexpected – this is Catalan cooking at its most experimental.

Koy Shunka (p69) Avant-garde Japanese fare, probably Barcelona's best.

Best for Tapas

Bormuth (p97) Serves both the classic and the new wave, plus tasty vermouths.

Quimet i Quimet (p182) Mouthwatering morsels served to a standing crowd.

Palo Cortao (p182) A new star in Poble Sec with outstanding sharing plates.

Bar Pinotxo (p80) Pull up a bar stool at this legendary Boqueria joint.

Tapas 24 (p132) Everyone's favourite gourmet tapas bar.

Best for Catalan

Vivanda (p169) Magnificent Catalan cooking with year-round garden dining.

El Glop (p156) A buzzing neighbourhood spot in Gràcia.

Roig Robí (p157) A pillar of traditional Catalan cooking.

Cafè de l'Acadèmia (p68) High-quality dishes that never disappoint.

Can Culleretes (p68) The city's oldest restaurant, with great-value traditional dishes.

Best for Eating Like a Local

Mitja Vida (p168) Mouthwatering tapas and vermouth.

El Tossal (Map p280) A nononsense Catalan spot with excellent cooking.

5º Pino (p169) Tapas and light fare with outdoor seating, near Sarrià.

La Cova Fumada (p111) Fight for a table at this scruffy little joint with outstanding food.

Best for Architecture

Els Quatre Gats (p69) Finely crafted interiors in a building where Picasso once supped.

El Asador de Aranda (p170) A beautiful spread of Modernista dining rooms.

Casa Calvet (p135) A stylish restaurant set in an early Gaudí building.

Best for Vegetarians

Aguaribay (p113) First-rate prix fixe lunches and a small but well-executed evening à la carte menu.

Cerería (p69) Pizzas and galettes in an old-fashioned setting.

Flax & Kale (p80) Vast, colourful salads and a truly creative approach.

Rasoterra (p68) Airy vegetarian charmer in Barri Gòtic.

Best Cafes

Copasetic (p130) Vintage-filled cafe.

Café Godot (p156) Friendly and easy-going, with tasty snacks and mains.

Federal (p68) Unnervingly hip, but the food is excellent and the service friendly.

Čaj Chai (p71) Teas and lively chatter in Barri Gòtic.

La Nena (p155) Kid-friendly cafe in Gràcia.

Best for Late-Night Eating

Alcoba Azul (p67) Tasty tapas and wine in an atmospheric setting.

Cafè de l'Òpera (p70) Stop in for late-night snacks on La Rambla.

Elisabets (p79) Offers late-night dining (till 1am) on Fridays.

Best for Chocolate Lovers

Granja La Pallaresa (p70) One of many chocolate-dispensing cafes on Carrer de Petritxol.

Cacao Sampaka (p139) Chocolate decadence comes in many forms at this L'Eixample shop and cafe.

Museu de la Xocolata (p97) Delve into the world of chocolate, then feast in the cafe.

Best for Brunch

Federal (p183) Excellent brunches and a small roof terrace.

En Aparté (p97) French eatery serving tasty brunch fare on weekends.

Milk (p68) Serves brunch daily (till 4.30pm).

Dos Trece (p81) Fabulous Sunday brunches in El Raval.

Best for Romantic Dining

La Vinateria del Call (p68) Flickering candles and medieval walls.

Can Recasens (p113) Romantic spot in Poblenou with market-fresh fare.

Pla (p69) Intimate setting and memorable meals.

Best Wine Lists

Viblioteca (p157) Heaven for wine and cheese lovers.

Monvínic (p135) A staggering number of wines on offer.

Onofre (p69) Run by wine lovers; good tapas to match.

Best for Historic Atmosphere

Can Cortada (p169) Peel back the centuries at this former country estate.

Can Travi Nou (p156) Upmarket Catalan cuisine in an 18th-century setting.

Restaurant 7 Portes (p113) Top seafood and art-deco elegance.

Best for Lunch Specials

Cafè de l'Acadèmia (p68) Rich lunch specials and great atmosphere.

La Esquina (p131) A new option with a classy lunch deal.

Chicha Limoná (p134) Gourmet eating at a pocket-friendly price.

Best for Desserts

Caelum (p70) Dine on sweet perfection in the pleasant cafe, or head downstairs for the medieval atmosphere.

Granja Petitbo (p134) Sink into a leather armchair and devour a homemade cake at this quaint cafe.

Escribà (p72) A household name in Barcelona for its beautiful pastries and other temptations.

Best for Seafood

Barraca (p112) A sparkling waterfront restaurant with unique and flavour-rich seafood combinations.

Can Majó (p112) Fine seafood in a pleasant outdoor setting.

Can Ros (p112) A family-run Barceloneta classic.

Can Maño (p112) An unfussy place with great dishes at low prices.

Best for Market Dining

Bar Pinotxo (p80) Celebrated tapas bar in La Boqueria.

Bar Joan (p98) Friendly staff and a relaxed neighbourhood feel in the Mercat de Santa Caterina.

El Guindilla (p112) A Mercat de la Barceloneta favourite with outdoor tables and tasty lunch specials.

Best for Views

Torre d'Alta Mar (p109) Seafood and waterfront views from the 75m Torre de Sant Sebastià.

Barraca (p112) Superb seafood to match the delicious sea views.

Can Majó (p112) Elegant Barceloneta seafood eatery with outdoor tables fronting the sea.

Best for Picnic Fare

Mercat de la Boqueria (p77) Barcelona's biggest and most inspiring market.

Mercat de Santa Caterina (p95) Cheeses, bakery items and other goodies, handily located near Parc de la Ciutadella.

Barcelona Reykjavik (p86) Branches of this bakery are the best place to pick up bread.

Best for Nueva Cocina Española

Disfrutar (p132) Set up by three alumni of El Bulli, this is one to watch.

Cinc Sentits (p132) Serves a magnificent tasting menu of the freshest, highest-quality ingredients.

Tickets (p184) Avant-garde gastronomy from Albert Adrià.

Wine and olives

Drinking & Nightlife

Barcelona is a nightlife-lovers' town, with an enticing spread of candlelit wine bars, old-school taverns, stylish lounges and kaleidoscopic nightclubs where the party continues until daybreak. For something a little more sedate, the city's atmospheric cafes and teahouses make a fine retreat when the skies turn grey.

NEED TO KNOW

Opening Hours
➡ **Bars** Typically open around 6pm and close at 2am (3am on weekends).

➡ **Clubs** Open from midnight until 6am, Thursday to Saturday.

➡ **Beach Bars** 10am to around midnight (later on weekends) from April to October.

When to Go
➡ Bars get lively around 11pm or midnight.

➡ Clubs don't start filling up until around 2am.

Getting In
Cover charges range from nothing to upwards of €20. If you go early, you'll often pay less. In most cases the admission price includes your first drink. Bouncers have the last say on dress code and your eligibility to enter. If you're in a big group, break into smaller groups.

Guides for the Latest Nightlife
➡ **Barcelonarocks.com** (www.barcelonarocks.com)

➡ **Clubbingspain.com** (www.clubbingspain.com)

➡ **Barcelona Connect** (www.barcelonaconnect.com)

➡ **Miniguide** (www.miniguide.es)

➡ **Metropolitan** (www.barcelona-metropolitan.com)

➡ **enBarcelona** (www.enbarcelona.com)

Drinking Glossary
Coffee
➡ *cafe con leche* – half coffee, half milk

➡ *cafe solo* – a short black or espresso

➡ *cortado* – a short black with a little milk

Beer
➡ *cerveza* – beer

➡ *caña* – a small draught beer

➡ *tubo* – a large draught beer

➡ *jarra* – a stein of beer (sometimes a pint)

➡ *quinto/tercio* – a 200/300ml bottle

➡ *clara* – a shandy; a beer with a hefty dash of lemonade (or lemon Fanta)

Wine
➡ *vino de la casa* – house wine

Bars & Lounges
Barcelona has a dizzying assortment of bars where you can start – or end – the night. The atmosphere varies tremendously – candlelit, mural-covered chambers in the medieval quarter, antique-filled converted storefronts and buzzing Modernista spaces are all part of the scene. Of course, where to go depends as much on the crowd as it does on ambience – and whether you're in the mood to drink with the hipsters (try Sant Antoni), the bohemian crowd (El Raval) or young expats (Gràcia), you'll find a scene that suits in Barcelona.

Wherever you end up, keep in mind that eating and drinking go hand in hand in Barcelona (as in other parts of Spain), and some of the liveliest bars serve up as much tapas as they do alcohol.

Wine & Cava Bars
A growing number of wine bars scattered around the city provide a showcase for the great produce from Spain and beyond. Vine-minded spots such as Monvínic (p135) serve a huge selection of wines by the glass, with a particular focus on stellar new vintages. A big part of the experience is having a few bites while you drink. Expect sharing plates, platters of cheese and charcuterie, and plenty of tapas.

Cava bars tend to be more about the festive ambience than the actual drinking of *cava*, a sparkling white or rosé, most of which is produced in Catalonia's Penedès region. At the more famous *cava* bars you'll have to nudge your way through the garrulous crowds and enjoy your bubbly standing up. Two of the most famous *cava* bars are El Xampanyet (p101) in La Ribera and Can Paixano (p114) in Barceloneta.

Drinks With a View
Barcelona has a handful of rooftop bars and hillside drinking spaces that provide an enchanting view over the city. Depending on the neighbourhood, the vista may take in the rooftops of the Ciutat Vella (Old City), the curving beachfront, or the entire expanse of the city centre with the Collserola Hills and Tibidabo in the distance. Most of these drinking spots are perched atop high-end hotels, but not solely the domain of visiting foreigners. An increasing number of style-minded *barcelonins* are drawn to these spaces. Late in the evening you'll find a mostly local crowd.

Drinking by Neighbourhood

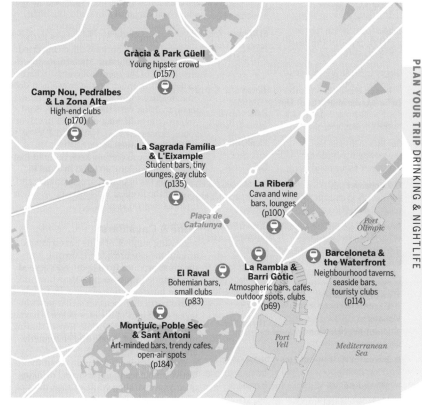

Gràcia & Park Güell
Young hipster crowd
(p157)

Camp Nou, Pedralbes & La Zona Alta
High-end clubs
(p170)

La Sagrada Família & L'Eixample
Student bars, tiny lounges, gay clubs
(p135)

La Ribera
Cava and wine bars, lounges
(p100)

Plaça de Catalunya

Port Olímpic

Barceloneta & the Waterfront
Neighbourhood taverns, seaside bars, touristy clubs
(p114)

La Rambla & Barri Gòtic
Atmospheric bars, cafes, outdoor spots, clubs
(p69)

El Raval
Bohemian bars, small clubs
(p83)

Montjuïc, Poble Sec & Sant Antoni
Art-minded bars, trendy cafes, open-air spots
(p184)

Port Vell

Mediterranean Sea

Beach Bars

During summer small wooden beach bars, affectionately known as *chiringuitos,* open up along the strand, from Barceloneta all the way up to Platja de la Nova Mar Bella. Here you can dip your toes in the sand and nurse a cocktail while watching the city at play against the backdrop of the deep-blue Mediterranean. Ambient grooves add to the laid-back environment. *Chiringuitos* are also great spots for a snack – particularly the Guingueta de la Barceloneta (p111) and Guingueta del Bogatell (p116) run by Michelin-starred chef Carles Abellan. The drink of choice at either is a refreshing *cava sangria.*

Clubs

Barcelona's *discotecas* (clubs) are at their best from Thursday to Saturday. Indeed, many open only on these nights. A surprising variety of spots lurk in the old-town

labyrinth, ranging from plush former dance halls to grungy subterranean venues that fill to capacity.

Along the waterfront it's another story. At Port Olímpic sun-scorched crowds of visiting yachties mix it up with tourists and a few locals at noisy, back-to-back dance bars right on the waterfront. The best spots are over on La Barceloneta side.

Cafes

The cafe scene in Barcelona is incredibly vibrant and makes a great setting for an afternoon pick-me-up. You'll find charming teashops hidden on the narrow lanes of Barri Gòtic, bohemian hang-outs in the Raval, hipster haunts in L'Eixample and Modernista gems on La Rambla. While coffee, tea or perhaps *xocolata calenta* (hot chocolate) are the main attractions, most places also serve snacks, while some serve beer, wine and cocktails.

Lonely Planet's Top Choices

Ocaña (p69) Stylish spot on pretty Plaça Reial with a beautifully designed interior.

Ginger (p69) An art-deco gem in the Barri Gòtic.

La Caseta del Migdia (p185) An open-air charmer, hidden in the thickets of Montjuïc.

Sor Rita (p70) Join festive crowds in a whimsical Almodovar-esque world.

El Xampanyet (p101) Sip *cava* and munch on tapas in this garrulous icon in El Born.

Dry Martini (p135) This elegant drinking den serves perfect martinis and goldfish-bowl-sized gin and tonics.

Best for Wine Lovers

Viblioteca (p157) A small modern space famed for its wine (and cheese) selections.

Monvínic (p135) With a staggering 3000 varieties of wines, you won't lack for options.

La Vinya del Senyor (p100) Outdoor wine-sipping facing Basílica de Santa Maria del Mar.

Best for Beer

La Cerveteca (p70) Great microbrews from around the globe (plus cured horsemeat).

BlackLab (p114) Creative microbrewery near the waterfront.

La Cervecita Nuestra de Cada Día (p116) A Poblenou brew bar for beer nerds.

Napar BCN (p135) The beautifully designed space makes a fine setting for sipping beers made on site.

Cat Bar (p98) Microbrews and vegan burgers make a winning combo in El Born.

El Drapaire (p83) Atmospheric tapas and creative microbrew joint in El Raval.

Best for Cocktails

Balius (p114) Beautifully mixed elixirs in Poblenou.

Elephanta (p157) The place to linger over a creative concoction.

Dry Martini (p135) Expertly made cocktails in a classy setting.

Juanra Falces (p100) White-jacketed waiters serve up artful elixirs.

Boadas (p84) An iconic drinking den that's been going strong since the 1930s.

Best for Old-World Ambience

Raïm (p159) Old-fashioned tavern with more than a hint of Havana.

Bar Marsella (p83) History lives on in this 1820 watering hole.

Bar Pastís (p83) Atmospheric little bar with the warble of French cabaret tunes playing overhead.

Casa Almirall (p83) Step back into the 1860s inside this atmospheric drinking den.

London Bar (p84) Former bohemian haunt of Picasso and Miró.

Best for Dancing

Marula Cafè (p70) Barri Gòtic favourite for its lively dance floor.

Moog (p84) A small Raval club that draws a fun, dance-loving crowd.

Antilla BCN (Map p274) The top name in town for salsa lovers.

City Hall (p135) A legendary Eixample dance club.

Best Bohemian Hang-Outs

Gran Bodega Saltó (p186) Poble Sec icon with psychedelic decor and an eclectic crowd.

Madame George (p114) Tiny, dramatically designed space with soulful DJs.

El Rouge (p184) Bordello-esque lounge with great people-watching.

Gipsy Lou (p85) For a night of surprises in El Raval.

Best for Views

La Caseta del Migdia (p185) Great hillside spot for a sundowner.

Mirablau (p171) The whole city stretches out beneath you from the foot of Tibidabo.

La Terrrazza (p186) Party beneath palms in Poble Espanyol.

Martínez (p184) Drinking and dining with views on Montjuïc.

Best Beachfront Settings

Santa Marta (Map p270) Sit at outdoor tables and watch the passing people parade.

CDLC (Map p270) Come early for a beach-facing outdoor table; stay for dancing.

Guingueta del Bogatell (p116) Sit on the seafront far from the mayhem.

⭐ Entertainment

Barcelona teems with stages hosting all manner of entertainment from underground cabaret and comic opera to high drama. Dance companies are thick on the ground and popular local theatre companies, when not touring the rest of Spain, keep folks strapped to their seats.

Live Music

Almost every big international act has passed through Barcelona at some point, more often than not playing at Razzmatazz (p116), Bikini (p171), Sala Apolo (p186) or BARTS (p186), although there are a number of other decent midsize venues. There are also abundant local gigs in institutions as diverse as CaixaForum (p178), La Pedrera (p128) and L'Ateneu (p71).

Classical Music & Opera

Barcelona is blessed with a fine line-up of theatres for grand performances of classical music, opera and more. The two historic – and iconic – music venues are the Gran Teatre del Liceu (p71) and the Palau de la Música Catalana (p101), while the L'Auditori (p117) is the modern concert hall par excellence and home to the city's orchestra, the OBC.

The main season for classical and opera runs from September to June, while in high summer you might find outdoor festivals or performances around town. Check with the tourist office for details.

Dance

Some fine local contemporary dance companies, along with international visiting companies from time to time, maintain a fairly busy performance program across town. Look for leaflets at Palau de la Virreina (p55) and watch theatre listings. For ballet and other big spectacles, you need to wait for acts to arrive from abroad.

FLAMENCO

Seeing good performances of this essentially Andalucian dance and music is not easy. The few *tablaos* are touristy and often tacky. You can catch flamenco on Friday and Saturday nights at the Jazz Sí Club (p85); also watch out for big-name performers at the Palau de la Música Catalana (p101).

The Festival de Flamenco de Ciutat Vella (ciutatflamenco.com) is held in May. A series of concerts can be seen from April to July as part of the Barcelona Guitar Festival (www.guitarbcn.com).

SARDANA

In Barcelona the best chance you have of seeing people dancing the *sardana* is either at noon on Sunday or 6pm on Saturday in front of La Catedral. It is also performed sometimes in Plaça de Sant Jaume. For more information, contact the **Agrupació Cultural Folklòrica de Barcelona** (☎93 315 14 96; www. acfbarcelona.cat).

Theatre

Most local theatre is performed in Catalan or Spanish, although physical theatre such as that performed by local group La Fura dels Baus (p40) is popular too. The monthly guide *Butxaca* can be picked up at the Palau de la Virreina (p55).

Cinemas

Outdoor cinema screens are set up in summer in the moat of the Castell de Montjuïc, on the beach and in the Fòrum. Foreign films with subtitles and original soundtracks are marked 'VO' *(versió original)* in movie listings.

NEED TO KNOW

Tickets

➡ The easiest way to get hold of tickets (*entradas*) for most venues throughout the city is through Ticketea (www.ticketea.com) or Ticketmaster (www.ticketmaster.es). Occasionally there are discounted tickets to be had on www.atrapalo.com.

➡ For exhibitions and other free activities, check out www.forfree.cat.

Listings

➡ The Palau de la Virreina (p55) cultural information office has oodles of information on theatre, opera, classical music and more.

➡ The Guía del Ocio (www.guiadelociobcn.es) has ample listings for all forms of entertainment, as does Time Out (www.timeout.cat).

➡ Good coverage of classical music is to be found on www.classictic.com (in English).

Football

Football in Barcelona has the aura of religion and for much of the city's population, support of FC Barcelona is an article of faith. But the city has another hardy (if less illustrious) side, RCD Espanyol. FC Barcelona is traditionally associated with the Catalans and even Catalan nationalism, while Espanyol is often identified with Spanish immigrants from other parts of the country.

A match at Barça's Camp Nou (p172) can be breathtaking; the season runs from September to May, and tickets can be bought at www.fcbarcelona.com or FC Botiga. If you can't make it to see Barça play, a trip to the multimedia museum (p164) with a tour through the locker room and out on to the field is a good secondary option.

Cycling

Barcelona's long enticing seafront makes a fine setting for a ride, and the bike lane separate from traffic and pedestrians ensures you can get going at a good clip (though you'll have to move slowly at peak times, like on summer weekends).

The city itself has over 180km of bike lanes, including lanes along Passeig de Sant Joan, Carrer del Consell de Cent, Avinguda Diagonal and Ronda de Sant Pau/Carrer del Comte d'Urgell, among other major streets. Avid mountain bikers will want to make their way up to the vast Parc de Collserola (p168), where rambling trails on a wooded massif overlook the city.

Entertainment by Neighbourhood

➡ **La Rambla & Barri Gòtic** (p71) This is where you'll find the Gran Teatre de Liceu and the weekly *sardana* dances.

➡ **El Raval** (p85) Great for theatre, jazz and flamenco on Friday and Saturday nights at the Jazz Sí Club.

➡ **La Ribera** (p101) The eclectic and spectacular Palau de la Música Catalana is here.

➡ **Montjuïc** (p186) This is where you'll find two of the best pop and rock venues, Sala Apolo and BARTS.

LA FURA DELS BAUS

Keep your eyes peeled for any of the eccentric (if not downright crazed) performances of Barcelona's La Fura dels Baus (www.lafura.com) theatre group. It has won worldwide acclaim for its brand of startling, often acrobatic, theatre in which the audience is frequently dragged into the chaos. The company grew out of Barcelona's street-theatre culture of the late 1970s and, although it has grown in technical prowess and received great international acclaim, it has not abandoned the rough-and-ready edge of street performances.

Lonely Planet's Top Choices

Palau de la Música Catalana (p101) This glittering Modernista gem, the city's traditional home for classical and choral music, is a multisensory delight.

Gran Teatre del Liceu (p71) Nineteenth-century style meets cutting-edge acoustics at Barcelona's elegant opera house.

Filmoteca de Catalunya (p85) This cinema and arts centre, situated in El Raval, also includes a film archive, a bookshop and an exhibition space.

Sala Apolo (p186) Characterful old dance hall with a great roster of live acts.

Best for Live Bands

Heliogàbal (p159) A quirky little bar where anything goes, from soulful singer-songwriters to pocket opera.

Music Hall (p138) The perfect midsize venue for up-and-coming local and international acts.

Sala Apolo (p186) Cosy booths and a warm red glow give this hugely popular venue something special.

BARTS (p186) The latest contender on the live music circuit, with superb sound and every mod con.

Best for Classical Music

Palau de la Música Catalana (p101) A Modernista fantasy, where the fabulous interior can distract from the finest musician.

Gran Teatre del Liceu (p71) One of Europe's most splendid opera houses, built to impress.

L'Auditori (p117) Fiercely modern concert venue, with a resident orchestra.

L'Ateneu (p71) This elegant old library is hard to enter if you're not a member – unless you catch one of its occasional concerts.

Best for Theatre

Teatre Nacional de Catalunya (p116) A neoclassical building hosting the best of Catalan theatre.

Teatre Romea (p85) Expect wacky (and not so wacky) versions of modern classics.

Teatreneu (p159) With three different stages, the Teatreneu dares to go where others dare not.

Sala Beckett (p116) With occasional shows in English, it's worth keeping an eye on the programming here.

Best for Jazz

Harlem Jazz Club (p72) Not just jazz, but also funk, blues, bossa nova and plenty more.

Jazz Sí Club (p85) Small, lively, cramped and never less than fun.

Jamboree (p72) A basement bar that's seen them all under its vaulted ceiling.

Best for Flamenco

Jazz Sí Club (p85) A tiny venue with impromptu jams and occasionally great performances.

Tablao Nervión (p101) A little bit touristy, but better than most for flamenco.

Sala Tarantos (p72) A cosy basement affair, good for up-and-coming acts.

Best for Cinema

Verdi (p159) Up-to-date releases, both commercial and less so.

Filmoteca de Catalunya (p85) The city's premier repertory cinema, with themed cycles and rock-bottom prices.

Méliès Cinemes (p139) Now showing nondubbed foreign films, the Méliès is a useful option for recent films.

Yelmo Cines Icària (p117) Huge multiscreen affair with all the latest releases.

Storefront on Carrer del Rec (p44)

Shopping

If your doctor has prescribed an intense round of retail therapy to deal with the blues, then Barcelona is the place. Across Ciutat Vella (Barri Gòtic, El Raval and La Ribera), L'Eixample and Gràcia is spread a thick mantle of boutiques, historic shops, original one-off stores, gourmet corners, wine dens and more designer labels than you can shake your gold card at. You name it, you'll find it here.

Design

Whether you are looking for homeware, gifts or decorations, you'll quickly realise that Barcelona is a stylish city – even the souvenirs have flair. High-end design shops are best found in L'Eixample and El Born, while arty places are scattered around El Raval, where you'll find, among other things, quirky furniture and homeware with a difference.

Boutique Barcelona

The heart of the Barri Gòtic has always been busy with small-scale merchants, but the area has come crackling to life since the mid-1990s. Some of the most curious old shops, such as purveyors of hats and candles, lurk in the narrow lanes around Plaça de Sant Jaume. The once-seedy Carrer d'Avinyó has become a minor young-fashion boulevard. Antique shops line Carrer de la Palla and Carrer dels Banys Nous.

La Ribera is nothing less than a gourmet's delight. Great old shops and some finger-licking newbies deal in speciality foodstuffs, from coffee and chocolate to roasted nuts. Amid such wonderful aromas, a crop of fashion and design stores caters to the multitude of fashionistas in the *barri* (neighbourhood).

Gràcia is also full of quirky little shops. In particular, check out Carrer de Verdi for anything from clothes to bric-a-brac.

El Raval is fantastic for unique boutiques and artists selling their own creations – fashion, prints and curios.

High-Street Chains

Everyone knows that across Europe (and further afield), Spain's chains rule the high street. This is the home of the ubiquitous Zara, Mango, Pull and Bear, Bershka, Massimo Dutti, and Zara Home (in fact, all owned by one company, Inditex) – and sure enough, you'll find all of them dotted around Barcelona. Women's underwear is stylish and affordable at Oysho and Women's Secret, while UK hits like Topshop also feature.

Department Stores

Spain's only surviving department store is El Corte Inglés – an enormous fortresslike main branch towers over Plaça de Catalunya. It covers everything from books, music and food to fashion, jewellery, kids' clothes and toys, technology and homeware. There are smaller branches across town. French chain FNAC is another biggie, selling books, CDs, DVDs, computers and mobile phones.

NEED TO KNOW

Where to Go

For high fashion, design, jewellery and department stores, the principal shopping axis starts on Plaça de Catalunya, proceeds up Passeig de Gràcia and turns left into Avinguda Diagonal, along which it extends as far as Plaça de la Reina Maria Cristina. The densely packed section between Plaça de Francesc Macià and Plaça de la Reina Maria Cristina is an especially good hunting ground.

Sale Time

The winter sales start after Reis (6 January) and, depending on the shop, can go on well into February. The summer sales start in July, with shops trying to entice locals to part with one last wad of euros before they flood out of the city on holiday in August. Some shops prolong their sales to the end of August.

Opening Hours

➡ In general, shops are open between 9am or 10am and 1.30pm or 2pm and then again from around 4pm or 4.30pm to 8pm or 8.30pm Monday to Friday. Many shops keep the same hours on Saturday, although some don't bother with the evening session.

➡ Large supermarkets, malls and department stores such as El Corte Inglés stay open all day Monday to Saturday, from about 10am to 10pm.

➡ Many fashion boutiques, design stores and the like open from about 10am to 8pm Monday to Saturday.

➡ A few shops open on Sundays and holidays, and the number increases in the run-up to key consumer holiday periods.

Vintage Fashion

El Raval is best for vintage fashion. You'll discover old-time stores that are irresistible to browsers, and a colourful array of affordable, mostly secondhand clothes boutiques. The central axis here is Carrer de la Riera Baixa, which plays host to '70s threads and military cast-offs. Carrer dels Tallers is also attracting a growing number of clothing and shoe shops (although CDs remain its core business). Small galleries, designer shops and arty bookshops huddle together along the streets running east of the MACBA towards La Rambla.

Designers

The heart of L'Eixample, bisected by Passeig de Gràcia, is known as the Quadrat d'Or (Golden Square) and is jammed with all sorts of glittering shops. Passeig de Gràcia is a bit of a who's who of international shopping – you'll find Spain's own high-end designers like Loewe, along with Armani, Chanel, Gucci, Stella McCartney and the rest.

El Born, particularly Carrer del Rec, is big on cool designers like Isabel Marant, Marni, Chloé and Hoss Intropia, in small, clean-line boutiques. Some Barcelona-based designs are also sold here. This is a great area if you have money to spend and hours to browse.

Markets

Barcelona's food markets are some of the best in Europe – just think of the inviting, glistening, aromatic and voluptuous offerings to be savoured in Mercat de la Boqueria (p77) or Mercat de Santa Caterina (p95). Every neighbourhood has its own central market, full of seasonal offers.

Several flea markets, like Els Encants Vells (p117), offer the opportunity to browse and enjoy the local buzz, and perhaps even find a good bargain.

Shopping Strips

Avinguda del Portal de l'Àngel This broad pedestrian avenue is lined with high-street chains, shoe shops, bookshops and more. It feeds into Carrer dels Boters and Carrer de la Portaferrissa, characterised by stores offering light-hearted costume jewellery and youth-oriented streetwear.

Avinguda Diagonal This boulevard is loaded with international fashion names and design boutiques, suitably interspersed with cafes to allow weary shoppers to take a load off.

Carrer d'Avinyó Once a fairly squalid old city street, Carrer d'Avinyó has morphed into a dynamic young fashion street.

Carrer de la Riera Baixa The place to look for a gaggle of shops flogging preloved threads.

Carrer del Consell de Cent The heart of the private art-gallery scene in Barcelona, between Passeig de Gràcia and Carrer de Muntaner.

Carrer del Petritxol Best for chocolate shops and art.

Carrer del Rec Another threads street, this one-time stream is lined with bright and cool boutiques. Check out Carrer del Bonaire and Carrer de l'Esparteria too. You'll find discount outlets and original local designers.

Carrer dels Banys Nous Along with nearby Carrer de la Palla, this is the place to look for antiques.

Passeig de Gràcia This is the premier shopping boulevard – chic with a capital 'C', and mostly given over to big-name international brands.

Shopping By Neighbourhood

➡ **La Rambla & Barri Gòtic** (p72) Excellent for all kinds of retail – boutiques, design and souvenirs.

➡ **El Raval** (p86) Haven for independent stores – vintage fashion and all kinds of original and arty shops – and home to the iconic Mercat de la Boqueria.

➡ **La Ribera** (p101) El Born is the place for cool designer boutiques that sell high-end fashion and excellent food shops for the gourmet traveller.

➡ **Port Vell & La Barceloneta** (p117) This area boasts the monster Maremàgnum shopping mall, and an occasional craft market alongside the port.

➡ **L'Eixample** (p138) High-end heart-stoppers, dazzling jewellery and high-street chains find a home along the wealthy streets of L'Eixample.

➡ **Gràcia** (p159) Dotted with fantastic little shops that sell anything from vintage cameras to unique fashion or food.

➡ **La Zona Alta** (p172) This is the city's Beverly Hills, so expect high prices and bijou boutiques.

SHOPPING MALLS

Barcelona has no shortage of shopping malls. One of the first to arrive was L'Illa Diagonal (p172), designed by star Spanish architect Rafael Moneo. The Centre Comercial Diagonal Mar (Map p272), by the sea, is one of the latest additions.

The city's other emporia include Centre Comercial de les Glòries (Map p272), in the former Olivetti factory; Heron City, just off Avinguda Meridiana, about 4km north of Plaça de les Glòries Catalanes; and the Centre Comercial Gran Via 2 in L'Hospitalet de Llobregat.

Lonely Planet's Top Choices

Mercat de la Boqueria (p77) Stock up on budget delicacies amid one of Europe's most vibrant food markets.

Vila Viniteca (p101) Oenophiles unite at this wonderful wine shop.

Coquette (p104) Simple and beautiful designer clothes for women.

Loisaida (p103) Men's and women's fashion, antiques and retro vinyl.

Best for Design & Craft

Drap Art (p74) Weird and wonderful recycled art and accessories.

Arlequí Màscares (p104) Handmade masks to rival any in Venice; the perfect souvenir.

Fantastik (p86) A temple to kitsch, with kooky wonders from all around the world.

Teranyina (p86) The 'Spider's Web', so called for its intricate designs in intricate textiles.

Best for Fashion

Coquette (p104) Offbeat women's clothes that share an ethereal elegance.

Holala! Plaza (p86) Today vintage is the new designer, and nowhere has a better selection than Holala!

Bagués-Masriera (p140) Exquisite jewellery from a company with a long tradition.

Custo Barcelona (p104) Quirky, colourful clothes that are not for the shy.

Loisaida (p103) Cute, smart and somewhat retro clothing for men and women.

Best Markets

Mercat de Santa Caterina (p95) A colourful alternative to La Boqueria, with fewer crowds and lower prices.

Els Encants Vells (p117) A sprawling flea market in a spanking new building.

El Bulevard dels Antiquaris (p140) A labyrinth of tiny antique shops that merits a morning's browsing.

Best for Souvenirs & Gifts

Born Centre de Cultura i Memòria (p95) The gift shop at this exhibition space stocks tasteful, well-made souvenirs, and books about the city.

Les Topettes (p86) Creams, oils, perfumes and soaps that look every bit as tantalising as they smell.

Galeri (p186) Tiny space selling one-of-a-kind prints and ceramics.

Sabater Hermanos (p72) Divinely fragranced shop selling handmade soaps in pretty gift boxes.

Best for Food & Wine

Casa Gispert (p103) The speciality is roast nuts of every type, but you'll also find chocolate, conserves and olive oils, attractively labelled.

Vila Viniteca (p101) A jaw-dropping cathedral of wines from Catalonia and elsewhere in Spain, tucked away in a Born side street.

Barcelona Reykjavik (p86) The place to come for that organic spelt loaf or buttery croissant.

Caelum (p70) Deliciously wicked sweet treats made by nuns, with a little tea room downstairs.

Best for Vintage

L'Arca (p73) Ethereal gowns, often used for film sets, in the heart of the Barri Gòtic.

El Bulevard dels Antiquaris (p140) A quirky hotchpotch of antique shops.

Els Encants Vells (p117) Stunningly remodelled flea market, where you can unearth retro homeware and kitschy bric-a-brac.

Port Antic (p117) A quirky street market with finds from vintage toys to tiny oil paintings.

☆ Gay & Lesbian Barcelona

Barcelona has a vibrant gay and lesbian scene, with a fine array of restaurants, bars and clubs in the area known as the 'Gaixample' (a clever conjoining of Gay and L'Eixample), an area about five to six blocks southwest of Passeig de Gràcia around Carrer del Consell de Cent.

Local Attitudes

Despite fierce opposition from the Catholic Church, Spain legalised same-sex marriage in 2005. It became the fourth country in the world to do so. A poll just prior to the legislation passing found that over 60% of Spaniards favoured the legalisation of same-sex marriage. Gay and lesbian married couples can also adopt children.

As a rule, Barcelona is pretty tolerant and the sight of gay or lesbian couples arm in arm is generally unlikely to raise eyebrows. Transgenderism, too, is increasingly accepted.

Gay Bars

Befitting a diverse city of its size, the bar scene in Barcelona offers plenty of variety, with stylish cocktail bars, leather bars, bear bars, easygoing pubs and theme bars (with drag shows and other events) all part of the mix.

Gay Clubs

As with all clubs in town, things don't get going until well into the early morning (around 2am). The bigger and better-known clubs, like Metro (p139), one of Barcelona's pioneers in the LGBTI club scene, host top-notch DJs, multiple bars, a dark room, drag shows and other amusements. Keep in mind that most of the clubs open only from Thursday to Saturday nights.

The Lesbian Scene

The lesbian bar scene is a little sparse compared to the gay scene, with more places catering to a mixed gay-lesbian crowd (and a few straights thrown in) than an exclusively lesbian clientele. The one place that's proudly lesbian is Aire (p136), which should be a requisite stop for every nightlife-loving lesbian visiting the city. Some nominally straight bars and clubs host periodic lesbian parties. Keep an eye out for party flyers in shops and bars in the Gaixample for the latest.

Special Events

The gay and lesbian community from Barcelona and beyond takes centre stage during the annual **Pride Barcelona** (www.pridebarcelona. org; ☺late Jun-early Jul). The week-long event takes place in late June and features concerts, campy drag shows, film screenings, art shows and open-air dance parties – complete with lots and lots of foam. It culminates with a festive parade along Carrer de Sepúlveda and ends at the Plaça d'Espanya, where the big events are held.

Also of note is the LGBTI film festival, Fire! (www.cinemalambda.com), hosted by the Casal Lambda (opposite) in July. Film lovers might also be able to catch a bit of the Sitges Film Festival (sitgesfilmfestival.com), which happens in early October.

Sitges: Catalonia's LGBTI Capital

Barcelona has a busy gay scene, but Spain's LGBTI capital is the saucily hedonistic Sitges, 35km southwest of Barcelona, a major destination on the international party circuit. The LGBTI community there takes a leading role in the wild Carnaval celebrations in February/March.

Lonely Planet's Top Choices

Metro (p139) The city's finest (and longest-running) gay club.

Aire (p136) Barcelona's best lesbian bar, with a fab dance floor.

Best LGBTI Stays

Room Mate Pau (Map p278) Stylish, budget-conscious hotel on the edge of Barri Gòtic.

Casa de Billy Barcelona Gay-friendly B&B with wildly decorated rooms in L'Eixample.

Hotel Axel Designer rooms, a sauna and a rooftop pool in the heart of the Gaixample.

Best LGBTI Clubs

Arena Madre (p138) With striptease shows and pumping beats, it's always a fun night at Arena.

Metro (p139) One of Barcelona's top gay clubs with multiple dance floors, dark rooms and shows.

Pervert Club (p185) A fit young crowd grooves to electronic beats at this weekly party.

Best Laid-Back LGBTI Bars

Átame (p135) Join the chatter over drinks early in the night; stay late as things heat up.

La Chapelle (p138) Casual spot for cocktails and a welcoming crowd.

Punto BCN (p136) A two-level bar with a good mix of ages and creeds.

Best Alternative Scene

New Chaps (p138) A leather bar with plenty of erotic intrigue.

Bacon Bear (Map p274) A man-cave retreat for burly folk and their admirers.

Best Mixed Clubs

Arena Classic (p138) Fun, dance-loving crowds of all persuasions flock here.

La Terrrrazza (p186) Open-air summer dance parties up on Montjuïc.

Best LGBTI-Friendly Beaches

Platja de la Mar Bella (p108) A buzzing beach scene that's clothing optional at its southern tip.

Sitges (p195) Hop on a train to this LGBTI seaside mecca.

Best LGBTI-Themed Shops

Antinous (Map p274) Spacious bookshop with cafe in L'Eixample.

Cómplices (p74) Mix of lit and grit at this inviting bookseller.

NEED TO KNOW

Gay Organizations

Casal Lambda (Map p268; 93 319 55 50; www.lambda.cat; Carrer de Verdaguer i Callís 10; 7-9pm Mon-Sat; Urquinaona) A gay and lesbian social, cultural and information centre in La Ribera.

Useful Websites

60by80 (www.60by80.com) An excellent website for gay travellers. Click on 'Barcelona' under 'City Guides' and take it from there.

VisitBarcelonaGay.com (www.visitbarcelonagay.com) A busy listings site for visitors to Barcelona, with everything from fetish sections through to saunas and gay accommodation tips.

Tillate (www.tillate.es) Discover upcoming parties in this nightlife guide to regions around Spain, including Catalonia.

GaySitges (www.gaysitges.com) A specific site dedicated to this LGBTI-friendly coastal town.

PLAN YOUR TRIP GAY & LESBIAN BARCELONA

Explore
Barcelona

BARCELONA'S TOP SIGHTS

Neighbourhoods at a Glance

① La Rambla & Barri Gòtic p52

La Rambla, Barcelona's most famous pedestrian strip, is a hive of activity, with buskers and peddlers, tourists and con artists mingling amid the cafes and shops on the boulevard. The adjoining Barri Gòtic is packed with historical treasures – relics of ancient Rome, 14th-century Gothic churches and cobblestone lanes lined with shops, bars and restaurants.

② El Raval p75

The once down-and-out district of El Raval is still seedy in parts, though it has seen remarkable rejuvenation in recent years, with the addition of cutting-edge museums and cultural centres, including the Richard Meier–designed Museu d'Art Contemporani de Barcelona. Other highlights include El Raval's bohemian nightlife and the sprawling culinary delights of Mercat de la Boqueria.

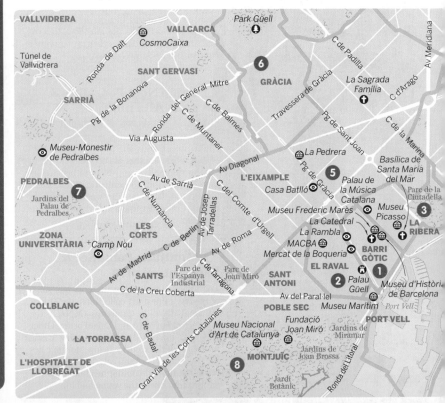

❸ La Ribera p88

This medieval quarter has a little of everything, from high-end shopping to some of Barcelona's liveliest tapas bars. Key sights include the superb Museu Picasso, the awe-inspiring Gothic Basílica de Santa Maria del Mar and the artfully sculpted Modernista concert hall of Palau de la Música Catalana. For a bit of fresh air, locals head to the manicured gardens of Parc de la Ciutadella.

❹ Barceloneta & the Waterfront p105

The formerly industrial waterfront has experienced a dramatic transformation in the last three decades, with sparkling beaches and seaside bars and restaurants, elegant sculptures, a 4.5km-long boardwalk, ultra-modern high-rises and yacht-filled marinas. Your gateway to the Mediterranean is the gridlike neighbourhood of Barceloneta,

an old-fashioned fishing quarter full of traditional seafood eateries.

❺ La Sagrada Família & L'Eixample p119

The elegant, if traffic-filled, district of L'Eixample (pronounced 'lay-sham-pluh') is a showcase for Modernista architecture, including Gaudí's unfinished masterpiece, La Sagrada Família. L'Eixample also has a celebrated dining scene, along with high-end boutiques and wildly diverse nightlife: university party spots, gilded cocktail lounges and the buzzing gay club scene of 'Gaixample' are all part of the mix.

❻ Gràcia & Park Güell p150

Gràcia was an independent town until the 1890s. Its narrow lanes and picturesque plazas still have a village-like feel, and it has long been a magnet to a young, hip, largely international crowd. Here you'll find well-worn cafes and bars, vintage shops and a smattering of multicultural eateries. On a hill to the north lies the outdoor Modernista storybook of Park Güell, yet another captivating work by Gaudí.

❼ Camp Nou, Pedralbes & La Zona Alta p162

Several of Barcelona's most sacred sights nestle inside the huge expanse beyond L'Eixample. One is the peaceful monastery of Pedralbes; another is the great shrine to Catalan football, Camp Nou. Other attractions include the amusement park and great views atop Tibidabo, the wooded trails of Parc de Collserola, and a kid-friendly science museum.

❽ Montjuïc, Poble Sec & Sant Antoni p173

The hillside overlooking the port has some of the city's finest art collections: the Museu Nacional d'Art de Catalunya (MNAC), the Fundació Joan Miró and CaixaForum. Other galleries, gardens and an imposing castle form part of the scenery. Below Montjuïc lies the lively tapas bars and eateries of Poble Sec, while the up-and-coming neighbourhood of Sant Antoni draws the young and hip.

La Rambla & Barri Gòtic

Neighbourhood Top Five

1 **La Rambla** (p54) Taking in Barcelona's liveliest street scene, with its human statues, open-air eateries, flower stalls and saunterers from every corner of the globe.

2 **La Catedral** (p58) Exploring the hidden nooks and crannies of this magnificent Gothic masterpiece.

3 **Museu d'Història de Barcelona** (p61) Walking amid the ruins of Roman-era Barcino.

4 **Museu Frederic Marès** (p63) Wandering through its strange and wondrous collections.

5 **Plaça Reial** (p62) Enjoying an alfresco meal or a drink in this picturesque square.

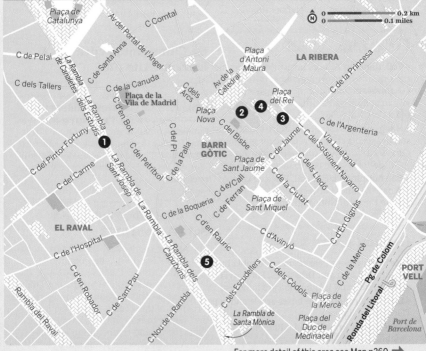

For more detail of this area see Map p260 ➡

Explore La Rambla & Barri Gòtic

La Rambla is Spain's most talked-about boulevard. It certainly packs a lot of colour into a short walk, with flower stands, historic buildings, a sensory-rich produce market, overpriced beers and tourist tat, and a ceaselessly changing parade of people from all corners of the globe. Once a river and sewage ditch on the edge of the medieval city, it still marks the southwest flank of the Barri Gòtic, the nucleus of old Barcelona. Come in the early morning to see it at its most peaceful, then return in the afternoon for the daily circus parade.

You can easily spend several days exploring the Barri Gòtic without leaving its medieval streets. In addition to major sights, the tangle of narrow lanes and tranquil plazas conceal atmospheric shops, cafes and bars. Despite the swarms of tourists Barri Gòtic has plenty of character.

Don't miss La Catedral and the smattering of Roman ruins inside the Museu d'Història de Barcelona. Another highlight is lingering over coffee or an alfresco meal at one of the Barri Gòtic's many outdoor plazas. The Plaça Reial, a wide, pretty square lined with restaurants, is perhaps the best-known spot for a bite, though Plaça del Pi and tiny Plaça de Sant Just are also quite charming.

By night, Barri Gòtic transforms into a maze-like collection of bars and clubs. The streets around Plaça Reial and Plaça George Orwell (also known as Plaça del Trippy) are good places to bar-hop, though you'll find nightspots all over the neighbourhood.

Local Life

→**Folk dancing** Although it's mostly old-timers dancing the *sardana,* a growing number of young folks are enjoying this Catalan dance. Learn a few moves and join in at 6pm on Saturday and noon on Sunday in front of La Catedral (p58).

→**Hang-outs** To escape the tourist masses, head to the southeast corner of Barri Gòtic for microbrews at La Cerveteca (p70), and cocktails and whimsy at Sor Rita (p70). Salterio (p70) is also much-loved.

→**Bar-hopping** Plaça Reial, Plaça de George Orwell and the narrow lanes between the two are the best spots to take in the local Gòtic nightlife.

Getting There & Away

→**Metro** Key stops near or on La Rambla include Catalunya, Liceu and Drassanes. For Barri Gòtic's east side, Jaume I and Urquinaona are handiest.

→**Bus** Airport and night buses arrive and depart from Plaça de Catalunya.

→**Taxi** Easiest to catch on La Rambla or Plaça de Catalunya.

Lonely Planet's Top Tip

For the best-value dining, plan to make lunch your main meal. Many restaurants in the Barri Gòtic offer three-course meals for €12 to €15, including wine.

Best Places to Eat

→ La Vinateria del Call (p68)
→ Cafè de l'Acadèmia (p68)
→ Pla (p69)
→ Koy Shunka (p69)
→ Onofre (p69)
→ Rasoterra (p68)

For reviews, see p67 →

Best Places to Drink

→ Ginger (p69)
→ Ocaña (p69)
→ Sor Rita (p70)
→ La Cerveteca (p70)
→ L'Ascensor (p69)
→ Polaroid (p70)

For reviews, see p69 →

Best Historical Treasures

→ Temple Romà d'August (p64)
→ Via Sepulcral Romana (p64)
→ Sinagoga Major (p64)
→ Domus de Sant Honorat (p66)

TOP SIGHT
LA RAMBLA

Barcelona's most famous street is both a tourist magnet and a window into Catalan culture, with cultural centres, theatres and intriguing architecture. The middle of La Rambla is a broad pedestrian boulevard, crowded every day with a wide cross-section of society. A stroll here is pure sensory overload, with souvenir hawkers, buskers, pavement artists, mimes and living statues all part of the ever-changing street scene.

DON'T MISS
....
→ Palau de la Virreina
→ Centre d'Art Santa Mònica
→ Església de Betlem
→ Palau Moja
→ Mosaïc de Miró

History

La Rambla takes its name from a seasonal stream (*raml* in Arabic) that once ran here. From the early Middle Ages, it was better known as the Cagalell (Stream of Shit) and lay outside the city walls until the 14th century. Monastic buildings were then built and, subsequently, mansions of the well-to-do from the 16th to the early 19th centuries. Unofficially La Rambla is divided into five sections, which explains why many know it as Las Ramblas.

PRACTICALITIES
....
→ Map p260
→ ⓂCatalunya, Liceu, Drassanes

La Rambla de Canaletes

The section of La Rambla north of Plaça de Catalunya is named after the **Font de Canaletes** (ⓂCatalunya), an inconspicuous turn-of-the-20th-century drinking fountain, the water of which supposedly emerges from what were once known as the springs of Canaletes. It used to be said that a proper *barcelonin* was one who 'drank the waters of Les Canaletes'. Nowadays people claim that anyone who drinks from the fountain will return to Barcelona, which is not such a bad prospect. Delirious football fans gather here to celebrate whenever the main home side, FC Barcelona, wins a cup or the league premiership.

A block east along Carrer de la Canuda is Plaça de la Vila de Madrid, with a sunken garden where Roman tombs lie exposed in the Via Sepulcral Romana (p64).

La Rambla dels Estudis

La Rambla dels Estudis, from Carrer de la Canuda running south to Carrer de la Portaferrissa, was formerly home to a twittering bird market, which closed in 2010 after 150 years in operation.

Església de Betlem

Just north of Carrer del Carme, this **church** (☑93 318 38 23; www.mdbetlem.net; Carrer d'en Xuclà 2; ⊘8.30am-1.30pm & 6-9pm; ⓂLiceu) was constructed in baroque style for the Jesuits in the late 17th and early 18th centuries to replace an earlier church destroyed by fire in 1671. Fire was a bit of a theme for this site: the church was once considered the most splendid of Barcelona's few baroque offerings, but leftist arsonists torched it in 1936.

Palau Moja

Looming over the eastern side of La Rambla, **Palau Moja** (ⓂLiceu) is a neoclassical building dating from the second half of the 18th century. Its clean, classical lines are best appreciated from across La Rambla. Unfortunately interior access is limited as it houses mostly government offices.

La Rambla de Sant Josep

From Carrer de la Portaferrissa to Plaça de la Boqueria, what is officially called La Rambla de Sant Josep (named after a now nonexistent monastery) is lined with flower stalls, which give it the alternative name La Rambla de les Flors. This stretch also contains the scurrilous Museu de l'Eròtica (p67).

Palau de la Virreina

The **Palau de la Virreina** (MLiceu) is a grand 18th-century rococo mansion (with some neoclassical elements) that now houses the **Centre de la Imatge** (☑93 316 10 00; www.ajuntament.barcelona.cat/lavirreina; ☉noon-8pm Tue-Sun; MLiceu) FREE, which has rotating photography exhibits.

Just south of the Palau, in El Raval, is the Mercat de la Boqueria (p77), one of the best-stocked and most colourful produce markets in Europe.

Mosaïc de Miró

At Plaça de la Boqueria, where four side streets meet just north of Liceu metro station, you can walk all over a Miró – the colourful mosaic in the pavement, with one tile signed by the artist. Miró chose this site as it's near the house where he was born on the Passatge del Crèdit. The mosaic's bold colours and vivid swirling forms are instantly recognisable to Miró fans, though plenty of tourists stroll right over it without realising.

La Rambla dels Caputxins

La Rambla dels Caputxins, named after a former monastery, runs from Plaça de la Boqueria to Carrer dels Escudellers. The latter street is named after the potters' guild, founded in the 13th century, the members of which lived and worked here. On the western side of La Rambla is the Gran Teatre del Liceu (p62); to the southeast is the entrance to the palm-shaded Plaça Reial (p62). Below this point La Rambla gets seedier, with the occasional strip club and peep show.

La Rambla de Santa Mònica

The final stretch of La Rambla widens out to approach the Mirador de Colom (p63) overlooking Port Vell. La Rambla here is named after the Convent de Santa Mònica, which once stood on the western flank of the street and has since been converted into the **Centre d'Art Santa Mònica** (☑93 567 11 10; www.artssantamonica.gencat.cat; La Rambla 7; ☉11am-9pm Tue-Sat, 11am-5pm Sun; MDrassanes), a cultural centre that mostly exhibits modern multimedia installations.

TAKE A BREAK

The best spot for breakfast – or coffee at any time of day – is the Cafè de l'Òpera (p70). For a proper sit-down meal, your best nearby bet is at one of the many restaurants ringing the Plaça Reial (p62).

CIVIL WAR

Many writers and journalists headed to Barcelona during the Spanish Civil War, including British author George Orwell who vividly described La Rambla gripped by revolutionary fervour in the early days of the war in his book *Homage to Catalonia*.

La Rambla

A TIMELINE

Look beyond the human statues and tourist-swarmed restaurants, and you'll find a fascinating piece of Barcelona history dating back many centuries.

13th century A serpentine seasonal stream (called *ramla* in Arabic) runs outside the city walls. As Barcelona grows, the stream will eventually become an open sewer until it's later paved over.

1500–1800 During this early period, La Rambla was dotted with convents and monasteries, including the baroque **Església de Betlem ①**, completed in the early 1700s.

1835 The city erupts in anticlericism, with riots and the burning of convents. Along La Rambla, many religious assets are destroyed or seized by the state. This paves the way for new developments, including the **Mercat de la Boqueria ②** in 1840, **Gran Teatre del Liceu ③** in 1847 and **Plaça Reial ④** in 1848.

Teatre Poliorama
Built in 1894 as the seat of the Royal Academy of Sciences and Arts, it later served as a cinema, and a strategic lookout for one communist faction during the Spanish Civil War.

RICHARD CUMMINS/GETTY IMAGES ©

Església de Betlem
Dedicated to the Holy Family, this is the last standing of the many churches once lining La Rambla. Its once sumptuous interior was gutted during the Spanish Civil War.

Font de Canaletes

Via Sepulcral Romana

Plaça del Pi

La Rambla

Palau Moja

Plaça de St Josep Oriol

Mercat de la Boqueria
The official name of Barcelona's most photogenic market is El Mercat de Sant Josep, which references the convent of St Josep that once stood here.

Centre de la Imatge ①

Palau de la Virreina

②

⑤

⑦

LUIS DAVILLA/GETTY IMAGES ©

HOLBOX/SHUTTERSTOCK ©

Gran Teatre del Liceu
Although badly damaged by fire in 1994, this gorgeous opera house was restored and reborn in 1999, and remains one of Europe's finest theatres.

1883 Architect Josep Vilaseca refurbishes the **Casa Bruno Cuadros 5**. As Modernisme is sweeping across the city, Vilaseca creates an eclectic work using stained glass, wrought iron, Egyptian imagery and Japanese prints.

1888 Barcelona hosts the Universal Exhibition. The city sees massive urban renewal projects, with the first electric lights coming to La Rambla, and the building of the **Mirador de Colom 6**.

1936–39 La Rambla becomes the site of bloody street fighting during the Spanish Civil War. British journalist and author George Orwell, who spends three days holed up in the **Teatre Poliorama 7** during street battles, later describes the tumultuous days in his excellent book, *Homage to Catalonia*.

Casa Bruno Cuadros
The Casa dels Paraigües (House of Umbrellas) – as it's known locally – prominently advertised its wares, with wall-mounted parasols and an ornate Chinese dragon.

Plaça Reial
Just off La Rambla lies one of Barcelona's prettiest plazas, home to outdoor cafes and bars, palm trees, a gurgling fountain and some unusual lampposts designed by a young Antoni Gaudí.

Mirador de Colom
Southern anchor of La Rambla, this Columbus monument was dedicated in 1888 as part of the Universal Exhibition. You can enjoy fine views from its 60m lookout.

BARRI GÒTIC

La Rambla

Palau Güell

La Rambla

Centre d'Art Santa Mònica

EL RAVAL

ISMAIL ÇIYDEM/GETTY IMAGE ©

TOP SIGHT
LA CATEDRAL

Barcelona's central place of worship presents a magnificent image. The richly decorated main facade, laced with gargoyles and the stone intricacies you would expect of northern European Gothic, sets it quite apart from other churches in Barcelona. The facade was actually added in 1870, although the rest of the building was built between 1298 and 1460.

The Interior

The interior is a broad, soaring space divided into a central nave and two aisles by lines of elegant, slim pillars. The cathedral was one of the few churches in Barcelona spared by the anarchists in the civil war, so its ornamentation, never overly lavish, is intact.

Coro

In the middle of the central nave is the late-14th-century, exquisitely sculpted timber *coro* (choir stalls). The coats of arms on the stalls belong to members of the Barcelona chapter of the Order of the Golden Fleece. Emperor Carlos V presided over the order's meeting here in 1519.

Crypt

A broad staircase before the main altar leads you down to the crypt, which contains the tomb of Santa Eulàlia, one of Barcelona's two patron saints and more affectionately known as Laia. The reliefs on the alabaster sarcophagus recount some of her tortures and, along the top strip, the removal of her body to its present resting place.

DON'T MISS

➡ The *claustre* and its 13 geese
➡ Views from the roof
➡ The crypt
➡ The *coro*

PRACTICALITIES

➡ Map p260
➡ ☎93 342 82 62
➡ www.catedralbcn.org
➡ Plaça de la Seu
➡ admission free, 'donation entrance' €7, choir €3, roof €3
➡ ⏰8am-12.45pm & 5.15-7.30pm Mon-Fri, 8am-8pm Sat & Sun, entry by donation 1-5.30pm Mon, 1-5pmSat, 2-5pm Sun
➡ Ⓜ Jaume I

The Roof

For a bird's-eye view (mind the poo) of medieval Barcelona, visit the cathedral's roof and tower by taking the lift (€3) from the Capella de les Animes del Purgatori near the northeast transept.

Claustre

From the southwest transept, exit by the partly Romanesque door (one of the few remnants of the present church's predecessor) to the leafy *claustre* (cloister), with its fountains and flock of 13 geese. The geese supposedly represent the age of Santa Eulàlia at the time of her martyrdom and have, generation after generation, been squawking here since medieval days. One of the cloister chapels commemorates 930 priests, monks and nuns martyred during the civil war.

In the northwest corner of the cloister is the **Capella de Santa Llúcia** (◷8am-7.30pm Mon-Fri, to 8pm Sat & Sun), one of the few reminders of Romanesque Barcelona (although the interior is largely Gothic).

Casa de l'Ardiaca

Upon exiting the Capella de Santa Llúcia, wander across the lane into the 16th-century **Casa de l'Ardiaca** (Arxiu Històric; ◷9am-9pm Mon-Fri, 9am-2pm Sat) , which houses the city's archives. Stroll around the supremely serene courtyard, cooled by trees and a fountain; it was renovated by Lluis Domènech i Montaner in 1902, when the building was owned by the lawyers' college. Domènech i Montaner also designed the postal slot, which is adorned with swallows and a tortoise, said to represent the swiftness of truth and the plodding pace of justice. You can get a good glimpse at some stout Roman wall in here. Upstairs, you can look down into the courtyard and across to La Catedral.

Palau Episcopal

Across Carrer del Bisbe is the 17th-century **Palau Episcopal** (Palau del Bisbat; Bishop's Palace). Virtually nothing remains of the original 13th-century structure. The Roman city's northwest gate was here and you can see the lower segments of the Roman towers that stood on either side of the gate at the base of the Palau Episcopal and Casa de l'Ardiaca. In fact, the lower part of the entire northwest wall of the Casa de l'Ardiaca is of Roman origin – you can also make out part of the first arch of a Roman aqueduct.

VISITING LA CATEDRAL

You may visit La Catedral in one of two ways. In the morning or afternoon, general admission is free, although you have to pay to visit the choir stalls or the roof. If you want to see more it's worth paying the extra euro for the so-called 'donation entrance' which gives access to the cathedral floor, the cloister, the roof, the choir, the chapter hall and the Saint Christ of Lepanto's Chapel.

SANT CRIST DE LEPANT

In the first chapel on the right from the northwest entrance, the main Crucifixion figure above the altar is Sant Crist de Lepant. It is said Don Juan's flagship bore it into battle at Lepanto and that the figure acquired its odd stance by dodging an incoming cannonball. Left from the main entrance is the baptismal font where, according to one story, six North American Indians brought to Europe by Columbus after his first voyage of accidental discovery were bathed in holy water.

SIGHTS

LA RAMBLA STREET
See p54.

LA CATEDRAL CATHEDRAL
See p58.

PALAU DEL LLOCTINENT HISTORIC SITE
Map p260 (Carrer dels Comtes; ⊙10am-2pm & 4-8pm Mon-Sat; Ⓜ Jaume I) FREE This converted 16th-century palace has a peaceful courtyard worth wandering through. Have a look upwards from the main staircase to admire the extraordinary timber *artesonado*, a sculpted ceiling made to seem like the upturned hull of a boat. Temporary exhibitions, usually related in some way to the archives, are often held here.

Next to the Plaça del Rei, the *palau* (palace) was built in the 1550s as the residence of the Spanish *lloctinent* (viceroy) of Catalonia and later converted into a convent. From 1853 it housed the Arxiu de la Corona d'Aragón, a unique archive with documents detailing the history of the Crown of Aragón and Catalonia, starting in the 12th century and reaching to the 20th.

MUSEU DIOCESÀ MUSEUM
Map p260 (Casa de la Pia Almoina; ☎ 93 315 22 13; www.cultura.arqbcn.cat; Plaça de la Seu 7; adult/concession/under 8yr €15/12/free; ⊙10am-6pm Nov-Easter, to 8pm Easter-Oct; Ⓜ Jaume I) Next to the cathedral, the Diocesan Museum has a handful of exhibits on Gaudí (including a fascinating documentary on his life and philosophy) on the upper floors. There's also a sparse collection of medieval and Romanesque religious art, usually supplemented by a temporary exhibition or two.

The building itself has fragments of Barcelona's Roman wall, as well as elements from its days as an 11th-century almshouse and its later use as an ecclesiastical residence in the 15th century.

PLAÇA DE SANT JAUME SQUARE
Map p260 (Ⓜ Liceu, Jaume I) In the 2000 or so years since the Romans settled here, the area around this square (often remodelled), which started life as the forum, has been the focus of Barcelona's civic life. This is still the central staging area for Barcelona's traditional festivals. Facing each other across the square are the Palau de la Generalitat (seat of Catalonia's regional government) on the north side and the Ajuntament (town hall) to the south.

Behind the Ajuntament rise the awful town-hall offices built in the 1970s over Plaça de Sant Miquel. Opposite is a rare 15th-century gem, **Palau Centelles** (Map p260; Plaça de Sant Miquel; Ⓜ Liceu, Jaume I), on the corner of Baixada de Sant Miquel. You can wander into the fine Gothic-Renaissance courtyard if the gates are open.

AJUNTAMENT ARCHITECTURE
Map p260 (Casa de la Ciutat; ☎ 93 402 70 00; www.barcelonaturisme.com; Plaça de Sant Jaume; ⊙10.30am-1.30pm Sun; Ⓜ Jaume I) FREE The Ajuntament, otherwise known as the Casa de la Ciutat, has been the seat of power for centuries. The Consell de Cent (the city's ruling council) first sat here in the 14th century, but the building has lamentably undergone many changes since the days of Barcelona's Gothic-era splendour.

Only the original, now disused, entrance on Carrer de la Ciutat retains its Gothic ornament. The main 19th-century neoclassical facade on the square is a charmless riposte to the Palau de la Generalitat. Inside, the Saló de Cent is the hall in which the town council once held its plenary sessions. The broad vaulting is pure Catalan Gothic and the *artesonado* (Mudéjar wooden ceiling with interlaced beams leaving a pattern of spaces for decoration) demonstrates fine work. In fact, much of what you see is comparatively recent. The building was badly damaged in a bombardment in 1842 and has been repaired and tampered with repeatedly. The wooden neo-Gothic seating was added at the beginning of the 20th century, as was the grand alabaster *retablo* (retable, or altarpiece) at the back. To the right you enter the small Saló de la Reina Regente, built in 1860, where the Ajuntament now sits. To the left of the Saló de Cent is the Saló de les

GRAFFITI ARTIST

Across Plaça Nova from La Catedral your eye may be caught by childlike scribblings on the facade of the **Col·legi de Arquitectes** (Architectural College; Map p260; Ⓜ Jaume I). It is, in fact, a giant contribution by Picasso from 1962. The artwork, which represents Mediterranean festivals, was much ridiculed by the local press when it was unveiled.

TOP SIGHT
MUSEU D'HISTÒRIA DE BARCELONA

One of Barcelona's most fascinating museums takes you back to the very foundations of Roman Barcino. You'll stroll amid extensive ruins of the town that flourished here following its founding by Emperor Augustus around 10 BC. Equally impressive is the setting inside the former Palau Reial Major (Grand Royal Palace) on Plaça del Rei (King's Sq, the former palace's courtyard), among the key locations of medieval princely power in Barcelona.

Below ground is a remarkable walk through about 4 sq km of excavated Roman and Visigothic Barcelona. After the display on the typical Roman *domus* (villa), you reach a public laundry. You pass dyeing shops, a public cold-water bath, shops dedicated to the making of *garum* (a fish sauce enjoyed across the Roman Empire), a 6th-century church and winemaking stores.

Ramparts then wind upward, past remains of the gated patio of a Roman house, the medieval Palau Episcopal (Bishops' Palace) and into two broad vaulted halls with displays on medieval Barcelona. The finale is the Saló del Tinell, the royal palace banqueting hall and a fine example of Catalan Gothic (built 1359–70). It was here that Fernando and Isabel heard Columbus' first reports of the New World.

DON'T MISS

➡ Public laundry
➡ Winemaking stores
➡ Saló del Tinell

PRACTICALITIES

➡ MUHBA
➡ Map p260
➡ 93 256 21 00
➡ www.museuhisto-ria.bcn.cat
➡ Plaça del Rei
➡ adult/concession/child €7/5/free, 3-8pm Sun & 1st Sun of month free
➡ 10am-7pm Tue-Sat, 10am-8pm Sun
➡ Jaume I

Croniques – the murals here recount Catalan exploits in Greece and the Near East in Catalonia's empire-building days.

PALAU DE LA GENERALITAT HISTORIC BUILDING
Map p260 (www.president.cat; Plaça de Sant Jaume; 2nd & 4th weekend of month; Jaume I) Founded in the early 15th century, the Palau de la Generalitat is open on limited occasions only (one-hour guided tours on the second and fourth weekends of the month, plus open-door days). The most impressive of the ceremonial halls is the Saló de Sant Jordi (Hall of St George), named after the region's patron saint. To see inside, book on the website (Catalan only).

Marc Safont designed the original Gothic main entrance on Carrer del Bisbe. The modern main entrance on Plaça de Sant Jaume is a late-Renaissance job with neoclassical leanings. If you wander by in the evening, squint up through the windows into the Saló de Sant Jordi and you will get some idea of the sumptuousness of the interior.

Normally you will have to enter from Carrer de Sant Sever. The first rooms you pass through are characterised by low vaulted ceilings. From here you head upstairs to

the raised courtyard known as the Pati dels Tarongers, a modest Gothic orangery (opened about once a month for concert performances of the palace's chimes). The 16th-century Sala Daurada i de Sessions, one of the rooms leading off the patio, is a splendid meeting hall lit up by huge chandeliers. Still more imposing is the Renaissance Saló de Sant Jordi, the murals of which were added last century – many an occasion of pomp and circumstance takes place here. Finally, you descend the staircase of the Gothic Pati Central to leave by what was originally the building's main entrance.

MUSEU D'IDEES I INVENTS DE BARCELONA MUSEUM
Map p260 (Museum of Ideas & Inventions; 93 332 79 30; www.mibamuseum.com; Carrer de la Ciutat 7; adult/concession/child under 4yr €8/6/free; 10am-2pm & 4-7pm Tue-Fri, 10am-8pm Sat, to 2pm Sun; Jaume I) Although the price is a bit steep for such a small museum (though they've now introduced a secondary system of €0.20 per minute), the collection makes for an amusing browse over an hour or so. You'll find both brilliant and bizarre inventions on display.

There are square egg makers, absorbent pillows for flatulent folks and a chair for inserting suppositories, as well as more useful devices like the Lifestraw (which filters contaminants from any drinking source) and gas glasses (adaptive eyecare for any prescription). There's also an exercise bike attached to a vending machine: you select the product, then pedal away – when your calorie output equals the calorie total of the crisps you want, the treat is yours! Don't miss the creatively configured toilets.

ESGLÉSIA DE SANTA MARIA DEL PI   CHURCH

Map p260 (☑93 318 47 43; www.basilicadelpi.com; Plaça del Pi; adult/concession/under 6yr €4/3/free; ☉10am-6pm; Ⓜ Liceu) This striking 14th-century church is a classic of Catalan Gothic, with an imposing facade, a wide interior and a single nave. The simple decor in the main sanctuary contrasts with the gilded chapels and exquisite stained-glass windows that bathe the interior in ethereal light. The beautiful rose window above its entrance is one of the world's largest. Occasional concerts are staged here (classical guitar, choral groups and chamber orchestras).

The third chapel on the left is dedicated to Sant Josep Oriol, who was parish priest here from 1687 to 1702. The chapel has a map showing the places in the church where he worked numerous miracles (he was canonised in 1909). According to legend, a 10th-century fisherman discovered an image of the Virgin Mary in a *pi* (pine tree) that he was intent on cutting down to build a boat. Struck by the vision, he instead built a little chapel, later to be succeeded by this Gothic church. A pine still grows in the square outside the church. There are guided tours, including of the bell towers, on Saturday and Sunday at noon, 1.30pm and 5pm (€10).

PLAÇA DE SANT JOSEP ORIOL   SQUARE

Map p260 (Ⓜ Liceu) This small plaza flanking the majestic Església de Santa Maria del Pi is one of the prettiest in the Barri Gòtic. Its bars and cafes attract buskers and artists and make it a lively place to hang out. It is surrounded by quaint streets, many dotted with appealing cafes, restaurants and shops.

PLAÇA REIAL   SQUARE

Map p260 (Ⓜ Liceu) One of the most photogenic squares in Barcelona, the Plaça Reial is a delightful retreat from the traffic and pedestrian mobs on the nearby Rambla. Numerous eateries, bars and nightspots lie beneath the arcades of 19th-century neoclassical buildings, with a buzz of activity at all hours.

It was created on the site of a convent, one of several destroyed along La Rambla (the street was teeming with religious institutions) in the wake of the Spain-wide disentailment laws that stripped the Church of much of its property. The lamp posts by the central fountain are Antoni Gaudí's first known works in the city.

GRAN TEATRE DEL LICEU   ARCHITECTURE

Map p260 (☑93 485 99 00; www.liceubarcelona.cat; La Rambla 51-59; tour 50min/25min €16/6; ☉50min tour 9.30am & 10.30am, 25min tour schedule varies; Ⓜ Liceu) If you can't catch a night at the opera, you can still have a look around one of Europe's greatest opera houses, known to locals as the Liceu. Smaller than Milan's La Scala but bigger than Venice's La Fenice, it can seat up to 2300 people in its grand horseshoe auditorium.

Built in 1847, the Liceu launched such Catalan stars as Josep (aka José) Carreras and Montserrat Caballé. Fire virtually destroyed it in 1994, but city authorities were quick to get it back into operation. Carefully

ROMAN WALLS

From Plaça del Rei it's worth taking a detour northeast to see the two best surviving stretches of Barcelona's **Roman walls** (Map p260; Ⓜ Jaume I), which once boasted 78 towers (as much a matter of prestige as of defence). One wall is on the southern side of Plaça Ramon de Berenguer Gran, with the **Capella Reial de Santa Àgata** (Map p260; Ⓜ Jaume I) atop. The square itself is dominated by a statue of count-king Ramon de Berenguer Gran done by Josep Llimona in 1880. The other wall is a little further south, by the northern end of Carrer del Sostinent Navarro. The Romans built and reinforced these walls in the 3rd and 4th centuries AD, after the first attacks by Germanic tribes from the north.

TOP SIGHT
MUSEU FREDERIC MARÈS

One of the wildest collections of historical curios lies inside this vast medieval complex, once part of the royal palace of the counts of Barcelona. A rather worn coat of arms on the wall indicates that it was also, for a while, the seat of the Spanish Inquisition in Barcelona.

Frederic Marès i Deulovol (1893–1991) was a rich sculptor, traveller and obsessive collector. He specialised in medieval Spanish sculpture, huge quantities of which are displayed in the basement and on the ground and 1st floors – including some lovely polychrome wooden sculptures of the Crucifixion and the Virgin. Among the most eye-catching pieces is a reconstructed Romanesque doorway with four arches, taken from a 13th-century country church in the Aragonese province of Huesca.

The top two floors comprise 'the collector's cabinet', a mind-boggling array of knick-knacks: medieval weaponry, finely carved pipes, delicate ladies' fans, intricate 'floral' displays made of seashells, and 19th-century daguerreotypes and photographs. A room that once served as Marès' study and library is now crammed with sculptures. The shady courtyard houses a pleasant summer cafe (Cafè de l'Estiu), well worth a visit after browsing the collections.

DON'T MISS

➡ Displays from the collector's cabinet
➡ Sculptures on the 1st floor
➡ Marès' study

PRACTICALITIES

➡ Map p260
➡ ☑93 256 35 00
➡ www.museumares. bcn.cat
➡ Plaça de Sant Iu 5
➡ adult/concession/ child €4.20/2.40/ free, after 3pm Sun & 1st Sun of month free
➡ ⊙10am-7pm Tue-Sat, 11am-8pm Sun
➡ Ⓜ Jaume I

---

reconstructing the 19th-century auditorium and installing the latest in theatre technology, technicians finalised its restoration in October 1999.

You can take a 25-minute guided tour around the main public areas of the theatre or join a longer guided tour. On the 50-minute tour you are taken to the grand foyer, with its thick pillars and sumptuous chandeliers, and then up the marble staircase to the Saló dels Miralls (Hall of Mirrors). These both survived the 1994 fire and the latter was traditionally where theatre-goers mingled during intermission. With mirrors, ceiling frescoes, fluted columns and high-and-mighty phrases in praise of the arts, it all exudes a typically neobaroque richness worthy of its 19th-century patrons. You are then led up to the 4th-floor stalls to admire the theatre itself.

The tour also takes in a collection of Modernista art, El Cercle del Liceu, which contains works by Ramon Casas. It is possible to book special tours, one that is similar to the guided tour but also including a half-hour music recital in the Saló dels Miralls, and another tour that penetrates the inner workings of the stage and backstage work areas.

MIRADOR DE COLOM   VIEWPOINT
Map p270 (☑93 302 52 24; www.barcelonaturisme.com; Plaça del Portal de la Pau; adult/concession €6/4; ⊙8.30am-8.30pm summer, 8.30am-7.30pm winter; ⓂDrassanes) High above the swirl of traffic on the roundabout below, Columbus keeps permanent watch, pointing vaguely out to the Mediterranean. Built for the Universal Exhibition in 1888, the monument allows you to zip up 60m in a lift for bird's-eye views back up La Rambla and across the ports of Barcelona.

It was in Barcelona that Columbus allegedly gave the delighted Catholic monarchs a report of his first discoveries in the Americas after his voyage in 1492. In the 19th century, it was popularly believed here that Columbus was one of Barcelona's most illustrious sons. Some historians still make that claim.

ESGLÉSIA DE SANTS
JUST I PASTOR   CHURCH
Map p260 (☑93 301 74 33; www.basilicasantjust. cat; Plaça de Sant Just; ⊙11am-2pm & 5-9pm Mon-Sat, 10am-1pm Sun; ⓂLiceu, Jaume I) FREE This somewhat neglected, single-nave church, with chapels on either side of the

ⓘ MANIC MONDAYS

Many attractions shut their doors on Monday, but there are plenty of exceptions, including the following:

Gran Teatre del Liceu (p62)

La Catedral (p58)

Museu de Cera (p67)

Museu de l'Eròtica (p67)

Sinagoga Major (p64)

buttressing, was built in 1342 in Catalan Gothic style on what is reputedly the site of the oldest parish church in Barcelona. Inside, you can admire some fine stained-glass windows. In front of it, in a pretty little square that was used as a film set (a smelly Parisian marketplace) in 2006 for *Perfume: The Story of a Murderer,* is what is claimed to be the city's oldest Gothic fountain.

On the morning of 11 September 1924, Antoni Gaudí was arrested as he attempted to enter the church from this square to attend Mass. In those days of the dictatorship of General Primo de Rivera, it took little to ruffle official feathers, and Gaudí's refusal to speak Spanish to the overbearing Guardia Civil officers who had stopped him earned him the better part of a day in the cells until a friend came to bail him out.

There are guided tours from Monday to Saturday (€10).

CENTRE D'INTERPRETACIÓ DEL CALL
HISTORIC SITE

Map p260 (☑93 256 21 22; www.museuhistoria. bcn.cat; Placeta de Manuel Ribé; adult/concession/child €2.20/1.50/free, 3-7pm Sun & 1st Sun of month free; ☺11am-2pm Mon, Wed, Fri, to 7pm Sat & Sun; ⓂJaume I, Liceu) Once a 14th-century house of the Jewish weaver Jucef Bonhiac, this small visitor centre is dedicated to the history of Barcelona's Jewish quarter, El Call. Glass sections on the ground floor allow you to inspect Mr Bonhiac's former wells and storage space. The house, also known as the Casa de l'Alquimista (Alchemist's House), hosts a modest display of Jewish artefacts, including ceramics excavated in the area of El Call, along with explanations and maps of the one-time Jewish quarter.

SINAGOGA MAJOR
SYNAGOGUE

Map p260 (☑93 317 07 90; www.calldebarcelona. org; Carrer de Marlet 5; ☺11am-5.30pm Mon-Fri, to 3pm Sat & Sun winter, 10.30am-6.30pm Mon-Fri, to 2.30pm Sat & Sun summer; ⓂLiceu) **FREE** When an Argentine investor bought a run-down electrician's store with an eye to converting it into central Barcelona's umpteenth bar, he could hardly have known he had stumbled onto the remains of what could be the city's main medieval synagogue (some historians cast doubt on the claim). A guide will explain what is thought to be the significance of the site in various languages.

Fragments of medieval and Roman-era walls remain in the small vaulted space that you enter from the street. Also remaining are tanners' wells installed in the 15th century. The second chamber has been spruced up for use as a synagogue. A remnant of late-Roman-era wall, given its orientation facing Jerusalem, has led some to speculate that there was a synagogue here even in Roman times. There were four synagogues in the medieval city, but after the pogroms of 1391, this one (assuming it was the Sinagoga Major) was Christianised by the placing of an effigy of St Dominic on the building.

TEMPLE ROMÀ D'AUGUST
RUIN

Map p260 (☑93 256 21 22; Carrer del Paradis 10; ☺10am-2pm Mon, to 7pm Tue-Sat, to 8pm Sun; ⓂJaume I) **FREE** Opposite the southeast end of La Catedral, narrow Carrer del Paradis leads towards Plaça de Sant Jaume. Inside No 10, an intriguing building with Gothic and baroque touches, are four columns and the architrave of Barcelona's main Roman temple, dedicated to Caesar Augustus and built to worship his imperial highness in the 1st century AD.

You are now standing on the highest point of Roman Barcino, Mont Tàber (a grand total of 16.9m – unlikely to induce altitude sickness). You may well find the door open outside the listed hours.

VIA SEPULCRAL ROMANA
ARCHAEOLOGICAL SITE

Map p260 (☑93 256 21 00; www.museuhistoria. bcn.cat; Plaça de la Vila de Madrid; adult/concession/child €2/1.50/free; ☺11am-2pm Tue & Thu, to 7pm Sat & Sun; ⓂCatalunya) Along Carrer de la Canuda, a block east of the top end of La Rambla, is a sunken garden where a series of Roman tombs lies exposed. A small-

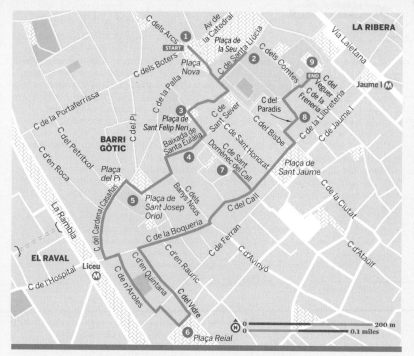

Neighbourhood Walk
Hidden Treasures in the Barri Gòtic

START LA CATEDRAL
END PLAÇA DEL REI
LENGTH 1.5KM; 1½ HOURS

This walk through the Barri Gòtic will take you back in time, from the early days of Roman-era Barcino through to the medieval era.

Before entering the cathedral, have a look at ❶ **three Picasso friezes** on the building facing the square. After noting his signature style, wander through ❷ **La Catedral** (p58); don't miss the cloister with its flock of 13 geese. Leaving the cathedral, enter the former gates of the ancient fortified city and turn right into ❸ **Plaça de Sant Felip Neri**. Note the shrapnel-scarred walls of the old church, damaged by pro-Francist bombers in 1939. A plaque commemorates the victims (mostly children) of the bombing.

Head out of the square and turn right. On this narrow lane is a small ❹ **statue of Santa Eulàlia**, one of Barcelona's patron saints who suffered various tortures during her martyrdom. Make your way west to the looming 14th-century ❺ **Església de Santa Maria del Pi** (p62), which is famed for its magnificent rose window. Follow the curving road and zigzag down to ❻ **Plaça Reial** (p62), one of Barcelona's prettiest squares. Flanking the fountain are lamp posts designed by Antoni Gaudí.

Stroll up to Carrer de la Boqueria and turn left on Carrer de Sant Domènec del Call. This leads into the El Call district, once the heart of the medieval Jewish quarter, until the bloody pogrom of 1391. The ❼ **Sinagoga Major** (p64), one of Europe's oldest, was discovered in 1996. Head across Plaça de Sant Jaume and turn left after Carrer del Bisbe. You'll soon pass the entrance to the remnants of a ❽ **Roman Temple**, with four columns hidden in a small courtyard.

The final stop is ❾ **Plaça del Rei**, a picturesque plaza where Fernando and Isabel received Columbus following his first New World voyage. The former palace today houses a superb history museum, with significant Roman ruins underground.

EL CALL

One of our favourite places in the Ciutat Vella (Old City) to wander is El Call (pronounced 'kye'), which is the name of the medieval Jewish quarter that flourished here until a tragic pogrom in the 14th century. Today its narrow lanes hide some surprising sites (including an ancient synagogue unearthed in the 1990s and the fragments of a women's bathouse inside the basement of the cafe Caelum; p70). Some of the old city's most unusual shops are here, selling exquisite antiques, handmade leather products and even kosher wine. Its well-concealed dining rooms and candelit bars and cafes make a fine destination in the evening.

El Call (which probably derives from the Hebrew word *kahal,* meaning 'community') is a tiny area, and a little tricky to find. The boundaries are roughly Carrer del Call, Carrer dels Banys Nous, Baixada de Santa Eulàlia and Carrer de Sant Honorat.

Though a handful of Jewish families remained after the bloody pogrom of 1391, the subsequent expulsion of all Jews in the country in the 15th century put an end to the Jewish presence in Barcelona. The Call Menor extended across the modern Carrer de Ferran as far as Baixada de Sant Miquel and Carrer d'en Rauric. The present Església de Sant Jaume on Carrer de Ferran was built on the site of a synagogue.

Even before the pograms of 1391, Jews in Barcelona were not exactly privileged citizens. As in many medieval centres, they were obliged to wear a special identifying mark on their garments and had trouble getting permission to expand their ghetto as El Call's population increased (as many as 4000 people were crammed into the tiny streets of the Call Major).

ish display in Spanish and Catalan by the tombs explores burial and funerary rites and customs. A few bits of pottery (including a burial amphora with the skeleton of a three-year-old Roman child) accompany the display.

The burial ground stretches along either side of the road that led northwest out of Barcelona's Roman predecessor, Barcino. Roman law forbade burial within city limits and so everyone, the great and humble, were generally buried along roads leading out of cities.

DOMUS DE SANT
HONORAT ARCHAEOLOGICAL SITE

Map p260 (☑93 256 21 00; www.museuhistoria. bcn.cat; Carrer de la Fruita 2; adult/concession/ child €2/1.50/free, 1st Sun of month free; ⊙10am-2pm Sun; MJaume I) The remains of a Roman *domus* (town house) have been unearthed and opened to the public. The house (and vestiges of three small shops) lies close to the Roman forum and the owners were clearly well off. Apart from providing something of an idea of daily Roman life through these remains, the location also contains six medieval grain silos installed when the Jewish quarter, El Call, was located in this area.

The whole site is housed in the mid-19th-century Casa Morell. So, in an unusual mix, one gets a glimpse of three distinct periods in history in the same spot.

HASH, MARIHUANA &
HEMP MUSEUM MUSEUM

Map p260 (☑93 319 75 39; www.hashmuseum. com; Carrer Ample 35; adult/under 13yr €9/free; ⊙10am-10pm; MJaume I) The world's largest museum dedicated to all things cannabis related opened to much fanfare in 2012 (even Virgin founder Richard Branson was at the opening). Set in the beautifully restored 16th-century Palau Mornau, exhibitions delve into the role the plant has played over the years, with 19th-century medicinal cannabis bottles, pulp film posters and consumer products made from hemp among the displays.

ESGLÉSIA DE LA MERCÈ CHURCH

Map p260 (☑93 315 27 56; www.basilicad-elamerce.cat; Plaça de la Mercè 1; ⊙10am-8pm Mon, Tue, Thu, Fri & Sun, 10am-1pm & 6-8pm Wed & Sat; MDrassanes) **FREE** Raised in the 1760s on the site of its Gothic predecessor, the baroque Església de la Mercè is home to Barcelona's most celebrated patron saint. It was badly damaged during the civil war. What remains is, however, quite a curiosity. The baroque facade facing the square contrasts with the Renaissance flank along Carrer Ample. Climb the steps behind the altar for a close-up view of the Virgin Mary statue for whom the church is named; it dates from 1361.

MUSEU DE L'ERÒTICA   MUSEUM

Map p260 (Erotica Museum; ☑93 318 98 65; www.erotica-museum.com; La Rambla 96; adult/concession €9/8; ☺10am-midnight; ⓂLiceu) Observe what naughtiness people have been getting up to since ancient times in this museum, with historical relics such as Indian bas-reliefs showing various aspects of tantric love, 18th-century wood carvings depicting Kama Sutra positions, Japanese porcelain porn and African fornication carvings. Despite the premise, overall it's a rather buttoned-up affair, and probably not worth the steep admission price (despite the free drink).

MUSEU DE CERA   MUSEUM

Map p260 (☑93 317 26 49; www.museocerabcn.com; Passatge de la Banca 7; adult/concession/under 4yr €15/9/free; ☺10am-10pm summer, 10am-1.30pm & 4-7.30pm Mon-Fri, 11am-2pm & 4.30-8.30pm Sat & Sun winter; ⓂDrassanes) Inside this late-19th-century building you can wander about looking at Frankenstein, Che Guevara, Lady Diana and lots of Spanish figures you probably won't recognise. It's unintentionally funny, with a price tag that's steep for often poorly executed representations, although small children are generally enthusiastic.

 EATING

LA PLATA   TAPAS €

Map p260 (☑93 315 10 09; www.barlaplata.com; Carrer de la Mercè 28; tapas €2.50-5; ☺9am-3.30pm & 6.30-11.30pm Mon-Sat; ⓂJaume I) Tucked away on a narrow lane near the waterfront, La Plata is a humble but well-loved bodega that serves just three plates: *pescadito frito* (small fried fish), *butifarra* (sausage) and tomato salad. Add in the drinkable, affordable wines (€1.10 per glass) and you have the makings of a fine predinner tapas spot.

BELMONTE   TAPAS €

Map p260 (☑93 310 76 84; Carrer de la Mercè 29; tapas €4-10, mains €12; ☺8pm-midnight Tue-Sat, plus 1-3.30pm Sat; ☎; ⓂJaume I) This tiny tapas joint in the southern reaches of Barri Gòtic whips up beautifully prepared

small plates – including an excellent *truita* (tortilla), rich *patatons a la sal* (salted new potatoes with *romesco* sauce) and tender *carpaccio de pop* (octopus carpaccio). Wash it down with the housemade *vermut* (vermouth).

TALLER DE TAPAS   CATALAN €

Map p260 (☑93 301 80 20; Plaça de Sant Josep Oriol 9; mains €7-10; ☺8.30am-1am Mon-Sat, noon-1am Sun; ⓂLiceu) A well-placed spot with outdoor seating on Plaça de Sant Josep Oriol, with a long list of tapas and more substantial bites.

ALCOBA AZUL   MEDITERRANEAN €

Map p260 (☑93 302 81 41; Carrer de Sant Domènec del Call 14; mains €7-8.50; ☺6pm-2.30am winter, noon-2am Sun-Thu, to 3am Fri & Sat summer; ☎; ⓂJaume I) Peel back the centuries inside this remarkably atmospheric watering hole, with medieval walls, low ceilings, wooden floors and flickering candles. Grab one of the seats at the tiny bar in front or slide into one of the table booths at the back, where you can enjoy good wines by the glass, satisfying plates of stuffed peppers, salads, *tostas* (sandwiches) and blood sausage with caramelised onions.

CERVECERÍA
TALLER DE TAPAS   TAPAS, CATALAN €

Map p260 (☑93 481 62 33; www.tallerdetapas.com; Carrer Comtal 28; mains €7-10; ☺8.30am-1am Mon-Sat, noon-1am Sun; ⓂUrquinaona) Amid white stone walls and a beamed ceiling, this buzzing, easy-going place serves a broad selection of tapas as well as changing daily specials like *cochinillo* (roast suckling pig). A smattering of beers from across the globe – Leffe Blonde, Guinness, Brahma (Brazil) and Sol (Mexico) – add to the appeal.

It has a few other locations around town, including a well-placed spot with outdoor seating on Plaça de Sant Josep Oriol.

XURRERIA   CHURROS €

Map p260 (☑93 318 76 91; Carrer dels Banys Nous 8; cone €1.20; ☺7.30am-1.30pm & 3.30-8.15pm; ⓂJaume I) It doesn't look much from the outside, but this brightly lit street joint is Barcelona's best spot for paper cones of piping-hot churros – long batter sticks fried and sprinkled with sugar and best enjoyed dunked in hot chocolate.

FORNERIA TIANA
BAKERY €

Map p260 (www.caltiana.cat; Carrer Ample 27; sandwiches around €3; ⊙7am-10pm; 🛜; Ⓜ Jaume I) Stop in this bright corner bakery and cafe for fresh pastries, croissants, cheese, charcuterie, quiches and other light bites. Staff whip up a decent coffee, though there's also wine and other refreshments.

★LA VINATERIA DEL CALL
SPANISH €€

Map p260 (✆93 302 60 92; www.lavinateriadelcall.com; Carrer de Sant Domènec del Call 9; small plates €7-12; ⊙7.30pm-1am; Ⓜ Jaume I) In a magical setting in the former Jewish quarter, this tiny jewel box of a restaurant (recently extended to add another dining room) serves up tasty Iberian dishes including Galician octopus, cider-cooked chorizo and the Catalan *escalivada* (roasted peppers, aubergine and onions) with anchovies. Portions are small and made for sharing, and there's a good and affordable selection of wines.

★CAFÈ DE L'ACADÈMIA
CATALAN €€

Map p260 (✆93 319 82 53; Carrer dels Lledó 1; mains €14-18; ⊙1-3.30pm & 8-11pm Mon-Fri; 🛜; Ⓜ Jaume I) Expect a mix of traditional Catalan dishes with the occasional creative twist. At lunchtime, local Ajuntament (town hall) office workers pounce on the *menú del día* (daily set menu; €14.30). In the evening it is more romantic, as low lighting emphasises the intimacy of the beamed ceiling and stone walls. On warm days you can also dine outside.

FEDERAL
CAFE €€

Map p260 (✆93 280 81 71; www.federalcafe.es; Passatge de la Pau 11; mains €9-12; ⊙9am-midnight Mon-Thu, to 1am Fri & Sat, 9am-5.30pm Sun; 🛜; Ⓜ Drassanes) Don't be intimidated by the industrial chic, the sea of open MacBooks or the stack of design mags – this branch of the Poble Sec Federal mothership is incredibly welcoming, with healthy, hearty and good-value food. Choose a salad and a topping (poached eggs, strips of chicken) or a yellow curry, say, and follow it up with a moist slab of carrot cake.

MILK
BRUNCH €€

Map p260 (✆93 268 09 22; www.milkbarcelona.com; Carrer d'en Gignàs 21; mains €8-12; ⊙9am-2am Sun-Thu, to 3am Fri & Sat; 🛜; Ⓜ Jaume I) Also known to many as an enticing cocktail spot, Irish-run Milk's key role for Barcelona night owls is providing morning-after brunches (served till 4.30pm). Tuck into pancakes, eggs Benedict and other hangover dishes in a cosy lounge-like setting.

CAN CULLERETES
CATALAN €€

Map p260 (✆93 317 30 22; www.culleretes.com; Carrer Quintana 5; mains €10-17; ⊙1.30-4pm & 9-11pm Tue-Sat, 1.30-4pm Sun; Ⓜ Liceu) Founded in 1786, Barcelona's oldest restaurant is still going strong, with tourists and locals flocking here to enjoy its rambling interior, old-fashioned tile-filled decor and enormous helpings of traditional Catalan food, including fresh seafood and sticky stews.

RASOTERRA
VEGETARIAN €€

Map p260 (✆93 318 69 26; www.rasoterra.cat; Carrer del Palau 5; mains €13; ⊙7-11pm Tue, 1-4pm & 7-11pm Wed-Sun; 🛜🖊; Ⓜ Jaume I) A delightful addition to the Gothic quarter, Rasoterra cooks up first-rate vegetarian dishes in a Zen-like setting with tall ceilings, low-playing jazz and fresh flowers on the tables. The creative, globally influenced menu changes regularly and might feature Vietnamese-style coconut pancakes with tofu and vegetables, beluga lentils with basmati rice, and pear and goat cheese quesadillas. Good vegan and gluten-free options.

MIRILLA
INTERNATIONAL €€

Map p260 (Carrer de Regomir 16; platillos €4.50-16; ⊙6pm-1am Mon-Thu, to 3am Fri & Sat; Ⓜ Jaume I) Mirilla is a great place to stumble upon, with excellent wines by the glass and well-executed cocktails, along with a range of *platillos* (somewhere between a tapa and a main course) that includes cod ceviche, pork with wild mushrooms and mackerel teriyaki. It's a cosy little place and fills up fast. Reserve if you can.

BEST CAFES

Some of Barcelona's most atmospheric cafes lie hidden in the old cobbled lanes of Barri Gòtic. A round-up of our favourite spots for a pick-me-up.

Salterio (p70)

Čaj Chai (p71)

La Clandestina (p71)

Caelum (p70)

Cafè de l'Òpera (p70)

La Granja (p70)

ONOFRE
SPANISH €€

Map p260 (☑93 317 69 37; www.onofre.net; Carrer de les Magdalenes 19; mains €9-14; ☺10am-4pm & 7.30pm-midnight Mon-Sat; ☎; ⓂJaume I) Famed for its (good, affordable) wine selections, Onofre is a small, modern eatery (and wine shop and delicatessen) that has a strong local following for its delicious tapas and great-value lunch specials (three-course prix fixé for €10.75, or €14.75 on Saturdays). Among the delectable tapas selections: Italian greens with foie shavings, duck confit, codfish carpaccio and oven-baked prawns.

CERERÍA
VEGETARIAN €€

Map p260 (☑93 301 85 10; Baixada de Sant Miquel 3; mains €7-11; ☺1pm-midnight Tue-Sat, 1pm-5pm Sun; ☎☑; ⓂJaume I) Black-and-white marble floors, a smattering of old wooden tables and ramshackle displays of musical instruments lend bohemian charm to this small vegetarian restaurant. The pizzas are delicious and feature organic ingredients – as do the flavourful galettes, dessert crêpes and bountiful salads. Vegan options too.

ALLIUM
CATALAN, FUSION €€

Map p260 (☑93 302 30 03; www.alliumrestaurant. es; Carrer del Call 17; mains €15-18; ☺8am-11pm Mon-Thu, to 11.30pm Fri, 10am-11.30pm Sat, noon-11pm Sun; ☎; ⓂLiceu) This bright, modern tapas bar and restaurant serves mostly Catalan dishes with varying specials (including seafood paella for one). The menu, which changes every two or threee weeks, focuses on seasonal, organic cuisine. Its kitchen is open all day, making it a good bet for those who don't want to wait until 9pm for a meal.

KOY SHUNKA
JAPANESE €€€

Map p260 (☑93 412 79 39; www.koyshunka.com; Carrer de Copons 7; multicourse menu €82-128; ☺1.30-3pm & 8.30-11pm Tue-Sat, 1.30-3pm Sun; ⓂUrquinaona) Down a narrow lane north of the cathedral, Koy Shunka opens a portal to exquisite dishes from the East – mouthwatering sushi, sashimi, seared Wagyu beef and flavour-rich seaweed salads are served alongside inventive cooked fushion dishes like steamed clams with sake or tempura of scallops and king prawns with Japanese mushrooms. Don't miss the house speciality of tender *toro* (tuna belly).

Set multicourse menus are pricey but well worth it for those seeking a truly extraordinary dining experience.

PLA
FUSION €€€

Map p260 (☑93 412 65 52; www.restaurant-pla.cat; Carrer de la Bellafila 5; mains €17-23; ☺7-11.30pm Sun-Thu, to midnight Fri & Sat; ⓂJaume I) One of Gòtic's long-standing favourites, Pla is a stylish, romantically lit medieval dining room where the cooks churn out such temptations as oxtail braised in red wine, seared tuna with oven-roasted peppers, and polenta with seasonal mushrooms. It has a tasting menu for €52 Sunday to Thursday.

ELS QUATRE GATS
CATALAN €€€

Map p260 (☑93 302 41 40; www.4gats.com; Carrer de Montsió 3; mains €21-29; ☺12.30-4.30pm & 6.30pm-1am; ☎; ⓂUrquinaona) Once the lair of Barcelona's Modernista artists, Els Quatre Gats is a stunning example of the movement, inside and out, with its colourful tiles, geometric brickwork and wooden fittings. The restaurant is not quite as thrilling as its setting, though you can just have a coffee and a croissant in the cafe (open from 9am to 1am) at the front.

🍷 DRINKING & NIGHTLIFE

★GINGER
COCKTAIL BAR

Map p260 (☑93 310 53 09; www.ginger.cat; Carrer de Palma de Sant Just 1; ☺7.30pm-2.30am Tue-Thu, 7.30pm-3am Fri & Sat; ⓂJaume I) Tucked away just off peaceful Plaça de Sant Just, Ginger is an art deco–style multilevel drinking den with low lighting, finely crafted cocktails and good ambient sounds (provided by vinyl-spinning DJs some nights). It's a mellow spot that's great for sipping wine and sampling from the gourmet tapas menu.

L'ASCENSOR
BAR

Map p260 (☑93 318 53 47; Carrer de la Bellafila 3; ☺6pm-2.30am Sun-Thu, to 3am Fri & Sat; ☎; ⓂJaume I) Named after the lift (elevator) doors that serve as the front door, this elegant drinking den with its vaulted brick ceilings, vintage mirrors and marble-topped bar gathers a faithful crowd that comes for old-fashioned cocktails and lively conversation against a soundtrack of up-tempo jazz and funk.

OCAÑA
BAR

Map p260 (☑93 676 48 14; www.ocana.cat; Plaça Reial 13; ☺noon-2.30am Mon-Fri, 11am-2.30am Sat & Sun; ☎; ⓂLiceu) Named after a flamboyant artist who once lived on Plaça Reial, Ocaña is a beautifully designed space with chandeliers and plush furnishings. Have a seat on the terrace and watch the passing people parade, or head downstairs to the Moorish-inspired Apotheke bar or the chic lounge a few steps away, where DJs spin for a mix of beauties and bohemians on weekend nights.

SOR RITA
BAR

Map p260 (📞93 176 62 66; www.sorritabar.es; Carrer de la Mercè 27; ⏱7pm-3am Sun-Thu, to 3.30am Fri & Sat; 📶; MJaume I) A lover of all things kitsch, Sor Rita is pure eye candy, from its leopard-print wallpaper to its high-heel-festooned ceiling and deliciously irreverent decorations inspired by the films of Almodóvar. It's a fun and festive scene, with special-event nights including tarot readings on Mondays, €5 all-you-can-eat snack buffets on Tuesdays, karaoke or cabaret on Wednesdays and gin specials on Thursdays.

LA GRANJA
CAFE

Map p260 (📞93 302 69 75; Carrer dels Banys Nous 4; ⏱9am-9pm; MJaume I) This long-running cafe serves up thick, rich cups of chocolate, in varying formats, but it doesn't make its own churros. Buy them a few doors down at Xurreria (p67) and bring them here for the perfect combo of churros dipped in chocolate. Also worth a look is the section of Roman wall visible at the back.

POLAROID
BAR

Map p260 (📞93 186 66 69; www.polaroidbar.es; Carrer dels Còdols 29; ⏱7pm-2.30am Sun-Thu, to 3am Fri & Sat; MDrassanes) For a dash of 1980s nostalgia, Polaroid is a blast from the past, with its wall-mounted VHS tapes, old film posters, comic-book-covered tables, action-figure displays and other kitschy decor. Not surprisingly, it draws a fun, unpretentious crowd who come for cheap *cañas* (draught beer), mojitos and free popcorn.

LA CERVETECA
BAR

Map p260 (www.lacerveteca.com; Carrer d'en Gignàs 25; ⏱6pm-midnight Tue-Fri, noon-3.30pm & 6pm-midnight Sat, noon-3.30pm Sun; MJaume I) An unmissable stop for beer lovers, La Cerveteca serves an impressive variety of global craft brews. In addition to scores of bottled beers, there's a frequent rotation of what's on draught. Cheeses, *jamón ibérico* and other charcuterie selections are on hand, including *cecina* (cured horse meat).

MARULA CAFÉ
BAR

Map p260 (📞93 318 76 90; www.marulacafe.com; Carrer dels Escudellers 49; ⏱11pm-6am Wed-Sun; MLiceu) A fantastic find in the heart of the Barri Gòtic, Marula will transport you to the 1970s and the best in funk and soul. James Brown fans will think they've died and gone to heaven. It's not, however, a monothematic place and DJs slip in other tunes, from breakbeat to house. Samba and other Brazilian dance sounds also penetrate here.

CAELUM
CAFE

Map p260 (📞93 302 69 93; www.caelumbarcelona.com; Carrer de la Palla 8; ⏱10.30am-8.30pm Mon-Thu, to 11pm Fri & Sat, to 9pm Sun; MLiceu) Centuries of heavenly gastronomic tradition from across Spain are concentrated in this exquisite medieval space in the heart of the city. The upstairs cafe is a dainty setting for decadent cakes and pastries, while descending into the underground chamber with its stone walls and flickering candles is like stepping into the Middle Ages.

Wherever you decide to sit, you'll also pass through the shop that sells sweets made by nuns in convents across the country.

SALTERIO
CAFE

Map p260 (Carrer de Sant Domènec del Call 4; ⏱11am-midnight, to 1am Fri & Sat; 📶; MJaume I) A wonderfully photogenic candlelit spot tucked down a tiny lane in El Call, Salterio serves Turkish coffee, authentic mint teas and snacks amid stone walls, incense and ambient Middle Eastern music. If hunger strikes, try the *sardo* (grilled flat-bread covered with pesto, cheese or other toppings).

CAFÈ DE L'ÒPERA
CAFE

Map p260 (📞93 317 75 85; www.cafeoperabcn.com; La Rambla 74; ⏱8.30am-2.30am; 📶; MLiceu) Opposite the Gran Teatre del Liceu is La Rambla's most intriguing cafe. Operating since 1929, it is pleasant enough for an early evening libation or coffee and croissants. Head upstairs for an elevated seat above the busy boulevard. Can you be tempted by the *cafè de l'Òpera* (coffee with chocolate mousse)?

GRANJA LA PALLARESA
CAFE

Map p260 (📞93 302 20 36; Carrer del Petritxol 11; ⏱9am-1pm daily, 4-9pm Mon, Sat & Sun; MLiceu) A buzzy cafe filled with families and specialising in cakes, churros and hot chocolate.

MANCHESTER BAR

Map p260 (www.manchesterbar.com; Carrer de Milans 5; ⊙6.30pm-2.30am Sun-Thu, to 3am Fri & Sat; ☎; MLiceu) ✐ A drinking den that has undergone several transformations over the years now treats you to the sounds of great Manchester bands, from Joy Division to Oasis. It has a pleasing rough-and-tumble feel, with tables jammed in every which way. There are DJs on Thursdays.

LA MACARENA CLUB

Map p260 (☎637 416647; www.macarenaclub. com; Carrer Nou de Sant Francesc 5; €5-10; ⊙midnight-5am Sun-Thu, to 6am Fri & Sat; MDrassanes) You won't believe this was once a tile-lined Andalucian flamenco musos' bar. Now it is a dark dance space, of the kind where it is possible to sit at the bar, meet people around you and then stand up for a bit of a shake to the DJ's electro and house offerings, all within a couple of square metres.

KARMA CLUB

Map p260 (☎93 302 56 80; www.karmadisco.com; Plaça Reial 10; ⊙6pm-5.30am; MLiceu) During the week Karma plays good, mainstream indie music, while on weekends the DJs spin anything from rock to disco. A golden oldie in Barcelona, tunnel-shaped Karma is small and becomes quite tightly packed (claustrophobic for some) with a good-natured crowd of locals and out-of-towners. The bar and terrace on the Plaça Reial open at 6pm, and the club opens at midnight.

LA CLANDESTINA CAFE

Map p260 (☎93 319 05 33; Baixada de Viladecols 2; ⊙10am-10pm Mon-Fri, to 11pm Sat, 11am-10pm Sun; ☎; MJaume I) Globally inspired options here include tea, Turkish coffee, mango lassi, quiche and panini, along with wine and beer. La Clandestina's white walls are enlivened with gold-painted beams and a changing display of local artwork for sale, under which sit youngish locals, often tapping away on laptops.

ČAJ CHAI CAFE

Map p260 (☎93 301 95 92; www.cajchai.com; Carrer de Sant Domènec del Call 12; ⊙10.30am-10pm; MJaume I) Inspired by Prague's bohemian tearooms, this bright and buzzing cafe in the heart of the old Jewish quarter is a tea connoisseur's paradise. Čaj Chai stocks over 100 teas from China, India, Korea, Japan, Nepal, Morocco and beyond. It's a much-loved local haunt.

OVISO BAR

Map p260 (☎637 589269; www.barnawood. com; Carrer d'Arai 5; ⊙10am-2.30am Sun-Thu, to 3am Fri & Sat; ☎; MLiceu) Oviso is a popular budget-friendly restaurant with outdoor tables on the plaza, but shows its true bohemian colours by night, with a mixed crowd, a rock-and-roll vibe and a rustic decorated two-room interior plastered with curious murals – geese taking flight, leaping dolphins and blue peacocks framing the brightly painted concrete walls.

BOSC DE LES FADES LOUNGE

Map p260 (☎93 317 26 49; Passatge de la Banca 5; ⊙10am-1am Mon-Fri, 11am-1.30am Sat & Sun; MDrassanes) The 'Forest of the Fairies' is touristy but offers a whimsical retreat from the busy Rambla nearby. Lounge chairs and lamplit tables are scattered beneath an indoor forest complete with fountain and grotto. Prices are steep (€10 for a cocktail).

⭐ ENTERTAINMENT

GRAN TEATRE DEL LICEU THEATRE, LIVE MUSIC

Map p260 (☎93 485 99 00; www.liceubarcelona. com; La Rambla 51-59; ⊙box office 9.30am-8pm Mon-Fri, 9.30am-6pm Sat & Sun; MLiceu) Barcelona's grand old opera house, restored after fire in 1994, is one of the most technologically advanced theatres in the world. To take a seat in the grand auditorium, returned to all its 19th-century glory but with the very latest in acoustics, is to be transported to another age. Tickets can cost anything from €10 for a cheap seat behind a pillar to €200 for a well-positioned night at the opera.

L'ATENEU CLASSICAL MUSIC

Map p260 (☎93 343 61 21; www.ateneubcn.org; Carrer de la Canuda 6; tickets free-€10; MCatalunya) This historic cultural centre (with roots dating back 150 years) hosts a range of high-brow fare, from classical recitals to film screenings and literary readings.

EL PARAIGUA LIVE MUSIC

Map p260 (☎93 302 11 31; www.elparaigua. com; Carrer del Pas de l'Ensenyança 2; ⊙noon-midnight Sun-Wed, to 2am Thu, to 3am Fri & Sat; MLiceu) A tiny chocolate box of dark tinted Modernisme, the 'Umbrella' has been serving up drinks since the 1960s. The turn-of-the-20th-century decor was transferred here from a shop knocked down elsewhere in the district and cobbled back together to create this cosy locale.

Take a trip in time from Modernisme to medieval by heading downstairs to the brick and stone basement bar area. Amid 11th-century walls, live bands – funk, soul, rock, blues – hold court on Fridays and Saturdays (from 11.30pm).

TEATRE PRINCIPAL   LIVE MUSIC

Map p260 (✆662 018517; www.teatreprincipalbcn.com; La Rambla 27; concerts €25-50; ⊙9.30-11.30pm Mon-Sat Café Principal, 8pm & 10pm Sala B; Ⓜ Liceu) Following a €6 million renovation, this historic theatre has been transformed into a lavish concert space, though most of it is currently used for one-off events. There are flamenco shows in the atmospheric Sala B, all columns and wood and red velvet banquettes.

SIDECAR FACTORY CLUB   LIVE MUSIC

Map p260 (✆93 302 15 86; www.sidecarfactoryclub.com; Plaça Reial 7; ticket prices vary; ⊙7pm-5am Mon-Sat; Ⓜ Liceu) Its entrance is on Plaça Reial, and you can come here for a meal before midnight or a few drinks at ground level (which closes by 3am at the latest), or descend into the red-tinged, brick-vaulted bowels for live music most nights. Just about anything goes here, from UK indie through to country punk, but rock and pop lead the way.

Most shows start around 10pm. DJs take over at 12.30am to keep things going.

JAMBOREE   LIVE MUSIC

Map p260 (✆93 319 17 89; www.masimas.com/jamboree; Plaça Reial 17; tickets €12-20; ⊙8pm-6am; Ⓜ Liceu) For over half a century, Jamboree has been bringing joy to the jivers of Barcelona, with high-calibre acts featuring jazz trios, blues, Afrobeats, Latin sounds and big-band sounds. Two concerts are held most nights (at 8pm and 10pm), after which Jamboree morphs into a DJ-spinning club at midnight. WTF jam sessions are held Mondays (entrance a mere €5).

Buy tickets online to save a few euros.

SALA TARANTOS   FLAMENCO

Map p260 (✆93 304 12 10; www.masimas.com/tarantos; Plaça Reial 17; tickets €15; ⊙shows 8.30pm, 9.30pm & 10.30pm; Ⓜ Liceu) Since 1963, this basement locale has been the stage for up-and-coming flamenco groups performing in Barcelona. These days Tarantos has become a mostly tourist-centric af-

fair, with half-hour shows held three times a night. Still, it's a good introduction to flamenco, and not a bad setting for a drink.

HARLEM JAZZ CLUB   JAZZ

Map p260 (✆93 310 07 55; www.harlemjazzclub.es; Carrer de la Comtessa de Sobradiel 8; tickets €6-10; ⊙10.30pm-3am Sun & Tue-Thu, to 5am Fri & Sat; Ⓜ Liceu) This narrow, old-city dive is one of the best spots in town for jazz, as well as funk, Latin, blues and gypsy jazz. It attracts a mixed crowd who maintains a respectful silence during the acts. Most concerts start around 10pm. Get in early if you want a seat in front of the stage.

BOULEVARD   DJ

Map p260 (✆622 438423; www.boulevardcultureclub.es; La Rambla 27; entry free to €15, depending on night; ⊙11.45pm-5am Sun-Thu, to 6am Fri & Sat; Ⓜ Drassanes) Boulevard (also known as Dome, depending on the night) is flanked by striptease bars (in the spirit of the lower Rambla's old days), and has undergone countless reincarnations. With three different dance spaces, one of them upstairs, it has a deliciously tacky feel, pumping out anything from 1980s hits to house music (especially on Saturdays in the main room). There's no particular dress code.

🛍 SHOPPING

TORRONS VICENS   FOOD

Map p260 (✆93 304 37 36; www.vicens.com; Carrer del Petritxol 15; ⊙10am-8.30pm Mon-Sat, 11am-8pm Sun; Ⓜ Liceu) You can find the *turrón* (nougat) treat year-round at Torrons Vicens, which has been selling its signature sweets since 1775.

SABATER HERMANOS   BEAUTY

Map p260 (✆93 301 98 32; www.shnos.com.ar; Plaça de Sant Felip Neri 1; ⊙10.30am-9pm; Ⓜ Jaume I) This fragrant little shop sells handcrafted soaps of all sizes. Varieties like fig, cinnamon, grapefruit and chocolate smell good enough to eat, while sandalwood, magnolia, mint, cedar and jasmine add spice to any sink or bathtub.

ESCRIBÀ   FOOD & DRINK

Map p260 (✆93 301 60 27; www.escriba.es; La Rambla 83; ⊙9am-10pm; ☎; Ⓜ Liceu) Chocolates, dainty pastries and mouth-watering cakes can be nibbled behind the Modernista mosaic facade here or taken away for

THE SWEET LIFE

Barcelona has some irresistible temptations for those with a sweet tooth. Chocolate lovers won't want to miss Carrer del Petritxol, which is home to several famous *granjas* (milk bars) that dole out thick cups of hot chocolate, best accompanied by churros. The recommended Granja La Pallaresa (p70) always draws a crowd.

At Christmas specialist pastry stores fill with *turrón*, the traditional holiday temptation. Essentially nougat, it comes in different varieties: softer blocks are *turrón de Valencia* and a harder version is *turrón de Gijón*. You can find the treat year-round at stores such as Torrons Vicens (left), which has been selling its signature sweets since 1775.

Other not-to-be-missed spots include Caelum (p70), and La Colmena (p74).

private, guilt-ridden consumption. This Barcelona favourite is owned by the Escribà family, a name synonymous with sinfully good sweet things. More than that, it adds a touch of authenticity to La Rambla.

FORMATGERIA LA SEU   FOOD

Map p260 (☑93 412 65 48; www.formatgerialaseu.com; Carrer de la Dagueria 16; ⏱10am-2pm & 5-8pm Tue-Sat, closed Aug; ⓜJaume I) Dedicated to artisan cheeses from all across Spain, this small shop is run by the knowledgeable Katherine McLaughlin and is the antithesis of mass production – it sells only the best from small-scale farmers and the stock changes regularly. Wine and cheese tastings in the cosy room at the back are fun.

EL CORTE INGLÉS   DEPARTMENT STORE

Map p260 (Portal de l'Àngel 19-21; ⏱9.30am-9.30pm Mon-Sat; ⓜCatalunya) A secondary branch of Spain's only remaining department store, selling electronics, fashion, stationery and sports gear.

L'ARCA   VINTAGE, CLOTHING

Map p260 (☑93 302 15 98; www.larca.es; Carrer dels Banys Nous 20; ⏱11am-2pm & 4.30-8.30pm Mon-Sat; ⓜLiceu) Step inside this enchanting shop for a glimpse of beautifully crafted apparel from the past, including 18th-century embroidered silk vests, elaborate silk kimonos, and wedding dresses and shawls from the 1920s. Thanks to its incredible collection, it has provided clothing for films including *Titanic, Talk to Her* and *Perfume: The Story of a Murderer*.

CERERIA SUBIRÀ   HOMEWARES

Map p260 (☑93 315 26 06; Baixada de la Llibreteria 7; ⏱9.30am-1.30pm & 4-8pm Mon-Thu, 9.30am-8pm Fri, 10am-8pm Sat; ⓜJaume I) Even if you're not interested in myriad mounds of colourful wax, pop in just so you've been

to the oldest shop in Barcelona. Cereria Subirà has been churning out candles since 1761 and at this address since the 19th century; the interior has a beautifully baroque quality, with a picturesque *Gone With the Wind*–style staircase.

HERBORISTERIA DEL REI   BEAUTY

Map p260 (☑93 318 05 12; www.herboristeriadelrei.com; Carrer del Vidre 1; ⏱2-8.30pm Mon, 10am-8.30pm Tue-Sat; ⓜLiceu) Once patronised by Queen Isabel II, this timeless corner store flogs all sorts of weird and wonderful herbs, spices and medicinal plants. It's been doing so since 1823 and the decor has barely changed since the 1860s. However, some of the products have, and you'll find anything from soaps to massage oil nowadays.

ARTESANIA CATALUNYA   HANDICRAFTS

Map p260 (☑93 342 75 20; www.bcncrafts.com; Carrer dels Banys Nous 11; ⏱10am-8pm Mon-Sat, to 2pm Sun; ⓜLiceu) A celebration of Catalan products, this nicely designed store is a great place to browse for unique gifts. You'll find jewellery with designs inspired by Roman iconography (as well as works that reference Gaudí and Barcelona's Gothic era), plus pottery, wooden toys, silk scarves, notebooks, housewares and more.

TALLER DE MARIONETAS
TRAVI   MARIONETTES

Map p260 (☑93 412 66 92; www.marionetastravi.com; Carrer de n'Amargós 4; ⏱noon-8pm Mon-Sat; ⓜUrquinaona) Opened in the 1970s, this atmospheric shop sells beautifully handcrafted marionettes. Don Quixote, Sancho Panza and other iconic Spanish figures are on hand, as well as unusual works from other parts of the world – including rare Sicilian puppets and pieces from Myanmar (Burma), Indonesia and elsewhere.

DRAP ART   ARTS & CRAFTS

Map p260 (☎93 268 48 89; www.drapart.org; Carrer Groc 1; ⊙11am-2pm & 5-8pm Tue-Fri, 6-9pm Sat; Ⓜ Jaume I) A nonprofit arts organisation runs this small store and gallery space, which exhibits wild designs from artists near and far. Works change regularly, but you might find sculptures, jewellery, handbags and other accessories made from recycled products.

ZOEN   ACCESSORIES

Map p260 (☎93 306 96 88; www.zoen.es; Carrer de Sant Domènec del Call 15; ⊙11am-2.30pm & 5-8.30pm Mon-Sat; Ⓜ Jaume I) In the heart of the old Jewish quarter, Zoen is a tiny shop selling finely crafted leather goods made on site. Handbags, wallets, belts, book covers and satchels are among the wares for sale.

LA COLMENA   FOOD

Map p260 (☎93 315 13 56; Plaça de l'Angel 12; ⊙9am-9pm; Ⓜ Jaume I) A pastry shop selling many delicacies including pine-nut-encrusted *panellets* (sweet almond cakes), flavoured meringues and feather-light *ensaïmadas* (soft, sweet buns topped with powdered sugar) from Mallorca.

CÓMPLICES   BOOKS

Map p260 (www.libreriacomplices.com; Carrer de Cervantes 4; ⊙10.30am-8pm Mon-Fri, noon-8pm Sat; Ⓜ Jaume I) One of the most extensive gay and lesbian bookstores in the city has a mix of erotica in the form of DVDs and comics as well as books.

SALA PARÉS   ARTS & CRAFTS

Map p260 (☎93 318 70 20; www.salapares.com; Carrer del Petritxol 5; ⊙4-8pm Mon, 10.30am-2pm & 4-8pm Tue-Sat; Ⓜ Liceu) This gallery has maintained its position as one of the city's leading purveyors of Catalan art since 1877, with works from the 19th century to the present. Increasingly it stocks more work from elsewhere in Spain and Europe.

LA MANUAL ALPARGATERA   SHOES

Map p260 (☎93 301 01 72; www.lamanualalpargatera.es; Carrer d'Avinyó 7; ⊙9.30am-1.30pm & 4.30-8pm Mon-Fri, from 10am Sat; Ⓜ Liceu) Clients from Salvador Dalí to Jean Paul Gaultier have ordered a pair of *espadrilles* (rope-soled canvas shoes) from this famous store. The shop was founded just after the Spanish Civil War, though the roots of the simple shoe design date back hundreds of years and originated in the Catalan Pyrenees.

ART & CRAFTS MARKET   MARKET

Map p260 (Mostra d'Art; Plaça de Sant Josep Oriol; ⊙11am-8.30pm Sat, 10am-3pm Sun; Ⓜ Liceu) The Barri Gòtic is enlivened by an art and crafts market on Saturday and Sunday.

XOCOA   FOOD

Map p260 (☎93 301 82 91; www.xocoa-bcn.com; Carrer del Petritxol 11-13; ⊙9.30am-9pm; Ⓜ Liceu) Tucked along 'chocolate street' Carrer del Petritxol, this den of dental devilry displays ranks and ranks of original bars in stunning designs, chocolates stuffed with sweet stuff, gooey pastries and more.

PAPABUBBLE   FOOD

Map p260 (☎93 268 86 25; www.papabubble.com; Carrer Ample 28; ⊙10am-2pm & 3.30-8pm Mon-Fri, 10am-8pm Sat; Ⓜ Jaume I) It feels like a step into another era in this sweet shop, which makes up pots of rainbow-coloured boiled lollies, just like some of us remember from corner-store days as kids.

FC BOTIGA   SOUVENIRS

Map p260 (☎93 269 15 32; Carrer de Jaume I 18; ⊙10am-9pm Mon-Sat; Ⓜ Jaume I) Need a Lionel Messi football jersey, a blue and burgundy ball, or any other football paraphernalia pertaining to what many locals consider the greatest team in the world?

OBACH   ACCESSORIES

Map p260 (☎93 318 40 94; Carrer del Call 2; ⊙10am-2pm & 4-8pm Mon-Sat; Ⓜ Jaume I) Since 1924 this store has been purveying all manner of headgear. You'll find Kangol mohair berets, hipsterish short-brimmed hats, fedoras, elegant straw sun hats and a full-colour spectrum of *barrets* (berets).

COIN & STAMP MARKET   MARKET

Map p260 (Mercat de Numismàtica i Filatèlia; Plaça Reial; ⊙9am-2.30pm Sun; Ⓜ Liceu) A relic of bygone Barcelona, in the shape of a dusty philatelic and coin market.

LA BASILICA GALERIA   JEWELLERY

Map p260 (☎93 304 20 47; www.labasilicagaleria.com; Carrer Sant Sever 7; ⊙11am-8.30pm; ☎; Ⓜ Jaume I) A pure wonderland for the senses, La Basilica Galeria is a whimsical jewellery store with artful displays. In addition to eye-catching necklaces, delicate rings and fairy-tale pendants, there are a few original paintings for sale, though there's more artwork a few doors down in Basilica's gallery and perfume shop.

El Raval

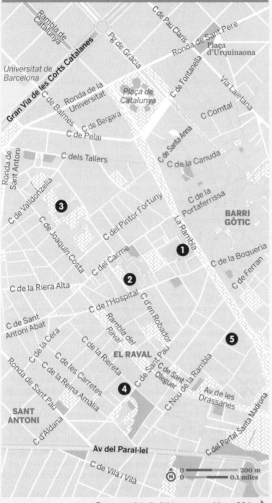

Neighbourhood Top Five

❶ Mercat de la Boqueria (p77) Shopping and browsing at this buzzing and beautiful market, and eating at one of the lively bars.

❷ Antic Hospital de la Santa Creu (p79) Exploring the historic building and relaxing with a coffee in its courtyard cafe.

❸ MACBA (p78) Getting to know the art collection here and watching the skaters in the front.

❹ Historical bars (p83) Partaking in a glass of cloudy absinthe.

❺ Palau Güell (p81) Walking around the artfully restored palace.

Lonely Planet's Top Tip

For a spot of sun away from the noisy El Raval streets, head for the garden cafe at the Antic Hospital de la Santa Creu (p79).

✕ Best Places to Eat

➡ Bar Pinotxo (p80)

➡ Caravelle (p80)

➡ Mam i Teca (p80)

➡ Suculent (p80)

➡ Elisabets (p79)

For reviews, see p79 ➡

🍷 Best Places to Drink

➡ Bar La Concha (p83)

➡ Casa Almirall (p83)

➡ La Confitería (p83)

➡ Negroni (p83)

For reviews, see p83 ➡

🔒 Best Gift Shops

➡ Les Topettes (p86)

➡ Fantastik (p86)

➡ Teranyina (p86)

For reviews, see p86 ➡

Explore El Raval

Long one of the most rough-and-tumble parts of Barcelona, El Raval is now so hip in a grungy, inner-city way that *barcelonins* have even invented a verb for rambling around El Raval: *ravalejar*.

The northern half of El Raval is the best place to start your ramble – this part of the *barri* (neighbourhood) has an almost respectable air about it. Spend a day wandering around the art shops on the streets around Carrer del Pintor Fortuny, lunching in the colourful Mercat de la Boqueria and dedicating a few hours to the fascinating MACBA.

Night-time is El Raval's forte, and not only because of all the illicit activities taking place under the shroud of darkness. This is where you will find some of Barcelona's more eccentric, trendy and downright ancient bars and clubs.

The area between Carrer de l'Hospital and the waterfront – also known as Barri Xino – is where El Raval retains its dodgy flavour of yore, and you should beware of boozy middle-of-the-night ramblings here. The national cinema and film archive, Filmoteca de Catalunya, has been relocated to just off the Rambla de Raval in an attempt to change the face of this area of town. Despite its slight edginess, you shouldn't miss this part of El Raval – several fine old bars have stood the test of time in these streets.

If you're curious about the fabric of life in multicultural Raval, take a stroll along Carrer de l'Hospital, home to the local mosque and numerous halal butchers' shops, cafes and barber shops.

Local Life

➡ **Market lunch** Don't miss the food at Mercat de la Boqueria (right) – either queue up and buy some fresh produce and cook it yourself, or sit down at a stall and let the local chefs shower you with Catalan delicacies.

➡ **Vintage shops** El Raval is the epicentre of Barcelona's fascination with all things vintage – you'll find plenty of secondhand shops along the pedestrian Carrer de la Riera Baixa, particularly.

➡ **Sugar rush** Locals swear that the best chocolate in town is to be had at Granja M Viader (p85).

Getting There & Away

➡ **Metro** El Raval is encircled by three metro lines. Línies 1, 2 and 3 stop at strategic points around the district, so nothing is far from a metro stop. The Línia 3 stop at Liceu is a convenient exit point.

TOP SIGHT
MERCAT DE LA BOQUERIA

Barcelona's most central produce market, the Mercat de la Boqueria, provides one of the greatest sound, smell and colour sensations in Europe. It spills over with the rich and varied colours of plentiful fruit and vegetable stands, and seemingly limitless varieties of sea critters, cheeses and meats.

La Boqueria has a handful of unassuming places to eat – and eat well – although they open only at lunchtime. It's worth trying some of Catalonia's gastronomical specialities, such as *bacallà salat* (dried salted cod), *calçots* (a cross between a leek and an onion), *cargols* (snails), *peus de porc* (pig's trotters) or *percebes* (goose-necked barnacles).

It is believed that there has been a market in this place since 1217, and, as much as it has become a modern-day attraction, it has always been the place where locals have come to shop. What is now known as La Boqueria didn't come to exist until the 19th century, and the iron Modernista gate was constructed in 1914.

Many of Barcelona's top restaurateurs buy their produce here, although nowadays it's no easy task getting past the seething crowds of tourists to snare a slippery slab of sole or tempting piece of goat's cheese.

DON'T MISS

➡ Digging into local specialities at a food stall

➡ Picking up fresh produce for a beach picnic

PRACTICALITIES

➡ Map p264
➡ ☎93 412 13 15
➡ www.boqueria.info
➡ La Rambla 91
➡ ⏰8am-8.30pm Mon-Sat
➡ Ⓜ Liceu

TOP SIGHT
MACBA

Designed by Richard Meier and opened in 1995, MACBA (Museu d'Art Contemporani de Barcelona) has become the city's foremost contemporary art centre. The permanent collection, displayed on the ground and first floors, features some 3000 pieces centred on three periods: post-WWII; circa 1968; and the years since the 1989 fall of the Berlin Wall, right up until the present day.

The emphasis is on Spanish and Catalan art from the second half of the 20th century, with works by Antoni Tàpies, Joan Brossa and Miquel Barceló, among others, though international artists, such as Paul Klee, Bruce Nauman and John Cage, are also represented.

The temporary visiting exhibitions are almost always challenging and intriguing. MACBA's philosophy is to do away with the old model of a museum where an artwork is a spectacle and to create a space where art can be viewed critically, so the exhibitions are usually tied in with talks and events. This is food for the brain as well as the eyes.

The library and auditorium stage regular concerts, talks and events, all of which are either reasonably priced or free. The bookshop has design objects and gifts as well as art books.

DON'T MISS

➜ The permanent collection of 20th-century Spanish and Catalan art
➜ The gallery's fascinating temporary exhibitions
➜ Richard Meier's extraordinary building

PRACTICALITIES

➜ Museu d'Art Contemporani de Barcelona
➜ Map p264, B3
➜ ☎93 481 33 68
➜ www.macba.cat
➜ Plaça dels Àngels 1
➜ adult/concession/under 12yr €10/8/free
➜ ⊙11am-7.30pm Mon & Wed-Fri, 10am-9pm Sat, 10am-3pm Sun & holidays
➜ Ⓜ Universitat

👁 SIGHTS

MERCAT DE LA BOQUERIA MARKET
See p77.

MACBA ARTS CENTRE
See p78.

**CENTRE DE CULTURA
CONTEMPORÀNIA DE BARCELONA** BUILDING
Map p264 (CCCB; ☑93 306 41 00; www.cccb.
org; Carrer de Montalegre 5; adult/concession/
under 12yr for 1 exhibition €6/4/free, 2 exhibitions €8/6/free, Sun 3-8pm free; ⊙11am-8pm
Tue-Sun; Ⓜ Universitat) A complex of audi-
toriums, exhibition spaces and conference
halls opened here in 1994 in what had
been an 18th-century hospice, the Casa de
la Caritat. The courtyard, with a vast glass
wall on one side, is spectacular. With 4500
sq metres of exhibition space in four separate areas, the centre hosts a constantly
changing program of exhibitions, film
cycles and other events.

**ANTIC HOSPITAL DE
LA SANTA CREU** HISTORIC BUILDING
Map p264 (Former Hospital of the Holy Cross;
☑93 270 16 21; www.bcn.cat; Carrer de l'Hospital
56; ⊙9am-8pm Mon-Fri, to 2pm Sat; Ⓜ Liceu) Behind La Boqueria stands the Antic Hospital
de la Santa Creu, which was once the city's
main hospital. Begun in 1401, it functioned
until the 1930s, and was considered one of
the best in Europe in its medieval heyday –
it is famously the place where Antoni Gaudí
died in 1926. Today it houses the **Biblioteca
de Catalunya**, and the **Institut d'Estudis
Catalans** (Institute for Catalan Studies).
The hospital's Gothic chapel, **La Capella** (☑93 256 20 44; www.bcn.cat/lacapella;
⊙noon-8pm Tue-Sat, 11am-2pm Sun & holidays)
FREE, shows temporary exhibitions.

Entering from Carrer de l'Hospital,
you find yourself in a peaceful **courtyard
garden** with a cheerful bar-cafe. Off the
garden lies the entrance to the prestigious
Massana conservatorium and, up a sweep
of stairs, the library. Approaching the complex from Carrer del Carme or down a narrow lane from Jardins del Doctor Fleming
(the little playground), you arrive at the
entrance to the institute, which was once
the 17th-century Casa de Convalescència
de Sant Pau. The public can visit the patio,
in the centre of which you'll find a statue
of St Paul. The building (especially the entrance vestibule) is richly decorated with
ceramics. Situated up on the 1st floor at
the far end is what was once an orange garden, now named after the Catalan novelist
Mercè Rodoreda.

RAMBLA DEL RAVAL STREET
Map p264 (Ⓜ Liceu) This broad boulevard was
laid out in 2000 as part of the city's plan to
open up this formerly gritty neighbourhood.
Now lined with palm trees and terrace cafes,
it hosts a craft market every weekend and is
overlooked by a glossy four-star hotel. Fernando Botero's huge sculpture of a plump
cat, which stands at the bottom of the Rambla, never fails to delight children.

**ESGLÉSIA DE SANT
PAU DEL CAMP** CHURCH
Map p264 (☑93 441 00 01; Carrer de Sant Pau
101; adult/concession €3/2; ⊙10am-1pm &
4-7pm Mon-Sat; Ⓜ Paral·lel) The best example of Romanesque architecture in the city
is the dainty little cloister of this church.
Set in a somewhat dusty garden, the 12th-
century church also boasts some Visigothic
sculptural detail on the main entrance.

🍴 EATING

ELISABETS CATALAN €
Map p264 (☑93 317 58 26; Carrer d'Elisabets
2-4; mains €8-10, menú del día €10.85;
⊙7.30am-11.30pm Mon-Sat Sep-Jul; Ⓜ Catalunya) This unassuming restaurant is popular
for no-nonsense local fare. The walls are
dotted with old radio sets and the *menú
del día* (daily set menu) varies daily. If you
prefer *a la carta,* try the *ragú de jabalí*
(wild boar stew) and finish with *mel i
mató* (Catalan dessert made from cheese
and honey).

Those with a post-midnight hunger on
Friday nights can probably get a meal here
as late as 1am.

EL COLECTIVO CAFE €
Map p264 (☑93 318 63 80; Carrer del Pintor Fortuny 22; bocadillos from €4; ⊙9am-9pm Mon-
Wed, 9am-midnight Thu, 9am-2am Fri & Sat; 🤙;
Ⓜ Catalunya) A relaxed little cafe on a quiet
Raval street, El Colectivo makes excellent
cake (carrot, pineapple, you name it), creative *bocadillos* (filled rolls) and good coffee. The shop-window seating is perfect
for street watching, the decor is simple
and minimal with a single row of wooden

tables, and there's always good jazz playing in the background. Tapas are served on Thursdays and Fridays.

SÉSAMO
VEGETARIAN €

Map p264 (📞93 441 64 11; Carrer de Sant Antoni Abat 52; tapas €6; ⊙8pm-midnight Tue-Sun; 🍴; MSant Antoni) Widely held to be the best veggie restaurant in the city (admittedly not as great an accolade as it might be elsewhere), Sésamo is a cosy, fun place. The menu is mainly tapas, and most people go for the seven-course tapas menu (€25, wine included), but there are a few more substantial dishes. Nice touches include the home-baked bread and cakes.

★MAM I TECA
CATALAN €€

Map p264 (📞93 441 33 35; Carrer de la Lluna 4; mains €9-12; ⊙1-4pm & 8pm-midnight Mon, Wed-Fri & Sun, 8pm-midnight Sat; MSant Antoni) A tiny place with half a dozen tables, Mam i Teca is as much a lifestyle choice as a restaurant. Locals drop in and hang at the bar, and diners are treated to Catalan dishes made with locally sourced products and that adhere to Slow Food principles (such as cod fried in olive oil with garlic and red pepper, or pork ribs with chickpeas).

★BAR PINOTXO
TAPAS €€

Map p264 (www.pinotxobar.com; Mercat de la Boqueria; mains €8-17; ⊙6am-4pm Mon-Sat; MLiceu) Bar Pinotxo is arguably La Boqueria's, and even Barcelona's, best tapas bar. It sits among the half-dozen or so informal eateries within the market, and the popular owner, Juanito, might serve up chickpeas with pine nuts and raisins, a soft mix of potato and spinach sprinkled with salt, soft baby squid with cannellini beans, or a quivering cube of caramel-sweet pork belly.

ARTICKET

Barcelona's best bargain for art lovers is the **Articket BCN** (www.articket bcn.org; €30), which gives you entry to six museums for a fraction of what you'd pay if you bought individual tickets. The museums are the MACBA, the CCCB, the Fundació Antoni Tàpies, Fundació Joan Miró, the MNAC and the Museu Picasso.

SUCULENT
CATALAN €€

Map p264 (📞93 443 65 79; www.suculent.com; Rambla del Raval 43; mains €13-21; ⊙1-4pm & 8.30-11.30pm Wed-Sun; MLiceu) Michelin-starred chef Carles Abellan adds to his stable with this old-style bistro, which showcases the best of Catalan cuisine. From the cod brandade to the oxtail stew with truffled sweet potato, only the best ingredients are used. Be warned that the prices can mount up a bit, but this is a great place to sample regional highlights.

The Taverna del Suculent next door is slightly cheaper and offers updated versions of traditional tapas.

FLAX & KALE
VEGETARIAN €€

Map p264 (📞93 317 56 64; www.teresacarles.com; Carrer dels Tallers 74; mains €12.50-16.50; ⊙10am-11.30pm; 📶🍴; MUniversitat) A far cry from the veggie restaurants of old, Flax & Kale marks a new approach (for Barcelona, at least) that declares that going meat-free does not mean giving up on choice or creativity, and is entirely possible in stylish surroundings. There are gluten-free and vegan options, and dishes include tacos with guacamole, aubergine, shiitake mushrooms and sour cashew cream, or Penang red curry.

BAR CAÑETE
TAPAS €€

Map p264 (📞93 270 34 58; www.barcanete.com; Carrer de la Unió 17; tapas from €3.50; ⊙1pm-midnight Mon-Sat; MLiceu) Part of a trend in creating upmarket versions of traditional bars with food to match. A long, narrow dining room holds an open kitchen along which runs a wooden bar, where diners sit and from here they can point at what they want or order from a long list of classic tapas and *raciones* (full-plate-size tapas serving; literally 'rations').

Many of the choices (such as the mussels with a citric dressing) have a modern twist.

CARAVELLE
INTERNATIONAL €€

Map p264 (📞93 317 98 92; www.caravelle.es; Carrer del Pintor Fortuny 31; mains €10-13; ⊙9.30am-5.30pm Mon, 9.30am-1am Tue-Fri, 10am-1am Sat, 10am-5.30pm Sun; MLiceu) A bright little joint, beloved of the hipster element of El Raval and anyone with a discerning palate. It dishes up tacos as you've never tasted them (cod, lime *alioli* and radish, and pulled pork with roast corn and avocado), a superior steak sandwich on homemade

TOP SIGHT
PALAU GÜELL

Gaudí built this palace off La Rambla in the late 1880s for his wealthy patron, the industrialist Eusebi Güell. Although sombre compared with some of his later whimsy, the Palau is still a characteristic riot of materials and styles (Gothic, Islamic, art nouveau). After the civil war the police tortured political prisoners in the basement, but the building was then abandoned, leading to its long-term disrepair. It was finally reopened in 2012 after several years of refurbishment.

Central to the structure of the building is the magnificent music room, with a rebuilt organ that is played during opening hours. The hall is a parabolic pyramid – each wall an arch stretching up three floors and coming together to form a dome, giving a magnificent sense of space in what is a surprisingly narrow building, constructed on a site of just 500 sq metres.

The attic now holds a detailed exhibition on the history of the building, and the roof is a tumult of tiled mosaics and fanciful design. The audioguide, included in the entry price, is worth getting for the detailed descriptions of the architecture, as well as the music and the illustrations of the Güell family's life.

DON'T MISS

➡ The music room
➡ The basement stables
➡ The tiled chimney pots

PRACTICALITIES

➡ Map p264
➡ 93 472 57 75
➡ www.palauguell.cat
➡ Carrer Nou de la Rambla 3-5
➡ adult/concession/under 10yr €12/9/free
➡ 10am-8pm Tue-Sun
➡ Ⓜ Drassanes

EL RAVAL EATING

---

brioche with pickled celeriac and all manner of soul food.

Drinks are every bit as inventive – try the homemade ginger beer or grapefruit soda.

EL QUIM
TAPAS €€

Map p264 (93 301 98 10; www.elquimdelaboqueria.com; Mercat de la Boqueria; ☺7am-4pm Tue-Thu, to 5pm Fri & Sat; Ⓜ Liceu) This classic counter bar in the Mercat de la Boqueria is ideal for trying traditional Catalan dishes such as fried eggs with baby squid (the house speciality) or *escalivada* (smoky grilled vegetables). Daily specials are prepared using whatever is in season, and might include artichoke chips or sautéed wild mushrooms.

DOS TRECE
INTERNATIONAL €€

Map p264 (93 301 73 06; www.dostrece.es; Carrer del Carme 40; mains €10-15; ☺10am-midnight; Ⓜ Liceu) Lively, sunny and fun, Dos Trece is great for brunches (including veggie and vegan options) that are available all day, as well as late-night bites. The menu ranges from juicy burgers to a more sophisticated rack of lamb, and the bar serves a

good array of cocktails. There are a few tables outside, next to the kids' playground.

EN VILLE
FRENCH €€

Map p264 (93 302 84 67; www.envillebarcelona.es; Carrer del Doctor Dou 14; menú del día €12.90, mains €14-18; ☺1-4pm & 8-11.30pm Tue-Sat, 1-4pm Sun & Mon; Ⓜ Universitat) You'll want to come here for the divine decor – the dramatic bouquets, the oil paintings and the antique details all around – as much as the food, though the *menú del día* is good value, and might include a platter of seafood and ample salads, as well as large glasses of wine. Turn up early for lunch to beat the queues.

CAN LLUÍS
CATALAN €€

Map p264 (www.restaurantcanlluis.cat; Carrer de la Cera 49; mains €9-20, menú del día €9.90; ☺1.30-4pm & 8.30-11.30pm Mon-Sat; Ⓜ Sant Antoni) Three generations have kept this spick-and-span old-time classic in business since 1929. Beneath the olive-green beams in the back dining room you can see the spot where an anarchist's bomb went off in 1946, killing the then owner. Expect fresh

EL RAVAL

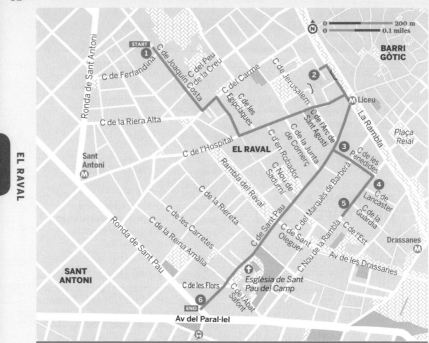

Neighbourhood Walk
Modernista Wining & Dining in El Raval

START CASA ALMIRALL
END LA CONFITERÍA
LENGTH 2KM; ONE HOUR

Run by the Almirall family who opened it in the mid-19th century, the corner tavern **1 Casa Almirall** on Carrer de Joaquín Costa preserves much of its Modernista decor, especially in the picture windows opening on to the street.

The **2 Mercat de la Boqueria** (p77), with half a dozen or so unassuming places to eat, dates back to the 13th century, but it wasn't until 1840 that it was officially inaugurated on this site. In 1914 it was capped with a metal roof and given its charming, wrought-iron, Modernista entrance sign, which is inset with colourful stained glass.

The **3 Hotel España** is known above all for its dining rooms, part of the 1903 design by Domènech i Montaner. The Sala Arnau (Arnau Room) features a magnificent alabaster fireplace designed by Eusebi Arnau. Moderately priced traditional Catalan fare is served.

While wandering around El Raval you should not miss its Modernista star, one of Gaudí's earlier big commissions, **4 Palau Güell** (p81), a remarkable building recently renovated to perfection. If passing by at night while doing a round of the bars, make a note to return here by day.

A classic of Barcelona nightlife for over a century, the **5 London Bar** (p84) displays Modernista decor and is run by the family of the waiter who founded it in 1910. In its heyday it stayed open 24 hours and attracted the likes of Pablo Picasso and Joan Miró for countless swift beers.

On Carrer de Sant Pau, walk south past the Romanesque church to **6 La Confitería** (p83), once a barber's shop and then a long-time confectioner's. It was lovingly restored for its reconversion into a bar in 1998. Most of the elements in the front section, including facade, bar counter and cabinets, are the real deal. The back room has been completely renovated more recently, but the style is sympathetic.

fish and seafood. The *llenguado* (sole) is oven-cooked with whisky and raisins.

RESTAURANT EL CAFETÍ CATALAN €€

Map p264 (☑93 329 24 19; www.elcafeti.com; Carrer de Sant Rafael 18; mains €12-18, menú del día €10; ☉1.30-3.30pm & 8.30-11.30pm Tue-Sun Sep-Jul; ⓜLiceu) This diminutive eatery is filled with antique furniture and offers traditional local cooking, with one or two unorthodox variations. Paella and other rice dishes dominate. The entrance is down the little Passatge de Bernardí Martorell.

🍷 DRINKING & NIGHTLIFE

★LA CONFITERÍA BAR

Map p264 (Carrer de Sant Pau 128; ☉7.30pm-2.30am Mon-Thu, 6pm-3.30am Fri, 5pm-3.30am Sat, 12.45pm-2.45am Sun; ⓜParal·lel) This is a trip into the 19th century. Until the 1980s it was a confectioner's shop, and although the original cabinets are now lined with booze, the look of the place barely changed with its conversion into a laid-back bar. A quiet enough spot for a house *vermut* (€3; add your own soda) in the early evening.

It fills with theatre-goers and local partiers later at night.

CASA ALMIRALL BAR

Map p264 (www.casaalmirall.com; Carrer de Joaquín Costa 33; ☉6pm-2.30am Mon-Thu, 6.30pm-3am Fri, noon-3am Sat, noon-12.30am Sun; ⓜUniversitat) In business since the 1860s, this unchanged corner bar is dark and intriguing, with Modernista decor and a mixed clientele. There are some great original pieces in here, such as the marble counter, and the cast-iron statue of the muse of the Universal Exposition, held in Barcelona in 1888.

BAR LA CONCHA BAR, GAY

Map p264 (http://laconchadelraval.com; Carrer de la Guàrdia 14; ☉5pm-2am; ⓜDrassanes) This place is dedicated to the worshipping of the actress Sara Montiel: the walls groan with more than 250 photos of the sultry star. La Concha used to be a largely gay and transvestite haunt, but anyone is welcome and bound to have fun – especially when the drag queens come out to play. Moroccan ownership means you're also likely to see belly dancing.

THE GREEN FAIRY

Bar Marsella (Map p264; ☑93 442 72 63; Carrer de Sant Pau 65; ☉10pm-2.30am Mon-Thu, 10pm-3am Fri & Sat; ⓜLiceu) has been in business since 1820, and has served the likes of Hemingway, who was known to slump here over an *absenta* (absinthe). The bar still specialises in absinthe, a drink to be treated with respect.

Your absinthe glass comes with a lump of sugar, a fork and a little bottle of mineral water. Hold the sugar on the fork, over your glass, and drip the water onto the sugar so that it dissolves into the absinthe, which turns yellow. The result should give you a warm glow.

Born in 1928, Sara Montiel bared all on the silver screen in an era that condemned nudity to shameful brazenness – hence 'la concha' (a word commonly used in Spanish slang) can be read as a sly salute to the female genitalia.

NEGRONI COCKTAIL BAR

Map p264 (www.negronicocktailbar.com; Carrer de Joaquín Costa 46; ☉7pm-2.30am Mon-Thu, 7pm-3am Fri & Sat; ⓜUniversitat) Good things come in small packages and this dark, teeny cocktail bar confirms the rule. The mostly black decor lures in a largely student set to try out the cocktails, among them, of course, the celebrated Negroni, a Florentine invention with one part Campari, one part gin and one part sweet vermouth.

EL DRAPAIRE BAR

Map p264 (☑607 466446; Carrer de les Sitges 11; ☉5pm-1am Sun-Thu, to 2am Fri & Sat; ⓜCatalunya) Part of the recent explosion in the craft-beer scene, this cosy, beamed tavern has been given a new lease of life and now has 13 taps, featuring Spanish and international beers of all styles. There are tapas and platters of cheese and charcuterie to share.

BAR PASTÍS BAR

Map p264 (www.barpastis.com; Carrer de Santa Mònica 4; ☉7.30pm-2am; ⓜDrassanes) A French cabaret theme (with lots of Piaf in the background) dominates this tiny, cluttered classic. It's been going, on and off, since the end of WWII. You'll need to be in here before 9pm to have any hope of sitting, getting near the bar or anything much else. On some nights it features live acts, usually performing French *chansons*.

33|45
BAR

Map p264 (Carrer de Joaquín Costa 4; ⊘4pm-2am Mon-Thu, 4pm-3am Fri & Sat, 4pm-1.30pm Sun; ⊚; MUniversitat) A super-trendy bar on a street that's not short of them, this place has excellent mojitos – even pink and strawberry ones – and a fashionable crowd. The main area has DJ music and lots of excited noisemaking, while the back room is scattered with sofas and armchairs for a post-dancing slump. On occasional Sundays the venue has lunchtime live gigs.

BAR KASPARO
CAFE

Map p264 (Plaça de Vicenç Martorell 4; ⊘9am-11pm; MCatalunya) A friendly outdoor cafe, which overlooks a traffic-free square with a playground, it's a favourite with the neighbourhood yummy mummies and daddies, and serves juices, tapas, salads and cakes.

MOOG
CLUB

Map p264 (www.masimas.com/moog; Carrer de l'Arc del Teatre 3; ⊘midnight-5am Mon-Thu & Sun, to 6am Fri & Sat; MDrassanes) This fun and minuscule club is a standing favourite with the downtown crowd. In the main dance area, DJs dish out house, techno and electro, while upstairs you can groove to a nice blend of indie and occasional classic-pop throwbacks. Admission is €5.

MARMALADE
BAR

Map p264 (www.marmaladebarcelona.com; Carrer de la Riera Alta 4-6; ⊘6.30pm-2.30am Mon-Wed, 10am-2.30am Thu-Sun; MSant Antoni) The golden hues of this backlit bar and restaurant beckon seductively through the glass facade. There are various distinct spaces, decorated in different but equally sumptu-

ous styles, and a pool table next to the bar. Cocktails are big business here, and a selection of them are €5 all night.

BETTY FORD'S
BAR

Map p264 (www.bettyfords.es; Carrer de Joaquín Costa 56; ⊘5pm-3am Sat-Tue, 1pm-3am Wed-Fri; MUniversitat) This enticing corner bar is one of several good stops along the student-jammed run of Carrer de Joaquín Costa. It puts together some nice cocktails and the place fills with an even mix of locals and foreigners, generally aged not much over 30. There's a decent line in burgers and soups, too.

LONDON BAR
BAR

Map p264 (Carrer Nou de la Rambla 34-36; ⊘6pm-3am Mon-Thu & Sun, 6pm-3.30am Fri & Sat; MLiceu) Open since 1909, this Modernista bar started as a hang-out for circus hands and was later frequented by the likes of Picasso, Miró and Hemingway. Today it fills to the brim with punters at the long front bar and rickety old tables. On occasion you can attend concerts at the small stage right up the back.

KENTUCKY
BAR

Map p264 (Carrer de l'Arc del Teatre 11; ⊘10pm-4am Wed-Sat; MDrassanes) Once a haunt of visiting US Navy boys, this exercise in Americana kitsch is the perfect way to finish an evening – if you can squeeze in. All sorts of odd bods from the *barri* and beyond gather here. An institution in the wee hours, this place often stays open until dawn.

BOADAS
COCKTAIL BAR

Map p260 (www.boadascocktails.com; Carrer dels Tallers 1; ⊘noon-2am Mon-Thu, noon-3am Fri & Sat; MCatalunya) One of the city's oldest cocktail bars, Boadas is famed for its daiquiris. Bow-tied waiters have been serving up unique, drinkable creations since Miguel

---

REVIVING EL RAVAL

The relocation of the **Filmoteca de Catalunya** (right) to El Raval from the neighbourhood of Sarrià is part of the 'Raval Revival', an ongoing project to set up the neighbourhood as one of Spain's most influential cultural centres. As part of the project, representatives from the MACBA, the Gran Teatre del Liceu, the Centre de Cultura Contemporània de Barcelona, the Biblioteca de Catalunya, Arts Santa Mònica, the Virreina Centre de la Imatge, the Institut d'Estudis Catalans and the Filmoteca de Catalunya meet every three months with the aim of creating a cultural network with El Raval as its nucleus. The idea is that these eight institutions will join forces, showing complementary exhibitions, organising cultural events and collaborating in creative projects.

Boadas opened it in 1933 – in fact Miró and Hemingway both drank here. Miguel was born in Havana, where he was the first barman at the immortal La Floridita.

GRANJA M VIADER   CAFE

Map p264 (☏93 318 34 86; www.granjaviader. cat; Carrer d'en Xuclà 6; ⊗9am-1.30pm & 5-9pm Mon-Sat; ⓂLiceu) For more than a century, people have flocked down this alley to get to the cups of homemade hot chocolate and whipped cream (ask for a *suís*) ladled out in this classic Catalan-style milk-bar-cum-deli. The Viader clan invented Cacaolat, a forerunner of kids' powdered-chocolate beverages. The interior here is delightfully vintage and the atmosphere always upbeat.

⭐ ENTERTAINMENT

★FILMOTECA DE
CATALUNYA   CINEMA

Map p264 (☏93 567 10 70; www.filmoteca. cat; Plaça de Salvador Seguí 1-9; adult/concession €4/3; ⊗screenings 5-10pm, ticket office 10am-3pm & 4-9.30pm Tue-Sun; ⓂLiceu) After almost a decade in the planning, the Filmoteca de Catalunya – Catalonia's national cinema – moved into this modern 6000-sq-metre building in 2012. It's a glass, metal and concrete beast that hulks in the midst of the most louche part of El Raval, but the building's interior shouts revival, with light and space, wall-to-wall windows, skylights and glass panels that let the sun in.

In addition to two cinemas totalling 555 seats, the Filmoteca comprises a film library, a bookshop, a cafe, offices and a dedicated space for exhibitions. This is mainly a film-archive space, though, and is being hailed as the marker of a cultural turning point for its new neighbourhood. The Filmoteca's screenings and exhibitions at the time of research included themes such as 'The Cinema and The Garden' and 'Popular Comedy'.

GIPSY LOU   LIVE MUSIC

Map p264 (www.gipsylou.com; Carrer de Ferlandina 55; ⊗8pm-2.30am Sun-Thu, 8pm-3am Fri & Sat; ⓂSant Antoni) A louche little bar that packs 'em in for live music from rumba and pop to flamenco, along with occasional storytelling events, and whatever else Felipe

feels like putting on. There are decent bar snacks to keep you going on a long night of pisco sours, the house speciality.

JAZZ SÍ CLUB   LIVE MUSIC

Map p264 (☏93 329 00 20; www.tallerdemusics. com; Carrer de Requesens 2; admission €4-10, incl drink; ⊗8.30-11pm Tue-Sat, 6.30-10pm Sun; ⓂSant Antoni) A cramped little bar run by the Taller de Músics (Musicians' Workshop) serves as the stage for a varied program of jazz jams through to some good flamenco (Friday and Saturday nights). Thursday night is Cuban night, Tuesday and Sunday are rock, and the rest are devoted to jazz and/or blues sessions. Concerts start around 9pm but the jam sessions can get going earlier.

23 ROBADORS   LIVE MUSIC

Map p264 (Carrer d'en Robador 23; admission varies; ⊗8pm-3am; ⓂLiceu) On what remains a sleazy Raval street, where streetwalkers, junkies and other misfits hang out in spite of all the work being done to gentrify the area, this narrow little bar has made a name for itself with its shows and live music. Jazz is the name of the game, but you'll also find live poetry, flamenco and plenty more.

CANGREJO   GAY

Map p264 (☏93 301 29 78; Carrer de Montserrat 9; ⊗11pm-3am Fri & Sat; ⓂDrassanes) This altar to kitsch, a dingy dance hall that has transgressed since the 1920s, is run by the luminous underground cabaret figure of Carmen Mairena and exudes a gorgeously tacky feel, especially with the midnight drag shows on Friday and Saturday. Due to its incredible popularity with tourists, getting in is all but impossible unless you turn up early.

TEATRE ROMEA   THEATRE

Map p264 (☏93 309 70 04; www.teatreromea. com; Carrer de l'Hospital 51; ticket prices vary; ⊗box office 4.30pm until start of show Tue-Fri, from 5.30pm Sat & Sun; ⓂLiceu) Just off La Rambla, this 19th-century theatre was resurrected at the end of the 1990s and is one of the city's key stages for quality drama. It usually fills up for a broad range of interesting plays, often classics with a contemporary flavour, in Catalan and Spanish.

TEATRE LLANTIOL
THEATRE

Map p264 (☎93 329 90 09; www.llantiol.com; Carrer de la Riereta 7; ticket prices vary; ⓂSant Antoni) At this charming little cafe-theatre, which has a certain scuffed elegance, all sorts of odd stuff, from concerts and theatre to magic shows, is staged. The speciality, though, is stand-up comedy, which is occasionally in English. Check the website for details.

🛍 SHOPPING

★LES TOPETTES
BEAUTY

Map p264 (☎93 500 55 64; www.lestopettes.com; Carrer de Joaquín Costa 33; ⊙11am-2pm & 4-9pm Tue-Sat; ⓂUniversitat) It's a sign of the times that such a chic little temple to soap and perfume can exist in El Raval. The items in Les Topettes' collection have been picked for their designs as much as the products themselves, and you'll find gorgeously packaged scents, candles and unguents from Diptyque, Cowshed and L'Artisan Parfumeur, among others.

FANTASTIK
ARTS & CRAFTS

Map p264 (☎93 301 30 68; www.fantastik.es; Carrer de Joaquín Costa 62; ⊙11am-2pm & 4-8.30pm Mon-Fri, noon-9pm Sat; ⓂUniversitat) Over 400 products, including a Mexican skull rattle, robot moon explorer from China and recycled plastic zebras from South Africa, are to be found in this colourful shop, which sources its items from Mexico, India, Bulgaria, Russia, Senegal and 20 other countries. It's a perfect place to buy all the things you don't need but can't live without.

BARCELONA REYKJAVIK
FOOD

Map p264 (☎93 302 09 21; www.barcelonareykjavik.com; Carrer del Doctor Dou 12; ⊙10am-9pm Mon-Sat, 9.30am-8pm Sun; ⓂCatalunya) Bread lovers, rejoice! Good bread can be hard to find in Barcelona, but Reykjavik saves the day. All loaves are made using organic flour – spelt, wholemeal, mixed cereals and

so on – and sourdough yeast, though this does make for fairly high prices. The bakery also produces excellent cakes. Three more shops can be found in the Born, Gràcia and L'Eixample.

HOLALA! PLAZA
FASHION

Map p264 (www.holala-ibiza.com; Plaça de Castella 2; ⊙11am-9pm Mon-Sat; ⓂUniversitat) Backing on to Carrer de Valldonzella, where it boasts an exhibition space (Gallery) for temporary art displays, this Ibiza import is inspired by that island's long-established (and somewhat commercialised) hippie tradition. Vintage clothes are the name of the game, along with an eclectic program of exhibitions and activities.

TERANYINA
ARTS & CRAFTS

Map p264 (www.textilteranyina.com; Carrer del Notariat 10; ⊙11am-3pm & 5-8pm Mon-Fri; ⓂCatalunya) Artist Teresa Rosa Aguayo runs this textile workshop in the heart of the artsy bit of El Raval. You can join courses at the loom, admire some of the rugs and other works that Teresa has created, and, of course, buy them.

LA PORTORRIQUEÑA
COFFEE

Map p264 (Carrer d'en Xuclà 25; ⊙9am-2pm & 5-8pm Mon-Fri, 9am-2pm Sat; ⓂCatalunya) Coffee beans from around the world, freshly ground before your eyes, have been the winning formula in this store since 1902. It also offers all sorts of chocolate goodies. The street it's on is good for little old-fashioned food boutiques.

JOAN LA LLAR DEL PERNIL
FOOD

Map p264 (☎93 317 95 29; Stalls 667, 669, 670 & 671, Mercat de la Boqueria; ⊙8am-3pm Mon-Thu, to 8pm Fri & Sat; ⓂLiceu) This stall in the Mercat de la Boqueria sells some of the best ham in the city, which can be sliced and sold as a snack.

🏃 ACTIVITIES

CICLOTOUR
BICYCLE TOUR

Map p264 (☎93 317 19 70; www.barcelonaciclotour.com; Carrer dels Tallers 45; tours €22; ⊙11am & 4.30pm daily mid-Apr–Oct, 11am Mon-Fri, Sat & Sun 11am & 4.30pm Nov, plus 7.30pm Thu-Sun Jun-Sep, Fri & Sat Oct; ⓂUniversitat) Daily bike tours around the city's main sights. The evening tour also includes a visit to the Font Màgica.

RUNNER BEAN TOURS   WALKING TOUR
Map p264 (📋636 108776; www.runnerbeantours.
com; Carrer del Carme 44; ☺tours 11am year-
round & 4.30pm Apr-Sep; Ⓜ Liceu) Runner Bean
Tours offers several daily thematic tours.
It's a pay-what-you-wish tour, with a collection taken at the end for the guide. The **Old
City tour** explores the Roman and medieval
history of Barcelona, visiting highlights in
the Ciutat Vella. The **Gaudí tour** takes in
the great works of Modernista Barcelona. It
involves two hops on the metro.

Both tours depart at 11am from Plaça
Reial (and also at 4.30pm from April
through September) and last for about 2½
hours. It's wise to book ahead, as numbers
are limited. Runner Beans also runs a Kids
and Family Walking Tour; check the website for departure times and to book a spot.

La Ribera

Neighbourhood Top Five

❶ Basílica de Santa Maria del Mar (p92) Admiring the simplicity and beauty of this Gothic church.

❷ Museu Picasso (p90) Being introduced to the origins of Picasso's genius at this fascinating museum.

❸ Palau de la Música Catalana (p93) Enjoying a show or just the Modernista interior of this beautiful concert hall.

❹ Parc de la Ciutadella (p94) Taking a stroll or having a picnic.

❺ Bormuth (p97) Tucking into old-school tapas.

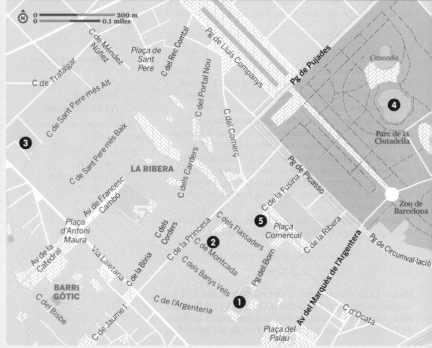

For more detail of this area see Map p268 ➡

Explore La Ribera

La Ribera is widely used to refer to the area covered by the city council's rather long-winded appellation of Sant Pere, Santa Caterina i la Ribera. Carrer de la Princesa, ramrod straight between the traffic-choked Via Laietana and Parc de la Ciutadella, cuts La Ribera in half. The gentrified southern half is generally known as El Born, after Passeig del Born, Barcelona's main drag from the 13th to the 18th centuries, now lined with bars and cafes. Capped at one end by the magnificent Gothic Basílica de Santa Maria del Mar, it runs along to the Born Centre de Cultura i Memòria, in what used to be the neighbourhood's market building. This area should be your first port of call, specifically a stroll down the Carrer de Montcada, a street rich in Gothic and baroque mansions as well as the location of one of the city's major museums, the Museu Picasso.

Northwest of Carrer de la Princesa, a mess of narrow streets wiggles northwards around the striking modern reincarnation of the Mercat de Santa Caterina and on towards the Modernista Palau de la Música Catalana. Some good eating and drinking options have opened up in these narrow streets.

Via Laietana marks the southwest side of La Ribera, while the Parc de la Ciutadella closes off its northeastern flank. The park is a rare green space in central Barcelona, where you can lounge on its stretches of grass, sit by the water at the grand fountain, visit the zoo and, if accompanied by tots, take advantage of its playgrounds.

Local Life

→ **Market secrets** Locals get their eggs at the Mercat de Santa Caterina (p95), where, in season, stand holders 'flavour' their eggs by stacking them up and placing truffles among them. Soft-boiled, they are divine.

→ **Catching the rays** Local favourite strip Passeig del Born is perfect for lazy Sunday morning sunbathing on the cafe terraces, as you enjoy a leisurely brunch.

→ **A slice of culture** Join the largely local clientele for a weekend lunchtime classical concert at the Palau de la Música Catalana (p93) and take advantage of the natural daylight to see the beautiful interior of the main auditorium.

→ **Barcelona style** Join the *barcelonins* and shop in some of the city's quirkiest fashion boutiques.

Getting There & Away

Metro Línia 4 coasts down the southwest flank of La Ribera, stopping at Urquinaona, Jaume I and Barceloneta. Línia 1 also stops nearby, at Urquinaona and Arc de Triomf (the nearest stop for the Parc de la Ciutadella).

Lonely Planet's Top Tip

Getting around all of Barcelona's museums can be anything but cheap, so take advantage of free Sunday afternoons, when entry into many of the city's museum will cost you zilch!

Best Places to Eat

→ Casa Delfín (p98)
→ El Atril (p98)
→ Nakashita (p99)
→ Bormuth (p97)
→ En Aparté (p97)

For reviews, see p97 ⇒

Best Places to Drink

→ Mudanzas (p100)
→ La Vinya del Senyor (p100)
→ Juanra Falces (p100)
→ Rubí (p100)
→ Miramelindo (p100)

For reviews, see p100 ⇒

Best for Architecture

→ Basílica de Santa Maria del Mar (p92)
→ Palau de la Música Catalana (p93)
→ Carrer de Montcada (p96)

LA RIBERA

TOP SIGHT
MUSEU PICASSO

The setting alone, in five contiguous medieval stone mansions, makes the Museu Picasso unique. The permanent collection is housed in Palau Aguilar, Palau del Baró de Castellet and Palau Meca, all dating from the 14th century. The 18th-century Casa Mauri, built over medieval remains (even some Roman leftovers have been identified), and the adjacent 14th-century Palau Finestres accommodate temporary exhibitions.

History of the Museum

Allegedly it was Picasso himself who proposed the museum's creation to his friend and personal secretary Jaume Sabartés, a Barcelona native, in 1960. Three years later, the 'Sabartés Collection' was opened, since a museum bearing Picasso's name would have been met with censorship – Picasso's opposition to the Franco regime was well known. The Museu Picasso we see today opened in 1983. It originally held only Sabartés' personal collection of Picasso's art and a handful of works hanging at the Barcelona Museum of Art, but the collection gradually expanded with donations from Salvador Dalí and Sebastià Junyer Vidal, among others, though most artworks were bequeathed by Picasso himself. His widow, Jacqueline Roque, also donated 41 ceramic pieces and the *Woman with Bonnet* painting after Picasso's death.

Sabartés' contribution and years of service are honoured with an entire room devoted to him, including Picasso's famous Blue Period portrait of him wearing a ruff.

DON'T MISS

➡ *Retrato de la Tía Pepa* (Portrait of Aunt Pepa)
➡ *Ciència i caritat* (Science and Charity)
➡ *Terrats de Barcelona* (Roofs of Barcelona)

PRACTICALITIES

➡ Map p268
➡ 📞 93 256 30 00
➡ www.museupicasso.bcn.cat
➡ Carrer de Montcada 15-23
➡ adult/concession/child all collections €14/7.50/free, permanent collection €11/7/free, temporary exhibitions €4.50/3/free, 3-7pm Sun & 1st Sun of month free
➡ ⊙9am-7pm Tue, Wed & Fri-Sun, to 9.30pm Thu
➡ Ⓜ Jaume I

The Collection

This collection concentrates on the artist's formative years, yet there is enough material from subsequent periods to give you a thorough impression of the man's versatility and genius. Above all, you come away feeling that Picasso was the true original, always one step ahead of himself (let alone anyone else) in his search for new forms of expression. The collection includes more than 3500 artworks, largely pre-1904, which is apt considering the artist spent his formative creative years in Barcelona.

It is important, however, not to expect a parade of his well-known works, or even works representative of his best-known periods. The holdings at the museum reflect Picasso's years in Barcelona and elsewhere in Spain, and what makes this collection truly impressive – and unique among the many Picasso museums around the world – is the way in which it displays his extraordinary talent at such a young age. Faced with the technical virtuosity of a painting such as *Ciència i caritat* (Science and Charity), for example, it is almost inconceivable that such a work could have been created at the hands of a 15 year old. Some of his self-portraits and the portraits of his parents, which date from 1896, are also evidence of his precocious talent.

Las Meninas Through the Prism of Picasso

From 1954 to 1962 Picasso was obsessed with the idea of researching and 'rediscovering' the greats, in particular Velázquez. In 1957 he created a series of renditions of the Velázquez masterpiece *Las meninas (The Ladies-in-Waiting)*, now displayed in rooms 12–14. It is as though Picasso has looked at the original Velázquez painting through a prism reflecting all the styles he had worked through until then, creating his own masterpiece in the process. This is a wonderful opportunity to see *Las meninas* in its entirety in this beautiful space.

Ceramics

What is also special about the Museu Picasso is its showcasing of his work in lesser-known media. The last rooms contain engravings and some 40 ceramic pieces completed throughout the latter years of his unceasingly creative life. You'll see plates and bowls decorated with simple, single-line drawings of fish, owls and other animal shapes, typical of Picasso's daubing on clay.

GETTING AROUND THE COLLECTION

The permanent collection is housed in Palau Aguilar, Palau del Baró de Castellet and Palau Meca. Casa Mauri and the adjacent 14th-century Palau Finestres accommodate temporary exhibitions.

ANNUAL PASS

Though ostensibly aimed at residents, the annual pass is also available to visitors on presentation of ID. The 'Carnet del Museu Picasso' cuts out the need to queue (and queues here can be long, if you haven't booked online ahead of time), and costs a mere €12, or €15 for a family pass.

LA RIBERA MUSEU PICASSO

TOP SIGHT
BASÍLICA DE SANTA MARIA DEL MAR

At the southwest end of Passeig del Born stands the apse of Barcelona's finest Catalan Gothic church, Santa Maria del Mar (Our Lady of the Sea). Built in the 14th century with record-breaking alacrity for the time (it took just 54 years), the church is remarkable for its architectural harmony and simplicity.

Its construction started in 1329, with Berenguer de Montagut and Ramon Despuig as the architects in charge. During construction the city's porters (*bastaixos*) carried the stone required to build the church from royal quarries in Montjuïc. Their memory lives on in reliefs of them in the main doors and stone carvings elsewhere in the church.

The exterior gives an impression of sternness, and the narrow streets surrounding it are restrictive and claustrophobic. It may come as a (pleasant) surprise then to find a spacious and light interior – the central nave and two flanking aisles separated by slender octagonal pillars give an enormous sense of lateral space.

The interior is almost devoid of imagery of the sort to be found in Barcelona's other large Gothic churches, but Santa Maria was lacking in superfluous decoration even before anarchists gutted it in 1909 and 1936. Keep an look out for music recitals, often baroque and classical.

DON'T MISS

➡ The church's architects portrayed in memorial stone relief
➡ A live-music performance

PRACTICALITIES

➡ Map p268
➡ ☎93 310 23 90
➡ www.santamaria-delmarbarcelona.org
➡ Plaça de Santa Maria del Mar
➡ incl guided tour 1-5pm €8
➡ ⊘9am-8pm
➡ Ⓜ Jaume I

TOP SIGHT
PALAU DE LA MÚSICA CATALANA

This concert hall is a high point of Barcelona's Modernista architecture, a symphony in tile, brick, sculpted stone and stained glass. Built by Domènech i Montaner between 1905 and 1908 for the Orfeo Català musical society, it was conceived as a temple for the Catalan Renaixença (Renaissance). The *palau* (palace) was built with the help of some of the best Catalan artisans of the time, and since 1990 it has undergone several major changes.

The *palau,* like a peacock, shows off much of its splendour on the outside. Take in the principal facade with its mosaics, floral capitals and the sculpture cluster representing Catalan popular music; wander inside the foyer and restaurant areas to admire the spangled, tiled pillars. Best of all, however, is the richly colourful auditorium upstairs, with its ceiling of blue-and-gold stained glass and shimmering skylight that looks like a giant, crystalline, downward-thrusting nipple. Above a bust of Beethoven on the stage towers a wind-blown sculpture of Wagner's Valkyries (Wagner was top of the Barcelona charts at the time it was created). This can only be savoured on a guided tour or by attending a performance – either is highly recommended.

DON'T MISS

➜ The principal facade's mosaics and columns

➜ The foyer and pillars in the restaurant

➜ The main auditorium

➜ A performance – day or night

PRACTICALITIES

➜ Map p268

➜ ☏93 295 72 00

➜ www.palaumusica. cat

➜ Carrer de Palau de la Música 4-6

➜ adult/concession/ child €18/11/free

➜ ⊘guided tours 10am-3.30pm, to 6pm Easter, Jul & Aug

➜ Ⓜ Urquinaona

⊙ SIGHTS

MUSEU PICASSO MUSEUM
See p90.

**BASÍLICA DE SANTA
MARIA DEL MAR** CHURCH
See p92.

**PALAU DE LA
MÚSICA CATALANA** ARCHITECTURE
See p93.

PARC DE LA CIUTADELLA PARK
Map p268 (Passeig de Picasso; ⚓; MArc de Triomf) Come for a stroll, a picnic, a visit to the zoo or to inspect Catalonia's regional parliament, but don't miss a visit to this, the most central green lung in the city. Parc de la Ciutadella is perfect for winding down.

After the War of the Spanish Succession, Felipe V razed a swath of La Ribera to build a huge fortress (La Ciutadella), designed to keep watch over Barcelona. It became a symbol of everything Catalans hated about Madrid and the Bourbon kings, and was later used as a political prison. Only in 1869 did the central government allow its demolition, after which the site was turned into a park and used for the Universal Exhibition of 1888.

The monumental **cascada** (waterfall) near the Passeig de Pujades park entrance, created between 1875 and 1881 by Josep Fontserè with the help of an enthusiastic young Gaudí, is a dramatic combination of statuary, rugged rocks, greenery and thundering water – all of it perfectly artificial. Nearby you can hire a rowing boat to paddle about in the small lake.

To the southeast, in what might be seen as an exercise in black humour, the fort's former arsenal now houses the **Parlament de Catalunya** (☎93 304 65 00; www.parlament.cat; ⊙guided tours 10am-1pm Sat, Sun & holidays) **FREE**. You can join free guided tours, in Catalan and Spanish only, on Saturdays and Sundays. The building is only open for independent visiting on 11 September from 10am to 7pm. On show to the public are the sweeping Escala d'Honor (Stairway of Honour) and the several solemn halls that lead to the Saló de Sessions, the semicircular auditorium where parliament sits. In the lily pond at the centre of the garden in front of the building is a statue of a seemingly heartbroken woman, *Desconsol* (Distress; 1907), by Josep Llimona.

The Passeig de Picasso side of the park is lined with several buildings constructed for, or just before, the Universal Exhibition. The medieval-looking caprice at the top end is the most engaging. Known as the **Castell dels Tres Dragons** (Castle of the Three Dragons), it long housed the Museu de Zoologia, which has since moved to the Fòrum area and is now known as the Museu Blau. Domènech i Montaner put the 'castle's' trimmings on a pioneering steel frame. The coats of arms are all invented and the whole building exudes a teasing, playful air. It was used as a cafe-restaurant during the Universal Exhibition.

To the south is L'Hivernacle, an elaborate greenhouse. Next come the former Museu de Geologia and L'Umbracle, a palm house. On Passeig de Picasso itself is Antoni Tàpies' typically impenetrable **Homenatge a Picasso** (Passeig de Picasso; MArc de Triomf, Jaume I). Water runs down the panes of a glass box full of bits of old furniture and steel girders.

Northwest of the park, Passeig de Lluís Companys is capped by the Modernista **Arc de Triomf** (Passeig de Lluís Companys), designed by Josep Vilaseca as the principal exhibition entrance, with unusual, Mudéjar-style brickwork. Josep Llimona did the main reliefs. Just what the triumph was eludes us, especially since the exhibition itself was a commercial failure. It is perhaps best thought of as a bricks-and-mortar embodiment of the city's general *fin de siècle* feel-good factor.

OLD FLAME

Opposite Basílica de Santa Maria del Mar's eastern flank, an eternal flame burns brightly over an apparently anonymous sunken square. This is **El Fossar de les Moreres** (The Mulberry Cemetery; Map p268; MJaume I), the site of a Roman cemetery. It's also where Catalan resistance fighters were buried after the siege of Barcelona ended in defeat in September 1714, for whom the flame burns.

PALAU DE LA MÚSICA CATALANA THROUGH THE AGES

The original Modernista creation, now a World Heritage Site, did not meet with universal approval in its day. The doyen of Catalan literature, Josep Pla, did not hesitate to condemn it as 'horrible', but few share his sentiments today. Domènech i Montaner himself was also in a huff. He failed to attend the opening ceremony in response to unsettled bills.

The *palau* (palace) was at the centre of a fraud scandal from 2009 to 2012, as its president, Felix Millet, who subsequently resigned, admitted to having siphoned off millions of euros of funds. He and his partner were ordered to repay the embezzled money to the *palau* in March 2012.

ZOO DE BARCELONA   ZOO

Map p268 (☑902 457545; www.zoobarcelona.cat; Parc de la Ciutadella; adult/child €19.90/11.95; ☺10am-5.30pm Nov-Mar, 10am-7pm Apr, May, Sep & Oct, 10am-8pm Jun-Aug; ♣; ⓂBarceloneta) The zoo is a great day out for kids, with 7500 critters that range from geckos to gorillas, lions and elephants – there are more than 400 species, plus picnic areas dotted all around and a wonderful adventure playground. There are pony rides, a petting zoo and a mini-train meandering through the grounds. Thanks to recent advances in legislation prohibiting the use of animals for performances (including circuses and bullfighting) the zoo called time on its dolphin shows in late 2015.

The zoo is also currently constructing a new living space seven times larger than the dolphins' current enclosure. There is a 20% discount if you book online.

BORN CENTRE
DE CULTURA I MEMÒRIA   HISTORIC BUILDING

Map p268 (☑93 256 68 51; http://elbornculturaimemoria.barcelona.cat; Plaça Comercial 12; centre free, exhibition spaces adult/concession/child €6/4.20/free; ☺10am-8pm Tue-Sun Mar-Sep, 10am-7pm Tue-Sat, to 8pm Sun Oct-Feb; ⓂBarceloneta) Launched to great fanfare in 2013, as part of the events held for the tercentenary of the Catalan defeat in the War of the Spanish Succession, this cultural space is housed in the former Mercat del Born, a handsome 19th-century structure of slatted iron and brick. Excavation in 2001 unearthed remains of whole streets flattened to make way for the much-hated citadel *(ciutadella)* – these are now on show on the exposed subterranean level.

On the ground floor there are panels giving information about the ruins, along with an exhibition space showing items from the period and explaining in greater depth the events surrounding the destruction of the area. There is also a stark and lofty restaurant serving Catalan cuisine, and a gift shop selling upmarket and high-design souvenirs, along with books about the region.

ARXIU FOTOGRÀFIC
DE BARCELONA   GALLERY

Map p268 (☑93 256 34 20; www.arxiufotografic. bcn.cat; Plaça de Pons i Clerch 2; ☺10am-7pm Mon-Sat; ⓂJaume I) FREE On the 2nd floor of the former Convent de Sant Agustí is the modest exhibition space of this photo archive. Photos on show are generally related to the city, as the photo collection is principally devoted to that theme, from the late 19th century until the late 20th century.

FUNDACIÓ FOTO COLECTANIA   GALLERY

Map p268 (☑93 217 16 26; www.colectania.es; Passeig de Picasso 14; adult/child €3/free, free first Sat of month; ☺11am-2pm & 4-8pm Mon-Sat Sep-Jul; ⓂArc de Triomf, Jaume I) Photography lovers should swing by here to see the latest exhibition from this non-profit foundation, which showcases thought-provoking works from across the globe. In 2016 the foundation moved from its base in Gràcia to this 500-sq-metre space in El Born. The exhibits may come from the foundation's extensive 3000-piece collection of Spanish and Portuguese photographers from the 1950s onwards, but more likely will be temporary exhibitions.

MERCAT DE SANTA CATERINA   MARKET

Map p268 (☑93 319 57 40; www.mercatsantacaterina.com; Avinguda de Francesc Cambó 16; ☺7.30am-3.30pm Mon, Wed & Sat, to 8.30pm Tue, Thu & Fri, closed afternoons Jul & Aug; ☎; ⓂJaume I) Come shopping for your tomatoes at this extraordinary-looking produce market, designed by Enric Miralles and Benedetta Tagliabue to replace its 19th-century predecessor. Finished in 2005, it is distinguished by its kaleidoscopic and undulating roof, held up above the bustling produce stands, restaurants, cafes and bars by twisting slender branches of what look like grey steel trees.

The multicoloured ceramic roof (with a ceiling made of warm, light wood) recalls the Modernista tradition of *trencadís* decoration (a type of mosaic, such as that in Park Güell). Indeed, its curvy design, like a series of Mediterranean rollers, seems to plunge back into an era when Barcelona's architects were limited only by their (vivid) imaginations. The market roof bears an uncanny resemblance to that of the Escoles de Gaudí at La Sagrada Família.

CARRER DE MONTCADA   STREET

Map p268 (MJaume I) An early example of town planning, this medieval high street was driven towards the sea from the road that in the 12th century led northeast from the city walls. It was the city's most coveted address for the merchant classes. The great mansions that remain today mostly date from the 14th and 15th centuries.

This area was the commercial heartland of medieval Barcelona. Five of the mansions on the east side of the street have been linked to house the Museu Picasso (p90). Across the road, others house what is now the Museu de Cultures del Món. Several other mansions on this street are commercial art galleries where you're welcome to browse. Make time for a cocktail in the courtyard of the originally medieval Palau de Dalmases.

At the corner of Carrer dels Corders and the northern end of the street, just beyond the 19th-century Carrer de la Princesa, stands a Romanesque chapel, the **Capella d'en Marcús** (93 310 23 90; www.hijosde-laiglesiabcn.com; Carrer de Montcada) FREE, once a wayfarers' stop on the road northeast out of medieval Barcelona.

FUNDACIÓ GASPAR   GALLERY

Map p268 (93 887 42 48; www.fundaciogaspar. org; Carrer de Montcada 25; adult/concession/ under 12yr €5/3/free; 10am-8pm Tue, Wed, Fri-Sun, to 9.30pm Thu; MJaume I) Set in a stunning Gothic palazzo next to the Museu Picasso, the Fundació Gaspar opened in November 2015 with the intention of complementing the works of other galleries and museums around town by bringing contemporary artists who have yet to exhibit here or whose work explores new concepts and styles. The exhibitions are on the 1st floor, while the ground floor is taken up with a graceful courtyard, where you'll find the Café Gaspar and a shop specialising in edgy, arty gifts.

MUSEU DE CULTURES DEL MÓN   MUSEUM

Map p268 (93 256 23 00; http://museuculturesmon.bcn.cat; Carrer de Montcada 12; adult/ concession/child €5/3.50/free, temporary exhibition €2.20/1.50/free, 3-8pm Sun & 1st Sun of month free; 10am-7pm Tue-Sat, to 8pm Sun; ; MJaume I) The Palau Nadal and the Palau Marquès de Llió, which once housed the Museu Barbier-Mueller and the Museu Tèxtil respectively, reopened in 2015 to the public as the site of a new museum, the Museum of World Cultures. Exhibits from private and public collections, including many from the Museu Etnològic on Montjuïc, take the visitor on a trip through the ancient cultures of Africa, Asia, the Americas and Oceania. There's a combined ticket with Museu Egipci (p129) and the Museu Etnològic (p180) for €12.

PALAU DE DALMASES   HISTORIC BUILDING

Map p268 (93 310 06 73; www.palaudalmases. com; Carrer de Montcada 20; adult/under 10yr €25/15 incl 1 drink; 8pm-2am Tue-Sat, 6-10pm Sun; MJaume I) You can sip wine or cocktails (both rather expensive) inside the baroque courtyard and theatrical interior of the originally medieval Palau de Dalmases at No 20, while listening to baroque music or operatic snippets.

MUSEU EUROPEU D'ART MODERN   MUSEUM

Map p268 (MEAM; 93 319 56 93; www.meam. es; Carrer Barra de Ferro 5; adult/concession/ under 10yr €9/7/free; 10am-8pm Tue-Sun; MJaume I) The European Museum of Modern Art opened in the summer of 2011 in the Palau Gomis, a handsome 18th-century mansion around the corner from the Museu Picasso. The art within is strictly representational (the 'Modern' of the name simply means 'contemporary') and is mostly from young Spanish artists, though there are some works from elsewhere in Europe.

ESGLÉSIA DE SANT PERE
DE LES PUELLES   CHURCH

Map p268 (93 268 07 42; www.parroquias-antpere.org; Plaça de Sant Pere; 9am-1pm & 5-7.45pm Mon-Fri, 9am-1pm & 4.30-6pm Sat, 11am-1.15pm Sun; MArc de Triomf) FREE It was around this church that settlement began in La Ribera. In AD 985 a Muslim raiding force under Al-Mansur attacked Barcelona and largely destroyed what was then a convent, killing or capturing the nuns. It was rebuilt in early medieval times, but not a great deal remains. The church's pre-Romanesque Greek-cross floor plan survives, as do some Corinthian columns, beneath the 12th-century dome and a much-damaged Renaissance vault leading into a side chapel.

MUSEU DE LA XOCOLATA   MUSEUM

Map p268 (☑93 268 78 78; www.museuxocolata.cat; Carrer del Comerç 36; adult/under 7yr €6/free; ⊙10am-7pm Mon-Sat, 10am-3pm Sun; ☎⌖; ⓂArc de Triomf) Chocoholics have a hard time containing themselves in this museum dedicated to the fundamental foodstuff – particularly when faced with tempting displays of cocoa-based treats in the cafe at the exit. The displays trace the origins of chocolate, its arrival in Europe, and the many myths and images associated with it. Among the informative stuff and machinery used in the production of chocolate are large chocolate models of emblematic buildings such as La Sagrada Família, along with various characters, local and international.

Kids and grown-ups can join guided tours and occasionally take part in chocolate-making and tasting sessions, especially at weekends.

CASA LLOTJA DE MAR   ARCHITECTURE

Map p268 (La Llotja; ☑93 547 88 49; www.casallotja.com; Passeig d'Isabel II 1; ⓂBarceloneta) ⬛ᴿᴱᴱ The centrepiece of the city's medieval stock exchange (more affectionately known as La Llotja) is the fine Gothic Saló de Contractacions (Transaction Hall), built in the 14th century. Pablo Picasso and Joan Miró attended the art school that was housed in the Saló dels Cònsols from 1849.

These and five other halls were encased in a neoclassical shell in the 18th century. The stock exchange was in action until well into the 20th century and the building remains in the hands of the city's chamber of commerce. Occasionally it opens its doors to the public but the rooms are more generally hired out for events.

MUSEU DEL REI DE LA MAGIA   MUSEUM

Map p268 (☑93 318 71 92; www.elreydelamagia.com; Carrer de les Jonqueres 15; adult/concession & child €5/3; ⊙11am-2pm & 4-8pm Tue-Sun, closed Sun morning Jul & Aug; ⌖; ⓂUrquinaona)

This museum is a timeless curio. It is the scene of magic shows, home to collections of material that hark back to the 19th-century origins of the associated magic shop (p103) at Carrer de la Princesa 11, and the place for budding magicians of all ages to enrol in courses. Seeing is believing.

✕ EATING

BORMUTH   TAPAS €

Map p268 (☑93 310 21 86; Carrer del Rec 31; tapas from €4; ⊙1pm-midnight; ☎; ⓂJaume I) Opened on the pedestrian Carrer del Rec in 2013, Bormuth has tapped into the vogue for old-school tapas with modern-day service and decor, and serves all the old favourites – *patatas bravas, ensaladilla* (Russian salad) and tortilla – along with some less predictable and superbly prepared numbers (try the chargrilled red pepper with black pudding).

The split-level dining room is never less than animated, but there's a more peaceful space with a single long table if you can assemble a group. A lunchtime deal offers three tapas and a drink for €8.90, or two tapas and a drink for €5.90.

EN APARTÉ   FRENCH €

Map p268 (☑93 269 13 35; www.enaparte.es; Carrer Lluís el Piados 2; mains €7-10; ⊙10am-1.30am Mon-Thu, to 2am Fri & Sat, to 12.30am Sun; ☎; ⓂArc de Triomf, Urquinaona) A great low-key place to eat good-quality French food, just off the quiet Plaça de Sant Pere. The restaurant is small but spacious, with sewing-machine tables and vintage details, and floor-to-ceiling windows that bring in some wonderful early-afternoon sunlight.

The lunch menu (€12.50) is excellent, offering a salad (such as beetroot, apple and walnut), and a quiche or another dish, such as stuffed peppers with a potato gratin. Brunch – including French toast, eggs Benedict and muesli with yoghurt – is served on weekends.

PARADISO   SMOKERY €

Map p268 (☑639 310671; www.rooftopsmokehouse.com; Carrer de Rera Palau 4; mains €8; ⊙cocktail bar 7pm-2am Sun-Thu, to 3am Fri & Sat, pastrami bar noon-2am Sun-Thu, to 3am Fri & Sat; ⓂBarceloneta) A kind of Narnia-in-reverse, Paradiso is fronted with a snowy-white space, not much bigger than a wardrobe, and in itself reason enough to linger, with pastrami sandwiches, smoked duck and other home-cured delights from the Rooftop Smokehouse team, best known for their food trucks.

But this is only the portal – pull open the huge wooden fridge door, and step through into a glam, sexy speakeasy of a cocktail bar guaranteeed to raise the most world-weary of eyebrows.

EUSKAL ETXEA   TAPAS €

Map p268 (☑93 310 21 85; Placeta de Montcada 1; tapas €1.95; ⊙10am-12.30am Sun-Thu, to 1am Fri & Sat; MJaume I) Barcelona has plenty of Basque and pseudo-Basque eateries, but this is the real deal. It captures the feel of San Sebastián better than many of its newer competitors. Choose your *pintxos* (Basque tapas piled on slices of bread), sip *txacolí* (Basque white wine), and keep the toothpicks so the staff can count them up and work out your bill.

CAT BAR   VEGAN €

Map p268 (Carrer de la Bòria 17; mains €6.50-8.50; ⊙6-11.30pm Mon-Wed, 1-11pm Thu-Sat; 🛜🍽; MJaume I) This tiny little joint squeezes in a vegan kitchen, a great selection of local artisanal beers and a smattering of live music. The food mostly centres on a list of different burgers, plus a gluten-free dish of the day, tapas and hummus. The beers change regularly, but there is always one wheat, one porter, one gluten-free and an IPA.

BAR JOAN   CATALAN €

Map p268 (☑93 310 61 50; Mercat de Santa Caterina; menú del día €12, tapas from €3; ⊙7.30am-3.30pm Mon, Wed & Sat, to 8.30pm Tue, Thu & Fri, closed afternoons Jul & Aug; 🛜; MJaume I) There are a couple of bar-eateries in the Mercat de Santa Caterina, with Bar Joan known especially to locals for its *arròs negre* (cuttlefish-ink rice) on Tuesday at lunchtime and paella on Thursdays. It's a simple spot, serving only tapas or the *menú del día* (daily set menu), but it's friendly and good value.

TANTARANTANA   MEDITERRANEAN €

Map p268 (☑93 268 24 10; www.gruposantelmo. com; Carrer d'en Tantarantana 24; mains €9-12; ⊙1pm-midnight; 🛜; MJaume I) There is something comforting about the old-style marble-top tables, upon which you can sample simple but well-prepared dishes such as risotto or grilled tuna served with vegetables and ginger. There's also a long list of tapas. It at-tracts a 30-something crowd who enjoy the outdoor seating in summer.

LA LLAVOR DELS ORÍGENS   CATALAN €

Map p268 (☑93 310 75 31; www.lallavordelsori-gens.com; Carrer de la Vidrieria 6-8; mains €8-12; ⊙1pm-midnight; MJaume I) In this treasure chest of Catalan regional products, the shop shelves groan under the weight of bottles. It also has a long menu of smallish dishes, such as *sopa de carbassa i castanyes* (pumpkin and chestnut soup) or *man-donguilles amb albergínies* (rissoles with aubergine), which you can mix and match over wine by the glass.

BUBÓ   PASTELERÍA €

Map p268 (☑93 268 72 24; www.bubo.es; Carrer de les Caputxes 6 & 10; tapas from €5; ⊙10am-9pm Mon-Thu & Sun, to 11pm Fri & Sat; MBarceloneta) Carles Mampel is a wizard of desserts. It is difficult to walk by his pastry shop (and adjacent tapas bar) without being sucked in to sample one of his fantasy-laden creations. Try saying no to a mousse of *gian-duia* (a dark hazelnut cream) with mango cream, caramelised hazelnuts with spices, and a hazelnut biscuit.

★CASA DELFÍN   CATALAN €€

Map p268 (☑93 319 50 88; www.tallerdetapas. com; Passeig del Born 36; mains €10-15; ⊙8am-midnight Sun-Thu, to 1am Fri & Sat; 🛜; MBarceloneta) One of Barcelona's culinary delights, Casa Delfín is everything you dream of when you think of Catalan (and Mediterranean) cooking. Start with the tangy and sweet *calçots* (a cross between a leek and an onion; February and March only) or salt-strewn *padron* peppers, moving on to grilled sardines speckled with parsley, then tackle the meaty monkfish roasted in white wine and garlic.

Or tease some mussels and clams out of their shells while crunching on the Catalan *coca* flatbread – done here to perfection and smeared with tomatoes and olive oil. For the finale, choose the Eton Mess (the English owner Kate's only tribute to her home-land) – a long glass of mashed-up cream, meringue and berries.

★EL ATRIL   INTERNATIONAL €€

Map p268 (☑93 310 12 20; www.atrilbarce-lona.com; Carrer dels Carders 23; mains €11-15; ⊙noon-midnight Mon-Thu, to 1am Fri & Sat, 11.30am-11.30pm Sun; 🛜; MJaume I) Aussie owner Brenden is influenced by culinary flavours from all over the globe, so while you'll see plenty of tapas (the *patatas bravas* are recommended for their homemade sauce), you'll also find kangaroo fillet, salmon and date rolls with mascarpone, chargrilled turkey with fried yucca, and plenty more.

If the weather is good or there's no space in the cosy dining room, there are tables outside in a lively square.

NAKASHITA   JAPANESE €€

Map p268 (☑93 295 53 78; www.nakashitabcn. com; Carrer del Rec Comtal 15; mains €15-20; ☺1.30-4.30pm & 8.30pm-midnight; ☎; MArc de Triomf) Brazil's particular immigration story means it has a tradition of superb Japanese food, and the Brazilian chef at Nakashita is no slouch, turning out excellent sashimi, maki rolls, soft shell crab and kakiage (a mix of tempura). One of the best Japanese restaurants in the city, with just a handful of tables – book if you can.

BAR DEL PLA   TAPAS €€

Map p268 (☑93 268 30 03; www.bardelpla.cat; Carrer de Montcada 2; mains €12-16; ☺noon-11pm Mon-Thu, to midnight Fri & Sat; MJaume I) At first glance, the tapas at informal Bar del Pla are traditionally Spanish, but the riffs on a theme display an assured touch. Try the ham and roasted-meat croquettes or the marinated salmon, yoghurt and mustard.

CAL PEP   TAPAS €€

Map p268 (☑93 310 79 61; www.calpep.com; Plaça de les Olles 8; mains €13-20; ☺7.30-11.30pm Mon, 1-3.45pm & 7.30-11.30pm Tue-Sat, closed last 3 weeks Aug; MBarceloneta) It's getting a foot in the door of this legendary fish restaurant that's the problem – there can be queues out into the square. And if you want one of the five tables out the back, you'll need to call ahead. Most people are happy elbowing their way to the bar for some of the tastiest seafood tapas in town.

Pep recommends *cloïsses amb pernil* (clams and ham) or the *trifàsic* (combo of calamares, whitebait and prawns). The restaurant's other *pièce de résistance* is a super-smooth *tortilla de patatas* (Spanish omelette) and tuna tartare.

SANTAGUSTINA   TAPAS €€

Map p268 (☑93 315 79 04; www.santagustina.com; Plaça Sant Agustí Vell 9; mains €9-12; ☺5pm-1am Mon, 9am-1am Tue-Thu, to 3am Fri & Sat; ☎; MArc de Triomf) This new tapas bar/restaurant has tables outside on a charm-

ing little plaza. Invoking a slightly wicked ecclesiastical theme, with menus sectioned into 'Blessed Tapas', 'Divine Tapas', 'Immaculate Tapas' and 'Temptations', it serves up well- executed Spanish and Catalan food – oxtail stew, 'Granny's meatballs', grilled octopus etc – in small portions designed for sharing. Service could be a little more attentive.

LE CUCINE MANDAROSSO   ITALIAN €€

Map p268 (☑93 269 07 80; www.lecucinemandarosso.com; Carrer de Verdaguer i Callís 4; mains €12-14, menú del día €11; ☺1.30pm-1am Tue-Sat, 1.30-5pm & 8pm-midnight Sun; MUrquinaona) This is comfort food done to perfection – the menu changes daily, with only a handful of mains to choose from, most of which are pasta, with one or two fish or meat. The antipasti can be vegetables, or fresh cheese, such as the wonderfully creamy *burrata* (fresh cheese made from mozzarella and cream), buffalo-milk mozzarella, or smoked *scamorza* and *provola* cheese.

Combine a good pasta dish – the *al forno* (baked) options are always outstanding – with a green salad, and follow up with the homemade cakes. The fresh produce is bought daily from the Mercat de Santa Caterina, and the rest is imported from Italy.

EL FORO   ARGENTINE €€

Map p268 (☑93 310 10 20; www.restauranteelforo.com; Carrer de la Princesa 53; mains €9-16; ☺10am-11.30pm Tue-Thu & Sun, to 1am Fri & Sat; ☎; MJaume I) Friendly El Foro does everything you'd expect an Argentine restaurant to do – huge slabs of red meat in a variety of cuts, *empanadas* (small pasties with various fillings) and the inevitable Italian element in the shape of pizzas and pasta dishes. Less predictable is the list of vegetarian dishes (such as vegetable curry with quinoa and coconut milk) and the range of salads.

It's a sunny, sprawling place with tables on the street, and is good for a coffee at any time of day.

CUINES DE SANTA
CATERINA   MEDITERRANEAN, ASIAN €€

Map p268 (☑93 268 99 18; www.grupotragaluz.com; Mercat de Santa Caterina; mains €12-16; ☺1-4pm & 6.30pm-midnight Sun-Thu, to 1am Fri & Sat; ☎; MJaume I) With a contemporary feel and open kitchens, this multifaceted restaurant inside the Mercat de Santa Caterina offers all sorts of food. Peck at the sushi bar, tuck

LA RIBERA EATING

into classic rice dishes or chargrilled meat, or go vegetarian. It does some things better than others (skip the hummus and tarte tatin). Reservations aren't taken, so you may have to queue.

A drawback is the speed with which barely finished plates are whisked away from you, but the range of dishes and bustling atmosphere are fun.

PASSADÍS DEL PEP
SEAFOOD €€€

Map p268 (☑93 310 10 21; www.passadis.com; Pla del Palau 2; mains €19-24; ◷1.15-3.45pm & 8.30-11.30pm Mon-Sat; MBarceloneta) There's no sign, but locals know where to head for a seafood feast. They say the restaurant's raw materials are delivered daily from fishing ports along the Catalan coast. There's no menu – what's on offer depends on what the sea has surrendered that day – but you can count on fresh seafood and/or fish, *jamón* (cured ham), tomato bread and grilled vegetables.

Just head down the long, ill-lit corridor and entrust yourself to its care.

🍷 DRINKING & NIGHTLIFE

MUDANZAS
BAR

Map p268 (☑93 319 11 37; Carrer de la Vidrieria 15; ◷10am-2am Sun-Thu, to 3am Fri & Sat; 🛜; MJaume I) This was one of the first bars to get things into gear in El Born and it still attracts a faithful crowd. With its chequered floor and marble-topped tables, it's an attractive, lively place for a beer and perhaps a sandwich or a tapa. It also has a nice line in rum and malt whisky.

LA VINYA DEL SENYOR
WINE BAR

Map p268 (☑93 310 33 79; www.lavinyadelsenyor.com; Plaça de Santa Maria del Mar 5; ◷noon-1am Mon-Thu, noon-2am Fri & Sat, noon-midnight Sun; 🛜; MJaume I) Relax on the *terrassa,* which lies in the shadow of the Basílica de Santa Maria del Mar, or crowd inside at the tiny bar. The wine list is as long as *War and Peace* and there's a table upstairs for those who opt to sample by the bottle rather than the glass.

JUANRA FALCES
COCKTAIL BAR

Map p268 (☑93 310 10 27; Carrer del Rec 24; ◷8pm-3am Tue-Sat, 10pm-3am Sun & Mon; MJaume I) Transport yourself to a Humphrey Bogart movie in this narrow little bar, formerly (and still, at least among the locals) known as Gimlet. White-jacketed bar staff with all the appropriate aplomb will whip you up a gimlet or any other classic cocktail (around €10) that your heart desires.

RUBÍ
BAR

Map p268 (☑647 773707; Carrer dels Banys Vells 6; ◷7.30pm-2.30am Sun-Thu, to 3am Fri & Sat; MJaume I) With its boudoir lighting and cheap mojitos, Rubí is where the Born's *cognoscenti* head for a nightcap – or several. It's a narrow, cosy space – push through to the back where you might just get one of the coveted tables, with superior bar food, from Vietnamese rolls to more traditional selections of cheese and ham.

MIRAMELINDO
BAR

Map p268 (☑93 310 37 27; www.barmiramelindobcn.com; Passeig del Born 15; ◷8pm-2am; 🛜; MJaume I) A spacious tavern in a Gothic building, this remains a classic on Passeig del Born for mixed drinks, while soft jazz and soul sounds float overhead. Try for a comfy seat at a table towards the back before it fills to bursting. A couple of similarly barn-sized places sit on this side of the *passeig.*

GUZZO
COCKTAIL BAR

Map p268 (☑93 667 00 36; www.guzzo.es; Plaça Comercial 10; ◷6pm-3am Tue-Thu, to 3.30am Fri & Sat, noon-3am Sun; 🛜; MBarceloneta) This swish but relaxed cocktail bar is run by much-loved Barcelona DJ Fred Guzzo, who is often to be found at the decks, spinning his delicious selection of funk, soul and rare groove. You'll also find frequent live-music acts of consistently decent quality, and a funky atmosphere at almost any time of day.

EL BORN BAR
BAR

Map p268 (☑93 319 53 33; Passeig del Born 26; ◷10am-2am Mon-Sat, noon-1.30am Sun; 🛜; MJaume I) El Born Bar effortlessly attracts everyone from cool thirty-somethings from all over town to locals who pass judgment on Passeig del Born's passing parade. Its staying power depends on a good selection of beers, spirits, and *empanadas* and other snacks.

BAR DEL CONVENT
CAFE

Map p268 (☑93 256 50 17; www.bardelconvent.com; Plaça de l'Acadèmia; ◷10am-9pm Tue-Thu, to 10pm Fri & Sat; MArc de Triomf) Alongside

MASTERS OF WINE

One of the best wine stores in Barcelona (and there are a few...), **Vila Viniteca** (Map p268; 902 327777; www.vilaviniteca.es; Carrer dels Agullers 7; 8.30am-8.30pm Mon-Sat; M Jaume I) has been searching out the best local and imported wines since 1932. On a couple of November evenings it organises what has become an almost riotous wine-tasting event in Carrer dels Agullers and surrounding lanes, at which cellars from around Spain present their young new wines.

At No 9 it has another store devoted to gourmet food products.

the Gothic arches of what remains of the Sant Agusti convent's cloister is this pleasant cafe-bar – particularly good for people with children. Kids often play football in the cloister grounds, and there are children's books and toys in the cafe itself. You can also enter at Carrer del Comerç 36 through James Turrell's light sculpture.

CACTUS BAR BAR
Map p268 (93 310 63 54; www.cactusbar.cat; Passeig del Born 30; 3pm-3am; M Jaume I) So many Barcelona nights end with a mojito, and El Born's biggest and best are to be found at Cactus Bar. The outdoor tables next to Passeig del Born are the perfect way to wind down the night.

EL XAMPANYET WINE BAR
Map p268 (93 319 70 03; Carrer de Montcada 22; noon-4pm & 7-11pm Tue-Sat, noon-4pm Sun; M Jaume I) Nothing has changed for decades in this, one of the city's best-known *cava* bars. Plant yourself at the bar or seek out a table against the decoratively tiled walls for a glass or three of the cheap house *cava* and an assortment of tapas, such as the tangy *boquerones en vinagre* (fresh anchovies in vinegar).

MAGIC CLUB
Map p268 (93 310 72 67; www.magic-club.net; Passeig de Picasso 40; 11pm-6am Thu-Sun; M Barceloneta) Although it sometimes hosts live acts in its sweaty, smoky basement, Magic is basically a straightforward, subterranean nightclub offering rock, mainstream dance faves and Spanish pop.

UPIAYWASI BAR
Map p268 (93 268 01 54; www.upiaywasi. com; Carrer d'Allada Vermell 11; 12.30pm-2am Mon-Thu, 11am-3am Fri & Sat, 11am-1am Sun; ; M Jaume I) Slide into this dimly lit bar, which crosses a chilled ambience with Latin American music and Peruvian textiles. A

mix of sofas and intimate tables, chandeliers and muted decorative tones lend the place a pleasingly conspiratorial feel. During the day most people will be found out on the terrace.

☆ **ENTERTAINMENT**

★ **PALAU DE LA MÚSICA CATALANA** CLASSICAL MUSIC
Map p268 (93 295 72 00; www.palaumusica. cat; Carrer de Palau de la Música 4-6; tickets from €15; box office 9.30am-9pm Mon-Sat, 10am-3pm Sun; M Urquinaona) A feast for the eyes, this Modernista confection is also the city's most traditional venue for classical and choral music, although it has a wide-ranging program, including flamenco, pop and – particularly – jazz. Just being here for a performance is an experience. In the foyer, its tiled pillars all a-glitter, sip a preconcert tipple.

Head up the grand stairway to the main auditorium, a whirlpool of Modernista whimsy.

TABLAO NERVIÓN DANCE
Map p268 (93 315 21 03; www.restaurante-nervion.com; Carrer de la Princesa 2; show incl 1 drink €17, show & set dinner €28; shows 8-10pm Thu-Sat; M Jaume I) For admittedly tourist-oriented flamenco, this unassuming bar (shows take place in the basement) is cheaper than most, and has good offerings. Check the website for further details.

🛍 **SHOPPING**

EL REI DE LA MÀGIA MAGIC
Map p268 (93 319 39 20; www.elreydelamagia. com; Carrer de la Princesa 11; 10.30am-2pm & 4-7.30pm Mon-Sat; M Jaume I) For more than 100 years, the people behind this box of

Local Life
Tapas & Bar Hopping in El Born

If there's one place that distils Barcelona's enduring cool to its essence and provides a snapshot of all that's irresistible about this city, it has to be El Born, the tangle of streets surrounding the Basílica de Santa Maria del Mar. Its secret is simple: this is where locals go for an authentic Barcelona night out.

❶ Passeig del Born
Most nights, and indeed most things, in El Born begin along the Passeig del Born, one of the prettiest little boulevards in Europe. It's a place to sit as much as to promenade. It's the graceful setting beneath the trees from which El Born's essential appeal is obvious – thronging people, brilliant bars and architecture that springs from a medieval film set.

❷ Catalan Tapas
Push through the crowd, order a *cava* (sparkling wine) and an assortment of tapas at El Xampanyet (p101), one of the city's best-known *cava* bars, in business since 1929. Star dishes include tangy *boquerones en vinagre* (white anchovies in vinegar) and there's high-quality seafood served from a can in the Catalan way.

❸ Best of Basque
Having taken your first lesson in Barcelona-style tapas it's time to compare it with the *pintxos* (Basque tapas of food morsels perched atop pieces of bread) lined up along the bar at Euskal Etxea (p98), a real slice of San Sebastián.

❹ Spain with a Twist
The detour to Bar del Pla (p99) on the northern limits of El Born is worth the walk. The tapas may look traditionally Spanish but a confident hand in the kitchen bestows deft touches of originality

❺ Tapas with a View
Back in the heart of El Born, in the shadow of Basílica de Santa Maria del Mar, pastry chef Carles Mampel operates Bubó (p98). If you're not already sated, try the salted cod

TRAVELSTOCK44/LOOK-FOTO ©

Tapas bar

croquettes at one of the outdoor tables inching onto the lovely square.

❻ Cal Pep

Boisterous Cal Pep (p99) is one of Barcelona's enduring stars. It can be difficult to snaffle a bar stool from which to order gourmet bar snacks such as *cloïsses amb pernil* (clams with ham); so if it's full, order a drink and wait. It's always worth it.

❼ El Born's Favourite Bar

El Born Bar (p100) effortlessly attracts everyone from cool thirty-somethings from all over town to locals who pass judgment on Passeig del Born's passing parade. Its staying power depends on a good selection of beers, spirits, and *empanadas* and other snacks.

❽ The Last Mojito

So many Barcelona nights end with a mojito, and El Born's biggest and best are to be found at Cactus Bar (p101). The outdoor tables next to Passeig del Born are the perfect way to wind down the night.

tricks have been keeping locals both astounded and amused. Should you decide to stay in Barcelona and make a living as a magician, this is the place to buy levitation brooms, glasses of disappearing milk and decks of magic cards.

HOFMANN PASTISSERIA   FOOD

Map p268 (☎93 268 82 21; www.hofmann-bcn.com; Carrer dels Flassaders 44; ⊙9am-2pm & 3.30-8pm Mon-Thu, 9am-8.30pm Fri & Sat, 9am-2.30pm Sun; MBarceloneta) With its painted wooden cabinets, this bite-sized gourmet patisserie, linked to the prestigious Hofmann cooking school, has an air of timelessness. Choose between jars of delicious chocolates, the renowned croissants (in various flavours) and more dangerous pastries, or an array of cakes and other sweet treats.

EL MAGNÍFICO   COFFEE

Map p268 (☎93 319 39 75; www.cafeselmagnifico.com; Carrer de l'Argenteria 64; ⊙10am-8pm Mon-Sat; MJaume I) All sorts of coffee has been roasted here since the early 20th century. The variety of coffee (and tea) available is remarkable – and the aromas hit you as you walk in. Across the road, the same people run the exquisite tea shop Sans i Sans (p104).

CASA GISPERT   FOOD

Map p268 (☎93 319 75 35; www.casagispert.com; Carrer dels Sombrerers 23; ⊙10am-2pm & 4-8pm Mon-Sat; MJaume I) The wonderful, atmospheric and wood-fronted Casa Gispert has been toasting nuts and selling all manner of dried fruit since 1851. Pots and jars piled high on the shelves contain an unending variety of crunchy titbits: some roasted, some honeyed, all of them moreish. Your order is shouted over to the till, along with the price, in a display of old-world accounting.

LOISAIDA   CLOTHING, ANTIQUES

Map p268 (☎93 295 54 92; www.loisaidabcn.com; Carrer dels Flassaders 42; ⊙11am-9pm Mon-Sat, 11am-2pm & 4-8pm Sun; MJaume I) A sight in its own right, housed in what was once the coach house and stables for the Royal Mint, Loisaida (from the Spanglish for 'Lower East Side') is a deceptively large emporium of colourful, retro and somewhat preppy clothing for men and women, costume jewellery, music from the 1940s and '50s and some covetable antiques.

LA RIBERA SHOPPING

ARLEQUÍ MÀSCARES
ARTS & CRAFTS

Map p268 (☑93 268 27 52; www.arlequimask.com; Carrer de la Princesa 7; ☺10.30am-8.30pm Mon-Sat, 10.30am-3pm & 4-7.30pm Sun; ⓂJaume I) A wonderful little oasis of originality, this shop specialises in masks for costume and decoration. Some of the pieces are superb, while stock also includes a beautiful range of decorative boxes in Catalan themes, and some old-style marionettes.

NU SABATES
SHOES, ACCESSORIES

Map p268 (☑93 268 03 83; www.nusabates.com; Carrer dels Cotoners 14; ☺11am-9pm Mon-Sat; ⓂJaume I) A couple of modern-day Catalan cobblers have put together some original handmade leather shoes for men and women (and a handful of bags and other leather items) in their friendly and stylish locale, which is enlivened by some inspired musical selections.

COQUETTE
FASHION

Map p268 (☑93 319 29 76; www.coquettebcn. com; Carrer del Rec 65; ☺11am-3pm & 5-9pm Mon-Fri, 11.30am-9pm Sat; ⓂBarceloneta) With its spare, cut-back and designer look, this friendly fashion store is attractive in its own right. Women can browse through casual, feminine wear by such designers as Humanoid, Vanessa Bruno, UKE and Hoss Intropia and others, with a further collection nearby at **Carrer de Bonaire 5** (Map p268; ☑93 310 35 35; Carrer de Bonaire 5; ☺11am-3pm & 5-9pm Mon-Fri, 11.30am-9pm Sat; ⓂBarceloneta).

OLISOLIVA
FOOD

Map p268 (☑93 268 14 72; www.olisoliva.com; Mercat de Santa Caterina; ☺9.30am-3.30pm Mon, Wed & Sat, to 8.30pm Tue & Thu; ⓂJaume I) Inside the Mercat de Santa Caterina, this simple, glassed-in store is stacked with olive oils and vinegars from all over Spain. Taste some of the products before deciding. Some of the best olive oils come from southern Spain. The range of vinegars is astounding too.

CUSTO BARCELONA
FASHION

Map p268 (☑93 268 78 93; www.custo.com; Plaça de les Olles 7; ☺10am-9pm Mon-Sat, noon-8pm Sun; ⓂBarceloneta) The psychedelic decor and casual atmosphere lend this avant-garde Barcelona fashion store a youthful edge. Custo presents daring new women's and men's collections each year on the New York catwalks. The dazzling colours and cut of everything from dinner jackets to hot pants are for the uninhibited. It has three other stores around town.

LA BOTIFARRERIA
FOOD

Map p268 (☑93 319 91 23; www.labotifarreria. com; Carrer de Santa Maria 4; ☺8.30am-2.30pm & 5-8.30pm Mon-Sat; ⓂJaume I) Say it with a sausage! Although this delightful deli sells all sorts of goodies, the mainstay is an astounding variety of handcrafted sausages – the *botifarra*. Not just the regular pork variety either – these sausages are stuffed with anything from green pepper and whisky to apple curry.

SANS I SANS
DRINK

Map p268 (☑93 310 25 18; Carrer de l'Argenteria 59; ☺10am-8pm Mon-Sat; ⓂJaume I) This exquisite tea shop is run by the same people who run El Magnífico (p103) across the road.

🏃 ACTIVITIES

AIRE DE BARCELONA
HAMMAM

Map p268 (☑93 295 57 43; www.airedebarcelona. com; Passeig de Picasso 22; thermal baths & aromatherapy Mon-Thu €31, Fri-Sun €33; ☺10am-10pm Mon-Thu & Sun, 10am-2am Fri & Sat; ⓂArc de Triomf) With low lighting and relaxing perfumes wafting around you, this basement hammam could be the perfect way to end a day. Hot, warm and cold baths, steam baths and options for various massages, including on a slab of hot marble, make for a delicious hour or so. Book ahead and bring a swimming costume.

BIKE TOURS BARCELONA
BICYCLE TOUR

Map p268 (www.biketoursbarcelona.com; Carrer de l'Esparteria 3; per person €23; ⓂJaume I) One of numerous operators offering daily three-hour tours of the Barri Gòtic, waterfront, La Sagrada Família and other Gaudí landmarks. Tours depart from the tourist office on Plaça de Sant Jaume; check the website for departure times.

BARCELONA SCOOTER
DRIVING TOUR

Map p268 (☑93 221 40 70; www.cooltra.com; Via Laietana 6; tour €50; ☺3.30pm Thu, 10.30am Sat; ⓂJaume I) Run by Cooltra, Barcelona Scooter offers a three-hour tour by scooter around the city, taking in architectural highlights (La Pedrera, La Sagrada Família) and great views (from Montjuïc). Departure is from the Cooltra rental outlet at 3.30pm on Thursdays and 10.30am on Saturdays.

Barceloneta & the Waterfront

PORT VELL & BARCELONETA | PORT OLÍMPIC, POBLENOU & EL FÒRUM

Neighbourhood Top Five

1 **Museu d'Història de Catalunya** (p108) Learning about Romans, Muslims, feudal lords and civil war freedom fighters, followed by drinks in the rooftop restaurant.

2 **Museu Marítim** (p107) Stepping back in time in this fascinating Gothic shipyard and exploring Barcelona's rich maritime past.

3 **Museu Can Framis** (p110) Studying avant-garde paintings by contemporary Catalan artists in up-and-coming Poblenou.

4 **Platja de la Nova Mar Bella** (p108) Basking on a sun-kissed sandy beach, followed by an invigorating dip in the Mediterranean.

5 **Teleférico del Puerto** (p109) Gazing out over the city on a scenic cable car ride from seaside to hilltop.

For more detail of this area see Maps p270 and p272 ➡

Lonely Planet's Top Tip

If you'd like to explore the sea and the mountains on the same day, take advantage of the Teleférico del Puerto, which whisks passengers from Barceloneta up to Montjuïc in a rather vintage-looking cable car. The tower also has a top-end restaurant, though the view is better than the food.

✕ Best Places to Eat

➡ El 58 (p113)
➡ Barraca (p112)
➡ Can Dendê (p113)
➡ Els Pescadors (p113)
➡ La Cova Fumada (p111)
➡ Kaiku (p112)

For reviews, see p111 ➡

🍷 Best Places to Drink

➡ Can Paixano (p114)
➡ Absenta (p114)
➡ The Mint (p114)
➡ Madame George (p114)
➡ Balius (p114)
➡ BlackLab (p114)

For reviews, see p114 ➡

🛍 Best Places to Shop

➡ Els Encants Vells (p117)
➡ Bazart (p117)
➡ Bestiari (p118)
➡ System Action (p117)

For reviews, see p117 ➡

Explore Barceloneta & the Waterfront

Barcelona's long, sun-drenched waterfront provides a pleasant escape when you need a break from Gothic lanes and Modernisme. Heading northeast from the old city, you'll soon find yourself amid tempting seafood restaurants and waterfront bars, with a palm-lined promenade taking cyclists, joggers and strollers out to the beaches running some 4km up to Parc del Fòrum.

At the foot of La Rambla, Port Vell is where many visitors first lay eyes on Barcelona's slice of the Mediterranean. This transformed area, once an industrial wasteland, draws locals and tourists alike who come to stroll the peaceful pedestrian bridge of Rambla de Mar, which leads out to the shops and restaurants in Maremàgnum mall and the aquarium next door.

East of there lie upmarket, open-air restaurants overlooking a marina and one of the city's best museums for learning about the Catalan experience, the Museu d'Historia de Catalunya. Nearby is Barceloneta, an old fishing quarter laid out in the mid-18th century with narrow gridlike lanes criss-crossed with laundry in the breeze. The few tourists venturing here stick mostly to the outdoor restaurants lining Passeig de Joan de Borbo. For something a little more memorable, head into the narrow lanes, which are dotted with festive tapas bars, old-fashioned seafood joints and bohemian drinking spots.

Where Barceloneta abuts the water, you'll find open-air restaurants offering views out over the promenade and the beaches beyond. Inland lies Poblenou. Although it's not a big draw for many tourists, in recent years this design and high-tech zone has brought new cafes, shops and eateries.

Local Life

➡ **Hang-outs** There are many great local haunts full of flowing *cava,* draught beer and delicious tapas: Vaso de Oro (p112) and Can Paixano (p114) are favourites.
➡ **Markets** Port Vell hosts Port Antic (p117), a small weekend antiques market; near the marina is the craft market of Feria de Artesanía del Palau de Mar (p117).

Getting There & Away

➡ **Foot** From the old city, La Rambla and Via Laietana are the main pedestrian access points across busy Ronda del Litoral.
➡ **Metro** Go to Drassanes (Línia 3) to reach Port Vell; Barceloneta (Línia 4) has its own stop for the neighbourhood. Línia 4 continues out to Ciutadella Vila Olímpica (best stop for Port Olímpic) and El Maresme Fòrum near Parc del Fòrum.

TOP SIGHT
MUSEU MARÍTIM

These mighty Reials Drassanes (Royal Shipyards) are an extraordinary piece of civilian architecture. From here, Don Juan of Austria's flagship galley was launched to lead a joint Spanish-Venetian fleet into the momentous Battle of Lepanto against the Turks in 1571. Today the broad arches shelter the Museu Marítim, the city's seafaring-history museum and one of Barcelona's most intriguing museums.

Royal Shipyards
The shipyards were, in their heyday, among the greatest in Europe. Begun in the 13th century and completed by 1378, the long, arched bays (the highest arches reach 13m) once sloped off as slipways directly into the water, which lapped the seaward side of the Drassanes until at least the end of the 18th century. Shipbuilding was later moved to southern Spain, and the Drassanes became a barracks for artillery.

Replica of Don Juan of Austria's Flagship
The centre of the shipyards is dominated by a full-sized replica (made in the 1970s) of Don Juan of Austria's flagship. A clever audiovisual display aboard the vessel brings to life the ghastly existence of the slaves, prisoners and volunteers (!) who, at full steam, could haul this vessel along at 9 knots. They remained chained to their seats, four to an oar, at all times. Here they worked, drank (fresh water was stored below decks, where the infirmary was also located), ate, slept and went to the loo. You could smell a galley like this from miles away.

Exhibitions
Fishing vessels, old navigation charts, models and dioramas of the Barcelona waterfront make up the rest of this engaging museum. Temporary exhibitions are also held (an intriguing show on the history of explorations in Antarctica was held here in 2014). The museum, which has seen major renovations in recent years, is scheduled to finally reopen in its entirety by early 2017. When it reopens, visitors will encounter a greatly expanded collection with multimedia exhibits evoking more of Spain's epic history on the high seas.

Ictíneo
In the courtyard, you can have a look at a swollen replica of the *Ictíneo,* one of the world's first submarines. It was invented and built in 1858 by Catalan polymath Narcis Monturiol, and was operated by hand-cranked propellers turned by friends of Monturiol who accompanied him on dozens of successful short dives (two hours maximum) in the harbour. He later developed an even larger submarine powered by a combustion engine that allowed it to dive to 30m and remain submerged for seven hours. Despite impressive demonstrations to awestruck crowds he never attracted the interest of the navy, and remains largely forgotten today.

DON'T MISS
➡ The replica of Don Juan of Austria's flagship
➡ Temporary exhibitions
➡ *Ictíneo*
➡ The courtyard cafe

PRACTICALITIES
➡ Map p270
➡ 93 342 99 20
➡ www.mmb.cat
➡ Avinguda de les Drassanes
➡ adult/child €7/3.50, 3-8pm Sun free
➡ 10am-8pm
➡ Drassanes

BARCELONETA & THE WATERFRONT MUSEU MARÍTIM

 **SIGHTS**

Port Vell & Barceloneta

MUSEU MARÍTIM   MUSEUM
See p107.

**MUSEU D'HISTÒRIA
DE CATALUNYA**   MUSEUM
Map p270 (Museum of Catalonian History; ☑93
225 47 00; www.mhcat.net; Plaça de Pau Vila 3;
adult/child €4.50/3.50, last Tue of the month Oct-
Jun free; ☺10am-7pm Tue & Thu-Sat, to 8pm Wed,
to 2.30pm Sun; Ⓜ Barceloneta) Inside the Palau de Mar, this worthwhile museum takes
you from the Stone Age through to the early
1980s. It is a busy hotchpotch of dioramas,
artefacts, videos, models, documents and
interactive bits: all up, an entertaining exploration of 2000 years of Catalan history.
Signage is in Catalan/Spanish.

See how the Romans lived, listen to Arab
poetry from the time of the Muslim occu-
pation of the city, peer into the dwelling of
a medieval family in the Pyrenees, and try
to mount a knight's horse or lift a suit of
armour.

When you have had enough of all this,
descend into a civil-war air-raid shelter,
watch a video in Catalan on post-Franco
Catalonia, or head upstairs to the first-rate
rooftop restaurant and cafe, 1881 (p113).

The temporary exhibitions are often as
interesting as the permanent display. Outside the museum, you'll find a string of elegant open-air restaurants serving classic
seafood dishes to harbourfront views.

L'AQUÀRIUM   AQUARIUM
Map p270 (☑93 221 74 74; www.aquariumbcn.
com; Moll d'Espanya; adult/child €20/15, dive
€300; ☺9.30am-11pm Jul & Aug, to 9pm Sep-Jun;
Ⓜ Drassanes) It is hard not to shudder at the
sight of a shark gliding above you, displaying its toothy, wide-mouthed grin. But this,
the 80m shark tunnel, is the highlight of one
of Europe's largest aquariums. It has the
world's best Mediterranean collection and
plenty of colourful fish from as far off as the
Red Sea, the Caribbean and the Great Bar-
rier Reef. All up, some 11,000 fish (including
a dozen sharks) of 450 species reside here.

Back in the shark tunnel, which you
reach after passing a series of themed fish
tanks with everything from bream to sea

⊙ TOP SIGHT
PLATJES

A series of pleasant beaches stretches northeast from the
Port Olímpic marina. They are largely artificial, but this
doesn't stop millions of bathers from piling in every year!

The southernmost beach, **Platja de la Nova Icària**,
is the busiest. Behind it, across the Avinguda del Litoral
highway, is the Plaça dels Campions, site of the rusting
three-tiered platform used to honour medallists in the
sailing events of the 1992 games.

The next beach is **Platja de Bogatell**. Just in from
the beach is **Cementiri del Poblenou** (p110), created in
1773. The cemetery is full of bombastic family memorials, but an altogether disquieting touch is the sculpture
El Petó de la Mort (the Kiss of Death), in which a winged
skeleton kisses a young kneeling lifeless body. There's
a good skateboard area with half-pipes at the north end
of the beach.

Platja de la Mar Bella (with its brief nudist strip
and sailing school) and **Platja de la Nova Mar Bella**
follow, leading into the new residential and commercial
waterfront strip, the Front Marítim, part of the Diagonal
Mar project in the Fòrum district. It is fronted by the
last of these artificial beaches to be created, **Platja del
Llevant**.

DON'T MISS

➡ The vibrant bustle
of Platja de la Nova
Icària

➡ The poignant *El
Petó de la Mort* sculp-
ture in Cementiri del
Poblenou

PRACTICALITIES

➡ Map p272
➡ 🚌36, 41,
Ⓜ Ciutadella Vila
Olímpic, Bogatell,
Llacuna, Selva de Mar

horses, various species of shark (white tip, sand tiger, bonnethead, black tip, nurse and sandbar) flit around you, along with a host of other critters, from flapping rays to bloated sunfish. An interactive zone, Planeta Aqua, is host to a family of Antarctic penguins and a tank of rays that you watch close up.

Those with a valid dive certificate may dive in the main tank with the sharks.

EDGE BREWING   BREWERY
Map p272 (www.edgebrewing.com; Carrer de Llull 62; tours incl beer tastings €20; ⊙tours by appointment; MBogatell) Founded by two Americans back in 2013, Edge Brewing has already racked up some impressive awards for its craft beers (among other things it was named top new brewer in the world in 2014 by RateBeer.com). On a brewery tour, you'll get a behind-the-scenes look at Edge's operations, and get to taste some of its classic (like the Hoptimista, an award-winning 6.6% IPA) and seasonal brews (the summertime Apassionada is a passionfruit sour ale).

Check the website for upcoming tours and other events – including 'members' nights in the tasting room (though you can become a member just by signing up online).

TELEFÉRICO DEL PUERTO   CABLE CAR
Map p270 (www.telefericodebarcelona.com; Passeig Escullera; one way/return €11/16.50; ⊙11am-7pm Mar-Oct, to 5.30pm Nov-Feb; 🚌17, 39, 64, MBarceloneta) This cable car strung across the harbour to Montjuïc provides a bird's-eye view of the city. The cabins float between the Torre de Sant Sebastià (in La Barceloneta) and Miramar (Montjuïc), with a midway stop at the Torre de Jaume I in front of the World Trade Center. At the top of the Torre de Sant Sebastià is a restaurant, **Torre d'Alta Mar** (Map p270; ☎93 221 00 07; www.torredealtamar.com; Passeig de Joan Borbó 88; prix-fixe lunch/dinner from €39/72; ⊙1-3.30pm Tue-Sat & 8-11.30pm daily; 🚌17, 39, 57, 64, MBarceloneta).

PAILEBOT DE SANTA EULÀLIA   SHIP
Map p270 (www.mmb.cat; Moll de la Fusta; adult/child €3/free; ⊙10am-8.30pm Tue-Fri & Sun, 2-8.30pm Sat; MDrassanes) This 1918 three-mast schooner, restored by the Museu Marítim, is moored along the palm-lined promenade Moll de la Fusta. You can see

109

LOCAL KNOWLEDGE

REMEMBERING THE VICTIMS OF FRANCO
Buried beneath the concrete expanses, bathing zone and marina created in El Fòrum lies the memory of more than 2000 people executed in the fields of Camp de la Bota between 1936 and 1952, most of them under Franco from 1939 onward. To their memory, *Fraternitat* (Brotherhood), a sculpture by Miquel Navarro, stands on Rambla de Prim.

it perfectly well without going aboard, and there's not an awful lot to behold below decks. Admission is free with a paid Museu Marítim ticket.

The ship makes a scenic three-hour cruise on some Saturdays, though ongoing maintenance has put a hold on its sailings until early 2017. Once the tours are again on offer (adult/child €12/6), you can book a spot by emailing reserves.mmaritim@diba.cat.

ESGLÉSIA DE SANT MIQUEL DEL PORT   CHURCH
Map p270 (☎93 221 65 50; Plaça de la Barceloneta; ⊙7am-1.30pm Mon-Fri, 8am-1.30pm Sat; MBarceloneta) Finished in 1755, this sober baroque church was the first building completed in La Barceloneta. Built low so that the cannon in the then Ciutadella fort could fire over it if necessary, it bears images of St Michael (Sant Miquel) and two other saints considered protectors of the Catalan fishing fleet: Sant Elm and Santa Maria de Cervelló.

Ferdinand Lesseps, the French engineer who designed the Suez Canal, did a stint as France's consul-general in Barcelona and lived in the house to the right of the church.

FÀBRICA DEL SOL   MUSEUM
Map p270 (☎93 256 44 30; Passeig de Salvat Papasseit 1; ⊙10am-2pm & 4.30-8pm Tue-Fri, 10am-2pm Sat; MBarceloneta) A relic from the industrial era, this striking Modernista building with its red brick and yellow details today houses an environmental education centre, with exhibitions on sustainable energy sources. You can wander around the building (and check out the solar panels on the roof), though all signage is in Catalan or Spanish.

BARCELONETA & THE WATERFRONT SIGHTS

⊙ Port Olímpic, Poblenou & El Fòrum

MUSEU DEL DISSENY DE BARCELONA   MUSEUM

Map p272 (☑93 256 68 00; www.museudeldisseny.cat; Plaça de les Glòries Catalanes 37; permanent/temporary exhibition €6/4.40, combination ticket €8; ☺10am-8pm Tue-Sun; MGlòries) Barcelona's design museum lies inside a new monolithic building with geometric facades and a rather brutalist appearance – it has already earned the nickname *la grapadora* (the stapler) by locals. Architecture aside, the museum houses a dazzling collection of ceramics, decorative arts and textiles, and is a must for anyone interested in the design world.

Start at the top and work your way down. On the 4th floor, you'll enter the terrain of the graphic arts, specifically posters from Catalan firms dating from the post-WWII years to the present. On the floor below, the museum provides a highly condensed overview of fashion from the 1500s onward. Among other things, you'll find a dramatically lit room with 19th-century crinolines (cage-like frames worn as an undergarment to hold up flouncy dresses), displayed like rare sea creatures inside giant glass tubes.

The 2nd floor is devoted to the decorative arts, with a wildly varied collection that includes 3rd-century Coptic works, an elaborate 16th-century Brussels tapestry, antique jewel-crusted pocket watches, and sculptural works by Picasso and Miró. Don't miss the glittering stained-glass panel created for the 1896 Expo. The 1st floor houses Catalan product design from the 20th century – worth a quick peek for the furniture.

Temporary exhibitions run the gamut from 17th-century Turkish ceramics to cutting-edge fashion photography of today.

MUSEU CAN FRAMIS   MUSEUM

Map p272 (☑93 320 87 36; www.fundaciovilacasas.com; Carrer de Roc Boronat 116; adult/student €5/2; ☺11am-6pm Tue-Sat, to 2pm Sun; MGlòries, Llacuna) Set in a former textile factory, this contemporary museum is a showcase for Catalan painting of the past 60 years. The galleries display some 300 works, arranged in thought-provoking ways – with evocative paintings by different artists (sometimes working in different time periods) creating fascinating intersections and collisions.

Highlights include the complex paintings (like tapestries in paint) of Victor Pérez-Porro, desolate black-and-white scenes of Gregori Iglesias, dreamlike sequences of Perejaume, photographic portraits by Pedro Madueño, Agustí Puig's ethereal *Menines* (whose point of departure is Velázquez' iconic *Las Meninas* created three centuries earlier) and the luminous works by self-taught painter Xevi Vilaro.

MUSEU DE LA MÚSICA   MUSEUM

Map p272 (☑93 256 36 50; www.museumusica.bcn.cat; Carrer de Lepant 150; adult/student/child €5/4/free, 3-8pm Sun free; ☺10am-6pm Tue-Sat, to 8pm Sun; MMonumental) Some 500 instruments (less than a third of those held) are on show in this museum, housed on the 2nd floor of the administration building in L'Auditori, the city's main classical-music concert hall.

Instruments range from a 17th-century baroque guitar through to lutes (look out for the many-stringed 1641 archilute from Venice), violins, Japanese kotos, sitars from India, eight organs (some dating from the 18th century), pianos and a varied collection of drums and other percussion instruments from across Spain and beyond, along with all sorts of phonographs and gramophones. There are some odd pieces indeed, like the *buccèn,* a snake-head-adorned brass instrument. Much of the documentary and sound material can be enjoyed through audiovisual displays as you proceed.

The museum periodically hosts daytime concerts, in which musicians perform on rare instruments held in the collection.

TORRE AGBAR   ARCHITECTURE

Map p272 (www.torreagbar.com; Av Diagonal 225; MGlòries) Barcelona's very own cucumber-shaped tower, Jean Nouvel's luminous Torre Agbar, is among the most daring additions to the skyline since the first towers of La Sagrada Família went up. Completed in 2005, it shimmers at night in shades of midnight blue and lipstick red. Talks have long been under way to transform the tower into a luxury hotel.

CEMENTIRI DEL POBLENOU   CEMETERY

Map p272 (Poblenou Cemetery; ☑93 225 16 61; Av d'Icària, near Carrer del Taulat; ☺8am-6pm; MLlacuna) Located just inland from the beach Platja de Bogatell, this cemetery dates from 1773. It's full of bombastic memorials, including the disquieting sculpture *El petó de la mort* (The Kiss of Death), in which a winged skeleton kisses a young kneeling lifeless body.

PARC DEL CENTRE DEL POBLENOU   PARK

Map p272 (Avinguda Diagonal; ⊘10am-sunset; ⓂPoblenou) Barcelona is sprinkled with parks whose principal element is concrete, and Jean Nouvel's Parc del Centre del Poblenou, with its stylised metal seats and items of statuary, is no exception. However, the park's Gaudí-inspired walls are increasingly covered by sprawling bougainvillea and, inside, some 1000 trees of mostly Mediterranean species are complemented by thousands of smaller bushes and plants. Nouvel's idea is that the trees, sustained by local ground water, will eventually form a natural canopy over the park.

MUSEU BLAU   MUSEUM

Map p272 (Blue Museum; ☑93 256 60 02; www.museuciencies.cat; Parc del Fòrum; adult/child €6/free; ⊘10am-6pm Tue-Fri, to 7pm Sat, to 8pm Sun; ⓂEl Maresme Fòrum) Set inside the futuristic Edifici Fòrum, the Museu Blau takes visitors on a journey all across the natural world. Multimedia and interactive exhibits explore topics like the history of evolution, the earth's formation and the great scientists who have helped shaped human knowledge. There are also specimens from the animal, plant and mineral kingdoms – plus dinosaur skeletons – all rather dramatically set amid the sprawling 9000 sq metres of exhibition space.

Science geeks of all ages will enjoy spending a few hours here.

✖ EATING

✖ Port Vell & Barceloneta

★LA COVA FUMADA   TAPAS €

Map p270 (☑93 221 40 61; Carrer del Baluard 56; tapas €4-8; ⊘9am-3.20pm Mon-Wed, 9am-3.20pm & 6-8.15pm Thu & Fri, 9am-1pm Sat; ⓂBarceloneta) There's no sign and the setting is decidedly downmarket, but this tiny, buzzing, family-run tapas spot always packs in a crowd. The secret? Mouthwatering *pulpo* (octopus), *calamar, sardinias* and 15 or so other small plates cooked to

perfection in the small open kitchen. The *bombas* (potato croquettes served with *alioli*) and grilled *carxofes* (artichokes) are good, but everything is amazingly fresh.

FILFERRO   TAPAS €

Map p270 (☑93 221 98 36; Carrer de Sant Carles 29; tapas €5-7, mains €8-13; ⊘10am-1am Tue-Sun; 🛜📶; ⓂBarceloneta) One of the few spots in Barceloneta where the focus isn't on seafood, Filferro has a loyal following for its good-value tapas, *bocadillos* (filled rolls), salads and pasta. It has a warmly lit and eclectically furnished interior, or you can dine at an outdoor table on the square (popular with families, with a playground just a few steps away).

GUINGUETA DE LA BARCELONETA   SPANISH €

Map p270 (Platja de Sant Sebastià; sandwiches €6-12; ⊘9am-midnight Mar-Nov; ⓂBarceloneta) Part of Carles Abellan's gastronomic empire, this open-sided beachside spot serves up snacks, sandwiches and salads, though cocktails (around €11) are the big draw (as is the sea view).

JAI-CA   SEAFOOD €

Map p270 (☑93 268 32 65; Carrer de Ginebra 13; tapas €4-8; ⊘9am-11.30pm Mon-Sat; ⓂBarceloneta) Jai-Ca is a much-loved eatery that serves up juicy grilled prawns, flavour-rich anchovies, tender octopus, decadent razor clams and other seafood favourites to ever-growing crowds as the evening progresses. The *turbio* (Galician white wine), sangria and cold draught are ideal refreshments after a day on the beach.

EL BEN PLANTAT   INTERNATIONAL €

Map p270 (☑93 624 38 32; Carrer de Sant Carles 21; tapas €5-10; ⊘1-4pm & 8.30-11.30pm Wed-Mon; 📶; ⓂBarceloneta) A welcome addition to seafood-centric Barceloneta, El Ben Plantat serves a varied menu of small plates, with excellent vegetarian choices (hummus, guacamole and chips, tofu pâté, stuffed marinated mushrooms). On weekdays you'll also find multicourse lunch specials – mussels with potatoes, homemade falafel, sausage with ratatouille, vegetable croquettes – good value at €9.

BALUARD BARCELONETA   BAKERY €

Map p270 (Carrer del Baluard 36; pastries €1-2.70; ⊘8am-9pm Mon-Sat; ⓂBarceloneta) One of the best bakeries in the city, Baluard serves up warm flaky croissants, perfect baguettes, moist muffins and a range of tempting pastries and tarts (try one with figs or wild berries).

BITÁCORA
TAPAS €

Map p270 (🖉93 315 35 88; Carrer de Balboa 1; tapas €4-9; ⊙10am-2am; Ⓜ Barceloneta) This youthful little gem is a neighbourhood favourite for its simple but congenial ambience and well-priced tapas plates, which come in ample portions. There's also a small hidden terrace at the back. Top picks: *ceviche de pescado* (fish ceviche), *chipirones* (baby squid) and *gambas a la plancha* (grilled prawns).

VASO DE ORO
TAPAS €

Map p270 (🖉93 319 30 98; www.vasodeoro. com; Carrer de Balboa 6; tapas €4-12; ⊙noon-midnight; Ⓜ Barceloneta) Always packed, this narrow bar gathers a festive, beer-swilling crowd who come for fantastic tapas. Fast-talking, white-jacketed waiters will serve a few quick quips with your plates of grilled *gambes* (prawns), *foie a la plancha* (grilled liver pâté) or *solomillo* (sirloin) chunks. Want something a little different to drink? Ask for a *flauta cincuenta* – half lager and half dark beer.

KAIKU
SEAFOOD €€

Map p270 (🖉93 221 90 82; www.restaurantkaiku. cat; Plaça del Mar 1; mains for 2 €28-36; ⊙1-3.30pm Tue-Sun; Ⓜ Barceloneta) Overlooking the waterfront at the south end of Barceloneta, Kaiku has a solid reputation for its creative seafood plates. Mouth-watering ingredients are sourced from the nearby fish market, and artfully prepared in dishes such as crayfish with mint, swordfish carpaccio with avocado and sundried tomatoes, chilli-smeared tuna with green apples and mushrooms, and the outstanding rice dishes for two.

EL GUINDILLA
CATALAN €€

Map p270 (🖉93 221 54 58; Carrer del Baluard 38; tapas €5-12, lunch specials €10; ⊙9.30am-1am; 🖉; Ⓜ Barceloneta) In the Mercat de la Barceloneta, this popular new eatery serves tasty lunch specials and draws a tapas-munching and beer-drinking crowd by night. Good vegetarian options as well. Peruse the market, then grab an outdoor table on the square.

CAN MAÑO
SPANISH €€

Map p270 (Carrer del Baluard 12; mains €8-14; ⊙9am-4pm Tue-Sat & 8-11pm Mon-Fri; Ⓜ Barceloneta) It may look like a dive, but you'll need to be prepared to wait before being squeezed in at a packed table for a raucous night of *raciones* (full-plate-size tapas serving; posted on a board at the back) over a bottle of *turbio* – a cloudy white plonk. The seafood is abundant with first-rate squid, prawns and fish served at rock-bottom prices.

CAN ROS
SEAFOOD €€€

Map p270 (🖉93 221 45 79; Carrer del Almirall Aixada 7; mains €16-30; ⊙1-4pm & 7-11pm Tue-Sun; 🚌45, 57, 59, 64, 157, Ⓜ Barceloneta) The fifth generation is now at the controls of this immutable seafood favourite, which first opened in 1911. In a restaurant where the decor is a reminder of simpler times, there's a straightforward guiding principle: serve juicy fresh fish cooked with a light touch.

Can Ros also does a rich *arròs a la marinera* (seafood rice), *fideuá* (similar to paella, but using vermicelli noodles as the base) with squid and mussels, and a grilled fish and seafood platter.

BARRACA
SEAFOOD €€€

Map p270 (🖉93 224 12 53; www.barraca-barcelona.com; Passeig Maritim de la Barceloneta 1; mains €19-24; ⊙12.30pm-midnight; Ⓜ Barceloneta) This buzzing space has a great location fronting the Mediterranean – a key reference point in the excellent seafood dishes served here. Start off with a cauldron of chilli-infused clams, cockles and mussels before moving on to the lavish paellas and other rice dishes, which steal the show.

The elegant upstairs dining room has mesmerising views over the waterfront.

CAN MAJÓ
SEAFOOD €€€

Map p270 (🖉93 221 54 55; www.canmajo.es; Carrer del Almirall Aixada 23; mains €19-29; ⊙1-4pm Tue-Sun & 8-11.30pm Tue-Sat; 🚌45, 57, 59, 64, 157, Ⓜ Barceloneta) Virtually on the beach (with tables outside in summer), Can Majó has a long and steady reputation for fine seafood, particularly its rice dishes and bountiful *suquets* (fish stews). The bouillabaisse of fish and seafood is succulent. Sit outside (there are heat lamps in winter) and admire the beach goers.

1881

SPANISH €€€

Map p270 (☎93 221 00 50; www.sagardi.com; Plaça de Pau Vila 3; mains €18-30; ☺1pm-1am Sun-Thu, to 3am Fri & Sat; ☞; ⓂBarceloneta) On the top floor of the Museu d'Història de Catalunya,1881 serves excellent seafood plates to lovely views over the waterfront. Standouts include Galician octopus, hearty fish stews for two and grilled beef tenderloin with wild mushrooms. It's also a fine place to stop in for cocktails (particularly around sunset), and the terrace transitions into a festive party space later on weekend nights.

RESTAURANT 7 PORTES

SEAFOOD €€€

Map p270 (☎93 319 30 33; www.7portes.com; Passeig d'Isabel II 14; mains €19-32; ☺1pm-1am; ⓂBarceloneta) Founded in 1836 as a cafe and converted into a restaurant in 1929, 7 Portes is a classic. It exudes an old-world atmosphere with its wood panelling, tiles, mirrors and plaques naming some of the famous – such as Orson Welles – who have passed through. Paella is the speciality, or try the surfeit of seafood in the *gran plat de marisc* (literally 'big plate of seafood').

✖ Port Olímpic, Poblenou & El Fòrum

CAN DENDÊ

AMERICAN €

Map p272 (☎646 325551; Carrer de la Ciutat de Granada 44; mains €6-11; ☺8.30am-5pm Mon-Fri, from 10.30am Sat & Sun; ⓂLlacuna) An eclectic crowd gathers at this bright, bohemian Brazilian-run eatery in Poblenou. Anytime brunch is the culinary star here, and you can tuck into eggs Benedict with smoked salmon, fluffy pancakes or pulled pork sandwiches while watching the cooks in action and listening to the mix of sounds at play – Latin tropicalia, American grooves, plus the various languages spoken at neighbouring tables.

EL TÍO CHÉ

SNACKS €

Map p272 (Rambla del Poblenou 44; snacks €2-4; ☺10am-10pm Sun-Thu, to 1am Fri & Sat; ⓂPoblenou) First opened back in 1912 (in El Born), this local icon is famed for its *horchata,* a sweet and refreshing if mildly grainy drink made of tigernut milk. Some love it, others less so, though you can also opt for sandwiches, ice cream and other homemade beverages.

EL 58

TAPAS €

Map p272 (Le cinquante huit; Rambla del Poblenou 58; sharing plates €4-11; ☺1.30pm-midnight Tue-Sat; ⓂLlacuna) This French-Catalan eatery serves imaginative, beautifully prepared tapas dishes that earn rave reviews from both locals and expats. Solo diners can grab a seat at the marble-topped front bar and get dining tips from the friendly multilingual baristas. The back dining room with its exposed brick walls, industrial light fixtures and curious artworks is a lively place to linger over a long meal.

Codfish balls with romesco sauce, scallop ceviche, *tartiflette* (a cheese, ham and potato casserole), salmon sashimi: you can't go wrong here, no matter what you order.

★CAN RECASENS

CATALAN €€

Map p272 (☎93 300 81 23; Rambla del Poblenou 102; mains €7-15; ☺9pm-1am Mon-Fri & 1-4pm & 9pm-1am Sat; ⓂPoblenou) One of Poblenou's most romantic settings, Can Recasens hides a warren of warmly lit rooms full of oil paintings, flickering candles, fairy lights and baskets of fruit. The food is outstanding, with a mix of salads, fondues, smoked meats, cheeses, and open-faced sandwiches piled high with delicacies like wild mushrooms and brie, *escalivada* (grilled vegetables) and gruyere, and spicy chorizo.

AGUARIBAY

VEGETARIAN €€

Map p272 (☎93 300 37 90; Carrer de Ramon Turró 181; mains €9-14; ☺1-4pm Mon-Wed, 1-4pm & 8.30-11pm Thu-Sun; ☞; ⓂLlacuna) Step into this polished eatery in Poblenou, and you can't help but feel that the vegetarian renaissance has arrived in Barcelona. Aguaribay serves a small well-executed a la carte menu by night: miso and smoked tofu meatballs, soba noodles with shitake mushrooms, and seasonal vegetables and a rich black rice. At lunchtime, stop in for the prix-fixe lunch specials, which change daily.

Craft beers and biodynamic wines round out the menu.

ELS PESCADORS

SEAFOOD €€€

Map p272 (☎93 225 20 18; www.elspescadors.com; Plaça de Prim 1; mains €19-40; ☺1-3.45pm & 8-11.30pm; ⓂPoblenou) Set on a picturesque square lined with low houses and *bella ombre* trees long ago imported from South America, this quaint family restaurant continues to serve some of the city's best grilled fish and seafood-and-rice dishes. There are three dining areas inside: two quite modern, while the main one preserves its old tavern flavour. On warm nights, try for a table outside.

🍷 DRINKING & NIGHTLIFE

🍷 Port Vell & Barceloneta

CAN PAIXANO WINE BAR
Map p270 (☎93 310 08 39; Carrer de la Reina Cristina 7; ⊗9am-10.30pm Mon-Sat; MBarceloneta) This lofty old champagne bar (also called La Xampanyeria) has long been run on a winning formula. The standard poison is bubbly rosé in elegant little glasses, combined with bite-sized *bocadillos* (filled rolls) and tapas (€3 to €7). Note that this place is usually packed to the rafters, and elbowing your way to the bar can be a titanic struggle.

ABSENTA BAR
Map p270 (www.absentabar.es; Carrer de Sant Carles 36; ⊗7pm-1am Tue & Wed, from 11am Thu-Mon; MBarceloneta) Decorated with old paintings, vintage lamps and curious sculpture (including a dangling butterfly woman and face-painted TVs), this whimsical and creative drinking den takes its liquor seriously. Stop in for the house-made vermouth or for more bite try one of the many absinthes on hand. Just go easy: with an alcohol content of 50% to 90%, these spirits have kick!

THE MINT COCKTAIL BAR
Map p270 (☎647 737707; Passeig d'Isabel II, 4; ⊗7.30pm-2.30am; MBarceloneta) Named after the prized cocktail ingredients, this mojito-loving drinkery has a little something for everyone. Linger upstairs with the grown-ups to peruse the first-rate house-infused gins (over 20 on hand, including creative blends like lemongrass and Jamaican pepper), or head downstairs with the kids to the brick-vaulted cellars, where red lights and driving beats create a more celebratory vibe.

It's a fun setting for a night out, and well located for a bar-hop through El Born before or after.

BLACKLAB MICROBREWERY
Map p270 (☎93 221 83 60; www.blacklab.es; Plaça Pau Vila 1; ⊗noon-1.30am; MBarceloneta)

Inside the historic Palau de Mar, BlackLab was Barcelona's first brewhouse to open way back in 2014. With 20 taps (including 18 housemade brews, including saisons, double IPAs and dry stouts), it's an impressive operation, and the brewmasters are constantly experimenting with new flavours.

There's plenty to eat: burgers and barbecued pulled pork as well as Asian dishes: *bahn mì* sandwiches, veggie dumplings and braised oxtail ramen.

BlackLab also runs tasting tours (currently on Sundays at 5pm), where you'll get a behind-the-scenes look at the brewers in action.

BAR LEO BAR
Map p270 (Carrer de Sant Carles 34; ⊗noon-9.30pm; MBarceloneta) Bar Leo is a hole-in-the-wall drinking spot plastered with images of late Andalucian singer and heart-throb Bambino, and a jukebox mostly dedicated to flamenco. For a youthful, almost entirely *barcelonin* crowd, Bar Leo is it! It's liveliest on weekends.

KÉ? BAR
Map p270 (Carrer del Baluard 54; ⊗noon-2am; MBarceloneta) An eclectic and happy crowd hangs about this small bohemian bar run by a friendly Dutchman. Pull up a padded 'keg chair' or grab a seat on one of the worn lounges at the back and join in the animated conversation wafting out over the street. Outdoor seating in summer, just a few steps from Barceloneta's market.

🍷 Port Olímpic, Poblenou & El Fòrum

BALIUS COCKTAIL BAR
Map p272 (☎93 315 86 50; www.facebook.com/BaliusBar; Carrer de Pujades 196; ⊗5pm-1am Tue-Fri, from 1pm Sat & Sun; MPoblenou) There's an old-fashioned jauntiness to this vintage cocktail den in Poblenou. Friendly barkeeps pour a fair mix of classic libations as well as vermouths, and there's a small tapas menu. Stop by on Sundays to catch live jazz, starting around 7.30pm.

MADAME GEORGE LOUNGE
Map p272 (www.madamegeorgebar.com; Carrer de Pujades 179; ⊗7pm-1am Sun-Thu, to 3am Fri & Sat; MPoblenou) A theatrical (veering towards campy) elegance marks the interior

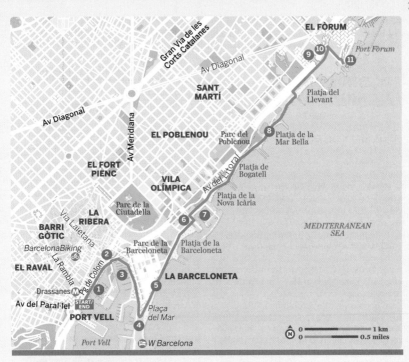

🏃 Cycling Tour
Barcelona's Waterfront Revamp

START PORT VELL
END PORT VELL
LENGTH 12KM RETURN, 1½ HOURS

This bike tour takes in boardwalks, beaches, sculpture and architecture along Barcelona's ever-changing waterfront. It's a flat and safe ride along a dedicated bike path separate from traffic – though watch out for pedestrians. There are several convenient bike hires nearby, including BarcelonaBiking (www. barcelonabiking.com) in the Barri Gòtic.

With Columbus at your back, make your way northeast along the waterfront. Keep an eye out for the three-mast schooner, ❶ **Pailebot de Santa Eulàlia** (p109), built in 1918. Another 400m up the road, you'll pass the colourful ❷ **Barcelona Head** sculpture by American pop artist Roy Lichtenstein.

As you make your way along the ❸ **Marina**, you may have to dismount amid the throng of strollers and open-air restaurants. Hop back on and pedal to the Plaça del Mar, which sports an elegant sculpture

entitled ❹ **Homenatge als Nedadors** (Homage to the Swimmers).

Follow the crowds north, past another well-known sculpture, the ❺ **Homenatge a la Barceloneta**, which commemorates the old-fashioned shacks that once lined the beach. Cycle another kilometre and you'll pass beneath the copper-hued ❻ **Peix sculpture**, designed by Frank Gehry.

Next up is ❼ **Port Olímpic**, which is lined with restaurants and bars. From here you'll pass more ❽ **beaches**, which fill with sunseekers in summer.

It's another 2.5km or so to the end, where you'll find the ❾ **Parc del Fòrum**. Dominating this empty plaza is the rather harsh-looking sculpture ❿ **Fraternitat**, dedicated to hundreds executed here during the Franco years.

The protected bathing area ⓫ **Zona de Banys** is a popular summer attraction for families. Just behind it looms the giant solar panel that powers the area. From here, retrace your journey back to Port Vell.

of this small, chandelier-lit lounge just off the Rambla del Poblenou. Deft bartenders stir up nicely balanced cocktails to a friendly, eclectic crowd, while off in the corner a DJ spins vintage soul and funk (bonus points for using vinyl).

LA CERVECITA NUESTRA DE CADA DÍA   BAR
Map p272 (Carrer de Llull 184; ⏱5.30-9.30pm Sun & Mon, 11.30am-2pm & 5.30-9.30pm Tue-Sat; Ⓜ Llacuna) Equal parts beer shop and craft brew bar, La Cervicita has a changing selection of unique beers from around Europe and the USA. You might stumble across a Catalan sour fruit beer, a rare English stout, a potent Belgian triple ale or half a dozen other draughts on hand – plus many more varieties by the bottle.

Low-playing music and minimal decorations keep the focus on beer chatter.

ESPAI JOLIU   CAFE
Map p272 (Carrer Badajoz 95; ⏱9am-7pm Mon-Fri; 📶; Ⓜ Llacuna) Further proof that Poblenou is fast becoming the Brooklyn of Barcelona are places like Espai Joliu, a charming little space with art mags, handmade stationery and ceramics sold up front and a peaceful cafe (blonde wood tables, melodic indie rock) tucked up the steps at the back.

SKYE   CAFE
Map p272 (Carrer de Pamplona 88; ⏱9am-1.30pm Mon-Wed, to 5pm Thu & Fri; 📶; Ⓜ Bogatell) Join expats at communal tables over tasty flat whites and *cortados* (espressos with a dribble of milk) inside a cavernous space that's emblematic of the creative rebirth of this once-industrial hood. Baristas whip up their concoctions inside the very adorable 1972 Citroen parked in the corner.

OPIUM MAR   CLUB
Map p270 (☎93 225 91 00; www.opiummar. com; Passeig Marítim de la Barceloneta 34; cover €10-20; ⏱club 11pm-5am, restaurant from noon; Ⓜ Ciutadella Vila Olímpica) This seaside dance place has a spacious dance floor that attracts a mostly North American crowd. It only begins to fill from about 3am and is best in summer, when you can spill onto a terrace overlooking the beach. The beachside outdoor section works as a chilled restaurant-cafe.

GUINGUETA DEL BOGATELL   BAR
Map p272 (Platja del Bogatell; ⏱9am-10.30pm May-Sep) At this summer-time spot, you can

dig your feet in the sand and enjoy a cold brew while watching the lapping waves.

☆ ENTERTAINMENT

RAZZMATAZZ   LIVE MUSIC
Map p272 (☎93 320 82 00; www.salarazzmatazz. com; Carrer de Pamplona 88; tickets €15-40; ⏱9pm-4am; Ⓜ Marina, Bogatell) Bands from far and wide occasionally create scenes of near hysteria in this, one of the city's classic live-music and clubbing venues. Bands can appear throughout the week (check the website), with different start times. On weekends the live music then gives way to club sounds.

Five different clubs in one huge postindustrial space attract people of all dance persuasions and ages. The main space, the Razz Club, is a haven for the latest international rock and indie acts. The Loft does house and electro, while the Pop Bar offers anything from garage to soul. The Lolita room is the land of house, hip-hop and dubstep, and upstairs in the Rex Room guys and girls sweat it out to experimental sounds. You can save a few euros by purchasing tickets to concerts in advance.

SALA MONASTERIO   LIVE MUSIC
Map p272 (☎616 287197; www.facebook.com/ sala.monasterio; Moll de Mestral 30; ⏱9pm-2.30am; Ⓜ Ciutadella-Vila Olímpica) Overlooking the bobbing masts and slender palm trees of Port Olímpic, this pocket-sized music spot stages an eclectic line-up of live bands, including jazz, *forró* (music from northeastern Brazil), blues jams and rock (usually on Fridays and Saturdays).

SALA BECKETT   THEATRE
Map p272 (☎93 284 53 12; www.salabeckett.com; Carrer de Pere IV 228; Ⓜ Poblenou) One of the city's principal alternative theatres, the Sala Beckett does not shy away from challenging theatre, and stages an eclectic mix of local productions and foreign drama. Formerly based in Gràcia, the theatre moved in 2016 to this lovely new space (in the building that formerly housed the Cooperativa Pau i Justícia Poblenou).

TEATRE NACIONAL DE CATALUNYA   PERFORMING ARTS
Map p272 (☎93 306 57 00; www.tnc.cat; Plaça de les Arts 1; tickets €12-30; ⏱box office 3-8pm

LOCAL KNOWLEDGE

WATERFRONT MARKETS

On weekends Port Vell springs to life with a handful of markets selling a mix of antiques and contemporary art and crafts at key points along the waterfront.

At the base of La Rambla, the small **Port Antic** (Map p270; Plaça del Portal de la Pau; ⊗10am-8pm Sat & Sun; Ⓜ Drassanes) market is a requisite stop for strollers and antique hunters. Here you'll find old photographs, frames, oil paintings, records, shawls, cameras, vintage toys and other odds and ends.

Near the Palau de Mar, you'll find **Feria de Artesanía del Palau de Mar** (Map p270; Moll del Dipòsit; ⊗11am-8.30pm Sat & Sun; Ⓜ Barceloneta), with artisans selling a range of crafty items, including jewellery, graphic T-shirts, handwoven hats, fragrant candles and soaps, scarves and decorative items. In July and August the market runs daily.

Take a stroll along the pedestrian-only Rambla de Mar to reach the weekend art fair **Mercado de Pintores** (Map p270; Passeig d'Ítaca; ⊗10am-8pm Sat & Sun; Ⓜ Drassanes), with a broad selection of paintings both collectable and rather forgettable.

Wed-Sat, to 6pm Sun & 1hr before show; Ⓜ Glòries, Monumental) Ricard Bofill's ultra-neoclassical theatre, with its bright, airy foyer, hosts a wide range of performances, including dramas, comedies, musicals and dance. Some shows are free.

L'AUDITORI
CLASSICAL MUSIC

Map p272 (☑93 247 93 00; www.auditori.org; Carrer de Lepant 150; tickets €7-80; ⊗box office 5-9pm Tue-Fri, 10am-1pm & 5-9pm Sat; Ⓜ Monumental) Barcelona's modern home for serious music lovers, L'Auditori puts on plenty of orchestral, chamber and other music. The ultramodern building (designed by Rafael Moneo) is home to the Orquestra Simfònica de Barcelona i Nacional de Catalunya.

YELMO CINES ICÀRIA
CINEMA

Map p272 (☑902 220922; www.yelmocines.es; Carrer de Salvador Espriú 61; Ⓜ Ciutadella Vila Olímpica) This vast cinema complex screens movies in the original language on 15 screens, making for plenty of choice. Aside from the screens, you'll find several cheerful eateries, bars and the like to keep you occupied before and after the movies.

🛍 SHOPPING

ELS ENCANTS VELLS
MARKET

Map p272 (Fira de Bellcaire; ☑93 246 30 30; www.encantsbcn.com; Plaça de les Glòries Catalanes; ⊗9am-8pm Mon, Wed, Fri & Sat; Ⓜ Glòries) In a gleaming open-sided complex near Plaça de les Glòries Catalanes, the 'Old Charms' flea market is the biggest of its kind in Barcelona. Over 500 vendors ply their wares beneath massive mirror-like panels. It's all here, from antique furniture through to secondhand clothes. A lot of it is junk, but occasionally you'll stumble across a *ganga* (bargain).

The most interesting time to be here is from 7.30am to 8.30am on Monday, Wednesday and Friday, when the *subastas* (public auctions) take place.

SYSTEM ACTION
CLOTHING

Map p272 (☑93 225 79 90; systemaction.es; Carrer de Pere IV 122; ⊗10am-7pm Mon-Sat; Ⓜ Llacuna) If you like discovering local producers, then look no further than this outlet store on Pere IV. Though System Action has stores all across Catalunya (and in Madrid), its design headquarters are a few blocks south in a former Poblenou ice factory. Fashions are feminine but rugged, and you'll find good basics here. Very wearable scarves, sweaters, skirts and even shoes.

Prices are reasonable – especially when sales are under way.

BAZART
ACCESSORIES

Map p272 (☑633 455378; Carrer de la Ciutat de Granada 44; ⊗10.30am-6pm Mon-Fri, to 2.30pm Sat; Ⓜ Llacuna) If you can't make it to the handicrafts market in South America, Bazart may be your next best option. This colourfully decorated shop stocks handcrafted goods from across the Andes. There are lots of great gift ideas, including silver jewellery from Ecuador, woven pillowcases from Bolivia, and alpaca gloves, scarves and blankets from Chile (the owner's birthplace).

ULTRA-LOCAL RECORDS
MUSIC

Map p272 (☑661 017638; www.ultralocalrecords.com; Carrer de Pujades 113; ⊗3-8.30pm Mon-Fri, from 11am Sat; Ⓜ Llacuna) Tucked along a fairly empty stretch of Poblenou, this small, well-curated shop sells mostly used records (plus some re-releases and albums by current indie rock darlings) from Catalan, Spanish, French, American and British artists. Vinyl aside, you'll find a smaller CD selection, plus zines and a few other curiosities. There's a €1 bargain bin out front.

BESTIARI
BOOKS, HANDICRAFTS

Map p270 (Plaça de Pau Vila 3; ⊙10am-7pm Tue-Sat, to 2.30pm Sun; MBarceloneta) On the ground floor of the Museu d'Història de Catalunya, this nicely stocked shop sells books in English, Spanish and Catalan for all ages, plus you'll find lots of Catalan-themed gift ideas: CDs, T-shirts, umbrellas, messenger bags, chess sets, mugs and toys (along the lines of the build-your-own Gothic or Gaudí structures).

MERCAT DE LA BARCELONETA
MARKET

Map p270 (☑93 221 64 71; www.mercatdelabarceloneta.com; Plaça de la Font 1; ⊙7am-3pm Mon-Thu & Sat, 7am-8pm Fri; MBarceloneta) Set in a modern glass and steel building fronting a long plaza in the heart of Barceloneta, this airy market has the usual array of fresh veg and seafood stalls, as well as several places where you can enjoy a sit-down meal. El Guindilla (p112) deserves special mention for its good-value lunch specials and outdoor seating on the plaza.

MAREMÀGNUM
MALL

Map p270 (☑93 225 81 00; www.maremagnum.es; Moll d'Espanya 5; ⊙10am-10pm; MDrassanes) Created out of largely abandoned docks, this buzzing shopping centre, with its bars, restaurants and cinemas, is pleasant enough for a stroll virtually in the middle of the old harbour. The usual labels are on hand, including the youthful Spanish chain Mango, mega-retailer H&M and eye-catching fashions from Barcelona-based Desigual. Football fans will be drawn to the paraphernalia at FC Botiga.

It's particularly popular on Sundays when most other stores in the city close.

🏃 ACTIVITIES

MOLOKAI SUP CENTER
WATER SPORTS

Map p270 (☑93 221 48 68; www.molokaisupcenter.com; Carrer de Meer 39; 2hr lesson €55, SUP rental per hour €15; MBarceloneta) This respected outfit will give you a crash course in stand-up paddleboarding (SUP). In addition to the two-hour beginner's class, Molokai can help you improve your technique (in intermediate and advanced lessons – all in two-hour blocks); gear and wetsuit are included. Or if you'd rather just hire a SUP board, they can get you out on the sea in no time.

ORSOM
CRUISE

Map p270 (☑93 441 05 37; www.barcelona-orsom.com; Moll de les Drassanes; adult/child from €16/11; ⊙May-Oct; MDrassanes) Aboard a large sailing catamaran, Orsom makes the 90-minute journey to Port Olímpic and back. There are three departures per day (four on weekends in July and August), and the last is a jazz cruise, scheduled around sunset. The same company also runs five daily, 50-minute speedboat tours (adult/child €13/11).

BOARDRIDERS
BARCELONETA
WATER SPORTS

Map p270 (☑93 221 44 91; Plaça del Mar 1; ⊙10am-8pm Mon-Sat, from 11am Sun; MBarceloneta) Facing the seafront, Boardriders rents out surfboards (per hour/half-day €12/25), stand-up paddleboards (per hour/half-day €15/30) and wetsuits. It also sells clothes and gear.

BASE NAUTICA
MUNICIPAL
SAILING, WINDSURFING

Map p272 (☑93 221 04 32; www.basenautica.org; Avinguda de Litoral; 2hr class €50-70; ⊙10am-7pm; MPoblenou) Have you come to Barcelona to become a sea dog? If so, head to this place, just back from Platja de la Mar Bella, where you can learn the basics of kayaking, windsurfing, catamaran sailing or stand up paddle boarding (90-minute class for €30 to €40). Prices are cheaper in groups of two or more.

Longer courses, running from eight to 12 hours over several days, are also available.

CLUB NATACIÓ
ATLÈTIC-BARCELONA
SWIMMING

Map p270 (☑93 221 00 10; www.cnab.cat; Plaça del Mar; day pass adult/child €12.20/7.10; ⊙7am-11pm Mon-Sat, 8am-8pm Sun; ☐17, 39, 57, 64, MBarceloneta) This athletic club has one indoor and two outdoor pools. Of the latter, one is heated for lap swimming in winter. Admission includes use of the gym and private beach access.

La Sagrada Família & L'Eixample

L'ESQUERRA DE L'EIXAMPLE | LA DRETA DE L'EIXAMPLE

Neighbourhood Top Five

1 La Sagrada Família (p121) Seeing history being made.

2 La Pedrera (p128) Witnessing ground-breaking architecture.

3 Casa Batlló (p127) Marvelling at its almost-alive, swirling facade.

4 Fundació Antoni Tàpies (p126) Deciphering the fascinating contemporary art.

5 Recinte Modernista de Sant Pau (p129) Admiring this lesser-known masterpiece of Modernisme.

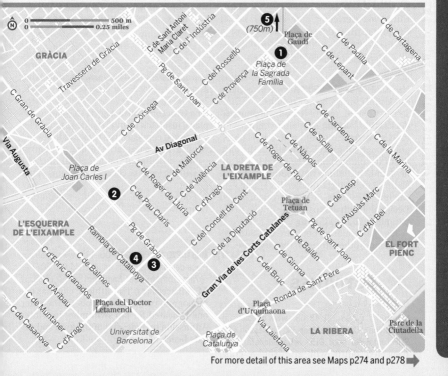

For more detail of this area see Maps p274 and p278 ➡

Lonely Planet's Top Tip

L'Eixample's restaurants can be quite pricey, but you can still sample their food at budget prices if you head over for the *menú del día* (daily set menu), which, although simpler in choice, is always good value.

⚔ Best Places to Eat

➡ Disfrutar (p132)
➡ Can Kenji (p134)
➡ Cinc Sentits (p132)
➡ Cata 1.81 (p131)
➡ Tapas 24 (p132)
➡ Cerveseria Catalana (p131)

For reviews, see p130 ➡

🍷 Best Places to Drink

➡ Dry Martini (p135)
➡ Monvínic (p135)
➡ Milano (p135)
➡ Les Gens Que J'Aime (p138)

For reviews, see p135 ➡

🛍 Best Places to Shop

➡ Cacao Sampaka (p139)
➡ Flores Navarro (p139)
➡ El Bulevard dels Antiquaris (p140)
➡ Joan Múrria (p141)

For reviews, see p139 ➡

Explore La Sagrada Família & L'Eixample

In the 1820s rows of trees were planted on either side of the road linking Barcelona and the town of Gràcia. Thus was born the Passeig de Gràcia, a strollers' boulevard that is now home to many of the city's most expensive shops and a range of restaurants. This is the street to head to for Modernista architecture, the best of which – apart from La Sagrada Família – is clustered on or near it. Eating is at the high end (though set-lunch options are available for lower budgets), and the emphasis is on designer fashion, though there are some notable exceptions. Drinking and nightlife in the area tend to be student- and gay-oriented – part of the area has even been dubbed 'Gaixample'.

La Dreta (the Right) de L'Eixample, stretching from Passeig de Gràcia to Passeig de Sant Joan, contains much sought-after real estate. Beyond it takes on a dowdy feel, even around La Sagrada Família. L'Esquerra (the Left) de L'Eixample, running southwest from Passeig de Gràcia, changes character several times. The whole area between Carrer d'Aribau, Passeig de Sant Joan, Avinguda Diagonal and the Ronda de Sant Pere has been known since the early 20th century as the Quadrat d'Or (Golden Square) thanks to its extravagant architecture and grand houses; it's now home to high-end shops.

The Modernista stars include Gaudí's La Pedrera and the Manzana de la Discordia, which comprises three gems by the three top architects of the period. Never is the old axiom about looking up as you wander more true than it is here.

Local Life

➡**Student life** The presence of the Universitat de Barcelona (p128) makes for a line of unpretentious hang-outs nearby on the Carrer d'Enric Granados.

➡**Coffee with a view** Take a lift to the very top of El Corte Inglés (p139) for a restaurant with a great view across the neighbourhood and beyond.

➡**Say it with flowers** Walking round the Flores Navarro (p139), a cathedral to colourful plant life, is quite a trip at 4am.

Getting There & Away

➡**Metro** Four metro lines criss-cross L'Eixample, three stopping at Passeig de Gràcia for the Manzana de la Discordia. Línia 3 stops at Diagonal for La Pedrera, while Línies 2 and 5 stop at Sagrada Família.

➡**Train** FGC lines from Plaça de Catalunya take you one stop to Provença, in the heart of L'Eixample.

TOP SIGHT
LA SAGRADA FAMÍLIA

If you have time for only one sightseeing outing, this should be it. La Sagrada Família inspires awe by its sheer verticality, and, in the manner of the medieval cathedrals it emulates, it's still under construction after more than 100 years. When completed, the highest tower will be more than half as high again as those that stand today.

A Holy Mission

The Temple Expiatori de la Sagrada Família (Expiatory Temple of the Holy Family) was Antoni Gaudí's all-consuming obsession. Given the commission by a conservative society that wished to build a temple as atonement for the city's sins of modernity, Gaudí saw its completion as his holy mission. As funds dried up, he contributed his own, and in the last years of his life he was never shy of pleading with anyone he thought a likely donor.

Gaudí devised a temple 95m long and 60m wide, able to seat 13,000 people, with a central tower 170m high above the transept (representing Christ) and another 17 of 100m or more. The 12 along the three facades represent the Apostles, while the remaining five represent the Virgin Mary and the four evangelists. With his characteristic dislike for straight lines (there were none in nature, he said), Gaudí gave his towers swelling outlines inspired by the weird peaks of the holy mountain Montserrat outside Barcelona, and encrusted them with a tangle of sculpture that seems an outgrowth of the stone.

At Gaudí's death, only the crypt, the apse walls, one portal and one tower had been finished. Three more towers were added by 1930, completing the northeast (Nativity) facade. In 1936 anarchists burned and smashed the interior, including workshops, plans and models.

DON'T MISS

➡ The apse, the extraordinary pillars and stained glass
➡ Nativity Facade
➡ Passion Facade
➡ Museu Gaudí

PRACTICALITIES

➡ Map p278
➡ ☎93 208 04 14
➡ www.sagradafamilia.cat
➡ Carrer de Mallorca 401
➡ adult/concession/under 11yr €15/13/free
➡ ⊙9am-8pm Apr-Sep, to 6pm Oct-Mar
➡ Ⓜ Sagrada Família

A HIDDEN PORTRAIT

Careful observation of the Passion Facade will reveal a special tribute from sculptor Josep Subirachs to Gaudí. The central sculptural group (below Christ crucified) shows, from right to left, Christ bearing his cross, Veronica displaying the cloth with Christ's bloody image, a pair of soldiers and, watching it all, a man called the evangelist. Subirachs used a rare photo of Gaudí, taken a couple of years before his death, as the model for the evangelist's face.

VISITOR NUMBERS

Unfinished it may be, but La Sagrada Família attracts around 2.8 million visitors a year and is the most visited monument in Spain. The most significant tourist in recent times was Pope Benedict XVI, who consecrated the church in a huge ceremony in November 2010.

Work began again in 1952, but controversy has always clouded progress. Opponents of the continuation of the project claim that the computer models based on what little of Gaudí's plans survived the anarchists' ire have led to the creation of a monster that has little to do with Gaudí's plans and style. It is a debate that appears to have little hope of resolution. Like or hate what is being done, the fascination it awakens is undeniable.

Guesses on when construction might be complete range from the 2020s to the 2040s. Even before reaching that point, some of the oldest parts of the church, especially the apse, have required restoration work.

The Interior & the Apse

Inside, work on roofing over the church was completed in 2010. The roof is held up by a forest of extraordinary angled pillars. As the pillars soar towards the ceiling, they sprout a web of supporting branches, creating the effect of a forest canopy. The tree image is in no way fortuitous – Gaudí envisaged such an effect. Everything was thought through, including the shape and placement of windows to create the mottled effect one would see with sunlight pouring through the branches of a thick forest. The pillars are of four different types of stone. They vary in colour and load-bearing strength, from the soft Montjuïc stone pillars along the lateral aisles through to granite, dark grey basalt and finally burgundy-tinged Iranian porphyry for the key columns at the intersection of the nave and transept. The stained glass, divided in shades of red, blue, green and ochre, creates a hypnotic, magical atmosphere when the sun hits the windows. Tribunes built high above the aisles can host two choirs: the main tribune up to 1300 people and the children's tribune up to 300.

Nativity Facade

The Nativity Facade is the artistic pinnacle of the building, mostly created under Gaudí's personal supervision. You can climb high up inside some of the four towers by a combination of lifts and narrow spiral staircases – a vertiginous experience. Do not climb the stairs if you have cardiac or respiratory problems. The towers are destined to hold tubular bells capable of playing complex music at great volume. Their upper parts are decorated with mosaics spelling out *'Sanctus, Sanctus, Sanctus, Hosanna in Excelsis, Amen, Alleluia'*. Asked why he lavished so much care on the tops of the spires, which no one would see from close up, Gaudí answered: 'The angels will see them.'

Three sections of the portal represent, from left to right, Hope, Charity and Faith. Among the forest of sculpture on the Charity portal you can see, low down, the manger surrounded by an ox, an ass, the shepherds and kings, and angel musicians. Some 30 different species of plant from around Catalonia are reproduced here, and the faces of the many figures are taken from plaster casts done of local people and the occasional one made from corpses in the local morgue.

Directly above the blue stained-glass window is the archangel Gabriel's Annunciation to Mary. At the top is a green cypress tree, a refuge in a storm for the white doves of peace dotted over it. The mosaic work at the pinnacle of the towers is made from Murano glass from Venice.

To the right of the facade is the curious Claustre del Roser, a Gothic-style mini-cloister tacked on to the outside of the church (rather than the classic square enclosure of the great Gothic church monasteries). Once inside, look back to the intricately decorated entrance. On the lower right-hand side you'll notice the sculpture of a reptilian devil handing a terrorist a bomb. Barcelona was regularly rocked by political violence, and bombings were frequent in the decades prior to the civil war. The sculpture is one of several on the 'temptations of men and women'.

Passion Facade

The southwest Passion Facade, on the theme of Christ's last days and death, was built between 1954 and 1978 based on surviving drawings by Gaudí, with four towers and a large, sculpture-bedecked portal. The sculptor, Josep Subirachs, worked on its decoration from 1986 to 2006. He did not attempt to imitate Gaudí, instead producing angular, controversial images of his own. The main series of sculptures, on three levels, are in an S-shaped sequence, starting with the Last Supper at the bottom left and ending with Christ's burial at the top right. Decorative work on the Passion Facade continues even today, as construction of the Glory Facade moves ahead.

To the right, in front of the Passion Facade, the Escoles de Gaudí is one of his simpler gems. Gaudí built this as a children's school, creating an original, undulating roof of brick that continues to charm architects to this day. Inside is a re-creation of Gaudí's modest office as it was when he died, and explanations of the geometric patterns and plans at the heart of his building techniques.

Glory Facade

The Glory Facade is under construction and will, like the others, be crowned by four towers – the total of 12 representing the Twelve Apostles. Gaudí wanted it to be the most magnificent facade of the church. Inside will be the narthex, a kind of foyer made up of 16 'lanterns', a series of hyperboloid forms topped by cones. Further decoration will make the whole building a microcosmic symbol of the Christian church, with Christ represented by a massive 170m central tower above the transept, and the five remaining planned towers symbolising the Virgin Mary and the four evangelists.

Museu Gaudí

Open at the same times as the church, the Museu Gaudí, below ground level, includes interesting material on Gaudí's life and other works, as well as models and photos of La Sagrada Família. You can see a good example of his plumb-line models that showed him the stresses and strains he could get away with in construction. A side hall towards the eastern end of the museum leads to a viewing point above the simple crypt in which the genius is buried. The crypt, where Masses are now held, can also be visited from the Carrer de Mallorca side of the church.

La Sagrada Família

A TIMELINE

1882 Francesc del Villar is commissioned to construct a neo-Gothic church.

1883 Antoni Gaudí takes over as chief architect, and plans a far more ambitious church to hold 13,000 faithful.

1926 Death of Gaudí; work continues under Domènec Sugrañes. Much of the **apse ❶** and **Nativity Facade ❷** is complete.

1930 **Bell towers ❸** of the Nativity Facade completed.

1936 Construction is interrupted by Spanish Civil War; anarchists destroy Gaudí's plans.

1939-40 Architect Francesc de Paula Quintana i Vidal restores the crypt and meticulously reassembles many of Gaudí's lost models, some of which can be seen in the **museum ❹**.

1976 Completion of **Passion Facade ❺**.

1986-2006 Sculptor Josep Subirachs adds sculptural details to the Passion Facade including the panels telling the story of Christ's last days, amid much criticism for employing a style far removed from what was thought typical of Gaudí.

2000 **Central nave vault ❻** completed.

2010 Church completely roofed over; Pope Benedict XVI consecrates the church; work begins on a high-speed rail tunnel that will pass beneath the church's **Glory Facade ❼**.

2020s–40s Projected completion date.

TOP TIPS

» **Light** The best light through the stained-glass windows of the Passion Facade bursts through into the heart of the church in the late afternoon.

» **Time** Visit at opening time on weekdays to avoid the worst of the crowds.

» **Views** Head up the Nativity Facade bell towers for the views, as long queues generally await at the Passion Facade towers.

KRZYSZTOF DYDYNSKI/GETTY IMAGES ©

Spiral staircase

Nativity Facade
Gaudí used plaster casts of local people and even of the occasional corpse from the local morgue as models for the portraits in the Nativity scene.

Central nave vault

①

Apse
Built just after the crypt in mostly neo-Gothic style, it is capped by pinnacles that show a hint of the genius that Gaudí would later deploy in the rest of the church.

JASON WALTMAN/500PX ©

Bell towers

The towers (eight completed) of the three facades represent the 12 Apostles. Lifts whisk visitors up one tower of the Nativity and Passion Facades (the latter gets longer queues) for fine views.

Completed church

Along with the Glory Facade and its four towers, six other towers remain to be completed. They will represent the four Evangelists, the Virgin Mary and, soaring above them all over the transept, a 170m colossus symbolising Christ.

③

②

⑥

Glory Facade

This will be the most fanciful facade of all, with a narthex boasting 16 hyperboloid lanterns topped by cones that will look something like an organ made of melting ice cream.

⑦

Museu Gaudí

Jammed with old photos, drawings and restored plaster models that bring Gaudí's ambitions to life, the museum also houses an extraordinarily complex plumb-line device he used to calculate his constructions.

⑤

④

Escoles de Gaudí

Crypt

The first completed part of the church, the crypt is in largely neo-Gothic style and lies under the transept. Gaudí's burial place here can be seen from the Museu Gaudí.

Passion Facade

See the story of Christ's last days from Last Supper to burial in an S-shaped sequence from bottom to top of the facade. Check out the cryptogram in which the numbers always add up to 33, Christ's age at his death.

◉ SIGHTS

◉ L'Esquerra de L'Eixample

FUNDACIÓ ANTONI TÀPIES   GALLERY

Map p274(☑93 487 03 15; www.fundaciotapies. org; Carrer d'Aragó 255; adult/concession €7/5.60; ⊙10am-7pm Tue-Sun; Ⓜ Passeig de Gràcia) The Fundació Antoni Tàpies is both a pioneering Modernista building (completed in 1885) and the major collection of leading 20th-century Catalan artist Antoni Tàpies. A man known for his esoteric work, Tàpies died in February 2012, aged 88; he left behind a powerful range of paintings and a foundation intended to promote contemporary artists.

The building, designed by Domènech i Montaner for the publishing house Editorial Montaner i Simón (run by a cousin of the architect), combines a brick-covered iron frame with Islamic-inspired decoration. Tàpies crowned it with the meanderings of his own mind, a work called *Núvol i cadira* (Cloud and Chair) that spirals above the building like a storm.

Although it's difficult to understand the art of Antoni Tàpies, it's worth seeing the one-hour documentary on his life, on the top floor, to learn about his influences and method, and the course of his interesting life. In his work, Tàpies expressed a number of themes, such as left-wing politics and humanitarianism; the practices of Zen meditation and its relationship between nature and insight; incarnation as seen in Christian faith; and art as alchemy or magic.

He launched the Fundació in 1984 to promote contemporary art, donating a large part of his own work. The collection spans the arc of Tàpies' creations (with more than 800 works) and contributions from other contemporary artists. In the main exhibition area (level 1, upstairs) you can see an ever-changing selection of around 20 of Tàpies' works, from early self-portraits of the 1940s to grand items like *Jersei negre* (Black Jumper; 2008). Level 2 hosts a small space for temporary exhibitions. Rotating exhibitions take place in the basement levels.

CASA AMATLLER   ARCHITECTURE

Map p274 (☑93 461 74 60; www.amatller.org; Passeig de Gràcia 41; adult/child 6-12yr/under 6yr 1hr tour €15/7.50/free, 30min tour €12/7/free;

⊙11am-6pm; Ⓜ Passeig de Gràcia) One of Puig i Cadafalch's most striking bits of Modernista fantasy, Casa Amatller combines Gothic window frames with a stepped gable borrowed from Dutch urban architecture. But the busts and reliefs of dragons, knights and other characters dripping off the main facade are pure caprice.

The pillared foyer and staircase lit by stained glass are like the inside of some romantic castle. The building was renovated in 1900 for the chocolate baron and philanthropist Antoni Amatller (1851-1910).

Recent renovation has seen the 1st (main) floor converted into a museum, with period pieces and original furniture and decor, which you can visit by guided tour. Amatller was a keen traveller and photographer (his absorbing shots of turn-of-the-20th-century Morocco are occasionally on show).

There is a one-hour visit in English at 11am; 30-minute express tours run throughout the day. Both tours also include a taste of Amatller chocolate in the original kitchen. You can wander into the foyer, and admire the staircase and lift for free.

CASA LLEÓ MORERA   ARCHITECTURE

Map p274 (☑93 676 27 33; www.casalleomorera. com; Passeig de Gràcia 35; guided tour adult/ concession/under 12yr €15/13.50/free, express tour adult/under 12yr €12/free; ⊙10am-1.30pm & 3-7pm Tue-Sun; Ⓜ Passeig de Gràcia) Domènech i Montaner's 1905 contribution to the Manzana de la Discordia, with Modernista carving outside and a bright, tiled lobby in which floral motifs predominate, is perhaps the least odd-looking of the three main buildings on the block. Since 2014 part of the building has been open to the public (by guided tour only – a one-hour tour in English at 11am, and 'express tours' every 30 minutes), so you can appreciate the 1st floor, giddy with swirling sculptures, rich mosaics and whimsical decor.

PALAU ROBERT   EXHIBITION

Map p274 (☑93 238 80 91; www.palaurobert. gencat.cat; Passeig de Gràcia 107; ⊙10am-8pm Mon-Sat, to 2.30pm Sun; Ⓜ Diagonal) **FREE** Catalonia's regional tourist office, which holds a huge range of books and leaflets, also serves as an exhibition space, mostly for shows with Catalan themes. In summer concerts are occasionally held in the peaceful gardens at the back of this fine building, or in its main hall.

SALA FUNDACIÓN MAPFRE
GALLERY

Map p274 (☎93 401 26 03; www.fundacionmapfre.org; Carrer de la Diputació 250; adult/student/under 6yr €6/3/free; ⊙2-8pm Mon, 10am-8pm Tue-Sat, 11am-7pm Sun; Ⓜ Passeig de Gràcia) **FREE** Formerly the Fundación Francisco Godia, this stunning, carefully restored Modernista residence was taken over in late 2015 by the charitable cultural arm of Spanish insurance giants MAPFRE as a space for art and photography exhibitions. Housed in the Casa Garriga i Nogués, it is a stunning, carefully restored Modernista residence originally built for a rich banking family by Enric Sagnier in 1902–05.

Exhibitions are shown on the ground floor and in a number of small rooms up the languidly curvaceous marble stairway. Look out for the fine Modernista stained-glass windows in room 8.

MUSEU DEL
MODERNISME BARCELONA
MUSEUM

Map p274 (☎93 272 28 96; www.mmbcn.cat; Carrer de Balmes 48; adult/concession/child 6-16yr/under 6yr €10/7/5/free; ⊙10.30am-7pm Tue-Sat, to 2pm Sun; Ⓜ Passeig de Gràcia) Housed in a Modernista building, the ground floor seems like a big Modernista furniture showroom. Several items by Antoni Gaudí, including chairs from Casa Batlló and a mirror from Casa Calvet, are supplemented by a host of items by his lesser-known contemporaries, including some typically whimsical, mock medieval pieces by Puig i Cadalfalch.

The basement, which has mosaic-coated pillars, bare-brick vaults and metal columns, is lined with Modernista art, including paintings by Ramon Casas and Santiago Rusiñol, and statues by Josep Llimona and Eusebi Arnau.

CASA GOLFERICHS
ARCHITECTURE

Map p274 (☎93 323 77 90; www.golferichs.org; Gran Via de les Corts Catalanes 491; ⊙10am-8pm Mon-Fri, 10am-2pm Sat; Ⓜ Rocafort) **FREE** This quirky mansion is an oddity of another era on one of the city's busiest boulevards, a Modernista villa owned by businessman Macari Golferichs. Brick, ceramics and wood are the main building elements of the house, which displays a distinctly Gothic flavour. It came close to demolition in the 1970s but was saved by the town hall and converted into a cultural centre. Opening times can vary depending on temporary exhibitions, concerts and other cultural activities.

◉ TOP SIGHT
CASA BATLLÓ

One of the strangest residential buildings in Europe, this is Gaudí at his hallucinatory best. The facade, sprinkled with blue, mauve and green tiles and studded with wave-shaped window frames and balconies, rises to an uneven blue-tiled roof. Locals know Casa Batlló variously as the *casa dels ossos* (house of bones) or *casa del drac* (house of the dragon). The balconies look like the bony jaws of some strange beast and the roof represents Sant Jordi (St George) and the dragon. The internal light wells shimmer with tiles of deep sea blue. Everything swirls: the ceiling is twisted into a vortex around its sun-like lamp; the doors, window and skylights are dreamy waves of wood and coloured glass.

It is one of the three houses on the block between Carrer del Consell de Cent and Carrer d'Aragó that gave it the playful name Manzana de la Discordia. Despite the Catalanisation of most Barcelona names, the Manzana de la Discordia is still known by its Spanish name to preserve a pun on *manzana*, which means 'block' and 'apple'. The other houses are the Casa Amatller and the Casa Lleó Morera. They were all renovated between 1898 and 1906 and show how eclectic a 'style' Modernisme was.

DON'T MISS

➡ The facade and balconies
➡ The swirling interior
➡ The dragon-back roof

PRACTICALITIES

➡ Map p274
➡ ☎93 216 03 06
➡ www.casabatllo.es
➡ Passeig de Gràcia 43
➡ adult/concession/under 7yr €22.50/19.50/free
➡ ⊙9am-9pm, last admission 8pm
➡ Ⓜ Passeig de Gràcia

MUSEU I CENTRE D'ESTUDIS DE L'ESPORT DR MELCIOR COLET MUSEUM
Map p274 (☎93 419 22 32; www.esports.gencat.cat; Carrer de Buenos Aires 56-58; ◷9am-2pm Mon-Fri; ⓂHospital Clínic) FREE Puig i Cadafalch's Casa Company (1911) looks like an odd Tyrolean country house and is marvellously out of place. A collection of photos, documents and other sports memorabilia stretches over two floors – from an incongruous 1930s pair of skis and boots to the skull-decorated swimming costume of a champion Catalan water-polo player.

A curio on the ground floor is the replica of a stone commemoration in Latin of Lucius Minicius Natal, a Barcelona boy who won a *quadriga* (four-horse chariot) race at the 227th Olympic Games...in AD 129.

MUSEU DEL PERFUM MUSEUM
Map p274 (☎93 216 01 21; www.museudelperfum.com; Passeig de Gràcia 39; adult/concession €5/3; ◷10.30am-8pm Mon-Fri, 11am-2pm Sat; ⓂPasseig de Gràcia) Housed in the back of the Regia perfume store (p140), this museum contains oddities from ancient Egyptian and Roman scent receptacles (the latter mostly from the 1st to 3rd centuries AD) to classic eau de cologne bottles – all in all, some 5000 bottles of infinite shapes, sizes and histories. Other items include ancient bronze Etruscan tweezers and little early-19th-century potpourri bowls made of fine Sèvres porcelain. Also on show are old catalogues and advertising posters.

UNIVERSITAT DE BARCELONA ARCHITECTURE
Map p274 (☎93 402 11 00; www.ub.edu; Gran Via de les Corts Catalanes 585; ◷8am-8pm Mon-Fri; ⓂUniversitat) Although a university was first set up on what is now La Rambla in the 16th century, the present, glorious mix of (neo) Romanesque, Gothic, Islamic and Mudéjar architecture is a caprice of the 19th century (built 1863–82). Wander into the main hall, up the grand staircase and around the various leafy cloisters, or take a stroll in the rear gardens.

On the 1st floor, the main hall for big occasions is the Mudéjar-style Paranimfo.

◉ TOP SIGHT
LA PEDRERA

This undulating beast is another madcap Gaudí masterpiece, built from 1905–10 as a combined apartment and office block. Formally called Casa Milà after the businessman who commissioned it, it is better known as La Pedrera (the Quarry) because of its uneven grey stone facade.

Pere Milà had married the older, far richer Roser Guardiola, and clearly knew how to spend his new wife's money. Milà was one of the city's first car owners and Gaudí built parking space into this building, itself a first.

The Fundació Caixa Catalunya has opened the top-floor apartment, attic and roof, together called the Espai Gaudí (Gaudí Space), to visitors. The roof is the most extraordinary element, with its giant chimney pots looking like multicoloured medieval knights. Gaudí wanted to put a tall statue of the Virgin up here too: when the Milà family said no, Gaudí resigned from the project in disgust.

The next floor down is the apartment (El Pis de la Pedrera). It's fascinating to wander around this elegantly furnished home, done up in the style a well-to-do family might have enjoyed in the early 20th century. There are sensuous curves and unexpected touches in everything from light fittings to bedsteads, and door handles to balconies.

DON'T MISS
➡ The marvellous roof
➡ The apartment
➡ The stone facade

PRACTICALITIES
➡ Map p278
➡ Casa Milà
➡ ☎902 202138
➡ www.lapedrera.com
➡ Passeig de Gràcia 92
➡ adult/concession/ under 13yr/under 7yr €20.50/16.50/ 10.25/free
➡ ◷9am-8.30pm Mar-Oct, to 6.30pm Nov-Feb
➡ ⓂDiagonal

☉ La Dreta de L'Eixample

LA SAGRADA FAMÍLIA
ARCHITECTURE
See p121.

RECINTE MODERNISTA
DE SANT PAU
ARCHITECTURE
Map p278 (☎93 553 78 01; www.santpaubar-celona.org; Carrer de Sant Antoni Maria Claret 167; adult/concession/under 16yr €10/7/free; ⊙10am-6.30pm Mon-Sat, to 2.30pm Sun; Ⓜ Sant Pau/Dos de Maig) Domènech i Montaner out-did himself as architect and philanthropist with the Modernista Hospital de la Santa Creu i de Sant Pau, redubbed in 2014 the 'Recinte Modernista'. It was long consid-ered one of the city's most important hospi-tals, and was only recently repurposed, its various spaces becoming cultural centres, offices and something of a monument. The complex, including 16 pavilions – together with the Palau de la Música Catalana, a joint World Heritage site – is lavishly deco-rated and each pavilion is unique.

Domènech i Montaner wanted to create an environment that would also cheer up patients. Among artists who contributed statuary, ceramics and artwork was the prolific Eusebi Arnau. The hospital facili-ties have been transferred to a new complex on the premises, freeing up the century-old structures, which are being restored to their former glory in a plan to convert the complex into an international centre on the Mediterranean.

Guided tours are available (adult/conces-sion €16/11.20) in a variety of languages, upon request.

PALAU DEL BARÓ QUADRAS
ARCHITECTURE
Map p278 (☎93 467 80 00; www.llull.cat; Aving-uda Diagonal 373; ⊙8am-8pm Mon-Fri; Ⓜ Diago-nal) FREE Puig i Cadafalch designed Palau del Baró Quadras (built 1902–06) in an exuberant Gothic-inspired style. The main facade is its most intriguing, with a soar-ing, glassed-in gallery. Take a closer look at the gargoyles and reliefs – the pair of toothy fish and the sword-wielding knight clearly have the same artistic signature as the ar-chitect behind Casa Amatller. Decor inside is eclectic, but dominated by Middle East-ern and East Asian themes.

The *palau* no longer houses the Casa Asia cultural centre, which means much of it is now closed to the public. However, you can visit the ground floor.

CASA DE LES PUNXES
ARCHITECTURE
Map p278 (Casa Terrades; Avinguda Diagonal 420; Ⓜ Diagonal) Puig i Cadafalch's Casa Terrades is better known as the Casa de les Punxes (House of Spikes) because of its pointed tur-rets. This apartment block, completed in 1905, looks like a fairy-tale castle and has the singular attribute of being the only fully detached building in L'Eixample.

MUSEU EGIPCI
MUSEUM
Map p278 (☎93 488 01 88; www.museuegipci.com; Carrer de València 284; adult/concession/under 15yr €11/8/5; ⊙10am-2pm & 4-8pm Mon-Fri, 10am-8pm Sat, to 2pm Sun; Ⓜ Passeig de Gràcia) Hotel magnate Jordi Clos has spent much of his life collecting ancient Egyptian artefacts, brought together in this private museum. It's divided into different themat-ic areas (the pharaoh, religion, funerary practices, mummification, crafts etc) and boasts an interesting variety of exhibits.

There are statuary, funereal implements and containers, jewellery (including a fabu-lous golden ring from around the 7th century BC), ceramics, and even a bed made of wood and leather. In the basement is an exhibition area and library, displaying volumes includ-ing original editions of works by Carter, the Egyptologist who led the Tutankhamun ex-cavations. On the rooftop terrace is a pleas-ant cafe, and there is a combined ticket with the Museu Cultural del Món (€12).

FUNDACIÓ SUÑOL
GALLERY
Map p278 (☎93 496 10 32; www.fundaciosunol.org; Passeig de Gràcia 98; adult/concession €4/3; ⊙11am-2pm & 4-8pm Mon-Fri, 4-8pm Sat; Ⓜ Diagonal) Rotating exhibitions of portions of this private collection of mostly 20th-century art (some 1200 works in total) offer anything from Man Ray's photography to sculptures by Alberto Giacometti. Over two floors, you are most likely to run into Span-ish artists, anyone from Picasso to Jaume Plensa, along with a sprinkling of interna-tional artists.

It makes a refreshing pause between the crush of crowded Modernista monuments on this boulevard. Indeed, you get an inter-esting side view of one of them, La Pedrera, from out the back.

ESGLÉSIA DE LA PURÍSSIMA
CONCEPCIÓ I ASSUMPCIÓ
DE NOSTRA SENYORA
CHURCH
Map p278 (☎93 457 65 52; www.parroquiacon-cepciobcn.org; Carrer de Roger de Llúria 70;

⊙7.30am-1pm & 5-9pm Mon-Fri, 7.30am-2pm & 5-9pm Sun; Ⓜ Passeig de Gràcia) One hardly expects to run into a medieval church on the grid-pattern streets of the late-19th-century city extension, yet that is just what this is. Transferred stone by stone from the old centre in 1871–88, this 14th-century church has a pretty 16th-century cloister with a peaceful garden.

Behind is a Romanesque-Gothic bell tower (11th to 16th century), moved from another old town church that didn't survive, Església de Sant Miquel. This is one of a handful of such old churches shifted willy-nilly from their original locations to L'Eixample.

PALAU MONTANER
ARCHITECTURE

Map p278 (☑93 317 76 52; www.fundaciotapies.org; Carrer de Mallorca 278; adult/child €7/free; ⊙guided tours 11am Sat; Ⓜ Passeig de Gràcia) Interesting on the outside and made all the more enticing by its gardens, this creation by Domènech i Montaner is spectacular on the inside. Completed in 1896, its central feature is a grand staircase beneath a broad, ornamental skylight. The interior is laden with sculptures (some by Eusebi Arnau), mosaics and fine woodwork. It is currently only open by guided tour, organised by the Fundació Tàpies and in Catalan only.

ESGLÉSIA DE LES SALESES
CHURCH

Map p278 (☑93 458 76 67; www.parroquiaconcepciobcn.org; Passeig de Sant Joan 90; ⊙10am-1pm & 5-7pm Mon-Fri, 10am-2pm Sun; Ⓜ Tetuan) A singular neo-Gothic effort, this church is interesting because it was designed by Joan Martorell i Montells (1833–1906), Gaudí's architecture professor. Raised in 1878–85 with an adjacent convent (badly damaged in the civil war and now a school), it offers hints of what was to come with Modern-isme, with his use of brick, mosaics and sober stained glass.

✗ EATING

✗ L'Esquerra de L'Eixample

COPASETIC
CAFE €

Map p274 (☑93 532 76 66; www.copaseticbarcelona.com; Carrer de la Diputació 55; mains €8-12; ⊙10.30am-midnight Tue & Wed, to 1am Thu, to 2am Fri & Sat, to 5.30pm Sun; 🛜📶; Ⓜ Rocafort) A fun and friendly cafe, decked out with retro furniture. The menu holds plenty for everyone, whether your thing is eggs Benedict, wild-berry tartlets or a juicy fat burger. There are lots of vegetarian, gluten-free and organic options, and superb (and reasonably priced) brunches on weekends. Wednesday night is ladies' night, with cheap cocktails. Lunch *menús* (Tuesday to Friday) cost between €9.50 and €11.

CREMERIA TOSCANA
GELATERIA €

Map p274 (☑93 539 38 25; www.cremeriatoscana.es; Carrer de Muntaner 161; ice cream from €2.80; ⊙1-10pm Sun-Thu, 1pm-midnight Fri & Sat winter, 1pm-midnight Easter-Oct; Ⓜ Hospital Clínic) Yes, you can stumble across quite reasonable ice cream in Barcelona, but close your eyes and imagine yourself across the Mediterranean with the real ice-cream wizards. Creamy *stracciatella* and wavy *nocciola* and myriad other flavours await at the most authentic gelato outlet in town. Buy a cone or a tub.

CRUSTO
BAKERY €

Map p274 (☑93 487 05 51; www.crusto.es; Carrer de València 246; pastries from €3; ⊙7.30am-9pm Mon-Fri, 8.30am-9pm Sat, 9am-3pm Sun; 🛜; Ⓜ Passeig de Gràcia) A French-inspired bakery and pastry shop, its wonderful perfume of freshly baked bread, baguettes, croissants and countless pastries will be enough to convince you that it's worth pulling up a stool here for a long and tasty breakfast.

EL RINCÓN MAYA
MEXICAN €

Map p274 (☑93 451 39 46; Carrer de València 183; mains €6-10; ⊙9pm-midnight Mon, 1.30-4pm & 8.30pm-midnight Tue-Sat; 🛜; Ⓜ Universitat) Getting a seat in this Mexican eatery can be a trial. The setting is warm, modest and simple. The pocket-sized serves of nachos,

---

LOCAL KNOWLEDGE

PLATJA DE L'EIXAMPLE

In a hidden garden inside a typical Eixample block is an old water tower and an urban 'beach', the **Platja de l'Eixample** (☑93 423 43 50; Carrer de Roger de Llúria 56; €1.55; ⊙10am-8.30pm late Jun–mid-Sep; ♿; Ⓜ Girona). In reality, this is a knee-height swimming pool, perfect for little ones, and surrounded by sand.

guacamole and fajitas all burst with flavour. You'll also discover lesser-known items like *tacos de pibil* (pork tacos) and *tinga* (little pasta pockets of chicken). There are also more substantial dishes.

The owner-chef spent much of his life in the restaurant business in Mexico City.

AMALTEA VEGETARIAN €

Map p274 (☑93 454 86 13; www.restaurantea-maltea.com; Carrer de la Diputació 164; mains €5-9; ☺1-4pm & 8-11.30pm Mon-Sat; ☎☑; ⓜUrgell) The ceiling fresco of blue sky sets the scene in this popular vegetarian eatery. The *menús del día* (€8.70 and €10.70) offer dishes that change frequently with the seasons. At night, the set dinners (€11.50 and €15.50) offer good value, and the homemade desserts are tempting. The place is something of an alternative lifestyle centre, with yoga, t'ai chi and belly-dancing classes.

★CERVESERIA CATALANA TAPAS €€

Map p274 (☑93 216 03 68; Carrer de Mallorca 236; tapas €4-11; ☺8am-1.30am Mon-Fri, 9am-1.30am Sat & Sun; ⓜPasseig de Gràcia) The 'Catalan Brewery' is good for breakfast, lunch and dinner. Come for your morning coffee and croissant, or enjoy the abundance of tapas and *montaditos* (canapés) at lunch. You can sit at the bar, on the pavement terrace or in the restaurant at the back. The variety of hot tapas, salads and other snacks draws a well-dressed crowd of locals and outsiders.

PARKING PIZZA PIZZA €€

Map p274 (☑93 633 96 45; www.parkingpizza.com; Carrer de Londres 98; mains €11-13.50; ☺1-4pm & 8-11pm Tue-Thu, 1-4pm & 8pm-midnight Fri & Sat; ⓜHospital Clínic) A new pizza restaurant in a high-ceilinged space, where you might well have to share a long unvarnished wooden table, squeezed in on a cardboard box stool. The food more than makes up for any forced intimacy, however, especially the starters, which include a creamy burrata 'stracciatella' and a superb red quinoa salad with guacamole and a poached egg.

KOYUKI JAPANESE €€

Map p274 (☑93 237 84 90; Carrer de Còrsega 242; mains €15-20; ☺1-3.30pm & 8.30pm-midnight Tue-Sat, 8-11pm Sun; ⓜDiagonal) This unassuming basement Japanese diner is one of those rough-edged diamonds that it pays to revisit. Sit at a long table and order from the cheesy menu complete with pictures courtesy of the Japanese owner – you

won't be disappointed. The variety of *sashimi moriawase* is generous and constantly fresh. The *tempura udon* is a particularly hearty noodle option. Wash it all down with Sapporo beer.

CATA 1.81 TAPAS €€

Map p274 (☑93 323 68 18; www.cata181.com; Carrer de València 181; tapas €5.50-8; ☺6pm-midnight Mon-Sat; ⓜPasseig de Gràcia) A beautifully designed venue (with lots of small lights, some trapped in birdcages), this is the place to come for fine wines and dainty gourmet dishes like *raviolis amb bacallà* (salt-cod dumplings) or *truita de patates i tòfona negre* (thick potato tortilla with a delicate trace of black truffle). The best idea is to choose from one of several tasting-menu options.

LA ESQUINA MEDITERRANEAN, BRITISH €€

Map p274 (☑93 768 72 42; www.laesquinabarcelona.com; Carrer de Bergara 2; meals €10-17; ☺9am-8pm Mon-Wed, 9am-1am Thu & Fri, 10am-1am Sat, 10am-6pm Sun; ☎; ⓜCatalunya) A new and superb eating option, in an unlikely spot next to Starbucks, near the Plaça Catalunya. British chef Alan Stewart rustles up cauliflower risotto with sage and almonds; clams with sherry, fennel and ham; and duck rillettes with pickles, among many other dishes. There is a €15 lunch deal – portions are smallish, but quality is high.

LA BODEGUETA PROVENÇA TAPAS €€

Map p274 (☑93 215 17 25; www.labodegueta.cat; Carrer de Provença 233; mains €9-19, tapas €6-14; ☺7am-1am Mon-Fri, 9am-1am Sat, 1pm-midnight Sun; ☎; ⓜDiagonal) The 'Little Wine Cellar' offers classic tapas presented with a touch of class, from *calamares a la andaluza* (lightly battered squid rings) to *cecina* (dried cured veal meat). The house speciality is *ous estrellats* (literally 'smashed eggs') – a mix of scrambled egg white, egg yolk, potato and ingredients ranging from foie gras to *morcilla* (black pudding).

Wash it all down with a good Ribera del Duero or *caña* (little glass) of beer. A lunchtime *menú* is €15.

CERVESERIA BRASSERIA GALLEGA SEAFOOD €€

Map p274 (☑93 439 41 28; Carrer de Casanova 238; mains €12-20; ☺1.30-3.30pm & 8.30-11.30pm Mon-Sat, closed Aug; ☎; ⓜHospital Clínic) You could walk right by this modest establishment without giving it a second

LA SAGRADA FAMÍLIA & L'EIXAMPLE EATING

MODERNISME UNPACKED

Travellers interested in running the gamut of L'Eixample's Modernista gems should consider the Ruta del Modernisme pack (€12; www.rutadelmodernisme.com). It includes a guide (in various languages) and discounted entry prices to the city's major Modernista sights.

glance. If you did, you'd notice it was chock-full of locals immersed in animated banter and surrounded by plates of abundant Galician classics. The fresh *pulpo a la gallega* (spicy octopus chunks with potatoes) as a starter marks this place as a cut above the competition.

Waiters have little time for loitering, but always a quick quip. The setting is simple, the meat dishes succulent and the *fideuà* (similar to paella but with vermicelli noodles as the base) full of seafood flavour.

TAKTIKA BERRI   BASQUE, TAPAS €€

Map p274 (☑93 453 47 59; Carrer de València 169; tapas from €3, mains €10-32; ☺1-4pm & 8.30-11pm Mon-Fri, 1-4pm Sat; 🖥; ⓂHospital Clínic) Get in early because the bar teems with punters from far and wide, anxious to wrap their mouths around some of the best Basque tapas in town. The hot morsels are all snapped up as soon as they arrive from the kitchen, so keep your eyes peeled. In the evening, it's all over by about 10.30pm.

The seated dining area out the back is also good.

★DISFRUTAR   MODERN EUROPEAN €€€

Map p274 (☑93 348 68 96; www.en.disfrutar barcelona.com; Carrer de Vilarroel 163; tasting menus €75/105/135; ☺1-4pm & 8-11pm Tue-Sat; ⓂHospital Clínic) In its first few months of life, Disfrutar rose stratospherically to become the city's finest restaurant – book now while it's still possible to get a table. Run by alumni of Ferran Adrià's game-changing El Bulli restaurant, it operates along similar lines.

Nothing is as it seems, from red and green peppers that are actually chocolate ganache coated in, respectively, chilli and mint-flavoured gelatine, to an iced hare consommé in a brandy snifter.

The decor is fabulously on point, with latticed brickwork and trademark geometric ceramics from Catalan design team Equipo Creativo, and the service is faultless.

★CINC SENTITS   INTERNATIONAL €€€

Map p274 (☑93 323 94 90; www.cincsentits.com; Carrer d'Aribau 58; tasting menus €100/120; ☺1.30-3pm & 8.30-10pm Tue-Sat; ⓂPasseig de Gràcia) Enter the realm of the 'Five Senses' to indulge in a jaw-dropping tasting menu consisting of a series of small, experimental dishes (there is no à la carte, although dishes can be tweaked to suit diners' requests). There is a lunch *menú* for €55.

The use of fresh local produce, such as fish landed on the Costa Brava and top-quality suckling pig from Extremadura, is key, along with the kind of creative genius that has earned chef Jordi Artal a Michelin star.

MONVÍNIC   SPANISH €€€

Map p274 (☑93 272 61 87; www.monvinic.com; Carrer de la Diputació 249; mains €24-32; ☺1.30-3.30pm & 8-10.30pm Tue-Fri, 8-10.30pm Mon & Sat; ⓂPasseig de Gracia) 🌱 Formerly known as Fastvínic, this is the 'espacio culinario' of world-famous wine emporium Monvínic. The menu has advanced from sandwiches and snacks to elaborate confections such as wild mushroom polenta with pigeon, and beetroot tatin. A project in sustainability all round, with ingredients, wine and building materials sourced from Catalonia.

Designed by Alfons Tost, there are air-purifying plants, energy-efficient LED lighting, and a water and food recycling system.

SPEAKEASY   INTERNATIONAL €€€

Map p274 (☑93 217 50 80; www.speakeasy-bcn. com; Carrer d'Aribau 162-166; mains €22-28; ☺1-4pm & 8pm-midnight Mon-Sat; ⓂDiagonal) This clandestine restaurant lurks behind the Dry Martini bar (p135). You will be shown a door through the open kitchen area to the 'storeroom', lined with hundreds of bottles of backlit, quality tipples. The menu has tempting options like the wild mushroom ravioli with langoustine or venison with puréed sweet potato.

Dark decorative tones, a few works of art, low lighting, light jazz music and smooth service complete the setting.

La Dreta de L'Eixample

★TAPAS 24   TAPAS €

Map p278 (☑93 488 09 77; www.carlesabellan.com; Carrer de la Diputació 269; tapas €4-9;

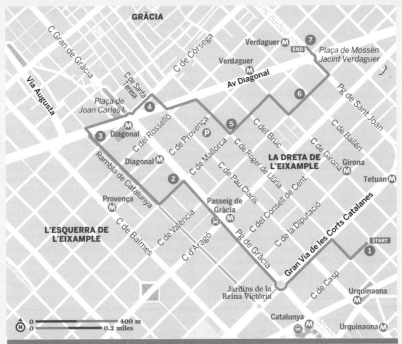

🏃 Walking Tour
More Modernisme in L'Eixample

START CASA CALVET
FINISH CASA MACAYA
LENGTH 4KM; ONE HOUR

Gaudí's most conventional contribution to L'Eixample is ① **Casa Calvet**, built in 1900. Inspired by baroque, the noble ashlar facade is broken up by protruding wrought-iron balconies. Inside, the main attraction is the staircase, which you can admire if you eat in the swanky restaurant.

② **Casa Enric Batlló** was completed in 1896 by Josep Vilaseca (1848–1910), part of the Comtes de Barcelona hotel. The brickwork facade is especially graceful when lit up at night.

Puig i Cadafalch let his imagination loose on ③ **Casa Serra** (1903–08), a neo-Gothic whimsy that is home to government offices. With its central tower topped by a conical roof, grandly decorated upper-floor windows and tiled roof, it must have been a strange house to live in!

④ **Casa Comalatis**, built in 1911 by Salvador Valeri (1873–1954), is similarly strik-

ing. Note Gaudí's obvious influence on the main facade, with its wavy roof and bulging balconies. Head around the back to Carrer de Còrsega to see a more playful facade, with its windows stacked like cards.

Completed in 1912, ⑤ **Casa Thomas** was one of Domènech i Montaner's earlier efforts – the ceramic details are a trademark and the massive ground-level wrought-iron decoration (and protection?) is magnificent. Wander inside to the Cubiñá design store to admire his interior work.

⑥ **Casa Llopis i Bofill** is an interesting block of flats designed by Antoni Gallissà (1861–1903) in 1902. The graffiti-covered facade is particularly striking to the visitor's eye. The use of elaborate parabolic arches on the ground floor is a clear Modernista touch, as are the wrought-iron balconies.

Puig i Cadafalch's ⑦ **Casa Macaya** (1901) has a wonderful courtyard and features the typical pseudo-Gothic decoration that characterises many of the architect's projects. It belongs to La Caixa bank and is occasionally used for temporary exhibitions, when visitors are permitted to enter.

⊘9am-midnight; 🖥; Ⓜ Passeig de Gràcia) Carles Abellan, master of the now-defunct Comerç 24 in La Ribera, runs this basement tapas haven known for its gourmet versions of old faves. Specials include the *bikini* (toasted ham and cheese sandwich – here the ham is cured and the truffle makes all the difference) and a thick black *arròs negre de sípia* (squid-ink black rice).

The inventive McFoie-Burger is fantastic and, for dessert, choose *xocolata amb pa, sal i oli* (delicious balls of chocolate in olive oil with a touch of salt and wafer). You can't book but it's worth the wait.

CAN KENJI   JAPANESE €€

Map p278 (☎93 476 18 23; www.cankenji.com; Carrer del Rosselló 325; mains €10-14; ⊘1-3.30pm & 8.30-11.30pm; Ⓜ Verdaguer) If you want to go Japanese in Barcelona, this is the place. The chef of this understated little *izakaya* (the Japanese version of a tavern) gets his ingredients fresh from the city's markets, with traditional Japanese recipes receiving a Mediterranean touch. This is fusion at its very best.

Choices include sardine tempura with an aubergine, miso and anchovy purée, or *tataki* (lightly grilled meat) of *bonito* (tuna) with *salmorejo* (a Cordoban cold tomato and bread soup).

CHICHA LIMONÁ   MEDITERRANEAN, PIZZERIA €€

Map p278 (☎93 277 64 03; www.chichalimona. com; Passeig de Sant Joan 80; mains €10-16; ⊘8.30am-1am Tue-Thu, 8.30am-2am Fri, 9.30am-2am Sat, 9.30am-5pm Sun; 🖥; Ⓜ Tetuan) Passeig de Sant Joan has become the newest haunt for the hussar-moustached, turned-up-cigarette-pants brigade, and bright, bustling Chicha Limoná has provided them with somewhere great to eat. Grilled octopus with quince jelly, pork with apple compote and pear tatin with crème anglaise are among the oft-changing dishes (set menu €12.90), along with homemade pizzas.

ENTREPANES DÍAZ   SANDWICHES €€

Map p278 (☎93 415 75 82; Carrer de Pau Claris 189; sandwiches €6-8, salads €12; ⊘11am-midnight Tue-Sat, 11am-6pm Sun; Ⓜ Diagonal) A new concept in upmarket gourmet sandwiches, from roast beef to suckling pig, along with sharing plates of Spanish specialities such as sea urchins and prawn fritters, in a sparkling old-style bar. The policy of only hiring experienced waiters over 50 lends a certain

gravitas to the operation and some especially charming service.

GRANJA PETITBO   MEDITERRANEAN €€

Map p278 (☎93 265 65 03; www.granjapetitbo. com; Passeig de Sant Joan 82; sandwiches €4-8, mains €10-12; ⊘8.30am-10pm Mon-Wed, 8.30am-midnight Thu & Fri, 10am-midnight Sat, 10am-5pm Sun; 🖥; Ⓜ Girona) High ceilings, battered leather armchairs and dramatic flower arrangements set the tone in this sunny little corner cafe, beloved of local hipsters and young families, who up until recently had been ill-served in this part of town. As well as an all-day parade of homemade cakes, freshly squeezed juices and superior coffee, there's a brunch menu on weekends.

LORIA   CATALAN, MEDITERRANEAN €€

Map p278 (☎93 412 33 72; www.restaurantloria. com; Carrer de Roger de Llúria 35; mains €9-12; ⊘1pm-midnight Mon-Thu, 1pm-2am Fri & Sat; Ⓜ Passeig de Gràcia) A smart, lively bistro that's good for brunch, tapas or a full meal. Dishes might include pork with a pumpkin *parmentier,* truffled chicken cannelloni or something a little more fusion – prawn wonton with basil mayonnaise, for example. The set lunch is €14.50.

CASA AMALIA   CATALAN €€

Map p278 (☎93 458 94 58; Passatge del Mercat 4-6; mains €9-20; ⊘1-3.30pm & 9-10.30pm Tue-Sat, 1-3.30pm Sun; Ⓜ Girona) This very local restaurant is popular for its hearty Catalan cooking that uses fresh produce, mainly sourced from the busy market next door. On Thursdays during winter it offers the mountain classic, *escudella*. Otherwise, you might try light variations on local cuisine, such as the *bacallà al allioli de poma* (cod in an apple-based aioli sauce). The three-course *menú del día* is €15.50.

This orange and white decorated joint has split-level dining that makes the most of its space.

CASA ALFONSO   SPANISH €€

Map p278 (☎93 301 97 83; www.casaalfonso.com; Carrer de Roger de Llúria 6; tapas from €4, mains €12-24; ⊘8am-1am Mon-Fri, 1pm-1am Sat; 🖥; Ⓜ Urquinaona) In business since 1934, Casa Alfonso is perfect for a morning coffee or a tapas stop at the long marble bar. Wood-panelled and festooned with old photos, posters and swinging hams, it attracts a faithful local clientele at all hours for its *flautas* (thin custom-made baguettes with choice of filling), hams, cheeses, hot dishes and homemade desserts.

There are also more substantial dishes, mostly involving huge hunks of grilled meat. Consider rounding off with an *alfonsito* (miniature Irish coffee).

CASA CALVET
CATALAN €€€

Map p278 (☏93 412 40 12; www.casacalvet.es; Carrer de Casp 48; mains €28-31; ☺1-3.30pm & 8.30-11pm Mon-Sat; MUrquinaona) An early Gaudí masterpiece loaded with his trademark curvy features houses a swish restaurant (just to the right of the building's main entrance). Dress up and ask for an intimate *taula cabina* (wooden booth). You could opt for scallops and razor clams with pesto and buckwheat, or venison with juniper and porcini sauce.

It has various tasting menus for up to €70, and a lunch menu for €36.

🍷 DRINKING & NIGHTLIFE

🍷 L'Esquerra de L'Eixample

★ MONVÍNIC
WINE BAR

Map p274 (☏93 272 61 87; www.monvinic.com; Carrer de la Diputació 249; ☺1-11pm Tue-Fri, 7-11pm Mon & Sat; MPasseig de Gràcia) Apparently considered unmissable by El Bulli's sommelier, Monvínic is an ode, a rhapsody even, to wine loving. The interactive wine list sits on the bar for you to browse, on a digital tablet similar to an iPad, and boasts more than 3000 varieties.

But that's not to say that it's for connoisseurs only; enthusiasts can also come here to taste wine by the glass – there are 60 selections. You can search by origin, year or grape, from a vast international range. Prices start at €3.50 for a glass of Albariño, and go up – and you can, of course, order by the bottle too. There is an emphasis on affordability, but if you want to splash out, there are fantastic vintage wines. Feel free to talk to one of the six sommeliers who work on the list. At the back is the restaurant, which specialises in Mediterranean cuisine, with ingredients that are sourced locally from Catalan farmers.

★ DRY MARTINI
BAR

Map p274 (☏93 217 50 80; www.drymartiniorg.com; Carrer d'Aribau 162-166; ☺1pm-2.30am Mon-Thu, 6pm-3am Fri & Sat, 7pm-2.30am Sun; MDiagonal) Waiters with a discreetly knowing smile will attend to your cocktail needs and make uncannily good suggestions, but the house drink, taken at the bar or in one of the plush green leather banquettes, is a safe bet. The gin and tonic comes in an enormous mug-sized glass – one will take you most of the night.

Out the back is a superb if pricy restaurant, Speakeasy (p132).

NAPAR BCN
BREWERY

Map p274 (☏606 546467; www.naparbcn.com; Carrer de la Diputació 223; ☺noon-midnight Tue-Thu, to 2am Fri & Sat, noon-5pm Sun; ☎; MUniversitat) The latest bar to open as part of Barcelona's burgeoning craft-beer scene, Napar has 12 beers on tap, six of which are beers brewed on site, including a mix of IPA, pale ale and stout. There's also an accomplished list of bottled beers. It's a stunning space, with a gleaming steampunk aesthetic, and serves some excellent food should hunger strike.

CITY HALL
CLUB

Map p274 (☏93 238 07 22; www.cityhallbarcelona.com; Rambla de Catalunya 2-4; cover €10-15, incl 1 drink; ☺midnight-5am Wed & Thu, midnight-6am Fri & Sat, 11pm-5am Sun; MCatalunya) A long corridor leads to the dance floor of this venerable and popular club, located in a former theatre. House and other electric sounds dominate, with occasional funk nights, and – on Sundays – a gay night, Black Room. Check the website for details.

MILANO
COCKTAIL BAR

Map p274 (☏93 112 71 50; www.camparimilano.com; Ronda de la Universitat 35; ☺noon-2.30am Mon-Sat, 6pm-2.30am Sun; MCatalunya) An absolute gem of hidden Barcelona nightlife, Milano is a subterranean old-school cocktail bar with velvet banquettes and glass-fronted cabinets, presided over by white-jacketed waiters and completely invisible from street level. Check the website for details on occasional live music.

ÁTAME
GAY

Map p274 (☏93 421 41 33; Carrer del Consell de Cent 257; ☺9pm-2.30am; MUniversitat) Cool for a coffee earlier on, Átame (Tie Me Up) heats up later in the night when the gay crowd comes out to play. There is usually a raunchy show on Friday nights and a happy hour on Thursdays.

AIRE
LESBIAN

Map p274 (Sala Diana; ☎93 487 83 42; www.grupoarena.com; Carrer de la Diputació 233; free Thu, cover €5/6 Fri/Sat; ⊗11pm-2.30am Thu-Sat; ⓂPasseig de Gràcia) A popular locale for lesbians; here the dance floor is spacious and there is usually a DJ in command of the tunes, which range from hits of the '80s and '90s to Latin and techno. As a rule, only male friends of the girls are allowed entry, although in practice the crowd tends to be fairly mixed.

COSMO
CAFE

Map p274 (www.galeriacosmo.com; Carrer d'Enric Granados 3; ⊗10am-10pm Sun-Wed, to 11pm Thu, to midnight Fri & Sat; ⓂUniversitat) This groovy cafe-gallery has bicycles hanging from the high, white walls, bright splashy murals and gaily painted ventilation pipes, and even makes a feature of its fire hose. It has a nice selection of teas, pastries and snacks, all set on a pleasant pedestrian strip just behind the university.

It's perfect for a morning session on your laptop (though be warned there is no wi-fi) or a civilised evening tipple while admiring the art.

QUILOMBO
BAR

Map p274 (☎93 439 54 06; Carrer d'Aribau 149; ⊗9.30pm-2.30am Wed-Sun; ⒭FGC Provença) Some formulas just work, and this place has been working since the 1970s. Set up a few guitars in the back room, which you pack with tables and chairs, add some cheapish pre-prepared mojitos and plastic tubs of nuts, and let the punters do the rest. They pour in, creating plenty of *quilombo* (fuss).

PUNTO BCN
GAY

Map p274 (☎93 451 91 52; www.grupoarena.com; Carrer de Muntaner 63-65; ⊗6pm-2.30am Sun-Thu, to 3am Fri & Sat; ⓂUniversitat) It's an oldie but a goody. A big bar over two levels with a slightly older crowd, this place fills to bursting on Friday and Saturday nights with its blend of Spanish pop and dance. It's a friendly early stop on a gay night out, and you can shoot a round of pool if you feel so inclined.

LA FIRA
BAR

Map p274 (☎682 323714; Carrer de Provença 171; cover €5, incl 1 drink; ⊗11.30pm-5.30am Fri & Sat;

🏃 Local Life
Shopping in the Quadrat d'Or

While visitors to L'Eixample do the sights, locals go shopping in the Quadrat d'Or, the grid of streets either side of Passeig de Gràcia. This is Barcelona at its most fashion- and design-conscious, which also describes a large proportion of L'Eixample's residents. All the big names are here, alongside boutiques of local designers who capture the essence of Barcelona cool.

❶ The New Wave

You could spend an entire day along Passeig de Gràcia but detour for a moment to Lurdes Bergada (p140), a boutique run by mother-and-son designer team Lurdes Bergada and Syngman Cucala. The classy men's and women's fashions use natural fibres and have attracted a cult following.

❷ A Pastry Stop

Time for a break. And few pastry shops have such a long-established pedigree as Mauri (☎93 215 10 20; www.pasteleri-asmauri.com; Rambla de Catalunya 102; pastries from €3.50; ⊗8am-midnight Mon-Sat, 9am-4pm Sun; ⓂDiagonal). The plush interior is capped by an ornate fresco dating back to Mauri's first days in 1929. Its croissants and feather-light *ensaïma-das* (sweet buns) are near perfect.

❸ Modernista Jewellery

This is more than just any old jewellery store. The boys from Bagués-Masriera (p140) have been chipping away at precious stones and moulding metal since the 19th century, and many of the classic pieces here have a flighty, Modernista influence. Bagués backs it up with service that can be haughty, but owes much to old-school courtesies.

Shop in L'Eixample district

④ Luxury Luggage

While bags and suitcases in every conceivable colour of buttersoft leather are the mainstay at Loewe (p140), there is also a range of clothing for men and women, along with some stunning – and stunningly priced – accessories. The shop itself is worth a visit, housed in the Casa Lleó Morera (p126), and with some interior details by Domènech i Montaner.

⑤ Say it With Chocolate

A sleek and modern temple to the brown stuff, Cacao Sampaka (p139) doubles as a shop and cafe and is the perfect place to stock up with gifts to take back home. Select from every conceivable flavour (rosemary, anyone, or curry?), either in bar form or as individual choccies to fill your own elegant little gift box.

⑥ Fine Wines

For superior souvenirs in liquid form, head to the state-of-the-art Monvínic (p135), a veritable palace of wine with more than 3000 wines in its cellar, including some extremely rare finds. Try before you buy in the wine bar, and ask them to make you up a gift box for someone special back home.

⑦ Chill Down

Cosmo (p136) is a bright, white cavernous space, dotted with colour from the exhibitions that adorn its high walls. It has a nice selection of teas, cakes and snacks. Set on a pleasant pedestrian strip, it's perfect for an evening tipple outside or in.

LA SAGRADA FAMÍLIA & L'EIXAMPLE

FGC Provença) Wander in past crazy mirrors, penny slot machines and other ancient fairground attractions from Germany, with glowing cuboid stools and other futuristic furniture added more recently. The music swings wildly from whiffs of house through '90s hits to Spanish pop classics. You can spend the earlier part of the night trying some of the bar's shots – it claims to have 500 varieties.

LA CHAPELLE GAY

Map p274 (93 453 30 76; Carrer de Muntaner 67; 4pm-2am Sun-Thu, to 2.30am Fri & Sat; Universitat) A typical long, narrow Eixample bar with white-tiled walls like a 1930s hospital, La Chapelle houses a plethora of crucifixes and niches that far outdo what you'd find in any other 'chapel'. This is a relaxed gay meeting place that welcomes all comers. No need for six-pack stomachs here.

ARENA CLASSIC CLUB

Map p274 (93 487 83 42; www.grupoarena. com; Carrer de la Diputació 233; cover €6/12 Fri/Sat; 2.30-5.30am Fri & Sat; Passeig de Gràcia) Arena Classic attracts a mixed gay crowd that tends not to get too wild. The dominant sound is handbag, and the vibe joyfully cheesy.

NEW CHAPS GAY

Map p274 (93 215 53 65; www.newchaps.com; Avinguda Diagonal 365; 9pm-3am Sun-Thu, to 3.30am Fri & Sat; Diagonal) Leather lovers get in some close-quarters inspection on the dance floor and more, especially in the dark room, downstairs past the fairly dark loos in the vaulted cellars. It's a classic handlebar-moustache gay-porn kinda place.

ARENA MADRE GAY

Map p274 (93 487 83 42; www.grupoarena. com; Carrer de Balmes 32; cover Sun-Fri €6, Sat €12; 12.30-5am; Passeig de Gràcia) Popular with a hot young crowd, Arena Madre is one of the top clubs in town for boys seeking boys. Mainly electronic and house, with a striptease show on Monday, handbag on Thursday, and live shows throughout the week. Heteros are welcome but a minority.

La Dreta de L'Eixample

CAFÈ DEL CENTRE CAFE

Map p278 (93 488 11 01; Carrer de Girona 69; 10am-midnight Mon-Fri, noon-midnight Sat;

Girona) Step back a century in this cafe that's been in business since 1873. The wooden bar extends down the right side as you enter, fronted by a slew of marble-topped tables and wooden chairs. It exudes an almost melancholy air by day but gets busy at night. Staff pride themselves on stocking 50 beers, and there is a lunchtime *menú* for €11.

LES GENS QUE J'AIME BAR

Map p278 (93 215 68 79; www.lesgensquejaime. com; Carrer de València 286; 6pm-2.30am Sun-Thu, 7pm-3am Fri & Sat; Passeig de Gràcia) This intimate basement relic of the 1960s follows a deceptively simple formula: chilled jazz music in the background, minimal lighting from an assortment of flea-market lamps and a cosy, cramped scattering of red-velvet-backed lounges around tiny dark tables.

EL VITI BAR

Map p278 (93 633 83 36; www.elvititaberna. com; Passeig de Sant Joan 62; noon-3.30pm & 7.30-11.30pm Tue-Fri, noon-4pm & 7.30pm-midnight Sat, 11am-4pm Sun; ; Tetuan) Another of the new bars to spring up along the Passeig de Sant Joan in recent months, El Viti checks all the boxes – high ceilings, brick walls both bare and glazed, black-clad staff and a barrel of artisanal vermouth on the bar. It also serves a good line in superior bar snacks, from a mini venison burger to a steamed pork bun.

MICHAEL COLLINS PUB PUB

Map p278 (93 459 19 64; www.michaelcollins-spubs.com; Plaça de la Sagrada Família 4; 1pm-2.30am Sun-Thu, 1pm-3am Fri & Sat; ; Sagrada Família) Locals and expats alike patronise this place, one of the city's best-loved Irish pubs. To be sure of a little Catalan-Irish *craic*, this barn-sized storming pub is just the ticket. It's ideal for football fans wanting big-screen action over their pints, too.

⭐ ENTERTAINMENT

MUSIC HALL CONCERT VENUE

Map p274 (93 238 07 22; www.musichall. es; Rambla de Catalunya 2-4; ticket prices vary; 7.30pm-midnight; Catalunya) The early-evening incarnation of City Hall, this former theatre is the perfect size and shape for live music, holding a crowd of around 500. The acoustics are also great and the layout means everyone gets a good view of the stage.

MÉLIÈS CINEMES
CINEMA

Map p274 (☑93 451 00 51; www.meliescinemes. com; Carrer de Villarroel 102; tickets €4-7; MUrgell) A cosy cinema with two screens, the Méliès specialises in the best of recent releases from Hollywood and Europe.

TEATRE TÍVOLI
THEATRE

Map p278 (☑93 412 20 63; www.grupbalana.com; Carrer de Casp 8; ticket prices vary; ☺box office noon-8pm; MCatalunya) A grand old theatre with three storeys of boxes and a generous stage, the Tívoli has a fairly rapid turnover of drama and musicals, with pieces often not staying on for more than a couple of weeks.

MEDITERRÁNEO
LIVE MUSIC

Map p274 (☑93 453 58 45; www.elmedi.net; Carrer de Balmes 129; ☺11pm-3am; MDiagonal) This jam joint is a great hang-out that attracts a mostly casual student set. Order a beer, enjoy the free nuts and chat at one of the tiny tables while waiting for the next act to tune up at the back. Sometimes the young performers are surprisingly good.

SHOPPING

FLORES NAVARRO
FLOWERS

Map p278 (☑93 457 40 99; www.floristerias-navarro.com; Carrer de València 320; ☺24hr; MDiagonal) You never know when you might need flowers, and this florist never closes. It's a vast space (or couple of spaces, in fact), and worth a visit just for the bank of colour and wonderful fragrance.

EL CORTE INGLÉS
DEPARTMENT STORE

Map p278 (☑93 306 38 00; www.elcorteingles. es; Plaça de Catalunya 14; ☺9.30am-9.30pm Mon-Sat; MCatalunya) This is now the city's only department store, with everything you'd expect, from computers to cushions, and high fashion to homewares. It's famous for its decent customer service (this isn't always the case in Spain). El Corte Inglés has other branches, including at Portal de l'Àngel 19-21 (p73), Avinguda Diagonal 617 (p172) and **Avinguda Diagonal 471-473** (☺9.30am-9.30pm Mon-Sat; MHospital Clínic) near Plaça de Francesc Macià.

The top floor is occupied by a so-so restaurant with fabulous city views.

THE GAIXAMPLE

The area just above Gran Via de les Corts Catalanes and to the left of Rambla de Catalunya is popularly known as the 'Gaixample', for its proliferation of gay bars and restaurants. We list some of the best, such as Átame (p135), **Are**na Classic (left) and Aire (p136) (this last one's for the ladies), but note that some old favourites are also to be found in adjoining neighbourhoods, such as **Metro** (Map p286; ☑93 323 52 27; www. metrodiscobcn.com; Carrer de Sepúlveda 185; before 2am from €6, after 2am €20; ☺12.15am-5.30am; MUniversitat) in Sant Antoni.

CACAO SAMPAKA
FOOD

Map p274 (☑93 272 08 33; www.cacaosampaka. com; Carrer del Consell de Cent 292; ☺9am-9pm Mon-Sat; MPasseig de Gràcia) Chocoholics will be convinced they have died and passed on to a better place. Load up in the shop or head for the bar out the back where you can have a classic *xocolata* (hot chocolate) and munch on exquisite chocolate cakes, tarts, ice cream, sweets and sandwiches. The bonbons make particularly good presents.

ALTAÏR
BOOKS

Map p274 (☑93 342 71 71; www.altair.es; Gran Via de les Corts Catalanes 616; ☺10am-8.30pm Mon-Sat; ☎; MCatalunya) Enter a wonderland of travel in this extensive bookshop, which is a mecca for guidebooks, maps, travel literature and all sorts of other books likely to induce a severe case of itchy feet. It has a travellers' noticeboard and, downstairs, a travel agent.

LAIE
BOOKS

Map p278 (☑93 318 17 39; www.laie.es; Carrer de Pau Claris 85; ☺9am-9pm Mon-Fri, 10am-9pm Sat; MCatalunya, Urquinaona) Laie has novels and books on architecture, art and film in English, French, Spanish and Catalan. It also has a great upstairs cafe where you can examine your latest purchases or browse through the newspapers provided for customers in true Central European style.

FNAC
DEPARTMENT STORE

Map p274 (☑902 100632; www.fnac.es; El Triangle, Plaça de Catalunya 4; ☺10am-9.30pm Mon-Sat; MCatalunya) FNAC, the French

WORTH A DETOUR

AN OUTLET OUTING

For the ultimate discount-fashion overdose, head out of town for some outlet shopping at **La Roca Village** (☑93 842 39 39; www.larocavillage.com; ⊗10am-9pm Mon-Sun). Here, a village has been given over to consumer madness. At a long line of Spanish and international fashion boutiques you'll find clothes, shoes, accessories and designer homewares at (they claim) up to 60% off normal retail prices.

To get here, follow the AP-7 tollway north from Barcelona, take exit 12 (marked Cardedeu) and follow the signs for 'Centre Comercial'. The **Sagalés Bus Company** (☑902 130014; www.sagales.com) organises shuttles from Plaça de Catalunya (€9 return, if bought online 24 hours in advance, 40 minutes, 12 daily). Alternatively, take a slower bus from the same company from Fabra i Puig metro station (€4 one way online, four departures Monday to Friday, three in August), or a *rodalies* train to Granollers and pick up the shuttle (Monday to Friday only) or a taxi there.

book, CD and electronics emporium, has a couple of branches around town, but this is the biggest.

LURDES BERGADA   CLOTHING
Map p274 (☑93 218 48 51; www.lurdesbergada.es; Rambla de Catalunya 112; ⊗10.30am-8.30pm Mon-Sat; ⓂDiagonal) Lurdes Bergada is a boutique run by mother-and-son designer team Lurdes Bergada and Syngman Cucala. The classy men's and women's fashions use natural fibres and have attracted a cult following.

REGIA   BEAUTY
Map p274 (☑93 216 01 21; www.regia.es; Passeig de Gràcia 39; ⊗9.30am-8.30pm Mon-Sat; ⓂPasseig de Gràcia) Reputed to be one of the best perfume stores in the city, and in business since 1928, Regia stocks all the name brands and also has a private perfume museum (p128) out the back. Aside from the range of perfumes, Regia sells all sorts of creams, lotions and colognes. It also has its own line of bath products.

PURIFICACIÓN GARCÍA   FASHION
Map p274 (☑93 496 13 36; www.purificaciongarcia.com; Carrer de Provença 292; ⊗10am-8.30pm Mon-Sat; ⓂDiagonal) Ms García has an enormous spread of offerings over two floors. Her collections are breathtaking as much for their breadth as anything else. You'll find all kinds of clothing, from women's cardigans to men's ties, as well as light summer dresses and jeans.

BAGUÉS-MASRIERA   JEWELLERY
Map p274 (☑93 216 01 74; www.bagues-masriera.com; Passeig de Gràcia 41; ⊗10am-8.30pm Mon-Fri, 11am-8pm Sat; ⓂPasseig de Gràcia) This

jewellery store, in business since the 19th century, is in thematic harmony with its location in the Modernista Casa Amatller. Some of the classic pieces to come out of the Bagués clan's workshops have an equally playful, Modernista bent.

LOEWE   FASHION
Map p274 (☑93 216 04 00; www.loewe.com; Passeig de Gràcia 35; ⊗10am-8.30pm Mon-Sat; ⓂPasseig de Gràcia) Loewe is one of Spain's leading and oldest fashion stores, founded in 1846. It specialises in luxury leather (shoes, accessories and travel bags), and also has lines in perfume, sunglasses, cuff links, silk scarves and jewellery. This branch opened in 1943 in the Modernista Casa Lleó Morera.

EL BULEVARD DELS ANTIQUARIS   ANTIQUES
Map p274 (☑93 215 44 99; www.bulevarddelsantiquaris.com; Passeig de Gràcia 55; ⊗10.30am-8.30pm Mon-Sat; ⓂPasseig de Gràcia) More than 70 stores (be warned most close for lunch) are gathered under one roof (on the floor above the more general Bulevard Rosa arcade) to offer the most varied selection of collector's pieces. These range from old porcelain dolls through to fine crystal, from Asian antique furniture to old French goods, and from African and other ethnic art to jewellery.

CUBIÑA   HOMEWARES
Map p278 (☑93 476 57 21; www.cubinya.es; Carrer de Mallorca 291; ⊗10am-2pm & 4.30-8.30pm Mon-Sat; ⓂVerdaguer) Even if interior design doesn't ring your bell, it's worth a visit to this extensive temple to furniture, lamps and just about any home accessory your heart might desire, just to see this

Domènech i Montaner building. Admire the enormous and whimsical wrought-iron decoration at street level before heading inside to marvel at the ceiling, timber work, brick columns and windows.

ADOLFO DOMÍNGUEZ
FASHION

Map p278 (☑93 487 41 70; www.adolfodominguez.com; Passeig de Gràcia 32; ☺10am-9pm Mon-Sat; ⓂPasseig de Gràcia) One of the stars of Spanish prêt-à-porter, this label produces classic men's and women's garments from quality materials. Encompassing anything from regal party gowns to kids' outfits (that might have you thinking of British aristocracy), the broad range generally oozes a conservative air, with elegant cuts that make no concessions to rebellious urban ideals.

CAMPER
SHOES

Map p274 (☑93 215 63 90; www.camper.com; Carrer de València 249; ☺10am-9pm Mon-Sat; ⓂPasseig de Gràcia) What started as a modest Mallorcan family business (the island has a long shoemaking tradition) has, over the decades, and particularly with the success of the 'bowling shoe' in the '90s, become the Clarks of Spain. The shoes, from the eminently sensible to the stylishly fashionable, are known for solid reliability and are sold all over the world. It now has shops all over Barcelona.

JOAN MÚRRIA
FOOD

Map p278 (☑93 215 57 89; www.murria.cat; Carrer de Roger de Llúria 85; ☺9am-2pm & 5-8pm Mon-Fri; ⓂPasseig de Gràcia) Ramon Casas designed the century-old Modernista shopfront advertisements featured at this culinary temple. For a century the gluttonous have trembled at this altar of speciality food goods from around Catalonia and beyond.

🏃 ACTIVITIES

ESPAI BOISÀ
COOKING COURSE

Map p274 (☑93 192 60 21; http://espaiboisa.com; Ptge Lluís Pellicer 8; cost varies; ⓂHospital Clínic) 🍴 Run by a young, multilingual Venezuelan-Catalan couple, this first-rate outfit offers cooking courses on various themes and of various lengths. They emphasise organic, seasonal ingredients from local producers outside of Barcelona – put to good use in dishes including paella, a range of tapas dishes and *crema catalana* (a Catalan version of *crème brûlée*).

The best part is eating your creations, served up with generous glasses of organic Catalan wine, or sangria on warm summer nights.

BARCELONA WALKING TOURS
WALKING TOUR

Map p274 (☑93 285 38 34; www.barcelonaturisme.com; Plaça de Catalunya 17; ⓂCatalunya) The Oficina d'Informació de Turisme de Barcelona organises guided walking tours. One explores the Barri Gòtic (adult/child €16/free; in English 9.30am daily); another follows in Picasso's footsteps (€22/7, in English 3pm Tuesday, Thursday and Saturday) and winds up at the Museu Picasso; and a third takes in the main jewels of Modernisme (€16/free, in English 6pm Wednesday and Friday).

Also offered is a gourmet tour of traditional purveyors of fine foodstuffs across the old city (€22/7, in English 10.30am Monday and Friday); it includes a couple of chances to taste some of the products.

There is a 10% discount on all tours if you book online.

Antoni Gaudí & Modernisme

Barcelona's architectural gift to the world was Modernisme, a flamboyant Catalan creation that erupted in the late 19th century. Modernisme was personified by the visionary work of Antoni Gaudí, a giant in the world of architecture. Imaginative creations by Gaudí and his contemporaries have filled Barcelona with dozens of masterpieces.

A Blank Canvas

In the 1850s a rapidly growing city fuelled by industrialisation meant notoriously crowded conditions in the narrow streets of the *ciutat vella*, Barcelona's old quarter. It was time to break down the medieval walls and dramatically expand the city. In 1869 the architect Ildefons Cerdà was chosen to design a new district, which would be called L'Eixample (the Enlargement).

He drew wide boulevards on a gridlike layout, and envisioned neighbourhoods with plenty of green space – an objective that city planners unfortunately overruled amid the rampant land speculation of the day. With a blank slate before them, and abundant interest from upper-class residents eager to custom design a new home, architects were much in demand. What developers could not have predicted was the calibre of those architects.

Antoni Gaudí

Leading the way was Antoni Gaudí. Born in Reus to a long line of coppersmiths, Gaudí was initially trained in metalwork. In childhood he suffered from poor health, including rheumatism, and became an early adopter of a vegetarian diet. He was not a promising student. In 1878, when he obtained his architecture degree, the school's headmaster is reputed to have said, 'Who knows if we have given a diploma to a nutcase or a genius. Time will tell.'

The Book of Nature

As a young man, what most delighted Gaudí was being outdoors, and he became fascinated by the plants, animals and geology beyond his door. This admiration for the natural world would heavily influence his designs. 'This tree is my teacher,' he once said. 'Everything comes from the book of nature.' Throughout his work, he sought to emulate the harmony he observed in the natural world, eschewing the straight line and favouring curvaceous forms and more organic shapes.

The spiral of a nautilus shell can be seen in staircases and ceiling details, tight buds of flowers in chimney pots and roof ornamentation, while undulating arches

....

1. Stained-glass ceiling at the Palau de la Música Catalana (p93)
2. Casa Batlló (p127)

GAUDÍ OFF THE BEATEN TRACK

Gaudí, like any freelancer, was busy all over town. While his main patron was Eusebi Güell and his big projects were bankrolled by the wealthy bourgeoisie, he also took on smaller jobs. One example is the Casa Vicens, a remarkable home with Moorish and Eastern motifs. Another is the Col·legi de les Teresianes, for which he created an unusual brick facade, topped with castle-like merlons. Gaudí fanatics might also want to reach Bellesguard, whose castle-like appearance is reinforced by heavy stonework, generous wrought iron and a tall spire.

Gaudí's Creations

The architect's work is an earthy appeal to sinewy movement, but often with a dreamlike or surreal quality. The private apartment house Casa Batlló is a fine example in which all appears a riot of the unnaturally natural – or the naturally unnatural. Not only are straight lines eliminated, but the lines between real and unreal, sober and dream-drunk, good sense and play are all blurred. Depending on how you look at the facade, you might see St George (one of Barcelona's patron saints) defeating a dragon, a magnificent and shimmering fish (a symbol of Mediterranean peoples) or elements of an effusive Carnaval parade.

Gaudí seems to have particularly enjoyed himself with rooftops. At Palau Güell he created all sorts of fantastical, multicoloured tile figures, as chimney pots resembling oversized budlike trees that seem straight out of *Alice in Wonderland* – or perhaps Dr Seuss.

evoke a cavern, overlapping roof tiles mimic the scales of an armadillo and flowing walls resemble waves on the sea. Tree branches, spider webs, stalactites, honeycombs, starfish, mushrooms, shimmering beetle wings and many other elements from nature – all were part of the Gaudían vernacular.

1. Park Güell (p152) 2. Ceiling of La Sagrada Família (p121)

La Sagrada Família

Gaudí's masterpiece was La Sagrada Família (begun in 1882), and in it you can see the culminating vision of many ideas developed over the years. Its massive scale evokes the grandeur of Catalonia's Gothic cathedrals, while organic elements foreground its harmony with nature.

The church is rife with symbols that tangibly express Gaudí's Catholic faith through architecture: 18 bell towers symbolise Jesus, the Virgin Mary, the four evangelists and the 12 apostles. Three facades cover Jesus' life, death and resurrection. Even its location: the Nativity Facade faces east where the sun rises; the Passion Facade depicting Christ's death faces west where the sun sets.

Gaudí: A Catholic & a Catalan

Gaudí was a devout Catholic and a Catalan nationalist. In addition to nature, Catalonia's great medieval churches were a source of inspiration to him. He took pride in utilising the building materials of the countryside: clay, stone and timber.

In contrast to his architecture, Gaudí's life was simple; he was not averse to knocking on doors, literally begging for money to help fund construction of the cathedral. As Gaudí became more adventurous he appeared as a lone wolf. With age he became almost exclusively motivated by stark religious conviction, and he devoted much of the latter part of his life to what remains Barcelona's call sign – the unfinished La Sagrada Família. He died in 1926, struck down by a streetcar while walking to the Sant Felip Neri church. Wearing ragged clothes with empty pockets – save for some orange peel – Gaudí was initially taken for a beggar and taken to a nearby hospital where he was left in a pauper's ward; he died two days later. Thousands attended his funeral, forming a half-mile procession to La Sagrada Família, where he was buried in the crypt.

Much like his work in progress, La Sagrada Família, Gaudí's story is far from over. In March 2000 the Vatican decided to proceed with the case for canonising him, and pilgrims already stop by the crypt to pay him homage. One of the key sculptors at work on the church, the Japanese Etsuro

Sotoo, converted to Catholicism because of his passion for Gaudí.

Domènech i Montaner

Although overshadowed by Gaudí, Lluís Domènech i Montaner (1850–1923) was one of the great masters of Modernisme. He was a widely travelled man of prodigious intellect, with knowledge of everything from mineralogy to medieval heraldry, and he was an architectural professor, a prolific writer and a nationalist politician. The question of Catalan identity and how to create a national architecture consumed Domènech i Montaner, who designed more than a dozen large-scale works in his lifetime.

The exuberant, steel-framed Palau de la Música Catalana is one of his masterpieces. Adorning the facade are elaborate Gothic-style windows, floral designs (Domènech i Montaner also studied botany) and sculptures depicting characters from Catalan folklore and the music world as well as everyday citizens of Barcelona. Inside, the hall leaves visitors dazzled with delicate floral-covered colonnades, radiant stained-glass walls and ceiling, and a rolling, sculpture-packed proscenium referencing the epics of musical lore.

His other great masterpiece is the Hospital de la Santa Creu i de Sant Pau, with sparkling mosaics on the facade

and a stained-glass skylight that fills the vestibule with golden light (like Matisse, Domènech i Montaner believed in the therapeutic powers of colour).

Puig i Cadafalch

Like Domènech i Montaner, Josep Puig i Cadafalch (1867–1956) was a polymath; he was an archaeologist, an expert in Romanesque art and one of Catalonia's most prolific architects. As a politician – and later president of the Mancomunitat de Catalunya (Commonwealth of Catalonia) – he was instrumental in shaping the Catalan nationalist movement.

One of his many Modernista gems is the Casa Amatller, a rather dramatic contrast to Gaudí's Casa Batlló next door. Here the straight line is very much in evidence, as is the foreign influence (the gables are borrowed from the Dutch). Blended with playful Gothic-style sculpture, Puig i Cadafalch has designed a house of startling beauty and invention.

Another pivotal work by Puig i Cadafalch was the Casa Martí (better known as Els Quatre Gats), which was one of Barcelona's first Modernista-style buildings (from 1896).

Materials & Decorations

Modernista architects relied on artisan skills that have now been all but relegated to history. There were no concrete pours (contrary to what is being done at La Sagrada Família today). Stone, unclad brick, exposed iron and steel frames, and the copious use of stained glass and ceramics in decoration were all features of the new style – and indeed it is often in the decor that Modernisme is at its most flamboyant.

The craftspeople required for these tasks were the heirs of the guild masters and had absorbed centuries of know-how about just what could and could not be done with these materials. Forged iron and steel were newcomers to the scene, but the approach to learning how they could be used was not dissimilar to that adopted for more traditional materials. Gaudí, in particular, relied on these old skills and even ran schools in La Sagrada Família workshops to keep them alive.

Exploring Modernisme

Barcelona is home to dozens of Modernista masterpieces, making for some tough decisions when it comes to deciding what to see. The following are two suggested half-day itineraries of the major highlights, though the very ambitious could combine these for a packed day of architectural gazing.

A MORNING OF MODERNISME

Start the day off with pastries and coffee at the Modernista gem **Escribà** ❶. From there walk a few blocks south and down Carrer Nou de Rambla to visit the **Palau Güell** ❷, one of

Gaudí's early masterpieces. Afterwards take the metro up to Passeig de Gràcia and have a look at the so-called Manzana de la Discordia – **Casa Batlló, Casa Amatller** ❸ and Casa Lleó Morera – deciding for yourself who among Gaudí, Puig i Cadafalch and Domènech i Montaner has created the most successful work of art. Afterwards, stroll up Passeig de Gràcia, a true architectural showcase, and end your tour at Gaudí's **La Pedrera** ❹ (Casa Milà). Don't miss the sentinel-like chimney pots on the roof – and the great view over the city.

La Sagrada Família
Still over a decade from completion, the magnificent basilica is an ever-changing work in progress. The beautifully sculpted Nativity Facade, with its rich symbolism, is a masterpiece unto itself.

GRÀCIA

SANT GERVASI

Park Güell
Gaudí's imagination runs wild here, with fairy-tale-like gatehouses, tilting tree-like columns, organic rock-strewn passageways and one much photographed lizard.

La Pedrera
Full of curving walls, La Pedrera presented challenges to one tenant, who complained there was no obvious place to put her piano. Gaudí's response: 'Madam, I suggest you take up the flute.'

AN AFTERNOON OF MODERNISME

Start the tour at **La Sagrada Família** ⑤ where you can gaze upon one of the world's most dynamic ecclesiastical designs. Afterwards, make your way up to **Park Güell** ⑥ for an afternoon stroll through the eye-catching park. If time allows, pay a visit to the Casa-Museu Gaudí in the park. Next head back down to the Ciutat Vella for a guided tour (or perhaps attend a concert) inside the luminescent **Palau de la Música Catalana** ⑦. Afterwards, stroll over to **Els Quatre Gats** ⑧ for a drink (or a meal) inside a whimsical building designed by Puig i Cadafalch.

TOP TIPS

» Go first thing in the morning or late in the day to beat the crowds at Gaudí sites.

» Buy La Sagrada Família tickets online to avoid long queues.

» La Pedrera also hosts rooftop evening concerts in the summer.

Palau de la Música Catalana
The sculptural facade is packed with folk symbols, with an open-armed nymph, a peasant, a fisherman, and other types gathered below a sword-bearing St George.

Escribà
This magnificent pastry shop has a stunning art nouveau exterior. Note the swirling mosaics and stained glass, key elements of Modernista design.

LA RIBERA

L'EIXAMPLE

Passeig de Gràcia

BARRI GÒTIC

La Rambla

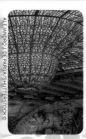

Casa Batlló & Casa Amatller
These two side-by-side buildings show how wildly different the Modernistas ranged in their inspirations. Puig i Cadafalch references Gothic Dutch architecture, while Gaudí's is a shimmering tile-covered fantasy.

Els Quatre Gats
From 1897 to 1903, this was the hang-out for avant-garde artists of the day. A young Picasso had his first exhibition here in 1900.

Palau Güell
There are many unusual features in this early work by Antoni Gaudí, including the massive entry doors, which allowed carriages to be driven right into the house.

Gràcia & Park Güell

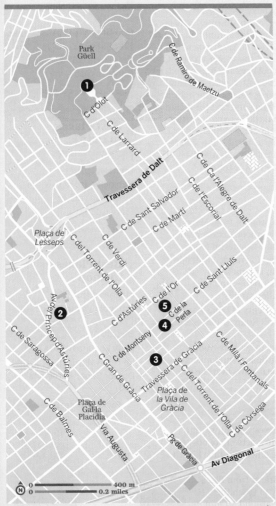

Neighbourhood Top Five

❶ **Park Güell** (p152) Getting lost along the winding paths and exploring the wild sculptures, mosaics and columns of Gaudí's verdant wonderland.

❷ **Casa Vicens** (p154) Admiring the strange interplay of brick, chequerboard patterns and Moorish elements on this castle mansion, Gaudí's first c ommission.

❸ **La Nena** (p155) Getting high on chocolate while playing a few board games and nibbling on crêpes.

❹ **Soda Acústic** (p159) Hearing Balkan gypsy beats, experimental jazz and other eclectic sounds in one of Gràcia's most innovative performance spaces.

❺ **Verdi** (p159) Watching an indie film at this neighbourhood icon, followed by tapas on the restaurant-lined lane out the front.

Explore Gràcia & Park Güell

Once a separate village north of L'Eixample, and an industrial district famous for its republican and liberal ideas, Gràcia was incorporated into the city of Barcelona in 1897, much to the disgust of the locals. The neighbourhood retains its distinct character today, with a boho feel that varies between chic and downtrodden – it's home to artists, young families and a fair number of tramps.

Start the day in Gràcia by exploring Park Güell and move down to the centre of the neighbourhood. If you walk from the park, cut across the traffic-choked Travessera de Dalt and go down Carrer de Verdi, into the heart of Gràcia – it's around 1km. Otherwise, Metro Línia 3 (Fontana stop) leaves you halfway up Carrer Gran de Gràcia and close to a network of busy squares.

Plunge into the atmosphere of its narrow streets and small plazas, and the bars and restaurants on and around them. The liveliest are Carrer de Verdi, where you will find wonderful cafes, bars and shops; Plaça del Sol, a raucous square populated by cool bars and (often loud) drunks; Plaça de la Vila de Gràcia, dotted with cafes and restaurants; Plaça de la Revolució de Setembre de 1868, a family-friendly square with a playground and ice-cream parlour; and the tree-lined Plaça de la Virreina, a particularly lovely square with cafes, shops and a chilled-out feel. Gràcia is great during the day or at night – the squares are sunny and relaxed for breakfast or lunch, and lively at night with scenesters enjoying a drink al fresco.

Local Life

➡**Markets** Locals get their fresh produce from Mercat de la Llibertat (p154), the neighbourhood's emblematic larder – queue up and sample some wonderful food.

➡**Independent stores** Wander up Carrer de Verdi and along Travessera de Gràcia for an insight into what Gràcia does best. Independent boutiques and food shops abound on these people-filled streets.

➡**Old-time bars** Gràcia still has plenty of tapas bars that have been around forever – El Roure (p155) is a fine example.

➡**Sunsets** Though it's a challenge to get here, your efforts will be well rewarded at little-known Bunkers del Carmel (p154), which offers magical views over the city.

Getting There & Away

➡**Metro** Línia 3 (Fontana stop) leaves you halfway up Carrer Gran de Gràcia and close to a network of busy squares. To enter Gràcia from the other side, take Línia 4 to Joanic.

➡**Foot** Strolling up Passeig de Gràcia from Plaça de Catalunya is a wonderful way to reach the neighbourhood, but it does take around 40 minutes.

Lonely Planet's Top Tip

A wonderful way to take in Gràcia's atmosphere is from a cafe or restaurant on one of its many squares. Arrive after dusk and watch as the place comes to life in the post-work hours.

GRÀCIA & PARK GÜELL

✕ Best Places to Eat

➡ TimeLine (p155)
➡ La Panxa del Bisbe (p155)
➡ Con Gracia (p156)
➡ Botafumeiro (p157)
➡ Sol i Lluna (p156)
➡ Chivuo's (p154)

For reviews, see p154 ➡

🍷 Best Places to Drink

➡ Elephanta (p157)
➡ Chatelet (p157)
➡ Rabipelao (p157)
➡ Viblioteca (p157)
➡ Raïm (p159)

For reviews, see p157 ➡

🛍 Best Places to Shop

➡ Magnesia (p160)
➡ Amapola Vegan Shop (p159)
➡ Be (p161)
➡ Lady Loquita (p160)
➡ La Festival (p160)
➡ Doctor Paper Barcelona (p160)

For reviews, see p159 ➡

TOP SIGHT
PARK GÜELL

Park Güell – north of Gràcia and about 4km from Plaça de Catalunya – is where Gaudí turned his hand to landscape gardening. It's a strange, enchanting place where this iconic Modernista's passion for natural forms really took flight, to the point where the artificial almost seems more natural than the natural.

City Park

Park Güell originated in 1900, when Count Eusebi Güell bought the tree-covered hillside of El Carmel (then outside Barcelona) and hired Gaudí to create a miniature city of houses for the wealthy, surrounded by landscaped grounds. The project was a commercial flop and was abandoned in 1914 – but not before Gaudí had created, in his inimitable manner, steps, a plaza, two gatehouses and 3km of roads and walks. In 1922 the city bought the estate for use as a public park. The park became a Unesco World Heritage site in 2004. The idea was based on the English 'garden cities', much admired by Güell, hence the spelling of 'Park'.

Just inside the main entrance on Carrer d'Olot, immediately recognisable by the two Hansel-and-Gretel gatehouses, is the park's newly refurbished Centre d'Interpretació, in the Pavelló de Consergeria, which is a typically curvaceous former porter's home that hosts a display on Gaudí's building methods and the history of the park. There are nice views from the top floor.

DON'T MISS

➡ Learning about Gaudí's building methods at the Centre d'Interpretació

➡ The Sala Hipóstila's stone forest

➡ The life of the artist at Casa-Museu Gaudí

➡ The undulating tiled bench with views across the city

PRACTICALITIES

➡ 📞 93 409 18 31

➡ www.parkguell.cat

➡ Carrer d'Olot 7

➡ admission to central area adult/child €8/6

➡ ⏰ 8am-9.30pm May-Aug, to 8pm Sep-Apr

➡ 🚌 24, 32, Ⓜ Lesseps, Vallcarca

Sala Hipóstila (The Doric Temple)

The steps up from the entrance, guarded by a mosaic dragon/lizard (a copy of which you can buy in many central souvenir shops), lead to the Sala Hipóstila (aka the Doric Temple). This forest of 88 stone columns – some leaning like mighty trees bent by the weight of time – was originally intended as a market. To the left curves a gallery whose twisted stonework columns and roof give the effect of a cloister beneath tree roots – a motif repeated in several places in the park. On top of the Sala Hipóstila is a broad open space. Its centrepiece is the Banc de Trencadís, a tiled bench curving sinuously around its perimeter, which was designed by one of Gaudí's closest colleagues, architect Josep Maria Jujol (1879–1949). With Gaudí, however, there is always more than meets the eye. This giant platform was designed as a kind of catchment area for rainwater washing down the hillside. The water is filtered through a layer of stone and sand, and it drains down through the columns to an underground cistern.

Casa-Museu Gaudí

The spired house above and to the right of the entrance is the **Casa-Museu Gaudí** (www.casa museugaudi.org; adult/student/child €5.50/4.50/free; ⊕9am-8pm Apr-Sep, 10am-6pm Oct-Mar; ☐24, 92, 116, Ⓜ︎Lesseps), where Gaudí lived for almost the last 20 years of his life (1906–26). It contains furniture he designed (including items that once lived in La Pedrera, Casa Batlló and Casa Calvet) along with other memorabilia. The house was built in 1904 by Francesc Berenguer i Mestres as a prototype for the 60 or so houses that were originally planned here.

Much of the park is still wooded, but it's laced with pathways. The best views are from the cross-topped Turó del Calvari in the southwest corner.

GETTING THERE

The walk from metro stop Lesseps is signposted. From the Vallcarca stop, the walk is marginally shorter and the uphill trek eased by escalators. Bus 24 drops you at an entrance near the top of the park.

TAKE A BREAK

Before or after making the trip up to the park, stop off at La Panxa del Bisbe (p155) for deliciously creative tapas and good wines. From the northeast exit of the park, it's a pleasant stroll over to Las Delicias (p155), a neighbourhood favourite for its classic, reasonably priced Spanish fare.

WORTH A DETOUR

BUNKERS DEL CARMEL

For a magnificent view over the city that's well off the beaten path, head to the neighbourhood of El Carmel and make the ascent up the hill known as Turó de la Rovira to the **Bunkers del Carmel** viewpoint. Above the weeds and dusty hillside, you'll find the old concrete platforms that were once part of anti-aircraft battery during the Spanish Civil War (in the post-War, it was a shanty town until the early 1990s, and has lain abandoned since then). Placards at the sight give an overview of what once stood here. These days, those old firing platforms are better used as seating for a mix of students and young travellers who come for the mesmerising 360-degree views over the city. It's a great place to watch the sunset. Before or after visiting here, you can stop for a bite and a drink at the charming, family-run Las Delicias (p155).

To get to the park, take the metro to El Carmel, take the Llobregas exit, and walk two blocks downhill to the bus stop, where you can catch the 86 bus; have the driver tell you when you're near the Bunkers. From the bus stop, it's a further 10-minute walk to the viewpoint.

⦿ SIGHTS

PARK GÜELL   PARK
See p152.

GAUDÍ EXPERIENCE   THEATRE
(⎆93 285 44 40; Carrer de Larrard 41; adult/child
€9/7.50; ☺10.30am-7pm Apr-Sep, to 5pm Oct-Mar;
Ⓜ Lesseps, Vallcarca) The 'Gaudí Experience'
is a fun-filled Disney-style look at the life
and work of Barcelona's favourite son, just
a stone's throw from Park Güell. There are
models of his buildings and achingly modern interactive exhibits and touchscreens,
but the highlight is the stomach-churning
4D presentation in its tiny screening room.
Not recommended for the frail or children
aged under six years.

MERCAT DE LA LLIBERTAT   MARKET
Map p280 (⎆93 217 09 95; www.mercatllibertat.
com; Plaça de la Llibertat 27; ☺8am-8pm Mon-Fri,
8am-3pm Sat; ☒ FGC Gràcia) Built in the 1870s,
the 'Market of Liberty' was covered over in
1893 in typically fizzy Modernista style, employing generous whirls of wrought iron. It
got a considerable facelift in 2009 and has
lost some of its aged charm, but the market
remains emblematic of the Gràcia district:
full of life and all kinds of fresh produce.

The man behind the 1893 remake was
Francesc Berenguer i Mestres (1866–1914),
Gaudí's long-time assistant.

CASA VICENS   ARCHITECTURE
(www.casavicens.org; Carrer de les Carolines 22;
☒ FGC Plaça Molina) The angular, turreted
1888 Casa Vicens was one of Gaudí's first
commissions. Tucked away west of Gràcia's
main drag, the richly detailed facade of this
private house is awash with ceramic colour
and shape. Recently purchased by a private
company (a subsidiary of the Andorran
Mora Banc), plans are under way to open
the house to the public by late 2016.

As was frequently the case, Gaudí sought
inspiration from the past, in this case the
rich heritage of building in the Mudéjar-
style brick, typical in those parts of Spain
reconquered from the Moors. Mudéjar architecture was created by those Arabs and
Berbers allowed to remain in Spain after
the Christian reconquests.

✕ EATING

CHIVUO'S   SANDWICHES €
Map p280 (⎆93 218 51 34; www.chivuos.com;
Carrer del Torrent de l'Olla 175; sandwiches €7-9;
☺1-5pm & 7pm-midnight Mon-Fri, 6pm-midnight
Sat; Ⓜ Lesseps, Fontana) Satisfying grilled
sandwiches and delicious craft brews make
a fine pair at this buzzing little snack den
in Gràcia. A mostly local crowd comes for
the slow-roasted pork, tuna melts, bacon-
covered burgers and 'philli cheese steaks' –
best ordered with *fritas* (chips). The rotating selection of eight craft brews includes
mostly Catalan and Spanish brews, including excellent ales from Barcelona-based
Edge Brewing (p109).

LA NENA
CAFE €

Map p280 (☑93 285 14 76; www.chocolateri-alanena.com; Carrer de Ramon y Cajal 36; desserts from €4.50; ☺9am-10pm; 🚻; MFontana) A French team has created this delightfully chaotic space for indulging in cups of *suïssos* (rich hot chocolate) served with a plate of heavy homemade whipped cream and *melindros* (spongy sweet biscuits), fine desserts and even a few savoury dishes (including crêpes). The place is strewn with books, and you can play with the board games on the shelves.

The area out the back is designed to keep kids busy, with toys, books and a blackboard with chalk, making it an ideal family rest stop.

CASA PORTUGUESA
BAKERY €

Map p280 (☑93 021 88 03; Carrer de l'Or 8; snacks from €2; ☺10am-10pm Tue-Sun; MFontana) Overlooking Plaça del Diamant, Casa Portuguesa is a delightful bakery and purveyor of delicacies. The *pasteis de belém* (Portuguese-style custard tarts) are magnificent, and you'll also find organic salads (which change daily), tarts, good coffee and Portuguese wines. For a kick, have a shot of *ginjinha* (cherry brandy).

CAFÈ CAMÈLIA
CAFE €

Map p280 (☑93 415 36 86; Carrer de Verdi 79; mains €8-11; ☺10am-midnight Mon-Sat, to 9pm Sun; 🐾🖉🚻; MFontana) This pretty little vegetarian cafe on Verdi makes a peaceful spot for coffee, set lunches and desserts. The menu, though small, features well-executed dishes – hummus, vegetable curry, open-faced sandwiches, quinoa burgers with roasted vegetables and a risotto of the day.

BAR BODEGA QUIMET
TAPAS €

Map p280 (☑93 218 41 89; Carrer de Vic 23; tapas from €3; ☺2-11.30pm Mon-Fri, 1-11.30pm Sat & Sun; MFontana) A remnant from a bygone age, Bar Bodega Quimet is a delightfully warm and atmospheric bar, with old bottles lining the walls, marble tables and a burnished wooden bar. The list of tapas and seafood is almost exhaustive, while another house speciality is *torrades* – huge slabs of toasted white bread topped with cured meats, fresh anchovies and sardines every which way.

In summer you'll be served a refreshing glass of chilled gazpacho.

EL ROURE
TAPAS €

Map p280 (☑93 218 73 87; Carrer de la Riera de Sant Miquel 51; tapas from €3.50; ☺7am-1am Mon-Sat; MFontana) This old-time locals' bar is what Hemingway meant by a 'clean, well-lighted place'. Sidle up to the bar or pull up a little wooden chair and tuck into good-value tapas from the bar, washed down by a few cold daroughts of Moritz. The *bunyols de bacallà* are delightful battered balls of cod that demand to be gobbled up.

The place is full to bursting most of the time. Time it right, and you can enjoy a first-rate paella (served only on Thursdays at lunchtime).

TIMELINE
SANDWICHES €

Map p280 (☑93 217 79 38; Carrer de la Providència 3; sandwiches €7-9; ☺7pm-2am Mon-Fri, from noon Sat & Sun; 🖉; MLesseps, Fontana) Like stepping into an enchanted cuckoo clock, TimeLine is a cosy candlelit eating and drinking cabin decked with curious artwork (roller skates, twisted light sculptures), black-and-white tile floors and a tiny train set scuttling along the bar. It draws a fun and multilingual crowd, who come for cocktails, sandwiches (curry chicken, meatballs, veggie barbecue), hummus platters and goat's cheese drizzled salads.

LA PANXA DEL BISBE
TAPAS €€

Map p280 (☑93 213 70 49; Carrer del Torrent de les Flors 156; tapas €8-14, tasting menus from €30; ☺1.30-3.30pm & 8.30pm-midnight Tue-Sat; MJoanic) With low lighting and an artfully minimalist interior, the 'Bishop's Belly' serves up creative tapas that earn high praise from the mostly local crowd. Feast on grilled razor clams, foie gras with pine nuts and pumpkin, tender morsels of tuna tataki or *picanya* (grilled rump steak) served with chips and Béarnaise sauce.

Top off the meal with a bottle of one of Spain's fine quaffs, like an Albariño white from Galicia (options by the glass are more limited).

LAS DELICIAS
SPANISH €€

(☑93 429 22 02; www.barrestaurantedelicias.com; Carrer de Mühlberg 1; tapas €6-14, mains €8-17; ☺10am-4pm Tue-Sun & 7-10.30pm Tue-Thu, 8-11pm Fri & Sat; MEl Carmel, then bus 86) This welcoming restaurant tucked away in El Carmel makes a fine add-on to an afternoon exploring either nearby Parc Güell or the Bunkers del Carmel. There's a decent selection of tapas on offer as well as heartier grilled meat and seafood dishes. Standouts include classics like *pulpo a gallega* (Galician-style octopus), *jamón ibérico* (cured Iberian ham) and fluffy paella.

PEPA TOMATE
TAPAS €€

Map p280 (☑93 210 46 98; www.pepatomate. com; Plaça de la Revolució de Setembre de 1868, 17; sharing plates €7-17; ☺8pm-1am Mon, 10am-1am Tue-Fri, from 11am Sat; ☻; ⓂFontana, ⓇFGC Gràcia) This casual tapas spot on Plaça de la Revolució de Setembre de 1868 is a popular go-to spot at all hours of the day. Fresh produce takes front and centre on the wide-ranging menu in dishes like penne with vegetables and trumpet mushrooms, fried green tomatoes, and Thai-style vegetable stir-fries. Carnivores can munch on tandoori lamb tacos, Iberian pork croquettes and beef tataki.

It's popular with families (crayons are available, and there's a mini playground at the front). Weekday multicourse lunch specials cost €12.50.

SOL I LLUNA
FRENCH €€

Map p280 (☑93 237 10 52; Carrer de Verdi 50; mains €12-18; ☺8pm-12.30am; ☝; ⓂFontana) Softly lit at night, Sol i Lluna is a peaceful, elegant place that has as its distinguishing feature a giant wooden hippo (frequently topped with a small child) in the window. The food is mostly French, but draws in influences from around the globe, such as the 'lasagne' of ratatouille with goat's cheese or the vegetarian Puy lentil 'meatballs'.

CAFÉ GODOT
INTERNATIONAL €€

Map p280 (☑93 368 20 36; www.cafegodot.com; Carrer de Sant Domènec 19; mains €10-17; ☺10am-1am Mon-Fri, 11am-2am Sat & Sun; ☝; ⓂFontana) Managing to combine spacious, stylish and friendly (especially if you have kids in tow), Godot is a relaxing place for a long lunch or Sunday brunch, with a mouthwatering list of snacks and more substantial dishes, from scallops with Thai-style green curry to to duck confit with lentils and spinach. There's plenty for vegetarians too.

CANTINA MACHITO
MEXICAN €€

Map p280 (☑93 217 34 14; Carrer de Torrijos 47; mains €12-16; ☺1pm-1am; ⓂFontana, Joanic) On the leafy Torrijos street, the colourful Machito – which seems devoted to the image of Frida Kahlo – gets busy with locals, and the outside tables are a great place to

eat and drink until late. You'll find all the standard Mexican delights like quesadillas, tacos and enchiladas, and some wonderfully refreshing iced water flavoured with honey and lime, mint and fruit.

EL GLOP
CATALAN €€

Map p280 (☑93 213 70 58; www.elglop.com; Carrer de Sant Lluís 24; mains €7-20; ☺1pm-midnight Mon-Fri, from noon Sat & Sun; ⓂJoanic) This raucous eatery is decked out in country Catalan fashion, with gingham tablecloths and no-nonsense, slap-up meals. The secret is hearty serves of simple dishes, such as *cordero a la brasa* (grilled lamb), *paella de pescado y marisco* (fish and seafood paella) and appetisers like *berenjenas rellenas* (stuffed aubergines) or *calçots* (spring onions) in winter. To finish try the *tocinillo,* a caramel dessert.

BANNA
THAI €€

Map p280 (☑93 213 30 44; www.bannagracia. es; Plaça de la Revolució de Setembre de 1868 15; mains €9-13; ☺1-4pm & 8pm-midnight Tue-Sun; ⓂFontana) Set on a pretty square in Gràcia, this enticing new eatery brings classical cooking from Thailand to a city much lacking in Southeast Asian options. The menu is quite large, with standouts like fish cakes, beef salad with vegetables and lime juice, prawn soup with coconut milk, fragrant curries, sizzling wok dishes with mixed vegetables, and sticky rice for dessert.

On warm evenings, the tables on the plaza are the place to be.

CON GRACIA
FUSION €€€

Map p280 (☑93 238 02 01; www.congracia.es; Carrer de Martínez de la Rosa 8; set menu €65, with wine pairing €95; ☺7-11pm Tue-Sat; ⓂDiagonal) This teeny hideaway (seating about 20 in total) is a hive of originality, producing delicately balanced Mediterranean cuisine with Asian touches. On offer is a regularly changing surprise tasting menu or the set 'traditional' one, with dishes such as squid stuffed with *jamón ibérico* and black truffle, and juicy black angus steak. Book ahead.

CAN TRAVI NOU
CATALAN €€€

(☑93 428 03 01; www.gruptravi.com; Carrer de Jorge Manrique 8; mains €18-28; ☺1-4pm & 8-11pm; Ⓟ; ⓂMontbau) This expansive 18th-century mansion has several dining areas that stretch out across two floors. The warm colours, grandfather clock and wholesome, rustic air make for a magical setting for a Catalan splurge. Reserve ahead.

It's a bit of a trek getting out here, so plan to make a day of it by visiting the Jardins del Laberint d'Horta (2km away), or Tibidabo or Parc Güell – both are in the general area, though not walkable.

ROIG ROBÍ
CATALAN €€€

Map p280 (🖉93 218 92 22; www.roigrobi.com; Carrer de Sèneca 20; mains €24-40; ⌚1.30-4pm & 8.30-11.30pm Mon-Fri, 8.30-11.30pm Sat; MDiagonal) This is an altar to refined traditional cooking. The menu changes seasonally, and serves as a showcase for beautifully presented creations with local and organic ingredients. Start off with sautéed baby squid with chickpeas or artichokes with foie gras, before moving on to outstanding seafood rice dishes, grilled market fresh fish baked with salt or slow roasted young lamb.

Call ahead to score a table on the elegant, vine-draped back patio.

BOTAFUMEIRO
SEAFOOD €€€

Map p280 (🖉93 218 42 30; www.botafumeiro.es; Carrer Gran de Gràcia 81; mains €20-48; ⌚noon-1am; MFontana) It is hard not to mention this classic temple of Galician shellfish and other briny delights, long a magnet for VIPs visiting Barcelona. You can bring the price down by sharing a few *medias raciones* (large tapas plates) to taste a range of marine offerings.

This is a good place to try *percebes,* the strangely twisted goose barnacles harvested along Galicia's north Atlantic coast, which many Spaniards consider the ultimate seafood delicacy.

🍷 DRINKING & NIGHTLIFE

RABIPELAO
COCKTAIL BAR

Map p280 (🖉93 182 50 35; www.elrabipelao.com; Carrer del Torrent d'En Vidalet 22; ⌚7pm-2am Mon-Sat, 1-4pm & 7pm-2am Sun; MJoanic, Fontana) An anchor of Gràcia's nightlife, Rabipelao is a celebratory space with a spinning disco ball and DJs spinning driving salsa beats. Patrons aside, there's much to look at here: a silent film plays in one corner beyond the red velvety wallpaper-covered walls and there's a richly hued mural above the bar – not to mention the tropical cocktails (mo-

jitos and caipirinhas) and snacks (arepas, ceviche).

There's also a covered patio at the back, and live music from time to time (currently Wednesdays from 8pm).

ELEPHANTA
BAR

Map p280 (🖉93 237 69 06; http://elephanta.cat; Carrer del Torrent d'en Vidalet 37; ⌚6pm-1.30am Mon-Wed, to 2.30am Thu-Sat, 5-10pm Sun; MJoanic, Fontana) This friendly and petite cocktail bar is a fine place to catch up with a friend. It has an old-fashioned vibe, with long plush green banquettes, art-lined walls and a five-seat bar topped with old vintage wooded stools.

Gin is the drink of choice, with more than 40 varieties on hand, and the cocktails are deftly mixed (though be patient, these things take time).

VIBLIOTECA
WINE BAR

Map p280 (🖉93 284 42 02; www.viblioteca.com; Carrer de Vallfogona 12; ⌚6pm-1am Mon-Sat, 7pm-midnight Sun; MFontana) If the smell of ripe cheese doesn't float your boat, this is not the place for you – a glass cabinet piled high with the stuff assaults your olfactory nerves as you walk into this small, white, cleverly designed space. The real speciality at Viblioteca, however, is wine, and you can choose from 150 mostly local labels, many of them available by the glass.

CHATELET
COCKTAIL BAR

Map p280 (🖉93 284 95 90; Carrer de Torrijos 54; ⌚6pm-2am Mon-Fri, noon-2am Sat & Sun; MJoanic, Fontana) A popular meeting point in the 'hood, Chatelet has big windows for watching the passing people parade, and a buzzing art-filled interior that sees a wide cross-section of Gràcia society. Blues or old-school American soul plays in the background, while friends chatter over drinks and light fare (hummus, nachos, sandwiches). The cocktails are excellent, and the drink prices fair (with discounts before 10pm).

LA CIGALE
BAR

Map p280 (🖉93 457 58 23; Carrer de Tordera 50; ⌚6pm-2am Tue-Sun; MJoanic) La Cigale is a very civilised place for a cocktail, with oil paintings on the walls, gilded mirrors and leatherbound volumes scattered about. Prop up the zinc bar, sink into a second-hand lounge chair around a teeny table or head upstairs.

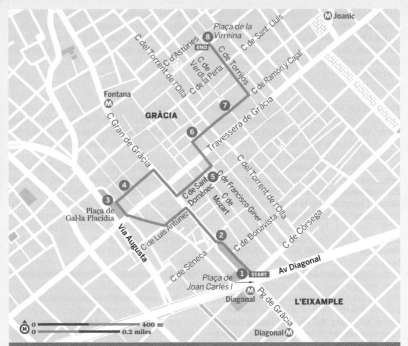

🏃 Neighbourhood Walk
The Squares of Gràcia

START PLAÇA DE JOAN CARLES I
END PLAÇA DE LA VIRREINA
LENGTH 1.9KM; 50 MINUTES

The obelisk at **①Plaça de Joan Carles I** honours Spain's present king for stifling an attempted coup d'état in February 1981, six years after Franco's death.

Where Carrer Gran de Gràcia leads you into Gràcia proper, a grand Modernista edifice now turned hotel, **②Casa Fuster** (p205), rises in all its glory.

③Plaça de Gal·la Placidia recalls the brief sojourn of the Roman empress-to-be Galla Placidia, captive and wife of the Visigothic chief Athaulf in the 5th century AD. She had been hauled across from Italy, where she hastily returned upon her captor-husband's death.

④Plaça de la Llibertat (Liberty Sq) is home to the bustling Modernista produce market of the same name. It was designed by one of Gaudí's colleagues, Francesc Berenguer, who was busy in this part of town de-

spite never having been awarded a diploma as an architect.

Popular **⑤Plaça de la Vila de Gràcia** was, until a few years ago, named after the mayor under whom Gràcia was absorbed by Barcelona, Francesc Rius i Taulet. It is fronted by the local town hall (designed by Berenguer).

Possibly the rowdiest of Gràcia's squares, **⑥Plaça del Sol** (Sun Sq) is lined with bars and eateries and comes to life on long summer nights. The square was the scene of summary executions after an uprising in 1870.

Busy, elongated **⑦Plaça de la Revolució de Setembre de 1868** commemorates the toppling of Queen Isabel II, a cause of much celebration in this working-class stronghold. Today locals gather on benches for a chat or pop into one of the bars or restaurants for refreshment.

Pleasant terraces adorn pedestrianised **⑧Plaça de la Virreina**, presided over by the 17th-century Església de Sant Joan. It was largely destroyed by anarchists during the unrest of the Setmana Tràgica (Tragic Week) of 1909. Rebuilt by Berenguer, it was damaged again during the civil war.

Music is chilled, conversation lively, and you're likely to see Charlie Chaplin in action on the silent flat-screen TV (though FC Barça games are also screened). You can also snack on wok-fried dishes and some of the city's best burgers.

EL SABOR BAR

Map p280 (☎674 997 073; Carrer de Francisco Giner 32; ⏱9pm-3am Tue-Sun; Ⓜ Diagonal) Ruled since 1992 by the charismatic Havana-born Angelito is this home of *ron y son* (rum and sound). A mixed crowd of Cubans and fans of the Caribbean island come to drink mojitos and shake their stuff in this diminutive, good-humoured hang-out. Stop by on Thursdays for a free two-hour salsa lesson (starting at 9.30pm).

LE JOURNAL BAR

Map p280 (☎93 368 41 37; Carrer de Francisco Giner 36; ⏱6pm-2am; Ⓜ Fontana) Students love the conspiratorial basement air of this narrow bar, whose walls and ceiling are plastered with newspapers (hence the name). Read the headlines of yesteryear while reclining in an old lounge. For a slightly more intimate feel, head upstairs to the rear gallery.

LA FOURMI BAR

Map p280 (☎93 213 30 52; Carrer de Milà i Fontanals 58; ⏱9am-2am Mon-Sat, from 10am Sun; Ⓜ Joanic) Just off the beaten path, La Fourmi is a small, cosy spot for a cocktail or a bite no matter the time of day. It draws a mix of students, old-timers and hipsters to its weekday breakfast (and more of the latter for weekend brunch).

RAÏM BAR

Map p280 (Carrer del Progrés 48; ⏱9pm-2am Tue-Sat; Ⓜ Diagonal) The walls in Raïm are alive with black-and-white photos of Cubans and Cuba. Weathered old wooden chairs of another epoch huddle around marble tables, while grand old wood-framed mirrors hang from the walls. It draws a friendly, garrulous crowd who pile in for first-rate mojitos and an excellent selection of rum.

☆ ENTERTAINMENT

SODA ACÚSTIC LIVE MUSIC

Map p280 (☎930 165 590; www.facebook.com/sodacustic; Carrer de les Guilleries 6; tickets from €3; ⏱8pm-2.30am Wed-Sun; Ⓜ Fontana) This low-lit modern space stages an eclectic lineup of bands and performing artists. Jazz, Balkan swing, Latin rhythms and plenty of experimental, not easily classifiable musicians all receive their due. The acoustics are excellent. Check its Facebook page for upcoming shows.

VERDI PARK CINEMA

Map p280 (☎93 238 79 90; www.cines-verdi.com; Carrer de Torrijos 49; Ⓜ Fontana) The Verdi Park is an art-house cinema.

HELIOGÀBAL LIVE MUSIC

Map p280 (www.heliogabal.com; Carrer de Ramón i Cajal 80; ⏱9.30pm-3am Wed-Sat; Ⓜ Joanic) This compact bar is a veritable hive of cultural activity where you never quite know what to expect. Aside from art exhibitions and poetry readings, you will be pleasantly surprised by the eclectic live-music program. Jazz groups are often followed by open jam sessions, and experimental music of all colours gets a run.

While many performers are local, international acts also get a look in.

TEATRENEU THEATRE

Map p280 (☎93 285 37 12; www.teatreneu.com; Carrer de Terol 26; ⏱box office 1hr before show; Ⓜ Fontana, Joanic) This lively theatre (with a bustling, rambling downstairs bar facing the street) dares to fool around with all sorts of material, from monologues to social comedy. Aside from the main theatre, two cafe-style spaces serve as more intimate stage settings for small-scale productions. Films are also shown.

VERDI CINEMA

Map p280 (☎93 238 79 90; www.cines-verdi.com; Carrer de Verdi 32; Ⓜ Fontana) A popular original-language cinema in the heart of Gràcia, handy to lots of local eateries and bars for pre- and post-film enjoyment.

SHOPPING

AMAPOLA VEGAN SHOP CLOTHING

Map p280 (☎93 010 62 73; www.amapolavegan-shop.com; Travessera de Gràcia 129; ⏱11am-2.30pm & 5-8.30pm Mon-Sat; Ⓜ Fontana, Diagonal) A shop with a heart of gold, Amapola proves that you need not toss your ethics aside in the quest for stylish clothing and accessories. You'll find sleek leather alternatives for wallets, handbags and messenger bags by Matt

& Nat, dainty ballerina-style flats by Victoria and elegant scarves by Barts.

Other finds: socks made from bamboo, soft but wool-free gloves and cheeky T-shirts – with slogans like 'Another Fucking Vegan' and 'No como mis amigos' (I don't eat my friends). Morrissey (a lifelong animal rights advocate) plays overhead.

LADY LOQUITA CLOTHING

Map p280 (☏93 217 82 92; www.ladyloquita. com; Travessera de Gràcia 126; ⊗11am-2pm & 5-8.30pm Mon-Sat; MFontana) Lady Loquita is a hip little shop, where you can browse through light summer dresses by Tirala-hilacha, evening wear by Japamala and handmade jewellery by local design label Klimbim. There are also whimsical odds and ends: dinner plates with dog people portraits and digital prints on wood by About Paola.

LA FESTIVAL WINE

Map p280 (☏93 023 22 81; Carrer de Verdi 67; ⊗5.30-9.30pm Mon, 10.30am-9.30pm Tue-Sat, 11am-2pm Sun; MFontana) This handsomely designed shop earns high marks for its knowledgeable (and English-speaking) staff who can give you a wealth of information about the many excellent wines for sale here. Most bottles are from Spanish producers, though there are a few French options, and some organic as well as bio-dynamic wines.

You can also refill your bottle with wine or vermouth from one of the casks at the front, starting at €3 a bottle.

MAGNESIA ACCESSORIES

Map p280 (☏93 119 01 87; www.magnesiabcn. com; Carrer del Torrent de l'Olla 192; ⊗10.30am-2pm & 4.30-8pm Mon-Fri, 10.30am-2pm Sat; MLesseps, Fontana) Tucked away on a quiet corner of Gràcia, Magnesia is a petite store so packed with intrigue that you might want to just giftwrap the whole thing and slip it into your handbag. There are fairy-tale-esque greeting cards, bespoke station-ery, one-of-a-kind framed illustrations, statement-piece jewellery and ceramics (tiny bowls, tea cups), herbal-infused can-dles and chunky puzzles (and other gift ideas) for kids.

PICNIC CLOTHING

Map p280 (☏93 016 69 53; www.picnicstore.es; Carrer de Verdi 17; ⊗11am-9pm Mon-Fri, 11am-2.30pm & 5-9pm Sat; MFontana) This tiny, beautifully curated boutique has many temptations: stylish sneakers by Meyba (a Barcelona brand), striped jerseys from Basque label Loreak Mendian and boldly patterned Mödernaked backpacks. Other finds include animal print ceramics for the home, small-scale art prints and fashion mags.

TINTIN SHOP CHILDREN

Map p280 (☏93 289 25 24; www.tintinshopbcn. com; Travessera de Gràcia 176; ⊗10.30am-2.30pm & 5-8.30pm Mon-Fri, 11am-2.30pm Sat) Fans of the French-speaking boy wonder should make a beeline to this Gràcia store, where you'll find Tintin T-shirts, posters, action figures, book bags, wristwatches, pencil cases, and even a soft, irresistible Milou (Tintin's wire fox terrier) – plus, of course, the books that made him famous (with titles in Spanish, Catalan and French).

**DOCTOR PAPER
BARCELONA** ACCESSORIES, TOYS

Map p280 (☏93 237 58 57; www.doctorpaperbcn. com; Travessera de Gràcia 130; ⊗10.30am-2pm & 5-8.30pm Mon-Sat; ℝFGC Gràcia) Doctor Paper is a fun little shop to explore, with shelves crammed full of whimsical objects and retro crafts. Wind-up robots, make-your-own-aeroplane kits, vintage postcards with irreverent sayings (in Spanish), action figures, painted enamel cups and teapots, glowing mushroom lamps and travel jour-nals with Barcelona street scenes are just a small part of the treasure trove.

SURCO MUSIC

Map p280 (☏93 218 34 39; Travessera de Gràcia 144; ⊗10.30am-2pm & 5.30-9pm Mon-Sat; MFon-tana, FGC Gràcia) Surco is an obligatory stop for music lovers – especially for fans of vinyl. You'll find loads of new and used records and CDs here, with a mix of Tom Waits, Mishima (a Catalan band), Calexico and more.

BE GIFTS

Map p280 (☏93 218 89 49; www.bethestore.com; Carrer de Bonavista 7; ⊗10.30am-9pm Mon-Sat; MDiagonal) Be is a fun place to browse for accessories and gift ideas. Among the eye candy waiting to be unearthed, you'll find rugged vintage-looking satchels, leather handbags, stylish (and reflective) Happy Socks, portable record players, sneakers (Vans, Pumas, old-school Nikes) and gadgets (including richly hued Pantone micro speakers and Polaroid digital cameras).

BODEGA BONAVISTA   WINE
Map p280 (☑93 218 81 99; Carrer de Bonavista 10; ⊙10am-2.30pm & 5-9pm Mon-Fri, noon-3pm & 6-9pm Sat, noon-3pm Sun; MFontana) An excellent little neighbourhood wine shop that endeavours to seek out great wines at reasonable prices. The stock is mostly from Catalonia and elsewhere in Spain, but there's also a good selection from France. The Bonavista also acts as a deli, and there are some especially good cheeses.

HIBERNIAN   BOOKS
Map p280 (☑93 217 47 96; www.hibernian-books. com; Carrer de Montseny 17; ⊙4-8.30pm Mon, 11am-8.30pm Tue-Sat; MFontana) The biggest secondhand English bookshop in Barcelona stocks thousands of titles covering all sorts of subjects, from cookery to children's classics. There is a smaller collection of new books in English too.

MERCAT DE L'ABACERIA CENTRAL   MARKET
Map p280 (Travessera de Gràcia 186; ⊙7am-2.30pm & 5.30-8pm Mon-Sat; MFontana) This sprawling iron and brick market, which dates back to the 1890s, is a fine place to browse for fresh produce, cheeses, bakery items and snack foods. There's also a sushi stand and several food stalls where you can grab a quick bite on the cheap.

🏃 ACTIVITIES

SWING MANIACS   COURSE
Map p280 (☑93 187 69 85; www.swingmaniacs. com; Carrer l'Església 4; group/private 55min class from €12/40; ⊙5pm-midnight Mon-Fri; MJoanic, Fontana) In the last few years, swing dancing has arrived in full force in the Catalan capital with old-fashioned dance parties happening in far-flung corners of the city every night. To learn the moves, sign up for a class at Swing Maniacs. You can join a drop-in class, and if you don't have a partner, one can be arranged for you.

The website lists upcoming events, and Swing Maniacs also hosts its own swing-dancing gatherings (click on School/Tickets for details).

FLOTARIUM   FLOTARIUM
Map p280 (☑93 217 36 37; www.flotarium.com; Plaça de Narcís Oller 3; 1hr session €40; ⊙10am-9pm Mon-Sat; MDiagonal) Be suspended in zero gravity and feel the stress ebb away. Each flotarium, like a little space capsule with water, is in a private room, with shower, towels and shampoo, and Epsom salts that allow you to float as if in the Dead Sea.

AQUA URBAN SPA   SPA
Map p280 (☑93 238 41 60; www.aqua-urbanspa. com; Carrer Gran de Gràcia 7; 90min session from €59; ⊙9am-9pm Mon-Sat; MDiagonal) With sessions for anything from stress to tired legs (helpful for diehard sightseers), this spa offers smallish pool and shower areas, along with steam baths, Roman-style baths and a series of beauty treatment options.

Camp Nou, Pedralbes & La Zona Alta

Neighbourhood Top Five

① **Camp Nou** (p172) Reliving the great moments of one of the world's legendary football teams at the multimedia museum – or, better yet, seeing a game live.

② **Museu-Monestir de Pedralbes** (p165) Walking the 14th-century cloister and gazing at exquisite murals.

③ **CosmoCaixa** (p167) Getting a taste of the Amazon, and travelling through Earth's evolution at warp speed.

④ **Bellesguard** (p166) Gazing upon imposing Gaudí's medieval-like masterpiece, only recently opened to the public.

⑤ **Tibidabo** (p168) Travelling by tram and funicular railway up to lovely views and an old-fashioned amusement park.

For more detail of this area see Maps p282 and p284 ➡

Explore Camp Nou, Pedralbes & La Zona Alta

This vast area, which runs north of L'Eixample and west of Gràcia, includes some intriguing sites. Football and fun parks aside, few people make the journey here, due to the area's relative remoteness and the longer distances between sights. On the upside, you'll have the chance to explore Barcelona off the tourist path.

Nearby Tibidabo is a more recognisable landmark, with the towering church of Temple del Sagrat Cor visible from all over the city. Tibidabo (512m) marks the city's highest point, and its old-fashioned amusement park and fine views are the big attraction. Getting here is half the fun – take an old tram past Modernista mansions, then a steeply inclined funicular railway to the top.

Upmarket Pedralbes has a mix of high-end gated residences and boxy apartment buildings, peaceful streets and manicured gardens hidden off the busy thoroughfares. Standouts include an atmospheric monastery, the elegant Jardins del Palau de Pedralbes, and Gaudí's little-visited Pavellons Güell.

Just south of Pedralbes is Camp Nou, the home of FC Barcelona. To the northeast lies Sarrià, a quaint neighbourhood of brick streets, tiny plazas and medieval buildings. Another area worth exploring is Sant Gervasi, with its handful of upmarket restaurants and bars.

Local Life

➡ **Outdoors** Going for a run or a mountain-bike ride in the vast reserve of Parc de Collserola (p168).

➡ **Nightlife** Having drinks and tapas in El Maravillas (p170) on the very charming Plaça de la Concòrdia, followed by a recital or mini-exhibition at Centre Cívic Can Deu (p172).

➡ **Village days** Wandering through the picturesque narrow lanes of Sarrià, stopping for cakes at Foix De Sarrià (p169), tapas at Bar Tomàs (p169) and a great meal at Vivanda (p169).

Getting There & Away

➡ **Metro** Línia 3 will get you to the Jardins del Laberint d'Horta (Mundet), and Camp Nou and Palau Reial de Pedralbes (Palau Reial).

➡ **Train** FGC trains are handy for getting close to sights in and around Tibidabo and Parc de Collserola.

➡ **Tram** Outside Avinguda Tibidabo station, the *tramvia blau* runs to Plaça del Doctor Andreu, where you can catch an onward funicular up to Tibidabo.

➡ **Funicular** Two funicular railways provide hilltop access: the funicular del Tibidabo runs between Plaça del Doctor Andreu and Plaça del Doctor Tibidabo. The funicular de Vallvidrera runs between Peu del Funicular and Vallvidrera Superior.

Lonely Planet's Top Tip

To make the most of the neighbourhood, try to visit on a weekend. Saturday and Sunday are the most reliable days for getting a tour (offered in English) inside the Pavellons Güell, near Palau Reial de Pedralbes. The weekend is also the best time to catch the tram up to Tibidabo.

✗ Best Places to Eat

➡ Ajoblanco (p169)
➡ Vivanda (p169)
➡ ABaC (p170)
➡ Hisop (p170)
➡ Metropolitan Iradier (p169)
➡ La Balsa (p170)

For reviews, see p167 ➡

🍷 Best Places to Drink

➡ Dô Bar (p171)
➡ El Maravillas (p170)
➡ Mirablau (p171)
➡ Berlin (p171)
➡ The Beer Shop (p171)

For reviews, see p170 ➡

◉ Best Parks & Gardens

➡ Parc de Collserola (p168)
➡ Jardins del Laberint d'Horta (p170)
➡ Jardins del Palau de Pedralbes (p166)
➡ Parc de la Creueta del Coll (p166)

CAMP NOU, PEDRALBES & LA ZONA ALTA

TOP SIGHT
CAMP NOU

A pilgrimage site for football fans from around the world, Camp Nou is one of Barcelona's most hallowed grounds. While nothing compares to the excitement of attending a live match, the Camp Nou Experience is a must for FC Barcelona fans. On this self-guided tour, you'll get an in-depth look at the club, starting with a museum filled with multimedia exhibits, trophies and historical displays, followed by a tour of the stadium.

Camp Nou Experience Museum

Camp Nou Experience begins in FC Barcelona's museum, which provides a high-tech view into the club. Massive touchscreens allow visitors to explore arcane aspects of the legendary team. You can also watch videos of particularly artful goals. Displays delve into the club's history, its social commitment and connection to Catalan identity, and in-depth stats of on-field action. Sound installations include the club's anthem (with translations in many languages) and the match-day roar of the amped-up crowds.

The best bits of the museum itself are the photo section, the goal videos and the views out over the stadium. You can admire the golden boots (in at least one case literally) of great goal scorers of the past and learn about the greats who have played for Barça over the years, including Maradona, Ronaldinho, Kubala and many others. There's even a special area devoted to Lionel Messi, considered by many to be the world's greatest footballer playing the game today.

DON'T MISS

➡ Hearing the rousing Barça anthem sung before FC Barcelona takes the field

➡ The museum's footage of the team's best goals

➡ A self-guided tour of the stadium

PRACTICALITIES

➡ Map p282

➡ ☎902 189900

➡ www.fcbarcelona. com

➡ Gate 9, Avinguda de Joan XXIII

➡ adult/child €23/18

➡ ⏱9.30am-7.30pm daily Apr-Sep, 10am-6.30pm Mon-Sat, to 2.30pm Sun Oct-Mar

➡ Ⓜ Palau Reial

The Stadium

Gazing out across Camp Nou is an experience in itself. The stadium, built in 1957 and enlarged for the 1982 World Cup, is one of the world's biggest, holding 99,000 people. The club has a world-record membership of 173,000.

The self-guided tour of the stadium takes in the team's dressing rooms, heads out through the tunnel, on to the pitch and winds up in the presidential box. You'll also get to visit the television studio, the press room and the commentary boxes. Set aside about 2½ hours for the whole visit. To make the tour, enter at Gate 9 (Avinguda de Joan XXIII near Carrer de Martí i Franquès).

Getting Tickets

Tickets to FC Barcelona matches are available at Camp Nou, online (through FC Barcelona's official website), and through various city locations. Tourist offices sell them – the **branch** (☎93 285 38 34; Plaça de Catalunya 17-S, underground; ⏱8.30am-8.30pm; Ⓜ Catalunya) at Plaça de Catalunya is a centrally located option – as do FC Botiga stores. Tickets can cost anything from €39 to upwards of €250, depending on the seat and match. On match day the ticket windows (at gates 9 and 15) open from 9.15am until kick off. Tickets are not usually available for matches with Real Madrid.

If you attend a game, go early so you'll have ample time to find your seat (this stadium is massive) and soak up the atmosphere.

You will almost definitely find scalpers lurking near the ticket windows. They are often club members and can sometimes get you in at a significant reduction. Don't pay until you are safely seated.

TOP SIGHT
MUSEU-MONESTIR DE PEDRALBES

This peaceful old convent was first opened to the public in 1983 and is now a museum of monastic life. It's full of architectural treasures and provides a fascinating glimpse into centuries past. Perched at the top of busy Avinguda de Pedralbes in what was once unpeopled countryside, the monastery remains a divinely quiet corner of Barcelona. Adjoining the monastery is the sober church, an excellent example of Catalan Gothic.

The Cloister & Chapel

The architectural highlight is the large, elegant, three-storey cloister, a jewel of Catalan Gothic, built in the early 14th century. Following its course to the right, stop at the first chapel, the Capella de Sant Miquel, the murals of which were done in 1346 by Ferrer Bassá, one of Catalonia's earliest documented painters. A few steps on is the ornamental grave of Queen Elisenda, who founded the convent. It is curious, as it is divided in two: the side in the cloister shows her dressed as a penitent widow, while the other part, an alabaster masterpiece inside the adjacent church, shows her dressed as queen.

The Refectory & Sleeping Quarters

As you head around the ground floor of the cloister, you can peer into the restored refectory, kitchen, stables, stores and a reconstruction of the infirmary – all giving a good idea of convent life. Eating in the refectory must not have been a whole lot of fun, judging by the inscriptions around the walls exhorting *Silentium* (Silence) and *Audi Tacens* (Listen and Keep Quiet).

Upstairs is a grand hall that was once the *dormidor* (sleeping quarters). It was lined by tiny night cells, but they were long ago removed. Today a modest collection of the monastery's art, especially Gothic devotional works, and furniture grace this space.

DON'T MISS

➡ Ferrer Bassá's murals
➡ The three-storey Gothic cloister
➡ The refectory's admonishing inscriptions

PRACTICALITIES

➡ Map p282
➡ ☏93 256 34 34
➡ monestirpedralbes. bcn.cat
➡ Baixada del Monestir 9
➡ adult/child €5/free, 3-8pm Sun free
➡ ⊙10am-5pm Tue-Fri, to 7pm Sat, to 8pm Sun
➡ ☐22, 63, 64, 75, ⓡFGC Reina Elisenda

⊙ SIGHTS

CAMP NOU EXPERIENCE　　　　MUSEUM
See p164.

**MUSEU-MONESTIR
DE PEDRALBES**　　　　MONASTERY
See p165.

PARC DE LA CREUETA DEL COLL　　PARK
(Passeig de la Mare de Déu del Coll 77; ⊙10am-sunset; ☻; MPenitents) Not far from Park Güell, this refreshing public park has a pleasant, meandering, splashing pool. The pool, along with swings, showers and a snack bar, makes for a relaxing family stop on hot summer days and is strictly a local affair. The park area is open all year; only the lake-pool closes outside summer.

From the Penitents metro station, it's a 15-minute walk. Enter from Carrer Mare de Déu del Coll. The park is set inside a deep crater left by long years of stone quarrying. On one side of it, an enormous concrete sculpture, *Elogio del Agua* (In Praise of Water) by Eduardo Chillida, is suspended. Wander the trails around the high part of this hill-park and enjoy views of the city and Tibidabo.

JARDINS DEL PALAU DE PEDRALBES　　PARK
Map p282 (Avinguda Diagonal 686; ⊙10am-8pm Apr-Oct, to 6pm Nov-Mar; MPalau Reial) A few steps from busy Avinguda Diagonal lies this small enchanting green space. Sculptures, fountains, citrus trees, bamboo groves, fragrant eucalyptus, towering cypresses and bougainvillea-covered nooks lie scattered along the paths criss-crossing these peaceful gardens. Among the little-known treasures here are a vine-covered parabolic pergola and a gurgling fountain of Hercules, both designed by Antoni Gaudí.

At the north end of the park is the Palau Reial de Pedralbes, an early-20th-century building that belonged to the family of Eusebi Güell (Gaudí's patron) until they handed it over to the city in 1926 to serve as a royal residence. Among its guests have been King Alfonso XIII, the president of Catalonia and General Franco. The *palau* (palace) itself is closed to the public.

BELLESGUARD　　　　ARCHITECTURE
Map p282 (☎93 250 40 93; www.bellesguard-gaudi.com; Carrer de Bellesguard 16; admission €9; ⊙10am-3pm Tue-Sun; ☒FGC Avinguda Tibidabo) This Gaudí masterpiece was recently rescued from obscurity, and opened to the public in 2013. Built between 1900 and 1909, this private residence (still owned by the original Guilera family) has a castle-like appearance with crenellated walls of stone and brick, narrow stained-glass windows, elaborate ironwork and a soaring turret mounted by a Gaudían cross. It's a fascinating work, which combines both Gothic and Modernista elements.

Guided tours in English (€16 per person) happen on weekends at 11am. At other times, you can visit the interior of the building and the grounds with an audioguide that gives historical background. The downside: it's a long walk to a train station, though many buses pass near (including bus 22 and bus 58 from Plaça de Catalunya). Be sure to call before making the trek out – Bellesguard sometimes closes for private events.

PAVELLONS GÜELL　　　　ARCHITECTURE
Map p282 (☎93 317 76 52; Avinguda de Pedralbes 7; guided tours adult/child €4/2; ⊙10am-4pm; MPalau Reial) A short stroll from the Jardins del Palau de Pedralbes are the stables and porter's lodge designed by Gaudí for the Fin-

---

A WANDER THROUGH OLD SARRIÀ

Hugging the left flank of thundering Via Augusta, the old centre of Sarrià is a largely pedestrianised haven of peace. Probably founded in the 13th century and incorporated into Barcelona only in 1921, ancient Sarrià is formed around sinuous **Carrer Major de Sarrià**, today a mix of old and new, with a sprinkling of shops and restaurants.

At its top end is pretty **Plaça de Sarrià** (from where Passeig de la Reina Elisenda de Montcada leads west to the medieval Museu-Monestir de Pedralbes), where you'll want to check out **Foix De Sarrià** (p169), an exclusive pastry shop. As you wander downhill, duck off into **Plaça del Consell de la Vila**, **Plaça de Sant Vicenç de Sarrià** and Carrer de Rocaberti, at the end of which is the **Monestir de Santa Isabel** (Map p282; Carrer de Rocaberti 12; ☒Sarrià), with a neo-Gothic cloister. Built in 1886 to house Clarissan nuns, whose order first set up in El Raval in the 16th century, it was abandoned during the civil war and used as an air-raid shelter.

TOP SIGHT
COSMOCAIXA

Kids (and kids at heart) are fascinated by displays here and the museum has become one of the city's most popular attractions. The single greatest highlight is the re-creation of over 1 sq km of flooded Amazon rainforest (*Bosc Inundat*). More than 100 species of Amazon flora and fauna (including anacondas, colourful poisonous frogs and caimans) prosper in this unique, living diorama in which you can even watch a tropical downpour. In another original section, the Mur Geològic, seven great chunks of rock (90 metric tons in all) have been assembled to create the Geological Wall.

Also worthwhile are the 3D shows in the Planetari (Planetarium), which are screened several times a day. Shows typically run for 35 minutes and cost €4; headsets provide commentary in English and other languages.

These and other displays on the lower 5th floor (the bulk of the museum is underground) cover many fascinating areas of science, from fossils to physics, and from the alphabet to outer space.

Outside, there's a nice stroll through the extensive Plaça de la Ciència, whose modest garden flourishes with Mediterranean flora.

DON'T MISS
➡ A tropical storm in the Amazon
➡ Geological Wall
➡ The Planetarium

PRACTICALITIES
➡ Museu de la Ciència
➡ Map p282
➡ 🕿93 212 60 50
➡ www.fundacio.lacaixa.es
➡ Carrer de Isaac Newton 26
➡ adult/child €4/free
➡ ⏱10am-8pm Tue-Sun
➡ 🚌60, 🚆FGC Avinguda Tibidabo

ca Güell, as the Güell estate here was called. The structures here were built in the mid-1880s, when Gaudí was strongly impressed by Islamic architecture. You can peer inside on guided visits, with English-language tours at 10.15am, 11.15pm and 3pm. Unexpected closures can occur, so it's wise to confirm opening hours before heading out.

One of the most eye-catching features here is the fantastical wrought-iron dragon gate near Avinguda de Pedralbes.

COL·LEGI DE LES TERESIANES ARCHITECTURE
Map p282 (🕿93 212 33 54; Carrer de Ganduxer 85-105; 🚆FGC Les Tres Torres) This striking work by Gaudí has exposed brick pillars and steep catenary arches, each of which is unique. It was built in 1889 for the Order of St Teresa.

OBSERVATORI FABRA OBSERVATORY
Map p282 (🕿93 170 17 97; www.fabra.cat; Carretera del Observatori; admission €15-25; 🚆FGC Avinguda Tibidabo) Inaugurated in 1904, this Modernista observatory is still a functioning scientific foundation. On certain evenings visitors can observe the stars through its grand old telescope (check the website for the latest schedule). Visits, generally in Catalan or Spanish, have to be booked.

From mid-June to mid-September an option is to join in with **Sopars amb Estrelles** (Dinner under the Stars; 🕿93 327 01 21; www.soparsambestrelles.com; Carretera del Observatori; meal & observatory packages €71-119; ⏱mid-Jun–mid-Sep; 🚗), an evening of high-end dining and astronomy.

 **ACTIVITIES**

RITUELS D'ORIENT SPA
Map p284 (🕿93 419 14 72; www.rituelsdorient.com; Carrer de Loreto 50; baths €29; ⏱11am-9pm Sun, Tue & Wed, to 10pm Thu-Sat; Ⓜ Hospital Clínic) Rituels d'Orient offers a setting that resembles a Moroccan fantasy, with dark woods, window grills, candle lighting and ancient-looking stone walls. It's a fine setting for luxuriating in a hammam and indulging in a massage, body scrub or other treatment.

EATING

COMAXURROS CHURROS €
Map p282 (🕿93 417 94 05; Carrer de Muntaner 562; churros from €2; ⏱4.30-8.30pm Tue, 9am-2pm & 5-8.30pm Wed-Sun; 🚆FGC El Putxet) At this

TIBIDABO: GARDENS OF EARTHLY DELIGHTS

Framing the north end of the city, the forest-covered mountain of Tibidabo, which tops out at 512m, is the highest peak in Serra de Collserola. Aside from the superb views from the top, the highlights of Tibidabo include an 8000-hectare **park** (Map p282; ☑93 280 35 52; www.parcnaturalcollserola.cat; Carretera de l'Església 92; ⊙Centre d'Informació 9.30am-3pm, Can Coll 9.30am-3pm Sun & holidays, closed Jul & Aug; ⓕFGC Baixador de Vall-vidrera, funicular Funicular de Vallvidrera), an old-fashioned **amusement park** (Map p282; ☑93 211 79 42; www.tibidabo.cat; Plaça de Tibidabo 3-4; adult/child €30/11; ⊙closed Jan & Feb; ⓠT2A from Plaça de Catalunya), a **telecommunications tower** (Map p282; ☑93 406 93 54; www.torredecollserola.com; Carretera de Vallvidrera al Tibidabo; adult/child €6/4; ⊙noon-2pm & 3.30-8pm Wed-Sun Jul & Aug, noon-2pm & 3.30-6pm Sat & Sun Sep-Dec & Mar-Jun, closed Jan & Feb; ⓠ111, funicular Funicular de Vallvidrera) with viewing platform and a **looming church** (Church of the Sacred Heart; Map p282; ☑93 417 56 86; Plaça de Tibidabo; lift €2.50; ⊙8am-8pm, lift 10am-2pm & 3-7pm; ⓠT2A from Plaça de Catalunya) **FREE** that's visible from many parts of the city. Tibidabo gets its name from the devil, who, trying to tempt Christ, took him to a high place and said, in Latin: *'Haec omnia tibi dabo si cadens adoraberis me'* ('All this I will give you if you fall down and worship me').

To reach the church and amusement park, take an FGC train to Avinguda Tibidabo. Outside Avinguda Tibidabo station, hop on the *tramvia blau*, which runs past fancy Modernista mansions to Plaça del Doctor Andreu (one way €5.50, 15 minutes, every 15 or 30 minutes 10am to 8pm daily late June to early September, 10am to 6pm Sat-urday, Sunday and holidays early September to late June – bus 196 runs the same path). From Plaça del Doctor Andreu the Tibidabo funicular railway climbs to the top of the hill (return €7.70, five minutes). Departures start around 10am and continue until shortly after the Parc d'Atraccions' closing time.

An alternative is bus T2A, the 'Tibibús', from Plaça de Catalunya to Plaça de Tibidabo (€3, 30 minutes, every 30 to 50 minutes on Saturday, Sunday and holidays year-round, and hourly from 10.15am Monday to Friday late June to early September). For Parc de Collserola, take an FGC train to Baixador de Vallvidrera. Alternatively, you can stop one station earlier at Peu del Funicular and ride to the top via funicular railway. Bus 111 runs between Tibidabo and Vallvidrera (passing in front of the Torre de Collserola).

eye-catching little cafe, brought to you by Barcelona's famous *pastelería* Canals, the humble churro receives a dramatic make-over: it's fried in olive oil to crispy (healthier) perfection and served with unique fillings and toppings (pistachio, strawberry sauce, dark chocolate – even cheese, mushrooms and *jamón ibérico* (Iberian ham).

MITJA VIDA   TAPAS €
Map p284 (Carrer de Brusi 39; tapas €3-7; ⊙6-11pm Mon-Thu, noon-4pm & 6-11pm Fri & Sat, noon-4pm Sun; ⓕFGC Sant Gervasi) A fun, youthful, mostly local crowd gathers around the stainless-steel tapas bar of tiny Mitja Vida. It's a jovial eating and drinking spot, with flavourful servings of anchovies, calamari, smoked her-ring, cheeses and *mojama* (salt-cured tuna). The drink of choice is house-made vermouth.

SANTAMASA   CATALAN €
Map p282 (☑93 676 35 74; Carrer Major de Sarrià 97; mains €7-12; ⊙9am-midnight; ⓕFGC Reina

Elisenda) Next door to Sarrià's pretty 18th-century church (Sant Vicenç de Sarrià), Santamassa is an enticing spot for a light meal at any time of day. The menu here is wide-ranging, with a mix of creatively topped *pizzetes* (small pizzas), salads, open-faced sandwiches, fondue, burgers, que-sadillas and good sharing appetisers like hummus and guacamole.

LIADÍSIMO   CAFE €
Map p284 (Carrer de Guillem Tell 23-25; mains €5-9; ⊙7.30am-9.30pm Mon-Fri, 8.30am-9.30pm Sat; ⓜSt Gervasi, Molina) This bright and enticing cafe has an art-loving soul with changing artwork adorning the walls, whimsical light fixtures and a backdrop of films playing silently against a textured back wall. There's also a lush garden, which is a relaxing retreat in which to en-joy the fresh juices and smoothies, sweet or savoury crêpes, pastas, grilled sandwiches and decent coffee.

FOIX DE SARRIÀ
PASTELERÍA €

Map p282 (☑93 203 04 73; www.foixdesarria.
com; Plaça de Sarrià 12-13; desserts €2-5; ⊙8am-
9pm; ⒭FGC Reina Elisenda) Since 1886 this
exclusive pastry shop has been selling the
most exquisite cakes and sweets. You can
take them away or head out the back to sip
tea, coffee or hot chocolate while sampling
the little cakes and other wizardry.

BAR TOMÀS
TAPAS €

Map p282 (☑93 203 10 77; Carrer Major de Sarrià 49; tapas €2.50-5.50; ⊙noon-4pm & 6-10pm
Mon-Sat; ⒭FGC Sarrià) Many *barcelonins* have
long claimed that Bar Tomàs is by far the
best place in the city for *patatas bravas* (potato chunks in a slightly spicy tomato sauce).
Despite the fluorescent lights and friendly
but gruff service, folks from all walks of life
pile in, particularly for lunch on weekends.

Potatoes aside, you'll find fried artichokes, anchovies and other snacks – all
of which go nicely with the ice-cold San
Miguel beer on tap.

METROPOLITAN IRADIER
SPANISH €€

Map p282 (☑93 254 00 55; clubmetropolitan.net;
Carrer de les Escoles Pies 105; prix-fixe lunches
€12-18, mains €11-18; ⊙1-4pm; 🛜☑; ⒭FGC
Sarrià) This lavish health club in the upper
reaches of Barcelona serves an excellent
prix-fixe lunch. It feels quite elegant, but the
friendly service keeps the place from feeling
too snooty. Quinoa salads, oven-baked fish
of the day, pasta with grilled artichokes and
tabbouleh with seasonal vegetables are a few
recent selections. Decent vegetarian options.

VIVANDA
CATALAN €€

Map p282 (☑93 203 19 18; www.vivanda.cat;
Carrer Major de Sarrià 134; sharing plates €8-18;
⊙1.30-3.30pm Tue-Sun & 9-11pm Tue-Sat; ⒭FGC
Reina Elisenda) With a menu designed by celebrated Catalan chef Jordi Vilà, diners are in
for a treat at this Sarrià classic. The changing dishes showcase seasonal fare (like eggs
with truffles, rice with cuttlefish, and artichokes with romesco sauce).

One of Vivanda's best features is the
gardenlike terrace hidden behind the restaurant. With heat lamps, it's open year-round –
blankets and hot broth are distributed to
diners in winter.

BANGKOK CAFE
THAI €€

Map p282 (☑93 339 32 69; Carrer d'Evarist Arnús
65; mains €10-13; ⊙7.45-11pm Tue-Sun & 1-3.30pm
Fri-Sun; ⓜPlaça del Centre) If you're craving

Thai cuisine, it's well worth making the
trip out to Bangkok Cafe, which serves up
spicy green papaya salad, tam yam kung
(spicy prawn soup), crispy prawns with plum
sauce, red curries and other standouts, with
more spice than you'll find in most Catalan
eateries.

It's a small buzzing place with an open
kitchen, photos of the royals (as in Thailand's
king and family), blackboard specials and
an oversized chandelier, which adds a bit of
drama to the space. Enter from the side lane.

AJOBLANCO
TAPAS €€

Map p284 (☑93 667 87 66; www.ajoblancorestau
rant.com; Carrer de Tuset 20; sharing plates €8-
21; ⊙noon-1am Sun-Wed, to 3am Thu-Sat; ☑;
⒭FGC Gràcia) This beautifully designed
space serves up a mix of classic and creative tapas plates that go nicely with the
imaginative cocktail menu. Sip the house
vermouth while munching on crispy aubergine with goat's cheese, slow-roasted lamb
shoulder, or wild sea bass ceviche with
mango and chilli.

5º PINO
CATALAN €€

Map p282 (Quinto Pino; ☑93 252 22 81; www.quinto
pino.es; Passeig de la Bonanova 98; sandwiches
€9-13, tapas €4-8; ⊙8.30am-1.30am Mon-Fri,
10am-1.30am Sat & Sun; 🛜; ⒭FGC Sarrià) While
exploring Sarrià, it's worth detouring a
few blocks east to this charming cafe and
restaurant, which is a favourite local spot
for tasty sandwiches, salads, tortillas, tapas and drinks. It's on a busy road, though
the outdoor, pine-shaded terrace is still a
pleasant spot for a bite. The adjoining playground (best for kids under six) adds to the
appeal for parents with little ones in tow.

CAN CORTADA
CATALAN €€

(☑93 427 23 15; www.gruptravi.com; Avinguda de
l'Estatut de Catalunya; mains €14-28; ⊙1.30-4pm
& 8.30-11.30pm; ⓟ; ⓜMundet) More than anything else, it is the setting and the hearty
welcome that make this 11th-century estate
(complete with the remains of a defensive
tower) worth the excursion. Try for a table in
the former cellars or on the garden terrace.

Grilled meats dominate the menu, though
you'll also find decent appetisers, and seasonal
dishes like artichokes fired up on the grill
and *calçots* (wild spring onions) in winter.

ABAC
CATALAN €€€

Map p282 (☑93 319 66 00; www.abacbarcelona.
com; Avinguda del Tibidabo 1; mains €45-75, tasting

JARDINS DEL LABERINT D'HORTA

These 18th-century gardens, **Jardins del Laberint d'Horta** (☑93 413 24 00; Passeig del Castanyers 1; adult/student €2.23/1.42, free Wed & Sun; ☺10am-sunset; ; ⓜMundet), take their name from the central maze; other paths take you past a pleasant artificial lake, waterfalls, a neoclassical pavilion and a false cemetery. The last is inspired by 19th-century romanticism, characterised by an obsession with a swooning, anaemic (some might say silly) vision of death.

To reach the gardens, take the right exit upstairs at Mundet Metro station; on emerging, turn right and then left along the main road (with football fields on your left), then the first left uphill to the gardens (about five minutes).

The labyrinth, in the middle of these cool gardens (somehow odd in this environment, with modern apartments and ring roads nearby), can be surprisingly frustrating! Aim to reach the centre from the bottom end, and then exit towards the ponds and neoclassical pavilion. This is a good one for kids. Scenes of the film adaptation of Patrick Süskind's novel *Perfume* were shot in the gardens.

Laid out in the twilight years of the 18th century by Antoni Desvalls, Marquès d'Alfarras i de Llupià, this carefully manicured park remained a private family idyll until the 1970s, when it was opened to the public.

Also in the area are two exceptional restaurants: Can Cortada (p169) and Can Travi Nou (p156).

menus €135-165; ☺1.30-4pm & 8.30-11pm Tue-Sat; FGC Av Tibidabo) Led by celebrated chef Jordi Cruz, ABaC offers one of Barcelona's most memorable dining experiences (and also one of its priciest). Expect creative, mouth-watering perfection in dishes like sea urchin curry with lime, guinea fowl with Norway lobster, and roasted sea bass with artichokes and oysters.

HISOP
MEDITERRANEAN €€€

Map p284 (☑93 241 32 33; www.hisop.com; Passatge de Marimon 9; tasting menus from €65; ☺1.30-4pm Mon-Fri & 8.30-11pm Mon-Sat; ⓜDiagonal) Black, white and burgundy dominate the dining room décor at this elegant little eatery just off the beaten path. The seasonal tasting menu is a work of art – you might wind up with a melt-in-your-mouth venison sirloin with a truffle sauce, and for dessert a light chocolate-and-olive ice-cream biscuit with a froth of tofu.

The wine list is impressive and service immaculate.

EL ASADOR DE ARANDA
SPANISH €€€

Map p282 (☑93 417 01 15; www.asadordearanda. com; Avinguda del Tibidabo 31; mains €17-24; ☺1-4.30pm daily, 7.45-11.30pm Mon-Sat; FGC Avinguda Tibidabo) A great place for a meal after visiting Tibidabo, El Asador de Aranda is set in a striking art-nouveau building, complete with stained-glass windows, Moorish-style brick arches and elaborate

ceilings. You'll find a fine assortment of tapas plates for sharing, though the speciality is the meat (roast lamb, spare ribs, beef), beautifully prepared in a wood oven.

LA BALSA
MEDITERRANEAN €€€

Map p282 (☑93 211 50 48; www.labalsarestaurant.com; Carrer de la Infanta Isabel 4; mains €20-28; ☺1.30-3.30pm Tue-Sun & 8.30-11pm Tue-Sat; FGC Avinguda Tibidabo) With its grand ceiling and the scented gardens that surround the main terrace dining area, La Balsa is one of the city's top dining experiences. The menu changes frequently and is a mix of traditional Catalan and off-centre inventiveness. Lounge over a cocktail at the bar before being ushered to your table.

🍷 DRINKING & NIGHTLIFE

EL MARAVILLAS
COCKTAIL BAR

Map p282 (☑93 360 73 78; Plaça de la Concòrdia 15; ☺noon-midnight Mon-Thu, to 2am Fri & Sat; ⓜMaria Cristina) Overlooking the peaceful Plaça de la Concòrdia, El Maravillas feels like a secret hideaway – especially if you've just arrived from the crowded lanes of the *ciutat vella* (old city). The glittering bar has just a few tables, with outdoor seating on the square when the weather warms. Creative cocktails, good Spanish red wines and easy-drinking vermouths are the drinks of choice.

There are several other nearby bars with outdoor seating on the plaza.

THE BEER SHOP
BAR

Map p284 (🖉93 250 84 28; www.thebeershop.es; Carrer d'Amigó 34; ⊙5-10.30pm Mon, 11am-10.30pm Tue & Wed, to 1am Thu-Sat, 11am-2.30pm Sun; 🐕; 🚈FGC Muntaner) Equal parts beer shop and drinking space, this Sant Gervasi spot gathers beer lovers at all hours of the day. If you come to drink (rather than shop), you can grab a table out on the footpath or sit inside chatting with knowledgeable staff while sampling a few of the rotating draughts available. Microbrews from Catalonia, England, Germany and the USA ensure wide variety.

Make the most of the experience by going for a tasting flight (six beers for €9).

DŌ BAR
BAR

Map p284 (🖉93 209 18 88; www.do-bcn.com; Carrer de Santaló 30, entrance on l'Avenir; ⊙7pm-1am Mon-Thu, 8pm-1am Fri & Sat; 🚈FGC Muntaner) This neighbourhood charmer has a warm and inviting interior, where friends gather over tall wooden tables to enjoy excellent gin and tonics, wines by the glass, craft beer and satisfying small plates (anchovies, mussels, tacos, charcuterie). On warm nights, arrive early for one of the terrace tables out the front.

MIRABLAU
BAR

Map p282 (🖉93 418 58 79; www.mirablaubcn.com; Plaça del Doctor Andreu; ⊙11am-4.30am Mon-Thu, 10am-4.30am Fri-Sun; 🚈FGC Avinguda Tibidabo) Gaze out over the entire city from this privileged balcony restaurant on the way up to Tibidabo. Wander downstairs to join the folk in the tiny dance space. In summer you can step out on to the even smaller terrace for a breather.

BERLIN
BAR

Map p284 (🖉93 200 65 42; Carrer de Muntaner 240; ⊙10am-2am Mon-Thu, to 3am Fri & Sat; Ⓜ Diagonal, Hospital Clínic) This elegant corner bar offers views over Avinguda Diagonal. There is a cluster of tables outside on the ground floor and designer lounges downstairs. Service can be harried, but the location is excellent for starting an uptown night. All ages and creeds snuggle in and many kick on to nearby clubs afterwards.

BIKINI
CLUB

Map p282 (🖉93 322 08 00; www.bikinibcn.com; Avinguda Diagonal 547; cover €10-25; ⊙midnight-6am Thu-Sat; 🚌6, 7, 33, 34, 63, 67, 68, Ⓜ Entença) This old star of the Barcelona nightlife scene has been keeping the beat since the darkest days of Franco. Every possible kind of music gets a run, from Latin and Brazilian beats to 1980s disco, depending on the night and the space you choose.

LIZARRAN
BAR

Map p282 (Carrer de Can Bruixa 6; ⊙8am-midnight Sun-Thu, to 2am Fri & Sat; Ⓜ Les Corts) This is a fine pre- or postgame drinking spot if you're catching an FC Barça game at Camp Nou. The beer is plentiful and cheap, there's a decent tapas selection, and on warm days you can sit on the pleasant terrace at the front.

From here it's about a 15-minute walk to the stadium.

CAFE TURÓ
CAFE

Map p284 (Carrer del Tenor Viñas 1; ⊙8.30am-midnight; 🚈FGC Muntaner) This pleasant cafe on the edge of Turó Parc is reminiscent of a Parisian-style cafe, with year-round seating on the footpath at the front – ideal for catching a bit of sun. There's a good selection of bistro plates and tapas.

SALA BECOOL
CLUB

Map p284 (🖉93 362 04 13; www.salabecool.com; Plaça de Joan Llongueras 5; cover €10-18; ⊙midnight-6am Thu-Sun; 🚌27, 32, 59, 66, 67, 68) Electro is the leitmotif in this middle-sized dance place dominated by a single giant mirror ball at the stage end, where earlier in the night you might catch a concert (from 9pm). The secondary Sala Redrum space runs at a slower pace, with indie music to the fore.

SUTTON CLUB
CLUB

Map p284 (www.thesuttonclub.com; Carrer de Tuset 13; cover from €15; ⊙midnight-5am Wed-Sat; Ⓜ Diagonal) A classic disco with mainstream sounds on the dance floor, some hopping house in a side bar and a fair spread of eye candy, this place inevitably attracts just about everyone pouring in and out of the nearby bars at some stage of the evening. The main dance floor is akin to a writhing bear pit. The people are mostly beautiful and the bouncers can be tough.

OTTO ZUTZ
CLUB

Map p284 (www.ottozutz.com; Carrer de Lincoln 15; cover €10-15; ⊙midnight-6am Thu-Sat; ⓇFGC Gràcia) Only beautiful people need apply for entry to this three-floor dance den. DJs come from the Ibiza rave mould.

Shake it all up to house on the ground floor, or head upstairs for funk and soul. The top floor is for VIPs (although at some ill-defined point in the evening the barriers all seem to come down).

☆ ENTERTAINMENT

CAMP NOU
FOOTBALL

Map p282 (☑902 189900; www.fcbarcelona.com; Carrer d'Arístides Maillol; Ⓜ Palau Reial) Among Barcelona's most-visited sites is the massive stadium of Camp Nou (which means New Field in Catalan), home to the legendary Futbol Club Barcelona. Attending a game amid the roar of the crowds is an unforgettable experience. Football fans who aren't able to see a game can get a taste of all the excitement at the Camp Nou Experience (p164), which includes a visit to interactive galleries and a tour of the stadium. The season runs from September to May.

LUZ DE GAS
LIVE MUSIC

Map p284 (☑93 209 77 11; www.luzdegas. com; Carrer de Muntaner 246; tickets up to €20; ⊙Thu-Sat; ☐6, 7, 15, 27, 32, 33, 34, 58, 64, Ⓜ Diagonal) Several nights a week this club, set in a grand former theatre, stages concerts ranging through rock, soul, salsa, jazz and pop. From about 2am, the place turns into a club that attracts a well-dressed crowd with varying musical tastes, depending on the night.

Check the website for the latest schedule. Concerts typically cost around €12, and kick off around 9pm.

CENTRE CÍVIC CAN DEU
CULTURAL CENTRE

Map p282 (☑93 410 10 07; www.cccandeu.com; Plaça de la Concòrdia 13; ⊙9am-10pm Mon-Sat, 10am-2pm Sun, closed Aug; Ⓜ Maria Cristina) Set in a late-19th-century neo-Gothic mansion, this cultural centre stages concerts, exhibitions and workshops throughout the year. It's located on a peaceful plaza, which is dotted with outdoor restaurants.

🛍 SHOPPING

LABPERFUM
BEAUTY

Map p284 (Carrer de Santaló 45; ⊙11am-2pm & 5-8pm Mon-Sat; ⓇFGC Muntaner) This tiny shop looks like an old apothecary, with its shelves lined with pretty glass bottles. What's for sale are extraordinary fragrances (for men and women) made in-house. Scents diverge from run-of-the-mill Obsession, with varieties like tobacco, black orchid and leather. You can also buy scented candles, soaps and creams. Beautiful packaging and fair prices (starting at €14 for 50ml).

TOMATES FRITOS
FASHION

Map p284 (☑93 209 26 17; tomatesfritos.es; Carrer del Tenor Viñas 7; ⊙10.30am-8.30pm Mon-Fri, 10.30am-3pm & 5-8.30pm Sat; ⓇFGC Muntaner) One of a growing number of boutiques along this street, Tomates Fritos is an obligatory stop for design-minded window shoppers, and carries a trove of unique wears.

The cache of global designers includes denim by IRO, handbags by Liebeskind, blouses and jackets by The Kooples and beautifully tailored tops by Scotch & Soda.

MERCAT DE GALVANY
MARKET

Map p284 (www.mercatgalvany.es; Carrer de Santaló 65; ⊙7am-2pm Mon-Sat; ⓇFGC Muntaner) Opened in the 1920s, Galvany is one of the city's most attractive markets, with a brick facade and glass- and cast-iron interior. Stop by for the usual assortment of bakery items, fresh produce and deli goods.

EL CORTE INGLÉS
DEPARTMENT STORE

Map p282 (☑93 366 71 00; www.elcorteingles.es; Avinguda Diagonal 617; ⊙9.30am-9.30pm Mon-Sat; Ⓜ Maria Cristina) A massive shopping centre on busy Avinguda Diagonal. With a supermarket and eateries on hand, it's not a bad option for grabbing a bite before a game at Camp Nou.

L'ILLA DIAGONAL
MALL

Map p282 (☑93 444 00 00; www.lilla.com; Avinguda Diagonal 549; ⊙10am-9.30pm Mon-Sat; Ⓜ Maria Cristina) One of Barcelona's best malls, this is a fine place to while away a few hours (or days), with high-end shops and a mesmerising spread of eateries.

Montjuïc, Poble Sec & Sant Antoni

Neighbourhood Top Five

1 **Museu Nacional d'Art de Catalunya (MNAC)** (p175) Dedicating a day to the world's most important collection of early-medieval art in the Romanesque halls, followed by a masterpiece-filled stroll through six centuries of Catalan art.

2 **Fundació Joan Miró** (p177) Gazing at brilliant works from one of the giants of the art world, all the more captivating inside the light-filled galleries designed by Josep Lluís Sert.

3 **CaixaForum** (p178) Taking in one of the city's best art spaces, a Modernista factory that serves as a showcase for groundbreaking exhibitions.

4 **Museu Etnològic** (p180) Going eye-to-eye with *gegants* (giant papier-mâché figures) while learning about the festivals and folklore of Catalonia.

5 **Cable car** (p179) Admiring the soaring view of the sea and city on a high-flying ride between Barceloneta and Montjuïc.

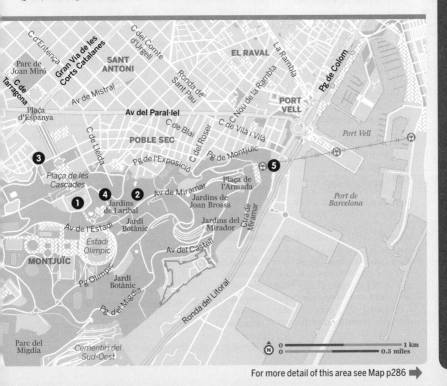

For more detail of this area see Map p286 ➡

Lonely Planet's Top Tip

The Arqueoticket is a special pass, available at tourist offices and participating museums for €14, that allows entry into the Museu d'Arqueologia de Catalunya (MNAC) (p180), the Museu Egipci (p129), the Born Centre de Cultura i Memòria (p95) and the Museu d'Història de Barcelona (p61).

✕ Best Places to Eat

➡ Casa Xica (p183)
➡ Palo Cortao (p182)
➡ Tickets (p184)
➡ Quimet i Quimet (p182)
➡ Tonka (p183)
➡ Federal (p183)

For reviews, see p182➡

🍷 Best Places to Drink

➡ La Caseta del Migdia (p185)
➡ La Terrrazza (p186)
➡ Tinta Roja (p185)
➡ Bar Calders (p184)

For reviews, see p184➡

◉ Best Art Museums

➡ Museu Nacional d'Art de Catalunya (MNAC; p175)
➡ Fundació Joan Miró (p177)
➡ CaixaForum (p178)

Explore Montjuïc, Poble Sec & Sant Antoni

Montjuïc is home to some of the city's finest art collections – the MNAC, the Fundació Joan Miró and CaixaForum – and it hosts several lesser museums, curious sights like Poble Espanyol, the sinister Castell de Montjuïc and the beautiful remake of Mies van der Rohe's 1929 German pavilion. The bulk of the Olympic installations of the 1992 games are also here. Come at night and witness the spectacle of the Font Màgica, several busy theatres and a couple of nightclubs. Throw in various parks and gardens and you have the makings of an extremely full couple of days.

You can approach the hill from Plaça d'Espanya on foot and take advantage of a series of escalators from the west side of the Palau Nacional up to Avingunda de l'Estadi; alternatively, and spectacularly, you can get on to a cable car from La Barceloneta and take in the beautiful aerial views. Another opportunity for a cable-car ride is from Estació Parc Montjuïc to Castell de Montjuïc.

Sloping down the north face of Montjuïc is the tight warren of working-class El Poble Sec. Though short on sights, it hides some of Barcelona's most creative bars and eateries. Cross busy Avinguda del Paral·lel to reach Sant Antoni, a formerly humdrum neighbourhood that's become the epicentre of Barcelona hipsterdom. Vintage-esque cafes, organic eateries and crafty tapas joints are in abundance – particularly along Carrer del Parlament.

Local Life

➡**Hang-outs** For inexpensive tapas with the student crowd, head for Carrer de Blai.

➡**Nightlife** Join the dance party at iconic Sala Apolo (p186), catch a concert at BARTS (p186) or see a cutting-edge performing arts piece at Hiroshima (p186).

➡**Greenery** Join the locals on a stroll through the gardens of Montjuïc and catch all that art on the way.

Getting There & Away

➡**Metro** The closest metro stops to Montjuïc are Espanya, Poble Sec and Paral·lel.

➡**Bus** Bus 150 does a circle trip from Plaça d'Espanya to Castell de Montjuïc. Bus 55 runs across town via Plaça de Catalunya past the Museu d'Arqueologia de Catalunya to the Estació Parc Montjuïc funicular station.

➡**Funicular** Take the metro to the Paral·lel stop and pick up the funicular railway, part of the metro fare system, to Estació Parc Montjuïc.

➡**Cable cars** The Teleférico del Puerto (p179) goes between Torre de Sant Sebastià in Barceloneta and the Miramar stop on Montjuïc. On Montjuïc (1.3km west of the other cable car), the Telefèric de Montjuïc runs from Estació Parc Montjuïc to the Castell de Montjuïc.

⊙ TOP SIGHT
MUSEU NACIONAL D'ART DE CATALUNYA

From across the city, the flamboyant neobaroque silhouette of the Mirador del Palau Nacional can be seen on the slopes of Montjuïc. Built for the 1929 World Exhibition and restored in 2005, it houses a vast collection of mostly Catalan art spanning the early Middle Ages to the early 20th century. The high point is the collection of extraordinary Romanesque frescoes.

The Romanesque Masterpieces

The Romanesque art section is considered the most important concentration of early medieval art in the world. Rescued from neglected country churches across northern Catalonia in the early 20th century, the collection consists of 21 frescoes, woodcarvings and painted altar frontals (low-relief wooden panels that were the forerunners of the elaborate altarpieces that adorned later churches). The insides of several churches have been recreated and the frescoes – in some cases fragmentary, in others extraordinarily complete and alive with colour – have been placed as they were when in situ.

The first of the two most striking frescoes, in Sala 7, is a magnificent image of Christ in Majesty done around 1123. Based on the text of the Apocalypse, we see Christ enthroned with the world at his feet. He holds a book open with the words *Ego Sum Lux Mundi* (I am the Light of the World) and is surrounded by the four Evangelists. The images were taken from the apse of the Església de Sant Climent de Taüll in northwest Catalonia. Nearby in Sala 9 are frescoes done around the same time in the nearby Església de Santa Maria de Taüll. This time the central image taken from the apse is of the Virgin Mary and Christ Child. These images were not mere decoration but tools of instruction in the basics of

DON'T MISS

➡ The Romanesque pieces
➡ Gothic artworks
➡ The paintings of the Cambo Bequest and Thyssen-Bornemisza collections
➡ 1930s Spanish Civil War posters

PRACTICALITIES

➡ Map p286
➡ ☎93 622 03 76
➡ www.museu nacional.cat
➡ Mirador del Palau Nacional
➡ adult/student/child €12/8.40/free, after 3pm Sat & 1st Sun of month free
➡ ⊙10am-8pm Tue-Sat, to 3pm Sun May-Sep, to 6pm Tue-Sat Oct-Apr
➡ Ⓜ Espanya

THE FRESCO STRIPPERS

The Stefanoni brothers, Italian art restorers, brought the secrets of *strappo* (stripping of frescoes from walls) to Catalonia in the early 1900s. The Stefanoni would cover frescoes with a sheet of fabric, stuck on with a glue made of cartilage. When dry, this allowed the image to be stripped off the wall and rolled up. For three years the Stefanoni roamed the Pyrenean countryside, stripping churches and sending the rolls back to Barcelona, where they were eventually put back up on walls to reflect how they had originally appeared.

TOP TIPS

➡ If you're on a museum rampage, you can save money by purchasing the Articket (p237), a pass that will give you discounted admission to six museums (including MNAC).

➡ Be sure to take in the fine view from the terrace just in front of the museum. It draws crowds around sunset.

➡ Another fine viewpoint is on the museum's roof terrace, where drinks are available.

Christian faith for the local population – try to set yourself in the mind of the average medieval citizen: illiterate, ignorant, fearful and in most cases eking out a subsistence living. These images transmitted the basic personalities and tenets of the faith and were accepted at face value by most.

The Gothic Collection

Opposite the Romanesque collection on the ground floor is the museum's Gothic art section. In these halls you can see Catalan Gothic painting and works from other Spanish and Mediterranean regions. Look out especially for the work of Bernat Martorell in Sala 25 and Jaume Huguet in Sala 26. Among Martorell's works figure images of the martyrdom of St Vincent and St Llúcia. Huguet's *Consagració de Sant Agustí,* in which St Augustine is depicted as a bishop, is dazzling in its detail.

The Cambò Bequest & the Thyssen-Bornemisza Collection

As the Gothic collection draws to a close, you pass through two separate and equally eclectic private collections. The Cambò Bequest by Francesc Cambó spans the history of European painting between the 14th century and the beginning of the 19th century, and the Thyssen-Bornemisza collection presents a selection of European painting and sculpture produced between the 13th and the 18th centuries on loan to the MNAC by the Museo Thyssen-Bornemisza in Madrid. The Thyssen-Bornemisza collection's highlight is Fra Angelico's *Madonna of Humility,* whereas the Cambò Bequest holds wonderful works by masters Veronese, Titian and Canaletto, particularly. Cranach, Titian, El Greco, Rubens and even Gainsborough also feature, but the collection's finale is examples of work by Francisco de Goya.

Modern Catalan Art

Up on the next floor, the collection turns to modern art, mainly but not exclusively Catalan. This collection is arranged thematically: Modernisme, Noucentisme, Art and the Civil War and so on. Among the many highlights: an early Salvador Dalí painting *(Portrait of My Father),* Juan Gris' collage-like paintings, the brilliant portraits of Marià Fortuny, and 1930s call-to-arms posters against the Francoist onslaught (nearby you'll find photos of soldiers and bombed-out city centres). There are works by Modernista painters Ramon Casas and Santiago Rusiñol, as well as Catalan luminary Antoni Tàpies.

Also on show are items of Modernista furniture and decoration, which include a mural by Ramon Casas (the artist and Pere Romeu on a tandem bicycle) that once adorned the legendary bar and restaurant Els Quatre Gats.

TOP SIGHT
FUNDACIÓ JOAN MIRÓ

Joan Miró, the city's best-known 20th-century artistic progeny, bequeathed this art foundation to his home town in 1971. Its light-filled buildings, designed by close friend and architect Josep Lluís Sert (who also built Miró's Mallorca studios), are crammed with seminal works, from Miró's earliest timid sketches to paintings from his last years.

Sert's Temple to Miró's Art

Sert's shimmering white temple to one of Spain's artistic luminaries is considered one of the world's most outstanding museum buildings. The architect designed it after spending many of Franco's dictatorship years in the USA as the head of the School of Design at Harvard University. The foundation rests amid the greenery of the mountains and holds the greatest single collection of the artist's work, containing around 220 of his paintings, 180 sculptures, some textiles and more than 8000 drawings spanning his entire life. Only a small portion is ever on display.

The Collection

The exhibits give a broad impression of Miró's artistic development. The first couple of rooms (11 and 12) hold various works, including a giant tapestry in his trademark primary colours. Along the way, you'll pass *Mercury Fountain* by Alexander Calder, a rebuilt work that was originally created for the 1937 Paris Fair and represented Spain at the Spanish Republic's Pavilion. Room 13, a basement space called Espai 13, leads you downstairs to a small room for temporary exhibitions.

After visiting Room 13, climb back up the stairs and descend to two other basement rooms 14 and 15. Together labelled Homenatge a Joan Miró (Homage to Joan Miró), this space is dedicated to photos of the artist, a 15-minute video on his life and a series of works from some of his contemporaries, like Henry Moore, Antoni Tàpies, Eduardo Chillida, Yves Tanguy, Fernand Léger and others.

Returning to the main level, you'll find Room 16, the Sala Joan Prats, with works spanning the early years until 1919. Here you can see how the young Miró moved away, under surrealist influence, from his relative realism (for instance his 1917 painting *Ermita de Sant Joan d'Horta*, with obvious Fauvist influences) towards his own unique style that uses primary colours and morphed shapes symbolising the moon, the female form and birds.

This theme is continued upstairs in Room 17, the Sala Pilar Juncosa (named after his wife), which covers the years 1932–55, his surrealist years. Rooms 18 and 19 contain masterworks of the years 1956–83, and Room 20 a series of paintings done on paper. Room 21 hosts a selection of the private Katsuta collection of Miró works from 1914 to 1974. Room 22 rounds off the permanent exhibition with some major paintings and bronzes from the 1960s and 1970s.

The museum library contains Miró's personal book collection.

The Garden

Outside on the eastern flank of the museum is the Jardí de les Escultures, a small garden with various pieces of modern sculpture. The green areas surrounding the museum, together with the garden, are perfect for a picnic in the shade, after a hard day's sightseeing.

DON'T MISS

→ Sert's architectural design
→ Masterworks in Rooms 18 and 19
→ Miró's move to surrealism, Room 17
→ The sculpture garden

PRACTICALITIES

→ Map p286
→ ☎93 443 94 70
→ www.fmirobcn.org
→ Parc de Montjuïc
→ adult/child €12/free
→ ⏰10am-8pm Tue-Sat, to 9pm Thu, to 2.30pm Sun & holidays
→ 🛜
→ 🚌55, 150, funicular Paral·lel

MONTJUÏC, POBLE SEC & SANT ANTONI FUNDACIÓ JOAN MIRÓ

◉ SIGHTS

**MUSEU NACIONAL D'ART
DE CATALUNYA (MNAC)**   MUSEUM
See p175.

FUNDACIÓ JOAN MIRÓ   MUSEUM
See p177.

CAIXAFORUM   GALLERY
Map p286 (✆93 476 86 00; www.fundacio.lacaixa.
es; Avinguda de Francesc Ferrer i Guàrdia 6-8;
adult/student & child €4/free, 1st Sun of month
free; ◔10am-8pm; P ✿; ⓜEspanya) The Caixa
building society prides itself on its involve-
ment in (and ownership of) art, in particular all that is contemporary. Its premier art
expo space in Barcelona hosts part of the
bank's extensive collection from around the
globe. The setting is a completely renovated
former factory, the Fàbrica Casaramona,
an outstanding Modernista brick structure
designed by Puig i Cadafalch. From 1940 to
1993 it housed the First Squadron of the police cavalry unit – 120 horses in all.

Now it is home to a major exhibition
space. On occasion portions of La Caixa's
own collection of 800 works of modern and
contemporary art go on display, but more
often than not major international exhibitions are the key draw.

In the courtyard where the police horses
used to drink is a steel tree designed by the
Japanese architect Arata Isozaki. Musical
recitals are sometimes held in the museum,
especially in the warmer months.

CASTELL DE MONTJUÏC   FORTRESS, GARDENS
Map p286 (✆93 256 44 45; www.bcn.cat/castellde
montjuic; Carretera de Montjuïc 66; adult/child
€5/free, after 3pm Sun free; ◔10am-8pm Apr-Oct,
to 6pm Nov-Mar; ⬚150, Telefèric de Montjuïc, Castell de Montjuïc) This forbidding *castell* (castle
or fort) dominates the southeastern heights
of Montjuïc and enjoys commanding views
over the Mediterranean. It dates, in its present form, from the late 17th and 18th centuries. For most of its dark history, it has been
used to watch over the city and as a political
prison and killing ground.

An exhibition space in several of the
rooms of the castle explains the history of
the place, with archaeological finds from
prehistoric days to its role as medieval bea-
con and its later days as a strategic bastion.
Most interesting (and disturbing) is the
exhibition devoted to the imprisonments,
trials and executions that happened here.

Don't miss the tombstones (some dating
from the 11th century) from the one-time
Jewish cemetery on Montjuïc.

The views from the castle and the surrounding area looking over the sea, port
and city below are the best part of making the trip here. Around the seaward foot
of the castle is an airy walking track, the
Camí del Mar, which offers breezy views of
the city and sea.

From the **Jardins del Mirador** (◔10am-
sunset; cable car Telefèric de Montjuïc, Mirador),
opposite the Mirador (Telefèric) station,
you have fine views over the port of Barcelona. A little further downhill, the **Jardins
de Joan Brossa** (◔10am-sunset; cable car Telefèric de Montjuïc, Mirador) FREE are charming,
landscaped gardens on the site of a former
amusement park near **Plaça de la Sardana**.
These gardens contain many Mediterranean
species, from cypresses to pines and a few
palms. There are swings and things, thematic walking trails and some good city views.

FONT MÀGICA   FOUNTAIN
Map p286 (✆93 316 10 00; Avinguda de la Reina
Maria Cristina; ◔every 30min 7-9pm Fri & Sat
Nov-Mar, 9.30-11pm Thu-Sun Apr-Oct; ⓜEspanya)
A huge fountain that crowns the long sweep
of the Avinguda de la Reina Maria Cristina
to the grand facade of the Palau Nacional,
Font Màgica is a unique performance in
which the water can look like seething fire-
works or a mystical cauldron of colour.

It is wonderful that an idea that was
cooked up for the 1929 World Exposition
has, since the 1992 Olympics, again become
a magnet. With a flourish, the 'Magic Fountain' erupts into a feast of musical, backlit
aquatic life. On hot summer evenings especially, this 15-minute spectacle (repeated
several times throughout the evening) mes-
merises onlookers. On the last evening of the
Festes de la Mercè in September, a particularly spectacular display includes fireworks.

**PAVELLÓ MIES
VAN DER ROHE**   ARCHITECTURE
Map p286 (✆93 423 40 16; www.miesbcn.com;
Avinguda de Francesc Ferrer i Guàrdia 7; adult/
child €5/free; ◔10am-6pm; ⓜEspanya) The
Pavelló Mies van der Rohe is a work of
artful simplicity that is emblematic of the
modernist movement. The structure has
been the subject of many studies and in-
terpretations, and it has inspired several
generations of architects. That said, unless
you're an avid architecture fan, there isn't

much to see inside beyond what you can glean from the building's exterior.

Designed in 1929 by Ludwig Mies van der Rohe (1886–1969) as the Pavelló Alemany (German Pavilion) for the World Exhibition, it was removed after the show and reconstructed only in 1980, after the building had been consistently referred to as one of the key works of modern architecture. The Pavelló was built using glass, steel and marble, reflecting Mies van der Rohe's originality in the use of materials – he admired their visual rigour and precision, and their embodiment of modernity.

POBLE ESPANYOL   CULTURAL CENTRE

Map p286 (www.poble-espanyol.com; Avinguda de Francesc Ferrer i Guàrdia 13; adult/child €12/7; ⊙9am-8pm Mon, to midnight Tue-Thu & Sun, to 3am Fri & Sat; ⬜13, 23, 150, ⓜEspanya) Welcome to Spain! All of it! This 'Spanish Village' is both a cheesy souvenir hunters' haunt and an intriguing scrapbook of Spanish architecture built for the Spanish crafts section of the 1929 World Exhibition. You can meander from Andalucía to the Balearic Islands in the space of a couple of hours, visiting surprisingly good copies of Spain's characteristic buildings.

You enter from beneath a towered medieval gate from Ávila. Inside, to the right, is an information office with free maps. Straight ahead from the gate is the Plaza Mayor (Town Sq), surrounded with mainly Castilian and Aragonese buildings. It is sometimes the scene of summer concerts. Elsewhere you'll find an Andalucian *barrio* (district), a Basque street, Galician and Catalan quarters, and even a Dominican monastery (at the eastern end). The buildings house dozens of restaurants, cafes, bars, craft shops and workshops (for glass artists and other artisans), and some souvenir stores.

Spare some time for the **Fundació Fran Daurel** (Map p286; www.fundaciofrandaurel. com; ⊙10am-7pm), an eclectic collection of 300 works of art, including sculptures, prints, ceramics and tapestries by modern artists ranging from Picasso and Miró to more contemporary figures, such as Miquel Barceló. The foundation also has a sculpture garden, boasting 27 pieces, nearby within the grounds of Poble Espanyol (look for the Montblanc gate). Frequent temporary exhibitions broaden the offerings further.

Children's groups can participate in the Joc del Sarró. Accompanied by adults, the kids go around the *poble* seeking the answers to various mysteries outlined in a kit distributed to each group. Languages catered for include English.

ⓘ MAR I MUNTANYA (SEA & MOUNTAIN)

The quickest way from the beach to the mountain is via the **Teleférico del Puerto** (Map p286; www.telefericodebarcelona.com; Av de Miramar, Jardins de Miramar; one way/return €11/16.50; ⊙11am-7pm Mar-Oct, to 5:30pm Nov-Feb; ⬜50, 153), a cable car that runs between Torre de Sant Sebastià in Barceloneta and the Miramar stop on Montjuïc. From Estació Parc Montjuïc, this cable car carries you to the Castell de Montjuïc via the Mirador (a lookout point).

JARDINS DE JOAN MARAGALL   GARDENS

Map p286 (Avinguda dels Montanyans 48; ⊙10am-3pm Sat & Sun; ⓜPlaça Espanya) FREE Near the Estadi Olímpic, make a detour to explore the lovely but little visited Jardins de Joan Maragall. Lush lawns, ornamental fountains, photogenic sculptures and a neo-classical palace (the Spanish royal family's residence in Barcelona) set these gardens apart from the other green spaces on Montjuïc. The catch: the grounds are only open on weekends.

ESTADI OLÍMPIC LLUÍS COMPANYS   STADIUM

Map p286 (☎93 426 20 89; www.estadiolimpic.cat; Avinguda de l'Estadi; ⊙8am-8pm May-Sep, 10am-6pm Oct-Apr; ⬜150) FREE The Estadi Olímpic was the main stadium of Barcelona's Olympic Games. If you saw the Olympics on TV, the 65,000-capacity stadium may seem surprisingly small. So might the Olympic flame holder into which an archer spectacularly fired a flaming arrow during the opening ceremony. The stadium was opened in 1929 and restored for the 1992 Olympics.

MUSEU OLÍMPIC I DE L'ESPORT   MUSEUM

Map p286 (☎93 292 53 79; www.museuolimpicbcn.com; Avinguda de l'Estadi 60; adult/student €5.10/3.20; ⊙10am-8pm Tue-Sat, 10am-2.30pm Sun; ⬜55, 150) The Museu Olímpic i de L'Esport is an information-packed interactive museum dedicated to the history of sport and the Olympic Games. After picking up tickets, you wander down a ramp that snakes below ground level and is lined

MONTJUÏC, POBLE SEC & SANT ANTONI SIGHTS

with displays on the history of sport, starting with the ancients.

MUSEU D'ARQUEOLOGIA
DE CATALUNYA
MUSEUM

Map p286 (MAC; ☎93 423 21 49; www.mac.cat; Passeig de Santa Madrona 39-41; adult/student €4.50/3.50; ⏱9.30am-7pm Tue-Sat, 10am-2.30pm Sun; ⓂPoble Sec) This archaeology museum, housed in what was the Graphic Arts palace during the 1929 World Exhibition, covers Catalonia and cultures from elsewhere in Spain. Items range from copies of pre-Neanderthal skulls to lovely Carthaginian necklaces and jewel-studded Visigothic crosses.

There's good material on the Balearic Islands (Rooms X to XIII) and Empúries (Emporion, the Greek and Roman city on the Costa Brava; Rooms XIV and XVII). The Roman finds upstairs were mostly dug up in and around Barcelona. The most beautiful piece is a mosaic depicting Les Tres Gràcies (The Three Graces), unearthed near Plaça de Sant Jaume in the 18th century. Another is of Bellerophon and the Chimera. In the final room, dedicated to the dying centuries of the Roman world, a beautiful golden disc depicting Medusa stands out. The museum has been renovated slowly over recent years, and the displays are now updated with a more modern design and interactive displays.

MUSEU ETNOLÒGIC
MUSEUM

Map p286 (www.museuetnologic.bcn.cat; Passeig de Santa Madrona 16-22; adult/child €5/3; ⏱10am-7pm Tue-Sat, to 8pm Sun; ⓐ55) Barcelona's ethnology museum presents an intriguing permanent collection that delves into the rich heritage of Catalunya. Exhibits cover origin myths, religious festivals, folklore, and the blending of the sacred and the secular (along those lines, don't miss the Nativity scene with that quirky Catalan character *el caganer*, aka 'the crapper').

The collection also has instruments and archive images of traditional dances from the Catalan Pyrenees, plus accoutrements of bygone days showcasing the region's blacksmiths, winemakers, weavers, apothecaries, shepherds, potters, toymakers and even *saurí* ('diviners'; those tasked with finding water and hidden things). There are also several *gegants* (massive figures made of papier-mâché) depicting King Jaume I and Queen Violant. You can also check out a dragon and devil costumes used in *correfocs*

(fire runs), which still figure prominently in Catalan festivals.

JARDÍ BOTÀNIC
GARDENS

Map p286 (www.museuciencies.cat; Carrer del Doctor Font i Quer 2; adult/child €3.50/free, after 3pm Sun free; ⏱10am-7pm Apr-Sep, to 5pm Oct-Mar; ⓐ55, 150) This garden is dedicated to Mediterranean flora and has a collection of some 40,000 plants and 1500 species that thrive in areas with a climate similar to that of the Mediterranean, such as the Eastern Mediterranean, Spain (including the Balearic and Canary Islands), North Africa, Australia, California, Chile and South Africa.

MUHBA REFUGI 307
HISTORIC SITE

Map p286 (☎93 256 21 22; www.museuhistoria. bcn.cat; Carrer Nou de la Rambla 169; incl tour adult/child €3.40/free; ⏱tours 10.30am, 11.30am & 2.30pm Sun; ⓂParal·lel) Part of the Museu d'Història de Barcelona (MUHBA), this is a shelter that dates back to the days of the Spanish Civil War. Barcelona was the city most heavily bombed from the air during the war and had more than 1300 air-raid shelters. Local citizens started digging this one under a fold of Montjuïc in March 1937.

Over the course of the next two years, the web of tunnels was slowly extended to 200m, with a theoretical capacity for 2000 people. People were not allowed to sleep overnight in the shelter – when raids were not being carried out work continued on its extension. Vaulted to displace the weight above the shelter to the clay brick walls (clay is porous, which allowed the bricks to absorb the shock waves of falling bombs without cracking), the tunnels were narrow and winding. Coated in lime to seal out humidity and whitewashed to relieve the sense of claustrophobia, they became a second home for many El Poble Sec folks.

It's open only on Sundays by tour only. Tours are conducted in English at 10.30am, Spanish at 11.30am and Catalan at 12.30pm. Reserve ahead.

JARDINS DE MOSSÈN
CINTO DE VERDAGUER
GARDENS

Map p286 (www.bcn.cat/parcsijardins; ⏱10am-sunset; ⓐ55, 150) Near the Estació Parc Montjuïc funicular/Telefèric station are the ornamental Jardins de Mossèn Cinto de Verdaguer. These sloping, verdant gardens are home to various kinds of bulbs and aquatic plants. Many of the former (some 80,000) have to be replanted each year.

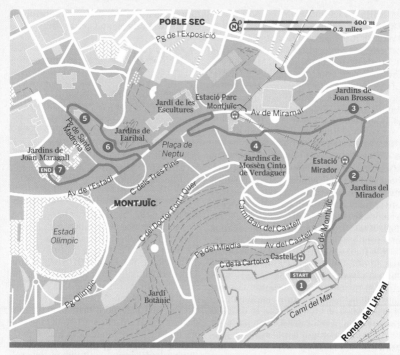

🏃 Neighbourhood Walk
Views & Gardens On Montjuïc

START CASTELL DE MONTJUÏC
END JARDINS DE JOAN MARAGALL
LENGTH 3KM; 1½ HOURS

Long synonymous with oppression, the dark history of ① **Castell de Montjuïc** (p178) is today overshadowed by the fine views it commands over the city and sea. (Don't miss the little sea-facing trail behind the fortress.) The ride up on the Telefèric is the perfect way to get there.

A short stroll down the road or the parallel Camí del Mar pedestrian trail leads to another fine viewpoint over the city and sea, the ② **Jardins del Mirador** (p178). Take the weight off on the park benches or pick up a snack.

Further downhill is the multitiered ③ **Jardins de Joan Brossa** (p178). The entrance is on the left just beyond Plaça de la Sardana, with the sculpture of people engaged in the classic Catalan folk dance. More fine city views can be had from among the many Mediterranean trees and plants.

Exiting the Jardins de Joan Brossa at the other (west) side, you cross Camí Baix del

Castello to the painstakingly laid-out ④ **Jardins de Mossèn Cinto de Verdaguer** (p180). This is a beautiful setting for a slow meander among tulip beds and water lilies.

Dropping away behind the Fundació Joan Miró, the ⑤ **Jardins de Laribal** comprise a combination of terraced gardens linked by paths and stairways. The pretty sculpted watercourses along some of the stairways were inspired by Granada's Muslim-era palace of El Alhambra.

While in the gardens, you can take a break for a meal if hunger strikes. ⑥ **La Font del Gat** has a lovely and spacious terrace dotted with orange trees and surrounded by greenery. It has a menu of fine dishes, which are a touch on the pricey side (you're paying for the view).

Continue walking west, past the Estadi Olímpic to reach ⑦ **Jardins de Joan Maragall** (p179), only open on weekends (10am to 3pm). Lush lawns, ornamental fountains, photogenic sculptures and a neo-classical palace (the Spanish royal family's residence in Barcelona) set these gardens apart.

JARDINS DE MOSSÈN COSTA I LLOBERA GARDENS

Map p286 (Carretera de Miramar 1; ⊙10am-sunset; cable car Transbordador Aeri, Miramar) FREE
Towards the foot of the part of Montjuïc below the castle, above the thundering traffic of the main road to Tarragona, the Jardins de Mossèn Costa i Llobera have a good collection of tropical and desert plants – including a veritable forest of cacti.

PLAÇA D'ESPANYA & AROUND SQUARE, NEIGHBOURHOOD

Map p286 (⊠Espanya) The whirling roundabout of Plaça d'Espanya, distinguished by its so-called Venetian towers (because they are vaguely reminiscent of the belltower in Venice's St Mark's Square), was built for the 1929 World Exhibition and is the junction of several major thoroughfares.

It is flanked on its northern side by the facade of the former Les Arenes bullring. Built in 1900 and once one of three bullrings in the city, it was recently converted into a shopping and leisure centre by Lord Richard Rogers. There are good views of the city from its 4th-floor rooftop terrace.

Behind the bullring is the **Parc de Joan Miró** (Carrer de Tarragona; ⊠Tarragona), created in the 1980s – worth a quick detour for Miró's phallic sculpture *Dona i Ocell* (Woman and Bird) in the western corner. Locals know the park (which apart from the Miró is a dispiriting affair) as the Parc de l'Escorxador (Abattoir Park), after the slaughterhouse that once stood here – unsurprisingly given the proximity to the bullring.

A couple of blocks west and just south of Estació Sants is **Parc d'Espanya Industrial** (Carrer de Sant Antoni, Sants; ⊙10am-sunset; ⊠Estació Sants) with ponds, little waterfalls and children's swings.

🏃 ACTIVITIES

PISCINES BERNAT PICORNELL SWIMMING

Map p286 (☎93 423 40 41; www.picornell.cat; Avinguda de l'Estadi 30-38; adult/child €12/8, nudist hours €7/5; ⊙6.45am-midnight Mon-Fri, 7am-9pm Sat, 7.30am-4pm Sun; ☐150) Barcelona's official Olympic pool on Montjuïc. Admission also includes use of fitness room, sauna, Jacuzzi, steam bath and track. On Saturday nights, between 9pm and 11pm, the pool (with access to sauna and steam bath) is open only to nudists. On Sundays between

October and May the indoor pool also opens for nudists only from 4.15pm to 6pm.

🍴 EATING

SPICE CAFE €

Map p286 (http://spicecafe.es; Carrer de Margarit 13; desserts around €4; ⊙4-9pm Tue-Thu, 11am-9pm Fri-Sun; 🎧; ⊠Poble Sec) Spice is a delightful cafe that's earned quite a following (among expats and locals) for its delicious homemade desserts – especially its moist, creamy carrot cake (the best in town). Good coffees, loose-leaf teas, friendly English-speaking staff and heavenly temptations in the glass front counter may inspire multiple visits.

SECO BAR SPANISH €

Map p286 (☎93 329 63 74; www.bar-seco.com; Passeig de Montjuïc 74; tapas €5-10, sandwiches €5-10; ⊙9am-5pm Mon, to 1am Tue-Sat, 10am-6pm Sun; 🎧🍴; ⊠Poble Sec) 🍴 A neighbourhood classic below Montjuïc, Seco Bar focuses on organic, sustainable and seasonal ingredients in its tasty but uncomplicated tapas plates, salads, sandwiches and daily specials. Top picks include a meaty vegan burger, best enjoyed with one of the craft beers, or perhaps a vermouth. On sunny days, you'll need to go early to score an outdoor table just opposite the restaurant. Outside of the warmer months Seco Bar opens during the day only.

★PALO CORTAO TAPAS €€

Map p286 (☎93 188 90 67; www.palocortao.es; Carrer de Nou de la Rambla 14; mains €10-15; ⊙8pm-1am Tue-Sun & 1-5pm Sat & Sun; ⊠Paral·lel) Palo Cortao has a solid reputation for its beautifully executed seafood and meat dishes, served at fair prices. Highlights include octopus with white bean hummus, skirt steak with foie armagnac, and tuna tataki tempura. You can order half sizes of all plates – which will allow you to try more dishes.

It has an eye-catching design, with geometric tile floors, exposed beams and a long wooden bar with metal stools (great for solo diners).

★QUIMET I QUIMET TAPAS €€

Map p286 (☎93 442 31 42; Carrer del Poeta Cabanyes 25; tapas €4-10, montaditos around €3; ⊙noon-4pm & 7-10.30pm Mon-Fri, noon-4pm Sat; ⊠Paral·lel) Quimet i Quimet is a family-run business that has been passed down from generation to generation. There's barely space to swing a *calamar* in this bottle-lined, standing-room-only place, but it is a treat for the palate, with *montaditos* (tapas on a slice of bread) made to order.

Try delectable combinations like artichoke, cheese and caviar, or tuna belly with sea urchin. Or let the folk behind the bar advise you, and order a drop of fine wine to accompany your meal.

JUICE HOUSE
HEALTH FOOD €€

Map p286 (☑93 117 15 15; http://thejuicehouse.es; Carrer del Parlament 12; mains €8-10; ☉10am-11pm; ☑; ⓂPoble Sec) Juice House ticks all the boxes in the healthy living camp. Whether you're a vegetarian, vegan, flexitarian, raw food fan or simply after a tasty, thoughtfully prepared meal, this cheery cafe should figure high on your itinerary. Oat and chia pancakes, açaí fruit bowls, and oven-baked eggs are fine ways to start the morning.

Later, you can nibble on open-faced sandwiches, tapas (like *corvina ceviche*) or changing daily specials (peppers stuffed with wild rice and goat's cheese, for example). Rustic wood tables, exposed Edison bulbs and fresh-cut flowers add to the Zen-like organic vibe.

CASA XICA
FUSION €€

Map p286 (☑93 600 58 58; Carrer de la França Xica 20; sharing plates €9-15; ☉1.30-3pm & 8.30-11.30pm Mon-Sat; ⓂPoble Sec) On the parlour floor of an old house, Casa Xica is a casual, artfully designed space that fuses elements of the Far East with fresh Catalan ingredients (owners Marc and Raquel lived and travelled in Asia).

The creative menu, which changes regularly, features sharing plates like prawn and cod liver gyoza (Japanese dumplings), Penang curry with foie gras and mushrooms, oxtail with sweet potato and ginger, and Iberian pork cured with kimchi and soy. It's a bit of an uphill slog from the metro station.

TONKA
INTERNATIONAL €€

Map p286 (☑93 127 05 44; www.tonkabar.com; Carrer del Marquès de Campo Sagrado 27; ☉5pm-midnight Tue-Fri, from 10am Sat & Sun; ☎☑; ⓂSant Antoni, Poble Sec) It's hard not to fall for this charming neighbourhood eatery. Fresh-cut flowers in vermouth jars, groovy music and a spray of colourful art prints on the wall set the stage for dining on delicious organic and veg-friendly dishes with Asian and Latin American accents.

You can assemble a meal on creative tapas, like fried yucca with salsa or brie, walnut and pear samosas, or opt for changing daily specials like braised octopus with potatoes and sweet-and-sour sauce, or mushroom risotto with thyme butter.

BODEGA 1900
TAPAS €€

Map p286 (☑93 325 26 59; www.bodega1900.com; Carrer de Tamarit 91; tapas €5-14; ☉noon-4pm & 7-11.30pm; ⓂSant Antoni) The latest venture from the world-famous Adrià brothers, Bodega 1900 mimics an old-school tapas and vermouth bar, but this is no ordinary spit-and-sawdust joint serving *patatas bravas* and tortilla. Witness, for example, the *mollete de calamars,* probably the best squid sandwich in the world, hot from the pan and served with chipotle mayonnaise, kimchi and lemon zest; or the 'spherified' false olives.

FEDERAL
CAFE €€

Map p286 (☑93 187 36 07; www.federalcafe.es; Carrer del Parlament 39; mains €9-12; ☉8am-11pm Mon-Thu, 8am-1am Fri, 9am-1am Sat, 9am-5.30pm Sun; ☎☑; ⓂSant Antoni) On a stretch that now teems with cafes, Australian-run Federal was the trailbazer, with its breezy chic and superb brunches. Later in the day there is healthy, tasty cooking from veggie burgers to grilled salmon with soba noodles, not to mention snacks (like prawn toast or polenta chips with gorgonzola) and good coffee (including a decent flat white).

Head to the roof for a small, leafy terrace on which to browse the day's papers.

PIZZA DEL SORTIDOR
PIZZA €€

Map p286 (http://lapizzadelsortidor.com; Carrer de Blasco de Garay 46; pizzas €8-13; ☉7pm-midnight Mon-Fri, from noon Sat & Sun; ☎☑; ⓂPoble Sec) Dive into this classic rock-loving pizzeria for delicious thin-crust pizza, served piping hot from the wood-burning oven. It's utterly pretension free – served without utensils or even plates for that matter (never mind the cardboard). Beer is served in plastic cups (just €2), but you won't leave dissatisfied, especially when you accept the complimentary shot of Limoncello at the meal's end.

BAR RAMÓN
TAPAS €€

Map p286 (☑93 325 02 83; www.barramon.com; Carrer del Comte Borrell 81; tapas €5-12; ☉8.30pm-midnight Mon-Sat & 9am-4pm Fri & Sat; ⓂSant Antoni) A much-loved local haunt in Sant Antoni, Bar Ramón serves mouthwatering tapas plates in a lively blues-filled joint near the market. Old photos of American musical R&B legends (and a few guitars) line the walls – a fine backdrop to tender slices of *jamón ibérico*, grilled prawns, homemade meatballs and cheese boards. This place fills up, so it's wise to reserve ahead.

FÀBRICA MORITZ CATALAN €€

Map p286 (☑93 426 00 50; www.moritz.com; Ronda de Sant Antoni 41; tapas from €4, sandwiches €8-11; ☺6am-3am; ☑; MSant Antoni) With the help of architect Jean Nouvel and chef Jordi Vilà, this microbrewery from the people behind Moritz beer has been rebuilt and opened with great fanfare as a vast food and drink complex, with wine bar and restaurant. The tapas and more substantial dishes comprise all the cornerstones of Catalan cuisine and plenty more, but be prepared to queue.

LA BELLA NAPOLI PIZZA €€

Map p286 (☑93 442 50 56; Carrer de Margarit 14; pizzas €10-12, mains €12-24; ☺1.30-4pm & 8.30pm-midnight; MParal·lel) There are pizza joints all over Barcelona. And then there's the real thing: the way they make it in Naples. This place even *feels* like Naples. The waiters are mostly from across the Med and have that cheeky southern Italian approach to food, customers and everything else.

The pizzas are good, ranging from the simple margherita to the more complex *tartufo nero* with gorgonzola and black truffles.

★TICKETS MODERN SPANISH €€€

Map p286 (☑606 225545; www.ticketsbar.es; Avinguda del Paral·lel 164; tapas €5-27; ☺6.30-10.30pm Tue-Fri, 1-3pm & 7-10.30pm Sat, closed Aug; MParal·lel) This is, literally, one of the sizzling tickets in the restaurant world, a tapas bar opened by Ferran Adrià, of the legendary El Bulli, and his brother Albert. And unlike El Bulli, it's an affordable venture – if you can book a table, that is: you can only book online, and two months in advance (or call for last-minute cancellations).

It's a fairly flamboyant and modern affair in terms of decor, playing with circus images and theatre lights, while the food veers towards the deliciously surreal in concoctions like spherical olives, 'airbaguette' with dry aged Rubia Gallega beef, or the wild carrot cone with cardamom yoghurt, sugared sesame and carrot ice cream. The seafood bar serves 14 varieties of oysters, with caviar, borscht and other unusual toppings.

MARTÍNEZ SPANISH €€€

Map p286 (☑93 106 60 52; www.martinezbarcelona.com; Carretera de Miramar 38; paella for two €38-62; ☺10am-1pm Sun-Thu, to 2.30am Fri & Sat; ☑D20) Boasting a fabulous view over the city and the port, Martínez is a standout among the lacklustre dining options atop Montjuïc. On warm days, head to the outdoor terrace for its signature rice and paella dishes. There's also oysters, calamari, fresh market fish and other seafood hits, plus *jamón* and a few grilled meat dishes.

If you're not up for the pricey main courses, Martínez is also a fine destination for drinks at any time of day.

ALKÍMIA CATALAN €€€

Map p286 (☑93 207 61 15; www.alkimia.cat; Ronda de Sant Antoni 41; mains €18-29; ☺1.30-3.30pm & 8-11pm Mon-Fri; MSant Antoni, Universitat) Jordi Vilà, a culinary alchemist, serves up refined Catalan dishes with a twist. Dishes such as his *arròs de nyora i safrà amb escamarlans de la costa* (saffron and sweet-chilli rice with crayfish) earned Vilà his first Michelin star. He presents a series of set menus starting around €70.

In 2016 Alkímia moved from its Eixample location to a space inside the Fàbrica Moritz.

🍷 DRINKING & NIGHTLIFE

BAR CALDERS BAR

Map p286 (☑93 329 93 49; Carrer del Parlament 25; ☺5pm-2am Mon-Fri, 11am-2.30am Sat, 11am-midnight Sun; MSant Antoni) It bills itself as a wine bar, but actually the wine selection at Bar Calders is its weak point. As an all-day cafe and tapas bar, however, it's unbeatable, with a few tables outside on a tiny pedestrian lane, and has become the favoured meeting point for the neighbourhood's boho element.

EL ROUGE BAR

Map p286 (☑666 251556; Carrer del Poeta Cabanyes 21; ☺11pm-2am Mon, 8pm-2am Tue & Thu, 10pm-3am Fri & Sat; ☎; MPoble Sec) Decadence is the word that springs to mind in this bordello-red lounge-cocktail bar, with acid jazz, drum and bass and other sounds drifting along in the background. The walls are laden with heavy-framed paintings, dim lamps and mirrors, and no two chairs are alike. You can sometimes catch DJs, risqué poetry soirées, cabaret shows or even nights of tango dancing.

PERVERT CLUB   CLUB
Map p286 (Avinguda Francesc Ferrer i Guàrdia 13, Poble Espanyol; cover €18; ⊙midnight-6am Sat; Ⓜ Espanya) This weekly fete takes place at The One club in Poble Espanyol. Electronic music dominates, and, in spite of the 6am finish, for many this is only the start of the 'evening'. Expect loads of tanned and buff gym bunnies – and plenty of topless eye candy.

LA CAMBICHA   BAR
Map p286 (🖉93 187 25 13; Carrer del Poeta Cabanyes 43; ⊙6pm-2am Mon-Wed, 1pm-2am Thu-Sun; Ⓜ Paral·lel) This shoebox-sized bar feels a bit like a lost cabin in the woods, what with the newspaper-covered walls, lantern-like lamps and old photos of sporting folk. Once you've wedged yourself alongside a tiny table, you can join the young James Brown–loving crowd over inexpensive empanadas and glasses of vermouth. A bands plays every now and again.

BACANAL   CAFE
Map p286 (Carrer de Sepúlveda 164; ⊙9am-midnight Mon & Wed-Fri, 10am-2am Sat, 10am-8.30pm Sun; 🛜; Ⓜ Urgell) This decidedly hip neighbourhood cafe invites lingering, with its spacious light-filled interior, artwork-lined walls and thoughtful touches (flowers on the tables) – never mind the concrete floors and columns. A mix of laptop users and chatterers stay fuelled on good coffees, smoothies, craft beers, wines, sandwiches and low-playing grooves.

REDRUM   BAR
Map p286 (Carrer de Margarit 36; ⊙7pm-3am Tue-Sun; Ⓜ Poble Sec) A fine escape from the tapas circus down on Carrer de Blai, Redrum doles out craft brews, cocktails and Mexican street food (including excellent tacos and ceviche). It has a low-lit interior, and the service is friendly – don't let the name deter you (a bone-chiller for anyone who's seen *The Shining*). Stop by for €3.50 drink specials from 7.30pm to 10.30pm.

BAR OLIMPIA   BAR
Map p286 (🖉606 200800; Carrer d'Aldana 11; ⊙7pm-1am Wed & Thu, to 2.30am Fri & Sat, 6-11pm Sun; Ⓜ Paral·lel) This great little neighborhood bar is a little slice of Barcelona history. It was here (and on the surrounding block), where the popular Olimpia Theatre Circus once performed way back in the 1930s. Today the vaguely retro bar draws a diverse crowd, who come for house-made vermouth, snacks (like quesadillas, cheese plates, tuna tartare) and satisfying gin and tonics.

PLATAFORMA   CLUB
Map p286 (🖉93 329 00 29; Carrer Nou de la Rambla 145; cover €6-12; ⊙10pm-6am Thu-Sat, 7pm-2am Sun; Ⓜ Paral.lel) With two adjoining if smallish dance spaces, 'Platform' has the sense of a slightly clandestine location in an otherwise quiet residential street. Inside this friendly, straightforward dance dive, far from the glitzy Ibiza look, you'll find popular '80s grooves, timeless rock and occasional nights of live bands – plus drum and bass that attract nostalgics in their 30s and younger partiers.

TINTA ROJA   BAR
Map p286 (🖉93 443 32 43; www.tintaroja.cat; Carrer de la Creu dels Molers 17; ⊙8.30pm-1am Wed, to 2am Thu, to 3am Fri & Sat; Ⓜ Poble Sec) A succession of nooks and crannies, dotted with flea-market finds and dimly lit in violets, reds and yellows, makes Tinta Roja an intimate spot for a drink and the occasional show in the back – with anything from actors to acrobats. This was once a *vaqueria* (small dairy farm), where they kept cows out the back and sold fresh milk at the front.

MONTJUÏC, POBLE SEC & SANT ANTONI DRINKING & NIGHTLIFE

DRINKS WITH A VIEW (NO SHOES REQUIRED)

The effort of getting to what is, for all intents and purposes, a simple *chiringuito* (makeshift cafe-bar) is well worth it. At **La Caseta del Migdia** (Map p286; 🖉617 956572; www.lacaseta.org; Mirador del Migdia; ⊙8pm-1am Wed-Fri, from noon Sat & Sun, weekends only in winter; 🚌150), you can sit at outdoor tables plonked on the shady, forest-backed hillside and stare out to sea over a beer or coffee by day. As sunset approaches the atmosphere changes, with melodic rhythms (from samba to funk) wafting out over the hillside. Drinks aside, you can also order barbecue, fired up on the outdoor grills.

To get here, walk along the walls of the Castell de Montjuïc along the dirt track or follow Passeig del Migdia – watch out for signs for the Mirador del Migdia.

LA TERRRAZZA   CLUB

Map p286 (📞687 969825; www.laterrrazza.com; Avinguda de Francesc Ferrer i Guàrdia; cover €15-20; ⏰12.30am-6am Thu-Sat, closed Oct-Apr; Ⓜ️Espanya) One of the city's top summertime dance locations, La Terrrazza attracts squadrons of beautiful people, locals and foreigners alike, for a full-on night of music and cocktails partly under the stars inside the Poble Espanyol complex.

 ⭐ **ENTERTAINMENT**

HIROSHIMA   LIVE PERFORMANCE

Map p286 (📞93 315 54 58; www.hiroshima.cat; Carrer de Vila i Vilà 67; ⏰5pm-1am Tue-Thu, to 3am Fri & Sat, noon-1am Sun; Ⓜ️Paral·lel) Hiroshima is a creative, new trailblazer in Poble Sec. In a former elevator factory, Hiroshima stages emerging and avant-garde musicians, dancers and performing artists. It has two stages (seating 130 and 250 people, respectively) and a lively ground-floor bar where you can grab a drink after the show. For unconventional fare, this is a good place to look.

BARTS   CONCERT VENUE

Map p286 (Barcelona Arts on Stage; 📞93 324 84 92; www.barts.cat; Avinguda del Paral·lel 62; tickets €12-40; ⏰5pm-midnight Mon-Thu & Sun, 5pm-2am Fri & Sat; Ⓜ️Paral·lel) BARTS hasn't been around long, but it has already earned a reputation for its innovative line-up of urban dance troupes, electro swing, psychedelic pop and other eclectic fare. BARTS has a smart design that combines a comfortable midsized auditorium with excellent acoustics.

TEATRE GREC   THEATRE

Map p286 (lameva.barcelona.cat/grec; Passeig de Santa Madrona; Ⓜ️Espanya) This lovely amphitheatre on Montjuïc stages one of the city's best festivals, with theatre, dance and music events running throughout the summer. Aside from the Teatre Grec, performances are held all over the city.

GRAN BODEGA SALTÓ   LIVE MUSIC

Map p286 (📞93 441 37 09; www.bodegasalto.net; Carrer de Blesa 36; ⏰7pm-2am Mon-Thu, noon-3am Fri & Sat, noon-midnight Sun; Ⓜ️Paral·lel) The ranks of barrels give away the bar's history as a traditional bodega. Now, after a little homemade psychedelic redecoration with odd lamps, figurines and old Chinese beer ads, it's a magnet for an eclectic barfly crowd. The crowd is mixed and friendly, and gets pretty animated on nights when there is live music.

SALA APOLO   LIVE MUSIC

Map p286 (📞93 441 40 01; www.sala-apolo.com; Carrer Nou de la Rambla 113; club €12-18, concerts vary; ⏰12.30am-5am Mon-Thu, 12.30am-6am Fri & Sat; Ⓜ️Paral·lel) This is a fine old theatre, where red velvet dominates and you feel as though you're in a movie-set dancehall scene featuring Eliot Ness. 'Nasty Mondays' and 'Crappy Tuesdays' are aimed at a diehard, we-never-stop-dancing crowd. Earlier in the evening, concerts generally take place, here and in 'La 2', a smaller auditorium downstairs.

Tastes are as eclectic as possible, from local bands and burlesque shows to big-name international acts.

🔒 **SHOPPING**

GALERI   ARTS

Map p286 (📞93 124 13 30; Carrer de Viladomat 27; ⏰11am-2pm & 5-9pm Tue-Sat; Ⓜ️Poble Sec) This boxy, brightly lit gallery sells prints by Catalan artists as well as unusual graphic T-shirts, canvas bags and small ceramics – delicate conversation pieces, just small enough to fit in a carry-on. There are also a few original paintings and sculptures, from an ever-changing collection.

MERCAT DE SANT ANTONI   MARKET

Map p286 (📞93 426 35 21; www.mercatdesantantoni.com; Carrer de Comte d'Urgell 1; ⏰7am-2.30pm & 5-8.30pm Mon-Thu, 7am-8.30pm Fri & Sat; Ⓜ️Sant Antoni) Just beyond the western edge of El Raval is Mercat de Sant Antoni, a glorious old iron and brick building that has been undergoing renovation since 2009. In the meantime, a huge marquee has been erected alongside to house a food market. The secondhand book market still takes place alongside on Sunday mornings.

The latest estimates for the market's re-opening is the end of 2017.

GI JOE   FASHION

Map p286 (📞93 329 96 52; www.gijoebcn.com; Ronda de Sant Antoni 49; ⏰10am-2pm & 4.30-8.30pm Mon-Sat; Ⓜ️Universitat) This is the best central army-surplus warehouse. Get your khakis here, along with urban army fashion T-shirts, and throw in a holster, gas mask or sky-blue UN helmet for a kinkier effect. You can also find vintage WWII items.

Day Trips from Barcelona

Girona p188
A splendid cathedral, a maze of narrow cobbled streets and Catalonia's finest medieval Jewish quarter are part of this riverside town's charms.

Figueres p191
The Teatre-Museu Dalí is Spain's most surreal sight, a place of pilgrimage for any fan of Salvador Dalí, and the artist's final resting place.

Montserrat p193
Catalonia's most important shrine is in this spectacularly sited mountain monastery, complete with Europe's oldest choir and superb scenic walks.

Sitges p195
A classy old town and eating scene, superb string of beaches, great nightlife and a hedonistic carnival await visitors at the south coast's premier seaside town.

Tarragona p196
This sunny port city has a beautiful medieval core, boasting some of Spain's most extensive Roman ruins and studded with tempting eating options.

Girona

Explore

Girona's big draw is its old town, a tight huddle of ancient arcaded houses, grand churches and climbing cobbled streets,so head first for the Catedral – either by strolling along the lazy Río Onyar or by taking the high road along the medieval walls. Follow this with a visit to El Call (the medieval Jewish quarter) and the excellent Museu d'Història dels Jueus de Girona before taking your pick of the numerous restaurants in the nearby streets. After lunch, continue your exploration of other old town sights, such as the wonderfully intact Banys Àrabs or the attractive cloisters of the Monestir de Sant Pere de Galligants, before finding a bar around the Plaça de l'Independència to put your feet up for a while.

The Best...

➜**Sight** Museu d'Història dels Jueus de Girona

➜**Place to Eat** El Celler de Can Roca (p191)

➜**Place to Drink** Bars on Plaça del'Independència

Top Tip

For the best city views, take a walk along Girona's medieval walls, known as the Passeig Arqueològic and accessed across from the Banys Àrabs or near Plaça de Catalunya.

Getting There & Away

➜**Car** Take the AP7 tollway via Granollers.

➜**Train** Trains and *rodalies* on the R11 line run from Barcelona (€11.25 to €16.20, 40 minutes to 1½ hours, up to 24 daily).

Need to Know

➜**Location** 85km northeast of Barcelona

➜**Tourist Office** (Map p190; ☑972 22 65 75; www.girona.cat/turisme; Rambla de la Llibertat 1; ⊙9am-8pm Mon-Fri, 9am-2pm & 4-8pm Sat, 9am-2pm Sun)

◉ SIGHTS

Most of Girona's sights are concentrated in the lanes of its old town.

★MUSEU D'HISTÒRIA DELS JUEUS DE GIRONA   MUSEUM

Map p190 (www.girona.cat/call; Carrer de la Força 8; adult/child €4/free; ⊙10am-6pm Mon-Sat, to 2pm Sun) Until 1492 Girona was home to Catalonia's second most important medieval Jewish community (after Barcelona), and one of the finest Jewish quarters in the country. The Call was centred on the narrow Carrer de la Força for 600 years, until relentless persecution forced the Jews out of Spain. This excellent museum shows genuine pride in Girona's Jewish heritage without shying away from the less salubrious aspects, such as persecution by the Inquisition and forced conversions.

Other well-presented displays deal with Girona's Jewish contribution to medieval astronomy and medicine, the synagogue, everyday life, and rituals in the Jewish community and the diaspora. Standout objects include funerary slabs and the original documents ordering the expulsion of Jews from Spain. Opens shorter hours in low season.

★CATEDRAL   CATHEDRAL

Map p190 (www.catedraldegirona.org; Plaça de la Catedral; adult/student incl Basílica de Sant Feliu €7/5, Sun free; ⊙10am-7.30pm Apr-Oct, 10am-6.30pm Nov-Mar) Towering over a flight of 86 steps rising from Plaça de la Catedral, this edifice is far more ancient than its billowing Baroque facade suggests. Built over an old Roman forum, parts of the cathedral's foundations date from the 5th century. Today Gothic styling – built over the Romanesque church during the 14th century – dominates, though a fine, double-columned Romanesque cloister dates from the 12th century. It's a surprisingly formidable sight to explore, but an audioguide is included in the price.

MUSEU D'HISTÒRIA DE GIRONA   MUSEUM

Map p190 (www.girona.cat/museuciutat; Carrer de la Força 27; adult/student/child €4/2/free; ⊙10.30am-5.30pm Tue-Sat, to 1.30pm Sun) This museum's setting within 18th-century cloisters lends an appropriately antique feel to your journey from Roman Girona to the present day. Standout displays include an exhibition illuminating the 3rd- to 4th-century Can Pau Birol mosaic, which depicts a lively circus scene with charioteers, and an explanation of the siege of Girona by Napoleonic troops. Many pieces on display are copies rather than originals, making this a place to unpeel the layers of Girona's history rather than goggle at sculpture and art.

MUSEU D'ART   GALLERY
Map p190 (www.museuart.com; Plaça de la Catedral 12; admission €4.50; ⊙10am-7pm Tue-Sat May-Sep, to 6pm Oct-Apr, 10am-2pm Sun) Next door to the cathedral, in the 12th- to 16th-century Palau Episcopal, this art museum impresses with the scale and variety of its collection. Around 8500 pieces of art, mostly from this region, make up the collection, which ranges from Romanesque woodcarvings and stained-glass tables to modernist paintings of the city by Mela Mutter and early-20th-century sculptures by influential Rafael Masó i Valentí.

MUSEU DEL CINEMA   MUSEUM
Map p190 (www.museudelcinema.cat; Carrer de Sèquia 1; adult/child €5/free; ⊙10am-6pm Tue-Fri, 10am-8pm Sat, 11am-3pm Sun; 🖩) There is much more to this museum than the silver screen. Displays examine the reasons why humanity longs to indulge its imagination, probing the origins of visual storytelling, such as Chinese and Indian shadow puppets. It's a whistle-stop tour taking in the invention of the camera obscura, the 19th-century debut of the Lumière brothers, and optical illusions using mirrors and trickery of light. There is a vast assortment of displays to poke, play with and peer through.

BANYS ÀRABS   RUIN
Map p190 (www.banysarabs.cat; Carrer de Ferràn el Catòlic; adult/child €2/1; ⊙10am-7pm Mon-Sat, to 2pm Sun Apr-Sep, 10am-2pm daily Oct-Mar) Although modelled on earlier Muslim and Roman bathhouses, the Banys Àrabs are a finely preserved, 12th-century Christian affair in Romanesque style. The baths contain an *apodyterium* (changing room), followed by a *frigidarium* and *tepidarium* (with cold and warm water, respectively) and a *caldarium* (a kind of sauna) heated by an underfloor furnace.

BASÍLICA DE SANT FELIU   CHURCH
Map p190 (Plaça de Sant Feliu; adult/student incl Catedral €7/5, Sun free; ⊙10am-5.30pm Mon-Sat, 1-5.30pm Sun) Just downhill from the cathedral is Girona's second great church, with its landmark truncated bell tower. The nave is majestic with Gothic ribbed vaulting, while St Narcissus, the patron of the city, is venerated in an enormous marble-and-jasper, late-Baroque side chapel. Underneath his reclining form you see scenes from his life including the conversion of women, martyrdom and expelling of an evil genie. To the side is the Gothic sepulchre, dating from 1328, that previously held his remains. A decent audioguide tour is included with admission.

MONESTIR DE SANT PERE DE GALLIGANTS   MONASTERY
Map p190 (www.mac.cat; Carrer de Santa Llúcia; adult/child €4.50/3.50; ⊙10am-6pm Tue-Sat, 10am-2pm Sun) This beautiful 11th- and 12th-century Romanesque Benedictine monastery has a sublime bell tower and a lovely cloister featuring otherworldly animals and mythical creatures on the capitals of its double columns – there are some great ones in the church too. It's also home to the **Museu Arqueològic**. Weekday opening hours from June to September run until 7pm.

🍴 EATING & DRINKING

Girona has an excellent range of old-town restaurants. For a beer or coffee on a sunny terrace, head to Plaça de l'Independència across the river from the old town.

+CUB   CAFE €€
Map p190 (www.mescub.cat; Carrer de l'Albereda 15; mains €10-14; ⊙8am-9pm Mon-Thu, 8am-midnight Fri, 9am-midnight Sat; 🛜🖉) This trendy cafe-bar is as good for a takeaway coffee as it is for a full-blown nosh on speciality burgers and veggie crêpes. Thirst-quenchers include fresh fruit-juice combos and shakes, and they have a range of Scottish, German and other beers, plus local Moska homebrew.

CUIDA'T   VEGETARIAN €€
Map p190 (Carrer del Nord 12; mains €10-12; ⊙1-4pm & 8-10.30pm Mon-Sat; 🖉) Cuida't prides itself on making mouth-watering meals for vegetarians, vegans and those with food allergies. Even carnivores might be tempted by their roasted tofu, stuffed cannelloni and boletus risotto.

Girona

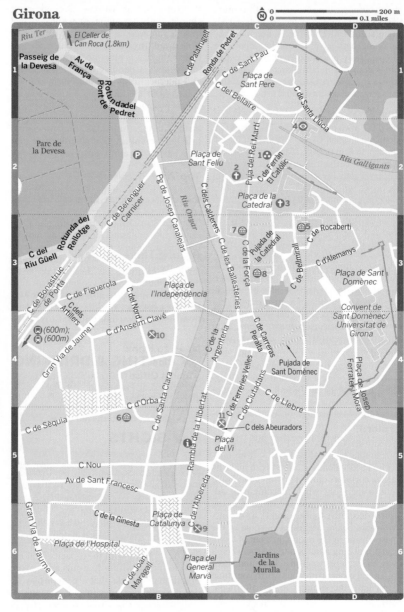

NU CATALAN €€

Map p190 (☑972 22 52 30; www.nurestaurant. cat; Carrer d'Abeuradors 4; mains €16-18; ⏱1.15-3.45pm & 8.15-10.45pm Mon-Sat; 🛜) Sleek and confident, this old-town spot has innovative, top-notch plates prepared in view by the friendly team. Flavour combinations keep things interesting: sample tuna *tataki* with red fruit glaze, tandoori pork cheeks with mango, and orange flower crème brulée. Great value for this quality.

Girona

★**EL CELLER DE CAN ROCA**   CATALAN €€€
(☎972 22 21 57; www.cellercanroca.com; Calle Can Sunyer 48; degustation menus €150-180; ⊙1-4pm & 8.30-11pm Wed-Sat, 8.30-11pm Sun) Ever-changing avant-garde takes on Catalan dishes have catapulted El Celler to global fame. Named the best restaurant in the world in 2015 by The World's 50 Best, each year brings new innovations from molecular gastronomy and multi-sensory food-art interplay to sci-fi dessert trolleys, all with mama's home cooking as the core inspiration. Run by three brothers, El Celler de Can Roca is set in a refurbished country house, 2km northwest of central Girona. Book online 11 months in advance or join a standby list.

Figueres

Explore
An early start is essential for visiting the incomparable Teatre-Museu Dalí – from mid-morning, coachloads of tourists can make its narrow corridors quite claustrophobic. You'll want to spend the whole morning here, admiring everything from the exterior to the bizarre decorative touches and Dalí's distinctive works before partaking in some of the finest cuisine in the region, just out of town, or just grabbing a quick bite nearby. There's more to Figueres than just Dalí, and there are several other attractions worth your time if you have the stamina in the afternoon: the vast Castell de Sant Ferran, perfect for a stroll around, or else the two entertaining museums in the centre.

The Best...
→**Sight** Teatre-Museu Dalí (p192)
→**Place to Eat** El Motel (p192)
→**Place to Drink** Sidrería Txot's (p192)

Top Tip
It pays to reserve online in advance for the Teatre-Museu Dalí, and to visit outside weekends and public holidays. Get here for opening time to avoid the worst of the crowds.

Getting There & Away
→**Car** Take the AP7 tollway via Granollers and Girona.
→**Train** Trains and *rodalies* on the R11 line run from Barcelona (€12 to €16, 1¾ to 2½ hours, at least hourly).

Need to Know
→**Location** 118km northeast of Barcelona
→**Tourist Office** (☎972 50 31 55; http://visitfigueres.cat; Plaça del Sol; ⊙9.30am-2pm & 4-6pm Tue-Sat, 10am-2pm Sun & Mon)

◎ SIGHTS

CASTELL DE SANT FERRAN   FORT
(www.lesfortalesescatalanes.info; adult/child €3/free; ⊙10.30am-6pm Apr–mid-Jul, 10.30am-8pm mid-Jul–mid-Sep, 10.30am-3pm Oct-Mar) This sturdy 18th-century fortress commands the surrounding plains from a low hill 1km northwest of the centre. The complex is a wonder of military engineering: it sprawls over 32 hectares, with the capacity for 6000 men to march within its walls and snooze in military barracks that are on display today. The admission fee includes a clanking audioguide (nearly as old as the castle) to help navigate the site. Book ahead for group guided tours (€10 to €15 per person).

MUSEU DE L'EMPORDÀ   MUSEUM
(www.museuemporda.org; La Rambla 2; adult/child €4/free; ⊙11am-8pm Tue-Sat, to 2pm Sun) Across four floors, this local museum time

travels from ancient amphorae and 7th-century sculptures to rotating installations of contemporary art. The 17th-century religious art is especially worthy of attention. There are signs in Spanish and Catalan, plus explanation on laminated cards in English and French. Admission is free with a Teatre-Museu Dalí ticket.

🍴 EATING & DRINKING

The restaurants closest to the Teatre-Museu Dalí are overpriced, mediocre tourist traps.

SIDRERÍA TXOT'S CATALAN, BASQUE €
(www.sidreriatxots.com; Avinguda Salvador Dalí 114; mains €10; ⏱noon-midnight; 🗗) Perch on a wooden seat and watch your Basque cider poured from on high from the barrel – the way it's supposed to be – before tucking into cold and hot *pintxos*, tasty burgers, cured meats, cheeses and salads, as well as dishes such as chorizo in cider and L'Escala anchovies on toast.

EL MOTEL CATALAN €€€
(Hotel Empordà; 📞972 50 05 62; www.elmotel.cat; Avinguda Salvador Dalí i Domènech 170; tast-ing menu €39.70; ⏱7.30-11am, 12.45-3.45pm & 9-11pm; 🅿🗗) Jaume Subirós, the chef and owner of this hotel-restaurant on a busy road 1km north of the centre, is a seminal figure of the transition from traditional Catalan home cooking to the polished, innovative affair it is today. Highlights are such dishes as sea urchins from Cadaqués, cod with truffle and calf's cheek in red wine. There are also appealing rooms in which to sleep off the gastronomic indulgence (single/double/suite €94/109/140).

🛏 SLEEPING

⭐**HOTEL DURÁN** HOTEL €€
(📞972 50 12 50; www.hotelduran.com; Carrer de Lasauca 5; d from €75; 🅿❄🗗🐾) For absolute immersion in the Dalí legend, a stay at this mid-19th-century hotel is a must. The artist and his wife were frequent guests here, and there's a fitting blend of old-style elegance with contemporary design and surrealist touches. Rooms are modern and great value, while the restaurant (mains €12 to €25) has the opulence of a royal banquet hall.

DAY TRIPS FROM BARCELONA FIGUERES

⊙ TOP SIGHT
TEATRE-MUSEU DALÍ

The first name that comes into your head when you sight this red castle-like building, bristling with giant eggs, Oscar-like statues and plaster croissants, is Dalí. An entirely appropriate final resting place for the master of surrealism, it has assured his immortality. Dalí converted Figueres' former theatre, ruined by fire in 1939, into this place full of surprises, tricks and illusions, which contains a substantial portion of his life's work.

Choice exhibits include *Taxi plujós* (Rainy Taxi): put a coin in the slot and water washes all over the occupant of the car. The **Palace of the Wind Room** is Dalí's heavenly reimagining of the Sistine Chapel. Beneath the former stage of the theatre is the crypt with Dalí's plain tomb, located at 'the spiritual centre of Europe' as Dalí modestly described it.

Gala – Dalí's wife and lifelong muse – is seen throughout, from the *Gala mirando el Mar Mediterráneo* (Gala Looking at the Mediterranean Sea) on the 2nd level, which also appears to be a portrait of Abraham Lincoln from afar, to the classic *Leda atómica* (Atomic Leda).

A separate entrance (same ticket and times) leads into Dalí Joies, a collection of 37 unique Dalí-designed jewels.

Don't Miss
➡ The museum's whimsical exterior
➡ The Palace of the Wind Room

Practicalities
➡ www.salvador-dali.org
➡ Plaça de Gala i Salvador Dalí 5
➡ adult/child under 9yr incl Museu de l'Empordà €12/free
➡ ⏱9am-8pm Tue-Sun Jul-Sep, 10.30am-6pm Tue-Sun Oct-Jun, closed Mon

DALÍ DELIRIUM

Salvador Dalí was born in Figueres in 1904, but his career took him to Madrid, Barcelona, Paris and the USA. He remained true to his roots and has left his mark in several locations around Catalonia, particularly at his seaside residence in Portlligat and his inland 'castle', Castell de Púbol.

Located by a peaceful cove in Portlligat, a tiny fishing settlement a 20-minute walk from Cadaqués, the **Casa Museu Dalí** (📱972 25 10 15; www.salvador-dali.org; adult/under 8yr €11/free; ⊙10.30am-6pm Tue-Sun, closed Jan–mid-Feb) was the lifelong residence of Dalí. The now expansive house started life as a mere fisherman's hut, and was steadily altered and enlarged by Dalí, who lived here with his wife from 1930 to 1982. If the Teatre-Museu Dalí is the mask that the showman presented to the world, then this is an intimate glimpse of his actual face. This splendid, bizarre whitewashed structure is a mishmash of cottages and sunny terraces, linked together by narrow labyrinthine corridors and containing an assortment of offbeat furnishings. Compulsory small group tours are conducted by multilingual guides; booking a day or three ahead – you can do this online or by phone – is essential.

The **Castell de Púbol** (www.salvador-dali.org; Plaça de Gala Dalí; adult/concession €8/6; ⊙10am-5pm Tue-Sun mid-Mar–Dec), in the village of La Pera, just south of the C66 road between Girona and Palafrugell, is a Gothic and Renaissance mansion, purchased by Dalí in 1969 as a retreat for his wife, Gala, who lived here until her death at 88 in 1982. An inconsolable Dalí then moved in himself, but was removed by friends after starting a fire in 1984. Though much of the castle was decorated according to Gala's taste, Dalí touches do creep in in the form of spindly legged elephant statues in the maze-like garden, a see-through table with a horse visible below and a stuffed giraffe staring at Gala's tomb in the crypt.

For Portlligat, take a Sarfa bus to Cadaqués from Figueres (€5.50, one hour, four weekdays); there are also connections from Barcelona and Girona. For the Castell de Púbol, catch a bus to Cruilla de la Pera from Girona (€3, 40 minutes) or Palafrugell, alight at the stop on the C66 and walk 2km to the castle, or take a train from Girona to Flaça (hourly, €3.30, 12 minutes) then take a taxi the last 5km.

Montserrat

Explore

Montserrat, 50km northwest of Barcelona, is at the heart of Catalan identity for its mountain, monastery and the natural park weaving among its distinctive rock formations. Montserrat mountain is instantly recognisable for its rock formations, sculpted over millennia by wind and frost. These turrets of rock, a coarse conglomerate of limestone and eroded fragments, extend like gnarled fingers from its 1236m-high bulk. More than halfway up the mountain lies the Benedictine Monestir de Montserrat, home to the Black Virgin, one of Spain's most revered icons. Extending from this sacred spot is the Parc Natural de de la Muntanya de Montserrat, superlative hiking terrain where brooks tumble into ravines and lookout points boast panoramas of rocky pillars.

Montserrat (often used interchangeably to mean the monastery and mountain) is a very popular day trip from Barcelona. The monastery complex throngs with visitors, but serenity can be found on the walking trails or by staying overnight.

The Best...

→**Sight** Monestir de Montserrat (p194)
→**Place to Eat** Hotel Abat Cisneros (p195)
→**Walk** Sant Jeroni (p194)

Top Tip

To commune with La Moreneta in solitude and enjoy the stillness and the silence of the mountain, stay overnight to make it to the chapel by the 7am opening time.

Getting There & Away

→**Train and cable car** The R5 line trains operated by FGC (www.fgc.net) run hourly from Plaça d'Espanya station, starting at 6.36am (55 minutes), to connect with the **AERI cable car** (☑938 35 00 05; www.aeridemontserrat.com; one-way/return €7/10; ⊕9.40am-7pm, closed mid-late Jan) at the Montserrat Aeri stop (every 15 minutes, five minutes). Alternatively take the **cremallera train** (☑902 31 20 20; www.cremallerademontserrat.com; 1-way/return €6.30/10) at the following stop, Monistrol de Montserrat. There are various train-cremallera combo tickets available.

→**Car** Take the C16 from Barcelona, then the C58 shortly after Terrassa, followed by the C55 to Monistrol de Montserrat. You can leave the car at the free car park and take the cremallera up to the top or drive up and park (cars €6.50).

Need to Know

→**Location** 50km northwest of Barcelona

→**Information Office** (☑938 77 77 77; www.montserratvisita.com; ⊕9am-5.45pm Mon-Fri, 9am-8pm Sat & Sun)

◉ SIGHTS

MONESTIR DE MONTSERRAT   MONASTERY
(www.abadiamontserrat.net; ⊕basilica 7.30-10.30am & 12.15-6.15pm) Catalonia's most renowned monastery was founded in 1025 to commemorate visions of the Virgin Mary, accompanied by celestial light and a chorus of holy music, experienced by shepherds. The monastery complex encompasses two blocks: on one side, the basilica and monastery buildings (housing a religious community of more than 100), and on the other, facilities for tourists and pilgrims. Admirable monastery architecture in Plaça de Santa Maria includes a gleaming late-19th-century facade depicting St George and St Benedict in relief, and 15th-century cloisters.

Most visitors make a beeline for the basilica to venerate La Moreneta (the 'Little Brown One' or 'Black Virgin'), a 12th-century Romanesque wooden sculpture of Mary with the baby Jesus (and Catalonia's official patroness since 1881).

MUSEU DE MONTSERRAT   MUSEUM
(www.museudemontserrat.com; Plaça de Santa Maria; adult/student €7/6, €11 with Espai Audiovisual; ⊕10am-5.45pm Mon-Fri, 10am-6.45pm Sat & Sun) This museum has an excellent collection, ranging from an Egyptian mummy and Gothic altarpieces to fine canvases by Caravaggio, El Greco, Picasso and several Impressionists, as well as a comprehensive collection of 20th-century classic Catalan art and some fantastic Orthodox icons.

SANTA COVA   CHAPEL
To see the 17th-century chapel built on the spot where holy visions of the Virgin Mary appeared to astonished shepherds, you can drop down the **Funicular de Santa Cova** (www.cremallerademontserrat.cat; one-way/return €2.20/3.50; ⊕every 20min btwn 10am-4pm, closed mid-late Jan). Otherwise walk down along a precipitous mountain path with stomach-plummeting views of the valley below. The chapel is open all day, but most visitors arrive during the funicular's operating hours.

WALKING IN MONTSERRAT

Beyond the touristic hubbub surrounding Montserrat's monastery and basilica, there's tranquillity to be found in the web of walking trails across the mountain. Take the **Funicular de Sant Joan** (one-way/return €2.40/3.70; ⊕every 20min 10am-4.50pm) for the first 250m uphill from the monastery; alternatively, it's a 45-minute walk along the road between the funicular's bottom and top stations. From the top, it's a further 20-minute stroll (signposted) to the Sant Joan chapel, with fine westward views.

More exciting is the one-hour walk northwest, along a path marked with some blobs of yellow paint, to Montserrat's highest peak, Sant Jeroni, from where there's a sheer drop on the north face. The walk takes you across the upper part of the mountain, with a close-up experience of some of the rock pillars. Before setting out, check ahead with the Information Office regarding weather and trail conditions, wear good walking boots, and bring water.

⭐ ENTERTAINMENT

ESCOLANÍA DE MONTSERRAT CHORAL MUSIC
(www.escolania.cat; ⊙performances 1pm Mon-Thu, 11am Sun, 6.45pm Sun-Thu) The clear voices of one of Europe's oldest boys' choirs have echoed through the basilica since the 14th century. The choir performs briefly on most days (except school holidays), singing *Virolai*, written by Catalonia's national poet Jacint Verdaguer, and *Salve Regina*. The 53 *escolanets*, aged between nine and 14, go to boarding school in Montserrat and must endure a two-year selection process to join the choir. Check performance times on the website.

🛏 SLEEPING & EATING

HOTEL ABAT CISNEROS HOTEL €€
(☎938 77 77 01; www.montserratvisita.com; s/d incl breakfast €63.75/109.90; 🅿🛜🌢) The only hotel in the monastery complex has a superb location next to the basilica. Rooms are comfortable though simple; some make up for the spartan decor with views overlooking Plaça de Santa Maria. There are also inexpensive basic apartments and family packages available. Its restaurant serves imaginative Catalan dishes (mains €17 to €20).

Sitges

Explore

Sitges is perfect for seafront promenading and sun worshipping, so in warmer weather you'll find the most central beaches quite crowded. Luckily there are quite a few to choose from, so pick your spot for a morning of sunbathing (or skinny dipping off the nudist beach) before choosing a seafood restaurant nearby. If you have an interest in contemporary art and in the Modernisme movement, the classy old centre's array of elegant buildings, many housing museums, is well worth some of your time. The gay scene in Sitges – and its vibrant party atmosphere in general – is legendary, so many a day trip ends up the morning after...

The Best...

➡ **Sight** Beaches
➡ **Place to Eat** Lady Green (p196)
➡ **Place to Drink** Casablanca (p196)

Top Tip

To find out the latest gay nightlife hot spots, head to the **Parrots Hotel** (☎938 94 13 50; www.parrotshotel.com; Calle de Joan Tarrida 16; d €99-130; ⊙mid-Feb–Oct; ❄@🛜); and if you're coming to Sitges for the bacchanalian weeklong Carnaval in February/March, book well ahead.

Getting There & Away

➡ **Train** From about 5am to 10pm regular R2 *rodalies* trains run to Barcelona's Passeig de Gràcia and Estació Sants (€4.10, 45 minutes).

➡ **Car** The best road from Barcelona is the C32 tollway. More scenic is the C31, which hooks up with the C32 after Castelldefels, but it is often busy and slow.

Need to Know

➡ **Location** 35km southwest of Barcelona
➡ **Tourist Office** (☎938 94 42 51; www.sitgestur.cat; Plaça de E Maristany 2; ⊙10am-2pm & 4-6.30pm Mon-Sat, 10am-2pm Sun)

⊙ SIGHTS

The main beach is flanked by the attractive seafront Passeig Maritim, dotted with *chiringuitos* (beachside bars) and divided into nine sections with different names by a series of breakwaters. West of the centre, **Anquines** and **Terramar** beaches have paddleboat rental and deck chairs during the summer. East of the headland find **St Sebastià**, **Balmins** and fine brown-sanded **D'aiguadolç** beaches. Though **Bassa Rodona** used to be the unofficial 'gay beach', gay sunbathers are now spread out pretty evenly, while Balmins is the sheltered bay favoured by nudists.

The most beautiful part of Sitges is the headland area, where noble Modernista palaces and mansions pose in the streets around the striking Església de Sant Bartomeu i Santa Tecla, with the blue sea as a backdrop.

★ MUSEU CAU FERRAT MUSEUM
(www.museusdesitges.cat; Carrer de Fonollar; incl Museu Maricel adult/reduced €10/7; ⊙10am-7pm Tue-Sun) Built in the 1890s as a house-cum-studio by artist Santiago Rusiñol, a pioneer of the Modernisme movement, this mansion is crammed with his own art and that of his contemporaries, including his friend Picasso,

as well as his own collection of ancient relics and antiques. The visual feast is piled high, from Grecian urns and a 15th-century baptismal font to 18th-century tilework that glitters all the way to the floral-painted wood-beamed ceiling.

MUSEU ROMÀNTIC
MUSEUM

(www.museusdesitges.cat; Carrer de Sant Gaudenci 1) Housed in a late-18th-century Can Llopis mansion, this faded museum recreates with its furnishings and dioramas the lifestyle of a 19th-century Catalan landowning family. Closed for renovations during our visit, the museum was due to reopen in 2016.

FUNDACIÓ STÄMPFLI ART CONTEMPORANI
GALLERY

(www.fundacio-stampfli.org; Plaça de l'Ajuntament 13; adult/child €5/3.50; ⊙3.30-7pm Fri, 10am-2pm & 5-7pm Sat, 11am-3pm Sun) Within an old wood-beamed fish-market building is this slick 20th-century art gallery. Whitewashed walls and shiny tiled floors draw all eyes to the primary colours of bold pop art and modern art within. Pucker up for Peter Stämpfli's *Rouge baiser* (an enormous cerise pair of lips), alongside works by Arroyo, Cueco and other greats. The lower floor has rotating temporary exhibitions. The museum runs extended hours in high season.

✖ EATING & DRINKING

EL POU
TAPAS €

(www.elpoudesitges.com; Carrer de Sant Pau 5; dishes €4-10; ⊙1.30-4pm & 8-11.30pm Thu-Sun, 8-11.30pm Mon & Wed; 🐾) Tiny Wagyu beef burgers, meatballs with cuttlefish, and classics like anchovies and local cheese crowd tables at this friendly gourmet tapas place. The presentation delights the eye as much as the flavours delight the palate.

EF & GI
FUSION €€€

(🖉938 11 33 07; Carrer Major 33; mains €18-25; ⊙1-4pm & 8-11.30pm Wed-Mon Mar-Jan; 🐾) Fabio and Greg (eF & Gi) are not afraid to experiment and the results are startlingly good: the mostly Mediterranean menu, with touches of Asian inspiration, throws out such delights as chargrilled beef infused with lemongrass and kaffir lime, and tuna loin encrusted with peanuts, and kalamata olives with mango chutney. Don't skip the dessert either.

★ BAR VORAMAR
BAR

(www.pub-voramar.com; Carrer del Port Alegre 55; ⊙4.30pm-1am Thu-Tue) On Platja de Sant Sebastià, this is a fabulous old-time bar decked out like a ship playing flamenco, jazz and more. It does brilliant caipirinhas, mojitos and more. The chummy booth seating is a Sitges classic.

Tarragona

Explore
In this effervescent port city, Roman history collides with beaches, nightlife and a food scene that perfumes the air with freshly grilled seafood. The biggest lure is the wealth of ruins in Spain's second most important Roman site, including mosaic-packed museums and a seaside amphitheatre. A roll-call of excellent places to eat gives you good reason to linger in the knot of lanes in the medieval centre, flanked by a broad cathedral with Gothic flourishes. Tarragona is also a gateway to the Costa Daurada's sparkling beaches and the feast of Modernisme architecture in nearby Reus.

The Best...
→ **Sight** Museu d'Història de Tarragona
→ **Place to Drink** Plaça de la Font

Top Tip
Don't visit Tarragona on a Sunday or Monday, as you'll find your sightseeing options drastically curtailed.

Getting There & Away
→ **Train** The local station is a 10-minute walk from the old town while fast AVE trains arrive at Camp de Tarragona station, a 15-minute taxi ride from the centre. Departures from Barcelona include normal trains and *rodalies* on the R14, R15 and R16 lines (€8.05 to €20.80, 35 minutes to 1½ hours, every 30 minutes).

→ **Bus** Services from Barcelona (€8.80, 1½ hours, up to 16 daily) stop at the bus station, a pleasant 20-minute walk from the centre.

→ **Car** Take the C32 toll road along the coast via Castelldefels or the AP7.

Need to Know

➡ **Location** 83km southwest of Barcelona

➡ **Tourist Office** (📞977 25 07 95; www.tarragonaturisme.es; Carrer Major 39; ⊙10am-2pm & 3-5pm Mon-Fri, to 7pm Sat, 10am-2pm Sun)

◉ SIGHTS

★**CATEDRAL DE TARRAGONA** CATHEDRAL
(www.catedraldetarragona.com; Plaça de la Seu; adult/child €5/3; ⊙10am-7pm Mon-Sat mid-Mar–Oct, 10am-5pm Mon-Fri, 10am-7pm Sat Nov–mid-Mar) Sitting grandly atop town, Tarragona's cathedral has both Romanesque and Gothic features, as typified by the main facade. The cloister has Gothic vaulting and Romanesque carved capitals, one of which shows rats conducting a cat's funeral...until the cat comes back to life! It's a lesson about passions seemingly lying dormant until they reveal themselves. Chambers off the cloister incorporate the **Museu Diocesà**, with its large collection extending from Roman hairpins to some lovely 12th- to 14th-century polychrome woodcarvings of a breastfeeding Virgin.

★**MUSEU NACIONAL ARQUEOLÒGIC DE TARRAGONA** MUSEUM
(www.mnat.cat; Plaça del Rei 5; adult/child €4.50/free; ⊙9.30am-6pm Tue-Sat, to 8.30pm Jun-Sep, 10am-2pm Sun) This excellent museum does justice to the cultural and material wealth of Roman Tarraco. The mosaic collection traces the changing trends – from simple black-and-white designs to complex full-colour creations; a highlight is the large, almost complete *Mosaic de Peixos de la Pineda*, showing fish and sea creatures. Explanation in the museum is in Catalan and Spanish, but there is a multilingual audioguide included in the price.

MUSEU D'HISTÒRIA DE TARRAGONA RUIN
(MHT; www.museutgn.com; adult/child per site €3.30/free, all sites €11.05/free; ⊙sites 9am-9pm Tue-Sat, 10am-3pm Sun Easter-Sep, 9am-7pm Tue-Sat, 9am-3pm Sun Oct-Easter) The Museu d'Història de Tarragona consists of various separate Unesco World Heritage Roman sites, as well as some other historic buildings around town: Forùm Provincial Pretori i Circ Romans, Amfiteatre Romà, Passeig Arqueològic Muralles and Fòrum de la Colònia. Buy a combined ticket and get exploring.

PASSEIG ARQUEOLÒGIC MURALLES WALLS
(adult/child €3.30/free; ⊙sites 9am-9pm Tue-Sat, 10am-3pm Sun Easter-Sep, 10am-7pm Tue-Sat, 10am-3pm Sun Oct-Easter) A peaceful walk takes you around part of the perimeter of the old town between two lines of city walls. The inner ones are mainly Roman and date back to the 3rd century BC, while the outer ones were put up by the British in 1709 during the War of the Spanish Succession. The earliest stretches are a mighty 4m thick. Prepare to be awed by the vast gateways built by the Iberians and clamber up onto the battlements from the doorway to the right of the entrance for all-encompassing views of the city. The walk starts from the Portal del Roser where Avenida Catalunya touches the old town.

✖ EATING

The quintessential Tarragona seafood experience can be had in Serrallo, the town's fishing port. Plaça de la Font in the old town is great for an outdoor drink.

AQ MEDITERRANEAN, FUSION €€
(📞977 21 59 54; www.aq-restaurant.com; Carrer de les Coques 7; mains €11-20; ⊙1.30-3.30pm & 8.30-11pm Tue-Sat) The crisp interior design of this stone-walled restaurant promises fine dining, and AQ amply delivers. Its impeccably crafted fusion dishes – taking inspiration from Catalan, Italian and Asian cuisines – are playfully executed. Treat your tastebuds to Iberico pork burgers, squid carbonara or chop suey lobster. The three-course lunch menu (€19.80) is excellent value.

BARQUET SEAFOOD €€
(📞977 24 00 23; www.restaurantbarquet.com; Carrer del Gasometre 16; mains €11-18; ⊙1-3.30pm & 9-10.30pm Tue-Sat, 1-3.30pm Mon) This popular neighbourhood restaurant is a short downhill stroll from the centre. It's deservedly famous for its excellent rice dishes bursting with maritime flavour, and also has great *raciones* of seafood. Don't be fooled by the nautical warehouse interior: fish dishes and jewel-like desserts are executed with finesse.

Sleeping

Barcelona has an excellent range of accommodation, with high-end luxury hotels, small-scale boutique lodgings, and a varied spread of midrange and budget selections. The settings offer some fine choices in historic districts, facing the seaside or in the thick of charming neighbourhoods packed with restaurants and nightlife.

Hotels

Hotels cover a broad range. At the bottom end there is often little to distinguish them from better *pensiones* and *hostales,* and from there they run up the scale to five-star luxury. Some of the better features to look out for include rooftop pools and lounges; views (either of the sea or a cityscape – La Sagrada Família, Montjuïc, Barri Gòtic); and of course proximity to the important sights.

For around €100 to €160 there are extensive options for good doubles across a wide range of hotels and areas. The top-end category starts at €250 for a double, and can easily rise to €500 (and beyond for suites).

Pensiones & Hostales

Depending on the season you can pay as little as €15 to €25 for a dorm bed in a youth hostel. If dorm living is not your thing, but you are still looking for a budget deal, check around the many *pensiones* (small private hotels) and *hostales* (budget hotels). These are family-run, small-scale hotels, often housed in sprawling apartments. Some are fleapits, others immaculately maintained gems.

You're looking at a minimum of around €35/55 for basic *individual/doble* (single/double) rooms, mostly without a private bathroom. (It is occasionally possible to find cheaper rooms, but they may be unappealing.)

Some places, especially at the lower end, offer triples and quads, which can be good value for groups. If you want a double bed (as opposed to two singles), ask for a *llit/cama matrimonial* (Catalan/Spanish). If your budget is especially tight, look at options outside the centre.

Apartment & Room Rentals

A cosier (and sometimes more cost-effective) alternative to hotels is short-term apartment rental. A plethora of firms organise short lets across town. Typical prices are around €80 to €100 for two people per night. For four people you might be looking at an average of €160 a night.

Travellers with Disabilities

Many hotels claim to be equipped for guests with disabilities but reality frequently disappoints. Check out www.accessiblebarcelona. com for help with finding genuinely accessible accommodation. The same people also run www.accessible.travel.

Useful Websites

➡ **Lonely Planet** (www.lonelyplanet.com) Neighbourhood profiles, plus extensive listings of hotels, hostels, guesthouses and apartments.

➡ **Oh Barcelona** (www.oh-barcelona.com) Hotel and apartment listings, plus tips on deciding where to stay.

➡ **Barcelona Bed and Breakfasts** (www. barcelonabedandbreakfasts.com) Listings of low-key, oft-overlooked lodging options.

Lonely Planet's Top Choices

DO (p201) Magnificent boutique option overlooking the Plaça Reial.

Hotel Casa Fuster (p205) Plush rooms in a Modernista mansion in Gràcia.

Hotel Brummell (p206) A stylish Poble Sec stay with soul.

Cotton House (p205) A beautifully designed L'Eixample hotel – you won't want to leave.

Serras Hotel (p202) Luxurious lodging in an ideal Barri Gòtic location.

Best by Budget

€

Casa Gràcia (p205) Stylish hostel with colourful rooms, communal dinners, film screenings and other events.

Amistat Beach Hostel (p203) Small, warm and welcoming hostel, near the beach and restaurants of Poblenou.

Tailor's Hostel (p206) A hip Sant Antoni option with a vintage vibe.

Pars Teatro Hostel (p206) Theatrically decorated space on the edge of Poble Sec.

€€

Five Rooms (p204) Small and charming with beautifully designed rooms.

Barceló Raval (p202) Hotel with design smarts and an appealing rooftop terrace.

Hotel Market (p206) Beautifully designed rooms in the very hot 'hood of Sant Antoni.

H10 Port Vell (p203) A plush boutique stay in a great location.

€€€

Hotel Neri (p201) Beautiful, historic hotel on a tranquil spot in Barri Gòtic.

Hotel Mercer (p201) Peaceful retreat with medieval details and atmospheric rooms.

Hotel Casa Fuster (p205) A photogenic Gràcia mansion with striking interiors.

Hotel Majèstic (p205) A grand dame of L'Eixample.

Best Rooms With a View

El Jardí (p201) Charming views over the picturesque Plaça de Sant Josep Oriol.

Ohla Hotel (p202) Staggering views over the old city from the rooftop terrace.

Hotel Miramar (p206) Fabulous views over the city from a hilltop icon.

Hotel Continental (p201) Get a room over the Rambla and imagine what Orwell felt when he stayed here in 1937.

Best Hotel Pools

Grand Hotel Central (p203) In a great location on Via Laietana, this place has a rooftop infinity pool.

W Barcelona (p108) Splendid poolside fun just a short stroll from the beach.

Hotel Arts Barcelona (p203) Take a swim while admiring the Mediterranean and Frank Gehry's shimmering Peix sculpture.

Best for Style

Cami Bed & Gallery (p204) Seven unique rooms in an art-filled Modernista building.

Chic & Basic Ramblas (p202) Boasts serious design cred – particularly the lobby with its vintage decor.

ABaC Barcelona (p206) Gorgeous rooms, a spa and a celebrated restaurant.

NEED TO KNOW

Price Ranges
The following price ranges refer to a double room per night during high season. Prices include private bathroom unless otherwise stated.

€ less than €75
€€ €75 to €200
€€€ more than €200

Room Tax
→ Most accommodation is subject to the IVA, a 10% value-added tax.
→ There's also an additional tax of between €0.72 and €2.48 per person per night.
→ These charges are usually included in the quoted rate.

Seasonal Rates
Some hotels, particularly at the lower and middle levels, maintain the same prices year-round. Others vary the rates for high, mid and low seasons. Low season is roughly November to Easter, except during the Christmas/New Year period. Whenever there is a major trade fair (they are frequent), high-season prices generally apply.

Reservations
→ Booking ahead is recommended, especially during peak periods such as Easter, Christmas/New Year, trade fairs and throughout much of summer (although August can be quite a slack month owing to the heat).
→ If you arrive without prebooked lodging, the Plaça de Catalunya's tourist office (p235) can help.

SLEEPING

Where to Stay

Neighbourhood	For	Against
La Rambla & Barri Gòtic	Great location, close to major sights; perfect area for exploring on foot; good nightlife and dining options	Very touristy; noisy; some rooms are small and lack windows
El Raval	Central option, with good local nightlife and access to sights; bohemian vibe with few tourists	Can be noisy; seedy and run-down in parts; many fleapits best avoided; feels unsafe to walk late at night
La Ribera	Great restaurant scene and neighbourhood exploring; central; top sights including the Museu Picasso and the Palau de la Música Catalana	Can be noisy; overly crowded; touristy
Barceloneta & the Waterfront	Excellent seafood restaurants; easygoing local vibe; handy access to the promenade and beaches	Very few sleeping options; outside of Barceloneta can be far from the action and better suited to business travellers
L'Eixample	Wide range of options for all budgets; close to Modernista sights; good restaurants and nightlife; prime LGBTI scene (in 'Gaixample')	Can be very noisy with lots of traffic; not a great area for walking; a little far from the old city
Gràcia	Youthful, local scene with lively restaurants and bars	Far from the old city; few formal options (but lots of rooms for rent)
Pedralbes & La Zona Alta	Good nightlife and restaurants in parts	Very far from the action; spread-out area requiring frequent metro travel; geared more towards business travellers
Montjuïc, Poble Sec & Sant Antoni	Near the museums, gardens and views of Montjuïc; great local exploring in Poble Sec; locations in Poble Sec are also convenient to El Raval	Somewhat out of the way; can be a bit gritty up by El Sants train station

🛏 La Rambla & Barri Gòtic

ALBERG HOSTEL ITACA
HOSTEL €

Map p260 (☎93 301 97 51; www.itacahostel.com; Carrer de Ripoll 21; dm €30, d without bathroom €76; ❄🕿; MJaume I) A bright, quiet hostel near the cathedral, Itaca has spacious dorms (sleeping six to 10 people) with parquet floors and spring colours, and two doubles. There's a lively vibe, and the hostel organises activities (pub crawls, flamenco concerts, free daily walking tours), making it a good option for solo travellers.

HOTEL COLÓN
HOTEL €€

Map p260 (☎93 301 14 04; www.colonhotelbarcelona.com; Avinguda de la Catedral 7; s/d from €135/175; ❄🕿⌫; MJaume I) Its position opposite the cathedral lends this hotel special grace. A range of rooms, from modest singles to light-filled doubles and suites, offers elegant accommodation, with a spa, sauna and rooftop plunge pool. Decoration varies considerably (tending towards the carpeted and plush) and the top-floor superior rooms with terrace are marvellous (and go for about €230).

BONIC BARCELONA
B&B €

Map p260 (☎mob 626 053434; www.bonic-barcelona.com; Carrer de Josep Anselm Clavé 9; s/d without bathroom €55/90; ❄🕿; MDrassanes) A small, cosy B&B that has eight rooms in varied styles, with wood or decorative tile floors, tall ceilings and attractive furnishings. Several are bright and cheerfully painted, and some lack exterior windows. Owing to the restrictive layout – all rooms share three bathrooms – maximum occupancy is six or seven guests a night, although groups of friends can book the whole place to themselves.

VRABAC
B&B €€

Map p260 (☎mob 663 494029; vrabacguesthouse.wordpress.com; Carrer de la Portaferrissa 14; s/d incl breakfast €65/75; ❄🕿; MLiceu, Catalunya) In a central location just off La Rambla, Vrabac is set in a beautifully restored heritage building complete with original decorative ceilings, exposed sandstone walls and large oil paintings. Rooms vary in size and features – the best have elegant ceramic tile floors and sizeable balconies with private bathrooms. The cheapest are small and basic, lack a bathroom and not recommended. Cash only.

EL JARDÍ
HOTEL €€

Map p260 (☎93 301 59 00; www.eljardi-barcelona.com; Plaça de Sant Josep Oriol 1; d incl breakfast €80; ❄🕿; MLiceu) 'The Garden' has no garden but a handful of boxy doubles with balcony overlooking one of the prettiest squares in Barcelona. If you can snag one of the rooms with a view, it is well worth climbing up the stairs. If you can't, you're better off looking elsewhere.

HOTEL CONTINENTAL
HOTEL €€

Map p260 (☎93 301 25 70; www.hotelcontinental.com; La Rambla 138; s/d from €107/116; ❄🕿; MCatalunya) In 1937 George Orwell stayed here on his return from the front during the Spanish Civil War, when Barcelona was tense with factional strife. The Continental's rooms are worn and rather spartan, but have romantic touches like ceiling fans, brass bedsteads and frilly bedclothes. An extra €20 yields a room with a small balcony overlooking La Rambla, and there is a 24-hour free buffet.

DO REIAL
BOUTIQUE HOTEL €€€

Map p260 (☎93 481 36 66; www.hoteldoreial.com; Plaça Reial 1; s/d incl breakfast from €220/270; ❄🕿⌫; MLiceu) Overlooking the magnificent plaza for which it is named, this 18-room property has handsomely designed rooms with beamed ceilings, wide plank floors and all-important soundproofing. The service is excellent and the facilities extensive, with a roof terrace (bar in summer), dipping pool, solarium and spa. Its excellent market-to-table restaurants draw in visiting foodies.

HOTEL MERCER
BOUTIQUE HOTEL €€€

Map p260 (☎93 310 74 80; www.mercerbarcelona.com; Carrer dels Lledó 7; s/d from €430; P❄🕿⌫; MJaume I) Set on a narrow medieval lane, Hotel Mercer is one of Barcelona's best new hotels. Famed Spanish architect Rafael Moneo stayed true to the building's original Gothic and even Roman elements while creating lavishly designed rooms, some of which overlook an interior garden. There's a lovely rooftop dip pool, stylish cocktail lounge, tapas bar and restaurant, plus wonderfully peaceful common areas.

HOTEL NERI
DESIGN HOTEL €€€

Map p260 (☎93 304 06 55; www.hotelneri.com; Carrer de Sant Sever 5; d €275; ❄🕿; MLiceu) This tranquil hotel occupies a beautifully adapted, centuries-old building backing

SLEEPING LA RAMBLA & BARRI GÒTIC

onto Plaça de Sant Felip Neri. The sandstone walls and timber furnishings lend a sense of history, while the rooms feature cutting-edge technology, including plasma-screen TVs and infrared lights in the stone-clad designer bathrooms. Choose from a menu of sheets and pillows, and sun yourself on the roof deck.

OHLA HOTEL   BOUTIQUE HOTEL €€€

Map p260 (📞93 341 50 50; www.ohlahotel.com; Via Laietana 49; d €285; P ❄ 🏠 ≋; MUrquinaona) This beautifully designed hotel gets almost everything right, from the top-notch service to the lovely rooftop terrace with pool and twinkling views of Montjuïc. The sleek modern rooms have lavish fabrics, long pendular bedside lights, iPod docks and separate shower cubes that face on to the room (take note if you're travelling with someone who needs a touch more privacy).

There's a Michelin-starred restaurant (Saüc) and an enticing cocktail bar presided over by an award-winning mixologist.

SERRAS HOTEL   BOUTIQUE HOTEL €€€

Map p260 (📞93 169 18 68; hoteltheserrasbarcelona.net; Passeig de Colom 9; r €299; ❄ 🏠 ≋; MBarceloneta) A fresh and funky five-star that has every comfort – including a rooftop bar with a small dipping pool and a terrific view over the port – but never feels stuffy. Rooms at the front are brighter and have a better view (from the bathtub, in some cases) but rooms at the side are spared the traffic noise.

🛏 El Raval

HOTEL PENINSULAR   HOTEL €

Map p264 (📞93 302 31 38; www.hotelpeninsular.net; Carrer de Sant Pau 34; s/d €40/60; ❄ 🏠; MLiceu) An oasis on the edge of the slightly dicey Barri Xino, this former convent (which was connected by tunnel to the Església de Sant Agustí) has a plant-draped atrium extending its height and most of its length. The 60 rooms are simple, with tiled floors and whitewash, but mostly spacious and well kept. There are some great bargains to be had during quiet periods.

★BARCELÓ RAVAL   DESIGN HOTEL €€

Map p264 (📞93 320 14 90; www.barceloraval.com; Rambla del Raval 17-21; r from €128; ❄ 🏠; MLiceu) Part of the city's plans to pull the El Raval district up by the bootstraps, this oval-shaped

designer hotel tower makes a 21st-century splash. The rooftop terrace offers fabulous views and the B-Lounge bar-restaurant is the toast of the town for meals and cocktails. Rooms have slick aesthetics (white with lime green or ruby-red splashes of colour), Nespresso machines and iPod docks.

CHIC & BASIC RAMBLAS   DESIGN HOTEL €€

Map p264 (📞93 302 71 11; www.chicandbasicramblashotel.com; Passatge Gutenberg 7; r €127-152; ❄ 🏠; MDrassanes) The latest in the Chic & Basic chain is the most riotous to date, with quirky and colourful interiors that hit you from the second you walk in and see a vintage Seat 600 car in the foyer. Note that the name is misleading – the hotel is a couple of blocks into the Raval.

The rooms themselves are solid blocks of colour, and each loosely pays homage to an aspect of Barcelona life in the 1960s. All have balconies and small kitchens.

HOTEL SANT AGUSTÍ   HOTEL €€

Map p264 (📞93 318 16 58; www.hotelsa.com; Plaça de Sant Agustí 3; r €138-155; ❄ 🏠; MLiceu) This former 18th-century monastery opened as a hotel in 1840, making it the city's oldest. The location is perfect – a quick stroll off La Rambla on a curious square. Rooms sparkle, and are mostly spacious and light filled. Consider an attic double with sloping ceiling and bird's-eye views.

🛏 La Ribera

PENSIÓ 2000   PENSIÓN €

Map p268 (📞93 310 74 66; www.pensio2000.com; Carrer de Sant Pere més Alt 6; d €70-80; ❄ 🏠; MUrquinaona) This 1st-floor, family-run place is opposite the anything-but-simple Palau de la Música Catalana. Seven reasonably spacious doubles have mosaic-tiled floors, and after a recent renovation all have private bathrooms. You can eat your breakfast in the little courtyard.

PENSIÓN FRANCIA   HOSTEL €

Map p268 (📞93 319 03 76; www.milisa.com/P.Francia; Carrer de Rera Palau 4; d with/without bathroom €99/60; 🏠; MBarceloneta) The homey smell of laundry pervades this quaint little hostel in a great location close to the shore, the Parc de la Ciutadella and the nightlife of El Born. The 11 simple rooms are kept spick and span, with nothing much in the way of frills. Rooms with balconies benefit from plenty of natural light but little noise, as the lane is set away from the busy nearby thoroughfares.

CHIC & BASIC
DESIGN HOTEL €€

Map p268 (📞93 295 46 52; www.chicandbasic. com/hotel-barcelona-born; Carrer de la Princesa 50; s/d €104/113; ✱🛜; Ⓜ Jaume I) This is a very cool hotel indeed, with its 31 spotlessly white rooms and fairy-light curtains that change colour, adding an entirely new atmosphere to the space. The rooms are small, but the ceilings are high and the beds enormous. Many beautiful old features of the original building have been retained, such as the marble staircase.

HOTEL BANYS ORIENTALS
BOUTIQUE HOTEL €€

Map p268 (📞93 268 84 60; www.hotelbanyso-rientals.com; Carrer de l'Argenteria 37; s/d €96/118; ✱🛜; Ⓜ Jaume I) Book well ahead to get into this magnetically popular designer haunt. Cool blues and aquamarines combine with dark-hued floors to lend this clean-lined, boutique hotel a quiet charm. All rooms, on the small side, look onto the street or back lanes. There are more spacious suites in two other nearby buildings.

GRAND HOTEL CENTRAL
DESIGN HOTEL €€€

Map p268 (📞93 295 79 00; www.grand-hotelcentral.com; Via Laietana 30; d €337; ✱🛜🏊; Ⓜ Jaume I) With super-soundproofed rooms no smaller than 21 sq metres, this design hotel, complete with rooftop infinity pool, is one of the standout hotel offerings along Via Laietana. Rooms are decorated in style, with high ceilings, muted colours (beiges, browns and creams), dark wooden floors and subtle lighting.

🛏 Barceloneta & the Waterfront

AMISTAT BEACH HOSTEL
HOSTEL €

Map p272 (📞93 221 32 81; www.amistatbeach-hostel.com; Carrer de l'Amistat 21; dm €21-34; ✱🛜; Ⓜ Poblenou) A stylish addition to Poblenou, Amistat has attractively designed common areas, with a beanbag-filled lounge with DJ set-up, a low-lit TV room and a guest kitchen. The rooms themselves, which sleep from four to 12, are clean but basic – aside from a splash of colour on the ceilings. Friendly staff organise pub crawls, club nights and other events.

BED & BEACH
GUESTHOUSE €€

Map p272 (📞630 528156; www.bedandbeachbar-celona.com; Passatge General Bassols 26; d €75-130, s/d without bathroom €40/70; ✱🛜; Ⓜ Bo-gatell) This pleasant eight-room guesthouse is set on a quiet narrow street just a five-minute walk to the beach. Rooms are clean and comfortable, and vary in size and equipment – some lack natural light, while others are bright, with simple modern furnishings and in-room kitchens. The rooftop terrace is a fine spot for an afternoon drink, and there's also a shared kitchen for self-caterers.

POBLENOU BED & BREAKFAST
HOTEL €€

Map p272 (📞93 221 26 01; www.hostalpoblenou. com; Carrer del Taulat 30; s/d from €55/88; ✱@🛜; Ⓜ Llacuna) Experience life in this colourful working-class neighbourhood, just back from the beach, a few steps from the restaurant-lined Rambla del Poblenou, and increasingly home to a diverse population of loft-inhabiting gentrifiers. The 1930s house, with its high ceilings and beautiful tile floors, has six appealing rooms, each unique and all with a fresh feel, light colours, comfortable beds and, occasionally, a little balcony.

H10 PORT VELL
BOUTIQUE HOTEL €€

Map p270 (📞93 310 30 65; www.h10hotels. com; Pas de Sota Muralla 9; d from €150; ✱@🛜🏊; Ⓜ Barceloneta) The location is excellent at this 58-room hotel within a short stroll of El Born and Barceloneta. Sleek, modern rooms have a trim, minimalist design with black and white bathrooms, and the best rooms (not all) have fine views over the marina. The rooftop terrace is the best feature, with sun loungers, a tiny plunge pool and cocktails by evening.

HOTEL ARTS BARCELONA
LUXURY HOTEL €€€

Map p272 (📞93 221 10 00; www.hotelarts-barcelona.com; Marina 19-21; r from €450; 🅿✱@🛜🏊; Ⓜ Ciutadella Vila Olímpica) Set in a sky-high tower looming above Port Olímpic, this is one of Barcelona's most fashionable hotels. It has more than 480 rooms each kitted out with high-end features (Bang & Olufsen entertainment systems, separate shower and soaking tub), plus unbeatable views. Services range from enticing spa facilities to fine dining in celebrated Enoteca, which has two Michelin stars.

MELIÁ SKY BARCELONA
LUXURY HOTEL €€€

Map p272 (📞93 367 20 50; www.melia. com; Carrer de Pere IV 272-286; r €175-315; 🅿✱@🛜🏊; Ⓜ Poblenou) This daring, slim tower, designed by Dominique Perrault, is made from two filigree slabs of glass. It overlooks Jean Nouvel's Parc del Centre del Poblenou and offers designer digs, with city or sea views. The amenities are extensive, including various bars and terraces, an enticing pool and a 24th-floor Michelin-starred restaurant (Dos Cielos).

🛏 L'Eixample

CAMI BED & GALLERY
B&B €€

Map p278 (☑93 270 17 48; www.camibedandgallery.com; Carrer de Casp 22, Prl 1º; s/d from €110, s/d without bathroom from €95; ☀☎; MCatalunya) A luxury B&B in a handsome Modernista building that could not be more central, just metres from the Plaça de Catalunya. Seven airy rooms, with high ceilings, are meticulously designed and each is slightly different in character, though only one has a private bathroom. It also functions as a gallery, staging exhibitions and cultural events.

CASA BONAY
HOTEL €€

Map p278 (☑93 545 80 70; casabonay.com; Gran Via de les Corts Catalanes 700; r €200; ☀☎; MTetuan) A new and very now midrange hotel that combines an indefinably New York aesthetic with Scandi-style wooden furniture and typically Barcelona tiled floors. Rooms are spare but stylish, but the hotel's unique selling point is the range of carefully selected 'guest' shops, bars and restaurants it houses downstairs. These include a specialist coffee bar, a Vietnamese barbecue and a juice bar.

CONDES DE BARCELONA
HOTEL €€

Map p274 (☑93 445 00 00; www.condesdebarcelona.com; Passeig de Gràcia 73-75; s/d €160-215; P☀☎☂; MPasseig de Gràcia) The most attractive half of the Condes de Barcelona occupies the 1890s Modernista Casa Enric Batlló. Across the road stands a more modern extension. Clean, designer lines dominate inside each, with luxurious rooms, hardwood floors and architectural touches reminiscent of the Modernista exterior. The rooftop pool is a great place to relax.

FASHION HOUSE
B&B €€

Map p278 (☑637 904044; www.bcnfashionhouse.com; Carrer del Bruc 13; s/d €120, without bathroom €55/75; ☀☎; MUrquinaona) The name is a little silly but this typical 1st-floor L'Eixample flat contains eight rooms of varying size done in tasteful style, with 4.5m-high ceilings, parquet floors and, in some cases, a little balcony onto the street.

Bathrooms are located along the broad corridor, one for every two rooms.

FIVE ROOMS
BOUTIQUE HOTEL €€

Map p278 (☑93 342 78 80; www.thefiverooms.com; Carrer de Pau Claris 72; s/d from €140/160; ☀☎; MUrquinaona) The Five Rooms is in fact 12 rooms nowadays (standard rooms and suites) in this 1st-floor flat on the border between L'Eixample and the old centre of town. Rooms are all different and features include broad, firm beds, stretches of exposed brick wall, restored mosaic tiles and minimalist decor. There are also two apartments.

HCC ST MORITZ
HOTEL €€

Map p278 (☑93 481 73 50; www.hcchotels.com; Carrer de la Diputació 264; s/d €140/155; P☀☎; MPasseig de Gràcia) This upmarket hotel, set in a late-19th-century building, has 91 fully equipped rooms and boasts an elegant restaurant, terrace bar and small gym. Some of the bigger rooms, with marble bathrooms, even have their own exercise bikes. You can dine in the modest terrace garden.

HOSTAL CENTER INN
HOTEL €€

Map p278 (☑93 265 25 60; www.centerinnbarcelona.com; Gran Via de les Corts Catalanes 688; s/d €75/85; ☀@☎; MTetuan) Simple rooms have quirky touches – wrought-iron bedsteads, Moroccan mosaic tables on the ample balconies, stripey Tim Burton wallpaper in one room, an antique escritoire in another. Get a back room if you can, as the Gran Via is noisy.

HOSTAL OLIVA
HOSTAL €€

Map p278 (☑93 488 01 62; www.hostaloliva.com; Passeig de Gràcia 32; s/d €55/95, without bathroom €41/71; ☀☎; MPasseig de Gràcia) A picturesque antique lift wheezes its way up to this 4th-floor *hostal*, a terrific, reliable cheapie in one of the city's most expensive neighbourhoods. Some of the single rooms can barely fit a bed but the doubles are big enough, and light and airy (some with tiled floors, others with parquet and dark old wardrobes).

HOTEL CONSTANZA
BOUTIQUE HOTEL €€

Map p278 (☑93 270 19 10; www.hotelconstanza.com; Carrer del Bruc 33; s/d €100/140; ☀☎; MGirona, Urquinaona) This boutique beauty has stolen the hearts of many a visitor to Barcelona. Design touches abound, and little details like flowers in the bathroom add charm. Suites and studios are further options. The terrace is a nice spot to relax for a while, looking over the rooftops of the L'Eixample.

PRAKTIK RAMBLA
BOUTIQUE HOTEL €€

Map p274 (☑93 343 66 90; www.hotelpraktikram-bla.com; Rambla de Catalunya 27; s/d €110-135; ✳️🛜; MPasseig de Gràcia) This Modernista gem hides a gorgeous little boutique number. While the high ceilings and the bulk of the original tile floors have been maintained, the 43 rooms have daring ceramic touches, spot lighting and contemporary art. There is a chilled reading area and deck-style lounge terrace. The handy location on a tree-lined boulevard is an added plus.

COTTON HOUSE
HOTEL €€€

Map p278 (☑93 450 50 45; www.hotelcotton-house.com; Gran Via de les Corts Catalanes 670; r from €332; ✳️🛜; MUrquinaona) This splendid new addition to the city's luxury hotels situated in the former headquarters of the Cottonmakers' Guild, something which is alluded to throughout, from the huge sprays of cotton bolls in the jaw-dropping lobby to the room names (Damask, Taffeta etc). There's even a space off the library where you can select fabric and have a shirt made.

All-white rooms are not quite as thrilling as the common areas, but are extremely comfortable, with wide beds, beautifully fragranced toiletries and large rainshowers.

HOTEL MAJÈSTIC
HOTEL €€€

Map p278 (☑93 488 17 17; www.hotelmajestic.es; Passeig de Gràcia 68; s/d €330; P✳️🛜; MPasseig de Gràcia) This sprawling, central option has the charm of a great European hotel. The rooftop pool is superb for views and relaxing, or you can pamper yourself in the spa after a workout in the gym. The standard rooms (no singles) are smallish but comfortable and come with marble bathrooms.

🛌 Gràcia

★CASA GRÀCIA
HOSTEL €

Map p280 (☑93 174 05 28; www.casagra-ciabcn.com; Passeig de Gràcia 116; dm/s/d from €27/90/103; ✳️@🛜; MDiagonal) A hostel with a difference, the tasteful Casa Gràcia has raised the bar for budget accommodation. There are some enticing common spaces, including a terrace, a library nook and an artfully decorated lounge – not to mention a restaurant and DJ-fuelled bar on hand.

Aside from the dorm rooms, there are a couple of private rooms, and all are decorated in crisp white with bursts of colour. Casa Gràcia hosts a wide range of activities and events: cocktail-making workshops, yoga classes, wine tastings and screenings of foreign films (and FC Barcelona games) on the big screen TV.

GENERATOR HOSTEL
HOSTEL €€

Map p280 (☑93 220 03 77; generatorhostels.com; Carrer de Còrsega 373; dm from €28/111; MVerdaguer, Diagonal) Part of the design-forward Generator brand, this stylish hostel has much to recommend it, including a quirky bar made from reclaimed lumber and recycled elevator parts and festooned with an explosion of paper lanterns. The rooms themselves are quite simple if adequately equipped – unless you opt for the penthouse room with a terrace offering panoramic views over the city.

HOTEL CASA FUSTER
DESIGN HOTEL €€€

Map p280 (☑93 255 30 00; www.hotelcasa-fuster.com; Passeig de Gràcia 132; r from €262; P✳️@🛜�❖; MDiagonal) This sumptuous Modernista mansion, built in 1908–11, is one of Barcelona's most luxurious hotels. Standard rooms are plush, if small. Period features have been restored at considerable cost and complemented by hydro-massage tubs, plasma TVs and king-size beds. The rooftop terrace (with pool) offers spectacular views.

The Café Vienès, once a meeting place for Barcelona's intellectuals, hosts excellent jazz nights (Thursdays from 9pm).

🛌 Pedralbes & La Zona Alta

INOUT HOSTEL
HOSTEL €

Map p282 (☑93 280 09 85; www.inouthostel.com; Major del Rectoret 2; dm €22; ✳️@🛜�❖♿; � FGC Baixador de Vallvidrera) 🌿 One of Spain's most extraordinary hostels, Inout is a beautifully located property with a strong social ethos. Over 90% of staff here have a disability. It's a friendly and welcoming place with extensive facilities, including an enticing pool, sports courts, and a low-key restaurant with panoramic views. It's a 12-minute uphill walk from the FGC Baixa-dor de Vallvidrera station.

SLEEPING GRÀCIA

206

Keep an eye out for the wild boars, which flourish in the surrounding Parc de Collserola, and can sometimes be spotted nearby.

HOTEL POL & GRACE BOUTIQUE HOTEL €€

Map p284 (✆93 415 40 00; www.polgracehotel. es; Carrer de Guillem Tell 49; r from €120; ❀🛜; ⓇFGC Molina, Sant Gervasi) This stylish new hotel has appealing, uniquely designed rooms, revolving around Barcelona themes (images and artefacts that celebrate a Catalan festival, key architectural icons, gastronomy etc). There's also a handsomely designed lounge where guests can unwind, and a roof terrace is in the works.

Staff aim to make guests feel at home here, and pride themselves on helping to arrange locally oriented experiences.

ABAC BARCELONA LUXURY HOTEL €€€

Map p282 (✆93 319 66 00; www.abacbarcelona.com; Avinguda del Tibidabo 1; d from €253; ❀@🛜; ⓇFGC Avinguda Tibidabo) This uberstylish hotel in Sant Gervasi receives high marks for its beautifully designed rooms, kitted out with Bang & Olufsen TVs, rainfall shower heads, Jacuzzi tubs with aromatherapy and luxury bed linens. A lovely spa and one of the city's best restaurants (p169; with two Michelin stars) add to the appeal.

🛏 Montjuïc, Poble Sec & Sant Antoni

TAILOR'S HOSTEL HOSTEL €

Map p286 (✆93 250 56 84; www.tailors-hostel. com; Carrer de Sepúlveda 146; dm €24-30; ❀🛜; ⓂUrgell, Sant Antoni) Decorated like a mid-20th-century tailor's shop, this popular hostel has uncommon style, with old sewing machines, lovingly framed brassieres and vintage fixtures adorning the common areas. Aside from admiring the aesthetics, there's much afoot at Tailor's: you can shoot a round on the old billiards table, mingle with other guests in the comfy lounge, or join one of the many activities on offer.

The hostel organises day trips and pub crawls, hires bikes, arranges cooking classes, and holds evening gatherings over tapas and drinks. The staff are friendly and have loads of local insight into Barcelona. The rooms themselves are as basic as can be.

PARS TEATRO HOSTEL HOSTEL €

Map p286 (✆93 443 94 66; www.teatrohostel.com; Carrer d'Albareda 12; dm €25-35; 🛜;

Ⓜ Drassanes) True to its name, Teatro Hostel has a theatrically decorated interior: old photos of actors of yesteryear hang on the walls of the vintage-filled main lounge, above an old row of velvety theatre seats. Rooms are less exciting, but clean and well-maintained. Friendly staff.

★HOTEL BRUMMELL BOUTIQUE HOTEL €€

Map p286 (✆93 125 86 22; www.hotelbrummell.com; Carrer Nou de la Rambla 174; d from €150; ❀🛜💦; ⓂParal·lel) This stylish addition to Barcelona has been turning heads since its 2015 opening. It's a thoughtfully designed hotel with a creative soul and great atmosphere. The 20 rooms are bright with a cheerful, minimalist design, and the best of the bunch have sizeable terraces with views and even outdoor soaking tubs. The smallest (the Brummell Classic rooms) feel a little tight.

Rooms are only a small part of Brummell's appeal. There's a great restaurant and cafe area, a terrace with a small dip pool, and kind-hearted staff who are happy to share insight into Barcelona's lesser-known gems. Don't miss the vending machines in the corridor with bottles of wine and gourmet snacks, in place of sodas and sweets. Weekend brunch at on-site Box Social is the hottest event in town.

HOTEL MARKET BOUTIQUE HOTEL €€

Map p286 (✆93 325 12 05; www.andilanahotels.com; Carrer del Comte Borrell 68; r €130; ❀@🛜; ⓂSant Antoni) Attractively located in a renovated building along a narrow lane just north of the grand old Sant Antoni market, this place has an air of simple chic, with wide plank floors, oversized armoires, bold art prints and nicely designed bathrooms (stone basins, rain showers). Some rooms have tiny (two-seat) balconies.

There's a first-rate restaurant and bar on the main floor, with outdoor seating on the lane.

HOTEL MIRAMAR HOTEL €€€

Map p286 (✆93 281 16 00; www.hotelmiramarbarcelona.com; Plaça de Carlos Ibáñez 3; r €230; ❀🛜💦; 🚌50,150) Welcome to the only hotel on Montjuïc, a designer five-star job. Local architect Oscar Tusquets took the shell of a building built for the 1929 World Fair and later the Barcelona HQ of Spanish national TV (1959–83), and created this hilltop configuration where all rooms have broad balconies and views over the port, city or park.

Understand Barcelona

Barcelona Today

Take a stroll through the streets of Barcelona, and you'll likely see more than a few *esteladas*, the flag with the lone star (and red and yellow bars) that symbolises Catalonia's drive towards independence. Talk of separatism has reached a fever pitch, and raised deep concerns across Europe. Of course, there's much more brewing in Barcelona than just self-rule. The city's deep commitment to innovation has led to improvements in transport, communications and urban design.

Best on Film

All About My Mother (director Pedro Almodóvar, 1999) One of Almodóvar's best-loved films is full of plot twists and dark humour, complete with transsexual prostitutes and doe-eyed nuns.

Vicky Cristina Barcelona (director Woody Allen, 2008) Allen gives Barcelona the *Manhattan* treatment, showing a city of startling beauty and neuroticism.

L'Auberge Espagnol (director Cédric Klapisch, 2002) A warmly told coming-of-age story about a mishmash of foreign-exchange students thrown together in Barcelona.

Barcelona (director Whit Stillman, 1994) A sharp and witty romantic comedy about two Americans living in Barcelona during the end of the Cold War.

Best in Print

Barcelona (Robert Hughes, 1992) Witty and passionate study of 2000 years of history.

The Shadow of the Wind (Carlos Ruiz Zafón, 2001) Page-turning mystery set in post-Civil-War Barcelona.

Homage to Catalonia (George Orwell, 1938) Orwell's classic account of the early days of the Spanish Civil War.

The Nation of Catalonia?

It's an historic moment in Barcelona. The drive towards independence is under way, with the very real possibility that Catalonia could break away from Spain and become a sovereign republic in 2018. With its own language, unique traditions and proud history (at least prior to its conquest by Spain in 1714), Catalonia has always thought of itself as distinct from other parts of the country. But until recently, only a small fringe group sought a permanent and irrevocable break from Madrid.

In the last few years, however, the number of self-proclaimed separatists has skyrocketed. Back in November 2014 Catalonia held a nonbinding referendum, and over 80% of those who voted backed Catalan independence (the turnout however, was low, with less than half of eligible voters participating). Spain's Constitutional Court wasted little time in declaring the vote (and all future votes) on independence to be illegal. Then in the following year (September 2015) Catalan nationalists won a majority of the 135-seat regional assembly, which they viewed as an implicit endorsement of secession. Catalan leader Artur Mas i Gavarró promised to press ahead with independence.

Hostilities quickly flared between Artur Mas and Spanish Prime Minister Mariano Rajoy, who vowed to use the judiciary to block any Catalan moves towards independence. This didn't deter the parliament of Catalonia, however. Shortly after the elections (November 2015) a resolution was passed laying out the road map to independence, with legislation under way to draft a Catalan constitution, create a new treasury and design a social security system. Self-rule was to be achieved within 18 months.

Fuelling the drive is the ongoing economic crisis – some 19% of Catalans are unemployed (versus 21%

nationally), and the feeling of injustice is pervasive. Catalonia has long claimed that it pays more in tax revenue than it gets back. According to a 2011 report (released only in 2015), Catalonia did in fact pay €8.5 billion more in taxes than it got back in transfers and investments (Catalan advocates claim the actual figure was above €11 billion).

The repercussions of Catalan independence would be wide-reaching. It could undermine the financial stability of Spain – and cause economic shock waves across the eurozone. Most damning to some would-be supporters: the president of the Spanish professional football league said Barcelona FC would no longer be part of La Liga. How it all shakes out is anybody's guess, but no one is expecting a smooth ride.

Land of Innovation

The city that gave birth to Gaudí and the ingenious creations of Modernisme continues to break new ground in other realms. In particular, Barcelona has become a global model as a Smart City – a place where technology is harnessed to create a more sustainable, efficient, and interconnected environment for both residents and visitors alike. Some 120 projects comprise the Smart City initiative, including wide-reaching innovations affecting transport, communications, public and social services, and even tourism.

Shrinking the city's carbon footprint is at the forefront of various new technologies. Self-powered lights installed along one stretch of beach use a combination of solar and wind energy, without needing to tap into the grid. Barcelona has the cleanest fleet of buses in Europe, with a large share of hybrids and natural-gas-powered vehicles (plus antipollution filters on its remaining diesel motors).

Speaking of buses, Barcelona has also launched new routes based on the flow of people using the system, creating a new more intuitive grid that moves vertically, horizontally and diagonally across the city. It has also been expanding its network for electric cars, with 300 existing charging stations and more in the works.

Barcelona also has a free, and growing, wi-fi network with nearly 500 hot spots and plans to add more than 1500 in the coming years – including inside buses and metro stations. Another innovation: smart traffic lights that turn green when emergency vehicles are approaching so they can reach their destination faster.

Fuelling much of the innovation is the 220-hectare district known as 22@ *(vint-i-dos arroba)*. This district in El Poblenou has seen enormous growth since its creation back in 2000. Over 90,000 jobs have been created under the 8000 firms at work, largely in the digital, creative and tech industries.

if Barcelona were 100 people

62 would be Catalan
24 would be other Spanish
14 would be non-Spanish

belief systems
(% of population)

90
Roman Catholic

10
Other

population per sq km

SPAIN   BARCELONA

🚹 ≈ 90 people

History

The layered settlement of Barcelona has seen waves of immigrants and conquerors over its 2000-plus years, including Romans, Visigoths, Franks and later Catalans. Barcelona's fortunes have risen and fallen; from the golden era of princely power in the 14th century to dark days of civil war and the Franco era. A fierce independent streak has always run through Barcelona, which has often led to conflict with the Kingdom of Castilla – an antagonism that continues today, with a desire for more autonomy (full independence, say some Catalans) from Spain.

The Romans

Barcelona's recorded history really begins with the Romans when Barcino (much later Barcelona) was founded in the reign of Caesar Augustus. The Romans were attracted to the location for the possibility of building a port here.

In 1991 the remains of 25 corpses, dating from 4000 BC, were found in Carrer de Sant Pau in El Raval. In those days much of El Raval was a bay and the hillock (Mont Tàber) next to Plaça de Sant Jaume may have been home to a Neolithic settlement.

Rome's legacy was huge, giving Hispania (as the Iberian Peninsula was known to the Romans) a road system, aqueducts, temples and the religion that still predominates today, Christianity. Before Rome embraced this monotheistic tradition, however, there were waves of persecutions of early Christians. Santa Eulàlia, who may or may not have existed, is one of the great martyrs of this time. She still plays a role in the city's folklore, with a major festival in her name happening in February each year. Her body is believed to be buried under La Catedral. Christian persecution ended a few years after her death, when Emperor Constantine declared Christianity the official religion in 312.

Wilfred the Hairy & the Catalan Golden Age

In the 9th century AD, when much of Spain was ruled by the Moors, Louis the Pious – the son of Charlemagne and the future Frankish ruler – conquered Barcelona and claimed it as part of his empire. Barcelona in those days was a frontier town in what was known as the Frankish or

TIMELINE	c 4000 BC	218 BC	AD 415
	A Neolithic settlement may have thrived around the present-day Plaça de Sant Jaume at this time, as indicated by jasper implements discovered around Carrer del Paradís.	In a move to block supplies to the Carthaginian general Hannibal, Roman troops under Scipio land at Empúries, found Tarraco (Tarragona) and take control of the Catalan coast.	Visigoths under Athaulf, with captured Roman empress Galla Placidia as his wife, make Barcino their capital. With several interruptions, it remains so until the 6th century.

Spanish March – a rough-and-ready buffer zone between the Pyrenees and the Moors who had conquered most of the lands to the south.

The March was under nominal Frankish control but the real power lay with local potentates who ranged across the territory. One of these rulers went by the curious name of Guifré el Pelós (Wilfred the Hairy). This was not a reference to uneven shaving habits: according to legend, old Guifré had hair in parts most people do not (exactly which parts was never specified!). He and his brothers gained control of most of the Catalan counties by 878 and Guifré entered the folk mythology of Catalonia.

Guifré consolidated power over Catalonia and ushered in an era of early building projects. He endowed churches and had a new palace for himself in Barcelona (of which nothing remains). His achievements were later described by medieval monks and Romantic poets, who credit him with transforming a minor town into the future seat of an empire. If Catalonia can be called a nation, then its 'father' was the hirsute Guifré. He founded a dynasty that lasted nearly five centuries, and which developed almost independently from the Reconquista wars that were playing out in the rest of Iberia.

Romanesque Beauties

At the beginning of the second millennium, Catalan culture entered a rich new age. Romanesque churches in the countryside fostered a powerful new style of architecture. Inside lay richly painted frescoes made of the finest pigments and bearing notable Byzantine influences. Some of these works – rescued from churches that later fell into ruin – are beautifully preserved inside the Museu Nacional d'Art de Catalunya (MNAC) on Montjuïc. Commerce was also on the rise, fuelled by a new class of merchants and tradespeople.

A Growing Empire

Shipbuilding, textiles and farming (grain and grapes) helped power expansion. An even bigger catalyst to Catalonia's growth came in 1137 when Ramon Berenguer IV, the Count of Barcelona, became engaged to Petronilla, heir to the throne of neighbouring Aragón, thus creating a joint state that set the scene for Catalonia's golden age.

In the following centuries the regime became a flourishing merchant empire, seizing Valencia and the Balearic Islands from the Moors, and later taking territories as far flung as Sardinia, Sicily and parts of Greece.

Barcelona's first patron saint, Santa Eulàlia (290–304), was martyred for her faith during the persecutory reign of Diocletian. Her death involved 13 tortures (one for each year of her life), including being rolled in a glass-filled barrel, having her breasts cut off and crucifixion. Some paintings depict her holding a tray containing her severed breasts.

According to a medieval legend, Barcelona was founded by Hercules himself. Although versions differ, all tell of nine *barcas* (boats), one of which separates from the others in a storm, and is piloted by Hercules to a beautiful spot on the coast where he founds a city, naming it Barca Nona (Ninth Boat).

878	985	1060	1137
Wilfred the Hairy consolidates power throughout Catalonia and founds a long-lasting dynasty with his capital in Barcelona.	Al-Mansur (the Victorious) rampages across Catalan territory and devastates Barcelona in a lightning campaign. Much of the population is taken as slaves to Córdoba.	Some 150 years before the Magna Carta, Count Ramon Berenguer I approves the 'Usatges de Barcelona', a bill of rights establishing all free men as equal before the law.	Count Ramon Berenguer IV is betrothed to one-year-old Petronilla, daughter of the king of Aragón, creating a new combined state that becomes known as the Corona de Aragón.

Barcelona's Golden Age

The 14th century marked the golden age of Barcelona. Its trading wealth paid for the great Gothic buildings that bejewel the city to this day. La Catedral, the Capella Reial de Santa Àgata (inside the Museu d'Història de Barcelona) and the churches of Santa Maria del Pi and Santa Maria del Mar were all completed during this time. King Pere III (1336–87) later created the breathtaking Reials Drassanes (Royal Shipyards) and also extended the city walls yet again, this time to include El Raval to the west.

Justice in feudal days was a little rough by modern standards. As prescribed in a 1060 bill: 'In regard to women, let the rulers render justice by cutting off their noses, lips, ears and breasts, and by burning them at the stake if necessary.'

Black Death & Pogroms

Preserving the empire began to exhaust Catalonia. Sea wars with Genoa, resistance in Sardinia, the rise of the Ottoman Empire and the loss of the gold trade all drained the city's coffers. Commerce collapsed. The Black Death and famines killed about half of Catalonia's population in the 14th century. Barcelona also lost some of its best merchants when bloodthirsty mobs attacked Jewish businesses and homes in 1391.

War of the Spanish Succession

Although Catalonia had only limited autonomy in the late 1600s, things grew worse at the turn of the 18th century when it supported the wrong side in the War of the Spanish Succession. Barcelona, under the auspices of British-backed archduke Charles of Austria, fell after an 18-month siege on 11 September 1714 to the forces of Bourbon king Felipe V, who established a unitary Castilian state.

Although 11 September reflects the tragic fall of the city, the day is still commemorated as the Diada, the National Day of Catalonia – often a day of political rallies and demonstrations, with independence very much on the agenda.

Catalonia Under a Repressive Regime

Angered at Catalonia's perceived treachery, the new king abolished the Generalitat and levelled a whole district of medieval Barcelona to make way for a huge fort (the Ciutadella) to watch over the city. The recently excavated ruins beneath El Born Centre Cultural (which opened in 2013) show what life was like for those living in the 1700s on the future site of the Ciutadella. Their lives changed irrevocably as their homes were destroyed and they were relocated to the new soulless geometric grid of Barceloneta. Not surprisingly, the citadel became the city's most hated symbol among most Catalans.

Teaching and writing in Catalan was banned, as Felipe V proceeded with a widespread plan of 'Castlianisation', in hopes of crushing future dissent. What was left of Catalonia's possessions were farmed out to the great powers.

1225–29	1283	1323	1348
At age 18 Jaume I takes command; four years later he conquers Muslim-held Mallorca, the first of several dazzling conquests that lead him to be called El Conqueridor (the Conqueror).	The Corts Catalanes, a legislative council for Catalonia, meets for the first time and begins to curtail unlimited powers of sovereigns in favour of nobles and the powerful trading class.	Catalan forces land in Sardinia and launch a campaign of conquest that would not end until 1409. Their fiercest enemy was Eleonora de Arborea, a Sardinian Joan of Arc.	Plague devastates Barcelona. Over 25% of the city's population dies. Further waves of the Black Death, a plague of locusts in 1358 and an earthquake in 1373 deal further blows.

A New Boom

After the initial shock, Barcelona found the Bourbon rulers to be comparatively light-handed in their treatment of the city. The big break came in 1778, when the ban on trade with the Spanish American colonies was lifted. In Barcelona itself, growth was modest but sustained. Small-scale manufacturing provided employment and profit, and wages were rising.

Barcelona's growth was briefly slowed by the French invasion in 1808, but gradually returned after Napoleon's defeat in 1814. The cotton trade with America helped fuel the boom. In the 1830s, the first steam-driven factories opened in Barcelona, heralding a wave of development that would last for most of the century. Wine, cork and iron industries flourished. From the mid-1830s onwards, steamships were launched off the slipways. In the following decade Spain's first railway line was opened between Barcelona and Mataró.

A Dramatic Redesign

Creeping industrialisation and prosperity for the business class did not work out so well down the line. Working-class families lived in increasingly putrid and cramped conditions. Poor nutrition, bad sanitation and disease were the norm in workers' districts, and riots, predictably, resulted. As a rule they were put down with little ceremony – the 1842 rising was bombarded into submission from the Castell de Montjuïc.

In 1869 a plan to expand the city was begun. Ildefons Cerdà designed L'Eixample (the Enlargement) as a grid, broken up with gardens and parks and grafted on to the old city, beginning at Plaça de Catalunya. The plan was revolutionary. Until then it had been illegal to build on the plains between Barcelona and Gràcia, as the area was a military zone. As industrialisation got under way this building ban also forced the concentration of factories in Barcelona itself (especially in Barceloneta) and surrounding towns like Gràcia, Sant Martí, Sants and Sant Andreu (all of which were subsequently swallowed up by the burgeoning city).

L'Eixample became the most sought-after chunk of real estate in Barcelona – but the parks were mostly sacrificed to an insatiable demand for housing and undisguised land speculation. The flourishing bourgeoisie paid for lavish, ostentatious buildings, many of them in the unique Modernista style.

A 19th-Century Renaissance

Barcelona was comparatively peaceful for most of the second half of the 19th century but far from politically inert. The relative calm and growing

HISTORY A NEW BOOM

Many Gothic masterpieces were built in the mid-14th century, a time of great suffering in Barcelona. When a wheat crop failed in 1333, the resulting famine killed 10,000 people (a quarter of the city's population). In the 1340s plague devastated the city, killing four of its five councillors along with many others.

1383	1387	1469	1640–52
After 50 or so years of frenzied construction, the massive Santa Maria del Mar rises above La Ribera. It is one of many Gothic architectural gems completed in the 14th century.	During the reign of Juan I Barcelona hosts its first bullfight, according to the city's historical archive. It isn't until the 19th century, however, that bullfighting gains widespread popularity.	Isabel, heir to the Castilian throne, marries Aragonese heir Fernando, uniting two of Spain's most powerful monarchies and effectively subjugating Catalonia to the Castilian state.	Catalan peasants, angered at having to quarter Castilian troops during the Thirty Years War, declare their independence under French protection. Spain eventually crushes the rebellion.

wealth that came with commercial success helped revive interest in all things Catalan.

The Renaixença (Renaissance) reflected the feeling of renewed self-confidence in Barcelona. Politicians and academics increasingly studied and demanded the return of former Catalan institutions and legal systems. The Catalan language was readopted by the middle and upper classes and new Catalan literature emerged as well.

In 1892 the Unió Catalanista (Catalanist Union) demanded the re-establishment of the Corts in a document known as the *Bases de Manresa*. In 1906 the suppression of Catalan news sheets was greeted by the formation of Solidaritat Catalana (Catalan Solidarity; a nationalist movement). It attracted a broad band of Catalans, not all of them nationalists.

Perhaps the most dynamic expression of the Catalan Renaissance occurred in the world of art. Barcelona was the home of Modernisme, Catalan art nouveau. While the rest of Spain stagnated, Barcelona was a hotbed of artistic activity – an avant-garde base with close links to Paris. The young Picasso spread his artistic wings here and drank in the artists' hang-out of Els Quatre Gats.

An unpleasant wake-up call came with Spain's short, futile war with the USA in 1898, in which it lost not only its entire navy but also its last colonies (Cuba, Puerto Rico and the Philippines). The blow to Barcelona's trade was enormous.

Working-Class Turmoil

Barcelona's proletariat was growing fast. The total population grew from 115,000 in 1800 to over 500,000 by 1900 and over one million by 1930 – boosted, in the early 19th century, by poor immigrants from rural Catalonia and, later, from other regions of Spain. All this made Barcelona ripe for unrest.

The city became a swirling vortex of poor workers, Republicans, bourgeois regionalists, gangsters, police terrorists and hired *pistoleros* (gunmen). Among the underclasses, who lived in some of the most abysmal conditions in Europe, there was a deep undercurrent of discontent towards the upper classes, the state and the Catholic church (which had long been viewed as an ally to the rich and powerful).

Anarchist Bombings & the Tragic Week

When the political philosophy of anarchism began spreading through Europe, it was embraced by many industrial workers in Barcelona, who embarked on a road to social revolution through violent means.

In Catalan folklore, the idea for the Catalan flag – alternating red-and-yellow bars – was born when, during a battle, King Louis the Pious dipped four fingers into the wound of a dying Wilfred the Hairy, and ran them across Wilfred's golden shield. Never mind that Louis died long before Wilfred was born!

1714	1770	1808	1869
Barcelona loses all autonomy after surrendering to the Bourbon king, Felipe V, on 11 September at the end of the War of the Spanish Succession.	A freak hurricane strikes Barcelona, causing considerable damage. Among other things, the winds destroy more than 200 of the city's 1500 gaslight street lamps.	In the Battle of Bruc, Catalan militiamen defeat occupying Napoleonic units, yet Barcelona, Figueres and the coast remain under French control until Napoleon's retreat in 1814.	Ildefons Cerdà designs L'Eixample (the Enlargement) district with wide boulevards and a grid pattern. Modernista architects of the day showcase their creations here.

One anarchist bomb at the Liceu opera house on La Rambla in the 1890s killed 22 people. Anarchists were also blamed for the Setmana Tràgica (Tragic Week) in July 1909 when, following a military call-up for Spanish campaigns in Morocco, rampaging mobs wrecked 70 religious buildings and workers were shot on the street in reprisal.

Class Struggle & the Coming War

In the post-WWI slump, unionism took hold. This movement was led by the anarchist Confederación Nacional del Trabajo (CNT; National Workers' Confederation), which embraced 80% of the city's workers. During a wave of strikes in 1919 and 1920, employers hired assassins to eliminate union leaders. The 1920s dictator General Miguel Primo de Rivera opposed bourgeois-Catalan nationalism and working-class radicalism, banning the CNT and even closing Barcelona's football club, a potent symbol of Catalanism. But he did support the staging of a second world fair in Barcelona, the Montjuïc World Exhibition of 1929.

Rivera's repression succeeded only in uniting, after his fall in 1930, Catalonia's radical elements. Within days of the formation of Spain's Second Republic in 1931, leftist Catalan nationalists of the Esquerra Republicana de Catalunya (ERC), led by Francesc Macià and Lluís Companys, proclaimed Catalonia a republic within an imaginary 'Iberian Federation'. Madrid pressured them into accepting unitary Spanish statehood, but after the leftist Popular Front victory in the February 1936 national elections, Catalonia briefly won genuine autonomy. Companys, its president, carried out land reforms and planned an alternative Barcelona Olympics to the official 1936 games in Nazi Berlin.

But things were racing out of control. The left and the right across Spain were shaping up for a showdown.

Civil War Erupts

On 17 July 1936, an army uprising in Morocco kick-started the Spanish Civil War. The main players in the conflict were the Nationalists and the Republicans. The Nationalists were allied with conservatives (and the Church). Angry at the new leftist direction in which Spain was heading, they staged a coup, led by General Franco and other rebels, and quickly gained the following of most of the army. On the opposite side was the Republican government, which was supported by those loyal to Spain's democratically elected government. Republican supporters were a loose coalition of workers' parties, socialists, anarchists, communists and other left-wing groups.

Historical Reads

....

Barcelona
(Robert Hughes)

*Barcelona –
A Thousand Years
of the City's Past*
(Felipe Fernández
Armesto)

*Homage to
Catalonia*
(George Orwell)

....

*Homage to
Barcelona*
(Colm Tóibín)

1873	1888	1895	1898
Antoni Gaudí, 21 years old and in Barcelona since 1869, enrols in architecture school, from which he graduates five years later, having already designed the street lamps in Plaça Reial.	Showcasing the grand Modernista touches of recent years (including L'Eixample), Barcelona hosts Spain's first International Exposition, held in the new, manicured Parc de la Ciutadella.	Málaga-born Pablo Picasso, aged 13, arrives in Barcelona with his family. His art-teacher father gets a job in the Escola de Belles Artes, where Pablo enrols as a pupil.	Spain loses its entire navy and last remaining colonies (the Philippines, Cuba and Puerto Rico) in two hopeless campaigns against the USA, dealing a heavy blow to Barcelona businesses.

Barcelona's army garrison attempted to take the city for General Franco, but was defeated by anarchists and police loyal to the government. Franco's Nationalist forces quickly took hold of most of southern and western Spain; Galicia and Navarra in the north were also his. Most of the east and industrialised north stood with Madrid. Initial rapid advances on Madrid were stifled and the two sides settled in for almost three years of misery.

Life Under the Anarchists

For nearly a year, Barcelona was run by anarchists and the Trotskyist militia of the Partido Obrero de Unificación Marxista (POUM; the Marxist Unification Workers' Party), with Companys president only in name. Factory owners and rightists fled the city. Unions took over factories and public services, hotels and mansions became hospitals and schools, everyone wore workers' clothes (in something of a foretaste of what would later happen in Mao's China), bars and cafes were collectivised, trams and taxis were painted red and black (the colours of the anarchists), and one-way streets were ignored as they were seen to be part of the old system.

The anarchists were a disparate lot ranging from gentle idealists to hardliners who drew up death lists, held kangaroo courts, shot priests, monks and nuns (over 1200 of whom were killed in Barcelona province during the civil war), and also burnt and wrecked churches – which is why so many of Barcelona's churches are today oddly plain inside. They in turn were shunted aside by the communists (directed by Stalin from Moscow) after a bloody internecine battle in Barcelona that left 1500 dead in May 1937.

Barcelona also suffered aerial bombing raids carried out by Italian bombers sympathetic to Franco. The pockmarked walls around Plaça Sant Felip Neri still bear the scars of one particularly gruesome day of bombardment when dozens of civilians – many of them children – were killed here.

Barcelona became the Republicans' national capital in autumn 1937. The Republican defeat in the Battle of the Ebro in southern Catalonia the following summer left Barcelona undefended. Republican resistance crumbled, in part due to exhaustion, in part due to disunity. In 1938 Catalan nationalists started negotiating separately with the Nationalists. The city fell to Franco's forces in January 1939.

Franco Takes the City

Franco's tanks rolled into a strangely silent and empty city. Almost half a million people had fled to the north. The first few months of occupa-

Barcelona nearly staged the Olimpíada Popular (People's Olympiad) in 1936, an alternative to the Olympics that were being held in fascist Germany. Around 6000 athletes from 23 countries registered. However, the civil war erupted just before the start. Some athletes who arrived stayed on and joined militias to help defend the republic.

July 1909	1914	July 1936	March 1938
After the call-up of reserve troops to fight a war in Morocco, *barcelonins* riot. Over 100 are reportedly killed in what's later known as Setmana Tràgica (Tragic Week).	The Mancomunitat de Catalonia, a first timid attempt at self-rule (restricted largely to administrative matters) and headed by Catalan nationalist Enric Prat de la Riba, is created in April.	General Franco launches the Spanish Civil War in Morocco. General Goded leads army units to take Barcelona for Franco, but is defeated by left-wing militia, workers and loyalist police.	In just three days of day-and-night air raids on Barcelona carried out by fascist Italian bombers based in Franco-controlled Mallorca, 979 people are killed and 1500 wounded.

tion were a strange hiatus before the onset of the full machinery of oppression. Within two weeks of the city's fall a dozen cinemas were in operation, and the following month Hollywood comedies were being shown between rounds of Nationalist propaganda. The people were even encouraged to dance the *sardana*, Catalonia's national dance, in public (the Nationalists thought such folkloric generosity might endear them to the people of Barcelona).

On the other hand, the city presented an exhausted picture. The metro was running but there were no buses (they had all been used on the front). Virtually all the animals in the city zoo had died of starvation or wounds. There were frequent blackouts, and would be for years.

Round-Ups & Executions

By 1940, with WWII raging across Europe, Franco had his regime more firmly in place and things turned darker for many. Catalan Francoists led the way in rounding up anarchists and former Republican supporters; up to 35,000 people were shot in purges. At the same time, small bands of resistance fighters continued to harry the Nationalists in the Pyrenees through much of the 1940s. Catalonia's president, Lluís Companys, was arrested in France by the Gestapo in August 1940, handed over to Franco, and shot on 15 October on Montjuïc. He is reputed to have died with the words 'Visca Catalunya!' ('Long live Catalonia!') on his lips.

The executions continued into the 1950s. Most people accepted the situation and tried to get on with living, while some leapt at opportunities, occupying flats abandoned by 'Reds' who had been forced to flee. Speculators and industrialists allied with Franco were able to earn a lucrative income, but the majority of *barcelonins* were affected by nationwide poverty.

Films Set in Franco's Spain

....

Pan's Labyrinth (2006)

....

The Spirit of the Beehive (1973)

....

¡Bienvenido, Mr Marshall! (Welcome, Mr Marshall!; 1952)

....

Las 13 Rosas (The 13 Roses; 2007)

Life Under Franco

Franco took a particularly hard line against Barcelona. Catalan monuments in the city were dismantled. He banned public use of Catalan, and had all town, village and street names rendered in Spanish (Castilian). Education, radio, TV and the daily press would henceforth be in Spanish. Independent political activity was banned, as was the celebration of traditional Catalan holidays.

In Barcelona, the Francoist Josep Maria de Porcioles became mayor in 1957, a post he held until 1973. That same year he obtained for the city a 'municipal charter' that expanded the mayor's authority and the city's capacity to raise and spend taxes, manage urban development and, ultimately, widen the city's metropolitan limits to absorb neighbouring

1939	1940	1957	1980
The first of Franco's troops, along with Italian tanks, roll into Barcelona and parade down Avinguda Diagonal. Thousands flee the city towards the French border.	Hitler's henchman and chief of the SS, Heinrich Himmler, visits Barcelona, stays at the Ritz, enjoys a folkloric show at Poble Espanyol and has his wallet stolen.	The Francoist Josep Maria de Porcioles becomes mayor of Barcelona and remains in charge until 1973. He presides over a willy-nilly building spree in the city.	Right-wing Catalan nationalist Jordi Pujol is elected president of the resurrected Catalan regional government at the head of the nationalist CiU coalition; he remains in power until 2003.

territory. He was responsible for such monstrosities as the concrete municipal buildings on Plaça de Sant Miquel in the Barri Gòtic. His rule marked a grey time for Barcelona.

Immigrants Pour Into Barcelona

Under Franco a flood of 1.5 million immigrants from poorer parts of Spain – chiefly Andalucía, Extremadura and the northwest – poured into Catalonia (750,000 of them to Barcelona) in the 1950s and '60s looking for work. Many lived in appalling conditions. While some made the effort to learn Catalan and integrate as fully as possible into local society, the majority came to form Spanish-speaking pockets in the poorer working-class districts of the city and in a ring of satellite towns. Even today, the atmosphere in many of these towns is more Andalucian than Catalan. Catalan nationalists will tell you it was all part of a Francoist plot to undermine the Catalan identity.

History Sites

....
Museu d'Història de Barcelona
....
Museu d'Història de Catalunya
....
Via Sepulcral Romana
....
Museu Marítim

The Road to Democracy

When the death of Franco was announced in 1975, *barcelonins* took to the streets in celebration. The next five years saw the gradual return of democracy. In 1977 Josep Tarradellas, who was head of Catalonia's government in exile, returned to Barcelona after Franco's death and was officially recognised by the Spanish government as head of a new Catalan coalition. *Barcelonins* who lived during that time will likely recall the historic words given from the balcony of the Palau de la Generalitat. Before a huge crowd gathered on Plaça de Sant Jaume, he said, *'Ciutadans de Catalunya, ja sóc aquí!'* (Citizens of Catalonia, I am here!).

Twenty years after his stint in Franco's jails, Jordi Pujol (an early ringleader in protests against the Francoists) was elected president of Catalonia in 1980. These were the first free regional elections since before the Civil War. A wily antagonist of the central authorities in Madrid, Pujol waged a quarter-century war of attrition, eking out greater fiscal and policy autonomy and vigorously promoting a re-Catalanisation program, with uneven success.

Barcelona's Olympian Moment

Politics aside, the big event in post-Franco Barcelona was the successful 1992 Olympic Games, planned under the guidance of the popular Socialist mayor, Pasqual Maragall. The games spurred a burst of public works and brought new life to areas such as Montjuïc, where the major events were held. The once-shabby waterfront was transformed with promenades, beaches, marinas, restaurants, leisure attractions and new housing.

1992	1994	2006	2010
Barcelona takes centre stage as it hosts the summer Olympic Games. In preparation the city undergoes a radical renovation program, the momentum of which continues today.	The Gran Teatre del Liceu, Barcelona's opera house, burns to the ground as a spark from a welder's blowtorch sets the stage alight. It is rebuilt and reopens in 1999.	The Catalan government negotiates a new autonomy statute with Madrid in a compromise that leaves many unsatisfied and ultimately leads to the fall of Maragall.	Pope Benedict XVI consecrates the basilica of La Sagrada Família before an audience of 6500, including King Juan Carlos I and Queen Sofia.

Urban Renewal

After the turn of the millennium, Barcelona continued to invest in urban renewal, with ambitious projects such as the 22@ high-tech zone in the once-industrial El Poblenou district, the major development around new trade fairgrounds between the city and the airport, and the Diagonal Mar waterfront development around the Parc del Fòrum at the northeast tip of the city.

A Move Towards Independence

Since the demise of Franco, Spain has devolved considerable powers to the regions, which are officially known as *comunidades autónomas* (autonomous communities). Catalans approved the new Estatut in a referendum in 2006, but within months the right-wing Partido Popular (warning of the 'Balkanisation' or break-up of Spain) launched an appeal in the Constitutional Court against the Estatut, which it claimed grants too much autonomy.

After four years of wrangling, in 2010 the court delivered a verdict, ruling that 14 of the articles were unconstitutional – including areas of language, taxes, the judiciary and self-recognition as a 'nation'. Catalans converged on the streets en masse to protest the decision, which was widely hailed as one more blow to relations between Barcelona and Madrid.

Separatism on the Rise

The economic crisis that erupted in 2007 has largely shifted the conversation to the realm of economic recovery. Soaring unemployment and painful austerity measures – not to mention Catalonia's heavy tax burden – has led to anger and resentment towards Madrid, and fuelled the drive towards independence.

The fervour to secede has only grown in the last few years. In 2013, on the Catalan National Day (11 September), hundreds of thousands of separatist supporters formed a 400km human chain across Catalonia. It even passed through the centre of Camp Nou, home stadium of FC Barcelona, long a symbol of pride among Catalans. Recent polls indicate about half of Catalans support the region becoming a new European state. Madrid, however, has clamped down, with Spanish judges ruling that a vote on independence is illegal, and in clear violation of the Spanish constitution. Many financial analysts and outside observers (such as Moody's Investors Service) believe independence is unlikely for Catalonia. Business interests, while mindful of the heavy tax burden, also don't want to be isolated – this could lead to an even greater economic crisis.

Ever at the vanguard, Barcelona had the first daily newspaper printed in Spain, plus its first cinema, public phone and airline (to Majorca). It also built the world's second metropolitan railway (London was first).

2010	2014	2015	2026
Hot on the heels of its victory in the European football championship in 2008, Spain defeats the Netherlands in the World Cup held in South Africa, its first-ever World Cup title.	Six months after a human chain stretches 400km across Catalonia, Spanish judges declare Catalonia's planned referendum on independence unconstitutional.	Following an election, separatists take control of Catalonia's government. They vow to continue the move towards full secession, laying out a route to achieve independence within 18 months.	Builders aim to finish La Sagrada Família on the centenary of the death of its creator, Gaudí (1852–1926), which is over 140 years after its construction began.

Catalan Culture

The fortunes of Catalonia have risen and fallen over the years, as Barcelona has gone from wealthy mercantile capital to a city of repression under the Franco regime, followed by the boom and bust of more recent years. Despite today's economic challenges, Catalan culture continues to flourish, with a lively festival calendar and abundant civic pride manifested in everything from the language spoken on the streets to Barcelona's much-loved football team.

Language

Above Human *castell* (castle) at Festes de la Mercè (p24)

In Barcelona, born and bred locals proudly speak Catalan, a Romance language related to French, Spanish (Castilian) and Italian. It was only relatively recently, however, that Catalan was deemed 'legitimate'. Since Barcelona was crushed in the War of the Spanish Succession in 1714, the use of Catalan has been repeatedly banned or at least frowned upon. Franco was the last of Spain's rulers to clamp down on its public use. All that changed in 1980, when the first autonomous regional parliament was assembled and adopted new laws towards *normalització lingüístico* (linguistic normalisation).

Today Catalonia's school system is based on bilingual education, with graduates showing equal skill in using either Catalan or Spanish. Around town, Catalan is the *lingua franca:* advertising and road signs tend to be in Catalan, while newspapers, magazines and other publications can be found in both languages (though you'll find about twice as many options in Catalan than in Spanish). You'll also find a mix of Catalan and Spanish programming on radio and TV stations.

Folk Dancing

On weekends year-round devotees of the folk dance *sardana* gather in front of La Catedral, while a 10-piece band puts everyone in motion. Catalans of all ages come out for the dance, which takes place in a circle with dancers holding hands. Together they move right, back and then left, hopping, raising their arms and generally building momentum as the tempo picks up. All are welcome to join in, though you'll have to watch a few rounds to get the hang of it.

Festivals

Catalonia's best celebrations tend to revolve around religious holidays. Fests dedicated to Nostra Senyora de la Mercè (Our Lady of Mercy) and Santa Eulàlia – Barcelona's two patron saints – are the city's biggest bashes. You'll see plenty of *sardana* and *castell*-building there. You'll also see *gegants* (huge papier-mâché giants: lords, princesses, sultans, fishers and historic and contemporary figures) and *capgrossos* (oversized heads worn by costumed actors).

Another feature of these Catalan fests is the *correfoc* (fire run): horned devils brandishing firework-spouting pitchforks wreak mayhem in the streets. They are sometimes accompanied by firework-spouting dragons, or even wooden carts that are set alight. Full coverings (hats, gloves, goggles) are highly recommended for anyone who wants to get near.

Castells

One of the highlights of a traditional Catalan festival is the building of human *castells* (castles), a Catalan tradition that dates back to the 18th century. Teams from across the region compete to build human towers up to 10 storeys tall. These usually involve levels of three to five people standing on each other's shoulders. A crowd of teammates forms a supporting scrum around the thickset lads at the base. To successfully complete the castle, a young (light!) child called the *anxaneta* must reach the top and signal with his or her hand.

FC Barcelona

One of the city's best-loved names is FC Barça, which is deeply associated with Catalans and even Catalan nationalism. The team was long a rallying point for Catalans when other aspects of Catalan culture were suppressed. The club openly supported Catalonia's drive towards autonomy in 1918, and in 1921 the club's statutes were drafted in Catalan. The pro-Catalan leanings of the club and its siding with the republic during the Spanish Civil War earned reprisals from the government. Club president Josep Sunyol was murdered by Franco's soldiers in 1936, and the club building was bombed in 1938.

In 1968 club president Narcís de Carreras uttered the now famous words, *El Barça: més que un club* ('more than a club'), which became the team's motto – and emphasised its role as an anti-Franco symbol and catalyst for change in the province and beyond. Today FC Barça is one of the world's most admired teams.

Essential Reading

Barcelona: The Great Enchantress (Robert Hughes; 2001)

Barcelonas (Manuel Vázquez Montalbán; 1992)

Barça: A People's Passion (Jimmy Burns; 1992)

CATALAN CULTURE FOLK DANCING

At Christmas some rather unusual Catalan characters appear. The *caganer* (crapper) is a chap with dropped pants who balances over his unsightly offering (a symbol of fertility for the coming year). There's also the *caga tío* (poop log), which on Christmas Day is supposed to *cagar* (crap) out gifts.

Architecture

Famed for its architectural treasures, Barcelona has striking Gothic cathedrals, fantastical Modernista creations and avant-garde works from more recent days. The city's great building boom first began in the late Middle Ages, when Barcelona was seat of the Catalan empire. The late 19th century was another time of great ferment, when the city began expanding beyond its medieval confines and bold new thinkers transformed the city. The third notable era of design began in the late 1980s and continues today.

The Gothic Period

Barcelona's first big building boom came at the height of the Middle Ages, when its imposing Gothic churches, mansions and shipyards were raised, together creating what survives to this day as one of the most extensive Gothic quarters in Europe. Most of these architectural treasures lie within the boundaries of the *ciutat vella,* but a few examples can be found beyond, notably the Museu-Monestir de Pedralbes in Sarrià.

Historical Roots

Catalonia's vast 14th-century mercantile empire fuelled Barcelona's boom. All manner of goods flowed to and from Sardinia, Flanders, North Africa and other places, with Catalan Jews carrying out much of this trade. The later pogroms, Inquisition and expulsion of Jews had devastating financial consequences and helped reduce Barcelona to penury.

This soaring style took off in France in the 12th century and spread across Europe. Its emergence coincided with Jaume I's march into Valencia and the annexation of Mallorca and Ibiza, accompanied by the rise of a trading class and a burgeoning mercantile empire. The enormous cost of building the grand new monuments could thus be covered by the steady increase in the city's wealth.

Perhaps the single greatest building spurt came under Pere III (1319–87). This is odd in a sense because, as Dickens might have observed, it was not only the best of times, but also the worst. By the mid-14th century, when Pere III was in command, Barcelona had been pushed to the ropes by a series of disasters: famine, repeated plagues and pogroms.

Maybe he didn't notice. He built, or began to build, much of La Catedral, the Drassanes, the Llotja stock exchange, the Saló del Tinell, the Casa de la Ciutat (which now houses the town hall) and numerous lesser buildings, not to mention part of the city walls. The churches of Santa Maria del Pi and Santa Maria del Mar were completed by the end of the 14th century.

Architectural Features

The style of architecture reflected the development of building techniques. The introduction of buttresses, flying buttresses and ribbed vaulting in ceilings allowed engineers to raise edifices that were loftier and seemingly lighter than ever before. The pointed arch became standard and great rose windows were the source of light inside these enormous spaces.

Think about the hovels that labourers on such projects lived in and the primitive nature of building materials available, and you get an idea of the awe such churches, once completed, must have inspired. They were not built in a day. It took more than 160 years, a fairly typical time frame, to finish La Catedral, although its facade was not erected until the 19th century. Its rival, the Basílica de Santa Maria del Mar, was one for the record books, taking only 59 years to build.

Catalan Gothic

Catalan Gothic did not follow the same course as the style typical of northern Europe. Decoration here tends to be more sparing and the most obvious defining characteristic is the triumph of breadth over height. While northern European cathedrals reach for the sky, Catalan Gothic has a tendency to push to the sides, stretching its vaulting design to the limit.

The Saló del Tinell, with a parade of 15m arches (among the largest ever built without reinforcement) holding up the roof, is a perfect example of Catalan Gothic. Another is the present home of the Museu Marítim, the Drassanes, Barcelona's medieval shipyards. In their churches, too, the Catalans opted for a more robust shape and lateral space – step into the Basílica de Santa Maria del Mar or the Església de Santa Maria del Pi and you'll soon get the idea.

Another notable departure from what you might have come to expect of Gothic north of the Pyrenees is the lack of spires and pinnacles. Bell towers tend to terminate in a flat or nearly flat roof. Occasional exceptions prove the rule – the main facade of Barcelona's La Catedral, with its three gnarled and knobbly spires, does vaguely resemble the outline that confronts you in cathedrals in Chartres or Cologne. But then it was a 19th-century addition, admittedly to a medieval design.

Late Gothic

Gothic had a longer use-by date in Barcelona than in many other European centres. By the early 15th century, the Generalitat still didn't have a home worthy of its name, and architect Marc Safont set to work on the present building on Plaça de Sant Jaume. Even renovations carried out a century later were largely in the Gothic tradition, although some Renaissance elements eventually snuck in – the facade on Plaça de Sant Jaume is a rather disappointing result.

Carrer de Montcada, in La Ribera, was the result of a late-medieval act of town planning. Eventually mansions belonging to the moneyed classes of 15th- and 16th-century Barcelona were erected along it. Many now house museums and art galleries. Although these former mansions appear forbidding on the outside, their interiors often reveal another world of pleasing courtyards and decorated external staircases. They mostly went through a gentle baroque makeover in later years.

Modernisme

Barcelona's Modernisme buildings arose during La Renaixença, a period of great artistic and political fervour that was deeply connected to Catalan identity, and which transformed early-20th-century Barcelona into a showcase for avant-garde architecture. Aiming to establish a new Catalan archetype, Antoni Gaudí and other visionary architects drew inspiration from the past, using elements from the Spanish vernacular – shapes, details and brickwork reminiscent of Islamic, Gothic and Renaissance designs.

The Modernistas also revived traditional artisan trades, which you can see in the exquisite stonework and stained-glass windows, and in their artful use of wrought iron, ceramics and mosaic tiles. Nature was celebrated and imitated to perfection in Gaudí's organic forms: leaning treelike columns, walls that undulate like the sea, and the use of native plants as decorative elements. Inside these buildings, the artistry and imaginative design continues.

Gothic Master-pieces

La Catedral

Basílica de Santa Maria del Mar

Església de Santa Maria del Pi

Saló del Tinell (in Museu d'Història de Barcelona)

The Drassanes (Museu Marítim)

For many, Modernisme is synonymous with Gaudí (1852–1926), but he was by no means alone. Lluís Domènech i Montaner (1850–1923) and Josep Puig i Cadafalch (1867–1956) left a wealth of remarkable buildings across the city. The Rome-trained sculptor Eusebi Arnau (1864–1934) was one of the most popular figures called upon to decorate Barcelona's Modernista piles. The appearance of the Hospital de la Santa Creu i de Sant Pau is one of his legacies and he also had a hand in the Palau de la Música Catalana and Casa Amatller.

The Arabs invented the ancient technique of *trencadís*, but Gaudí was the first architect to revive it. The procedure involves taking ceramic tiles or fragments of broken pottery or glass and creating a mosaic-like sheath on roofs, ceilings, chimneys, benches, sculptures or any other surface.

Olympic & Contemporary Architecture

Barcelona's latest architectural revolution began in the 1980s. The appointment then of Oriol Bohigas, who was regarded as an elder statesman for architecture, as head of urban planning by the ruling Socialist party marked a new beginning. The city set about its biggest phase of renewal since the heady days of L'Eixample.

The Olympic Games Building Boom

The biggest urban makeover in 100 years happened in the run-up to the 1992 Olympics, when more than 150 architects beavered away on almost 300 building and design projects. The city saw dramatic transformations, from the construction of huge arterial highways to the refurbishment of whole neighbourhoods in dire need of repair. In a rather crafty manoeuvre, the city government used national monies to fund urban improvements the capital would never normally have approved. Several kilometres of waterfront wasteland that included Port Vell was beautifully transformed into sparkling new beaches – suddenly Barcelona had prime beachfront real estate. The long road to resurrecting Montjuïc took off with the refurbishment of the Olympic stadium and the creation of landmarks like Santiago Calatrava's Torre Calatrava.

Post-1992, landmark buildings still went up in strategic spots, usually with the ulterior motive of trying to pull the surrounding area up by its bootstraps. One of the most emblematic of these projects is the gleaming white Museu d'Art Contemporani de Barcelona, better known as MACBA, which opened in 1995. The museum was designed by Richard Meier and incorporates the characteristic elements for which the American architect is so well known – the geometric minimalism and the pervasive use of all white with glass and steel – and remains much debated in architectural circles.

More widely hailed, the Teatre Nacional de Catalunya, which opened in 1996, is a splendid blend of the neoclassical and the modern. Framed by 26 columns with a single gabled roof and grand entrance steps, the theatre takes the form of a Greek temple, though its all-glass exterior gives it a light and open appearance.

Henry Cobb's World Trade Center, at the tip of a quay jutting out into the waters of Port Vell, has been overshadowed by Ricardo Bofill's hotel, W Barcelona, whose spinnakerlike front looks out to sea from the south end of La Barceloneta's beach strip.

Best Contemporary Buildings

Torre Agbar

Teatre Nacional de Catalunya

Mercat de Santa Caterina

Edifici Fòrum

W Barcelona

Santos Porta Fira Hotel (Llobregat)

Les Arenes (Plaça d'Espanya)

The New Millennium

One of the first big projects of the 21st century has occurred around Diagonal Mar. A whole district has been built in the northeast coastal corner of the city where before there was a void. High-rise apartments, waterfront office towers and five-star hotels – among them the eye-catching Hotel Me (completed in 2008) by Dominique Perrault – mark this new district. The hovering blue, triangular Edifici Fòrum by Swiss architects

Herzog & de Meuron is the most striking landmark here, along with a gigantic photovoltaic panel that provides some of the area's electricity.

Much of the district was completed in 2004, though the area continues to evolve as new buildings are added to the mix. Among the most notable recent additions is a 24-storey whitewashed trapezoidal prism that serves as the headquarters for the national telephone company, Telefónica. Designed by Enric Massip-Bosch and dubbed the Torre ZeroZero, it has a deceivingly two-dimensional appearance upon initial approach. Shortly after its completion in 2011, the Torre was awarded the respected Leading European Architects Forum (LEAF) award for commercial building of the year.

Another prominent addition to the skyline came in 2005. The shimmering, cucumber-shaped Torre Agbar is a product of French architect Jean Nouvel, emblematic of the city's desire to make the developing high-tech zone of 22@ a reality.

Southwest, on the way to the airport, the new Fira M2 trade fair along Gran Via de les Corts Catalanes is now marked by red twisting twin landmark towers (one the Santos Porta Fira Hotel, the other offices) designed by Japanese star architect and self-confessed Gaudí fan Toyo Ito.

The heart of La Ribera got a fresh look with its brand-new Mercat de Santa Caterina. The market is quite a sight, with its wavy ceramic roof and tubular skeleton, designed by one of the most promising names in Catalan architecture until his premature death, Enric Miralles. Miralles' Edifici de Gas Natural, a 100m glass tower near the waterfront in La Barceloneta, is extraordinary for its mirrorlike surface and weirdly protruding adjunct buildings, which could be giant glass cliffs bursting from the main tower's flank.

Modernista Masterpieces
....
La Pedrera
....
La Sagrada Família
....
Palau de la Música Catalana
....
Casa Batlló
....
Palau Güell
....
Casa Amatller
....
Hospital de la Santa Creu i de Sant Pau

The City of Tomorrow

Big projects have slowly taken shape around the city, although the continuing economic crisis has dramatically slowed the pace of construction.The redevelopment of the area near Plaça de les Glòries Catalanes is one of the latest completed projects, with the goal of revitalising the neighbourhood and making it a draw for tourists.

The centrepiece is the new Disseny Hub (which now houses Barcelona's design museum), a building completed in 2013, which incorporates sustainable features in its cantilevered, metal-sheathed building. Vaguely futuristic (though some say it looks like a stapler), it has a rather imposing, anvil-shaped presence over the neighbourhood.

Nearby stands Els Encants Vells ('the Old Charms' flea market), which was given a dramatic new look by local architecture firm b720 Fermín Vázquez Arquitectos. Traders now sell their wares beneath a giant, mirrored canopy made up of geometric panels and held aloft with long, slender poles. It opened to much acclaim in 2013.

In a rather thoughtful bit of recycling, British architect Lord Richard Rogers transformed the former Les Arenes bullring on Plaça d'Espanya into a singular, circular leisure complex, with shops, cinemas and more, which opened in 2011. He did so while still maintaining its red-brick, 19th-century Moorish-looking facade. Perhaps its best feature is the rooftop with 360-degree views from the open-air promenade and cafes and restaurants.

In the *ciutata vela* (old city), El Raval continues to be the focal point for urban renewal. The Filmoteca de Catalunya is a hulking rather brutalist building of concrete and glass, with sharp angles. It was designed by Catalan architect Josep Lluís Mateo and completed in 2011. It sits near the Richard Meier-designed MACBA, which opened in 1995.

No one longs for the pre-Olympic days when the waterfront was a dangerous and polluted wasteland. However, some old timers still bemoan the loss of its old rickety restaurant shacks, which sat on stilts over the water and served delectable if utterly unfussy seafood.

Picasso, Miró & Dalí

Three of Spain's greatest 20th-century artists have deep connections to Barcelona. Picasso spent his formative years in the city and maintained lifelong friendships with Catalans. It was Picasso's own idea to create a museum of his works here. Joan Miró is one of Barcelona's most famous native sons. His instantly recognisable style can be seen in public installations throughout the city. Although Salvador Dalí is more commonly associated with Figueres, Barcelona was a great source of inspiration for him, particularly the fantastical architectural works of Antoni Gaudí.

Pablo Picasso

Born in Málaga in Andalucía, Pablo Ruiz Picasso (1881–1973) was already sketching by the age of nine. As a young boy, he lived briefly in La Coruña (in Galicia), before landing in Barcelona in 1895. His father had obtained a post teaching art at the Escola de Belles Artes de la Llotja (then housed in the stock exchange building) and had his son enrolled there too. It was in Barcelona and Catalonia that Picasso matured, spending his time ceaselessly drawing and painting.

After a stint at the Escuela de Bellas Artes de San Fernando in Madrid in 1897, Picasso spent six months with his friend Manuel Pallarès in bucolic Horta de Sant Joan, in western Catalonia – he would later claim that it was there he learned everything he knew. In Barcelona, Picasso lived and worked in the Barri Gòtic and El Raval (where he was introduced to the seamier side of life in the Barri Xinès).

By the time Picasso moved to France in 1904, he had explored his first highly personal style. In this so-called Blue Period, his canvases have a melancholy feel heightened by the trademark dominance of dark blues. Some of his portraits and cityscapes from this period were created in and inspired by what he saw in Barcelona. A number of pieces from this period hang in the Museu Picasso.

By the mid-1920s, he was dabbling with surrealism. His best-known work is *Guernica* (in Madrid's Centro de Arte Reina Sofia), a complex painting portraying the horror of war, inspired by the German aerial bombing of the Basque town Gernika in 1937.

Picasso worked prolifically during and after WWII and he was still cranking out paintings, sculptures, ceramics and etchings until the day he died in 1973.

With *Les Demoiselles d'Avignon* (Ladies of Avignon; 1907), Picasso broke with all forms of traditional representation, introducing a deformed perspective that would later spill over into cubism. The subject was supposedly taken from the Carrer d'Avinyó in the Barri Gòtic, in those days populated with a series of brothels.

Joan Miró

At the time the 13-year-old Picasso arrived in Barcelona, his near contemporary, Joan Miró (1893–1983), was still learning to crawl in the Barri Gòtic, where he was born. He spent a third of his life in Barcelona but later divided his time between France, the Tarragona countryside and the island of Mallorca, where he ended his days.

Like Picasso, Miró attended the Escola de Belles Artes de la Llotja. He was initially uncertain about his artistic vocation – in fact he studied commerce. In Paris from 1920, he mixed with Picasso, Hemingway, Joyce and friends, and made his own mark, after several years of struggle, with an exhibition in 1925. The masterpiece from this, his so-called realist period, was *La Masia* (Farmhouse).

It was during WWII, while living in seclusion in Normandy, that Miró's definitive leitmotifs emerged. Among the most important images that appear frequently throughout his work are women, birds (the link between Earth and the heavens), stars (the unattainable heavenly world, the source of imagination) and a sort of net entrapping all these levels of the cosmos. The Miró works that most people are acquainted with emerged from this time – arrangements of lines and symbolic figures in primary colours, with shapes reduced to their essence.

He lived in Mallorca, home of his wife Pilar Juncosa, from 1956 until his death in 1983.

Salvador Dalí

The great Catalan artist Salvador Dalí i Domènech (1904–89) was born and died in Figueres, where he left his single greatest artistic legacy, the Teatre-Museu Dalí. Although few of his famed works reside in Barcelona, the city provided a stimulating atmosphere for Dalí, and places like Park Güell, with its surrealist-like aspects, had a powerful effect on him.

Prolific painter, showman, shameless self-promoter or just plain weirdo, Dalí was nothing if not a character – probably a little too much for the conservative small-town folk of Figueres. Every now and then a key moment arrives that can change the course of one's life. Dalí's came in 1929, when the French poet Paul Éluard visited Cadaqués with his Russian wife, Gala. The rest, as they say, is histrionics. Dalí shot off to Paris to be with Gala and plunged into the world of surrealism.

In the 1930s Salvador and Gala returned to live at Port Lligat on the north Catalan coast, where they played host to a long list of fashionable and art-world guests until the war years – the parties were by all accounts memorable. They started again in Port Lligat in the 1950s. The stories of sexual romps and Gala's appetite for local young men are legendary. The 1960s saw Dalí painting pictures on a grand scale, including his 1962 reinterpretation of Marià Fortuny's *Batalla de Tetuán*. On his death in 1989, he was buried (according to his own wishes) in the Teatre-Museu he had created on the site of the old theatre in central Figueres, which also houses an awe-inspiring Dalí collection.

The Fundació Joan Miró, housed in an extensive gallery atop Montjuïc, has the single largest collection of Miró's work in the world today.

PICASSO, MIRÓ & DALÍ SALVADOR DALÍ

ART ON THE STREETS

Barcelona hosts an array of street sculpture, from Miró's 1983 *Dona i Ocell* (Woman and Bird), in the park dedicated to the artist, to *Peix* (Fish), Frank Gehry's shimmering, bronze-coloured headless fish facing Port Olímpic. Halfway along La Rambla, at Plaça de la Boqueria, you can walk all over Miró's *Mosaïc de Miró*.

Picasso left an open-air mark with his design on the facade of the Col·legi Arquitectes opposite La Catedral in the Barri Gòtic. Other works include the *Barcelona Head* by Roy Lichtenstein at the Port Vell end of Via Laietana and Fernando Botero's tumescent *El Gat* on Rambla del Raval.

Wander down to the Barceloneta seaside for a gander at Rebecca Horn's 1992 tribute to the old shacks that used to line the waterfront. The precarious stack is called *Homenatge a la Barceloneta* (Tribute to La Barceloneta). A little further south is the 2003 *Homenatge als Nedadors* (Tribute to the Swimmers), a complex metallic rendition of swimmers and divers in the water by Alfredo Lanz.

Heading a little further back in time, in 1983 Antoni Tàpies constructed *Homenatge a Picasso* (Homage to Picasso) on Passeig de Picasso; it's essentially a glass cube set in a pond and filled with, well, junk. Antoni Llena's *David i Goliat* (David and Goliath), a massive sculpture of tubular and sheet iron, in the Parc de les Cascades near Port Olímpic's two skyscrapers, looks like an untidy kite inspired by Halloween.

Music & Dance

Barcelona's vibrant music and dance scene has been shaped by artists both traditional and cutting-edge. From Nova Cançó, composed during the dark years of the dictatorship, to the hybridised Catalan rumba to hands-in-the air rock ballads of the 1970s and '80s, Barcelona's music evolves constantly. Today's groups continue to push musical boundaries, blending rhythms from all corners of the globe. In the realm of dance, flamenco has a small loyal following, while the old-fashioned folk dance *sardana* continues to attract growing numbers.

Contemporary Music

Nova Cançó

Curiously, it was probably the Franco repression that most helped foster a vigorous local music scene in Catalan. In the dark 1950s the Nova Cançó (New Song) movement was born to resist linguistic oppression with music in Catalan (getting air time on the radio was long close to impossible), throwing up stars that in some cases won huge popularity throughout Spain, such as the Valencia-born Raimon.

More specifically loved in Catalonia as a Bob Dylan–style 1960s protest singer-songwriter was Lluís Llach, much of whose music was more or less antiregime. Joan Manuel Serrat is another legendary figure. His appeal stretches from Barcelona to Buenos Aires. Born in the Poble Sec district, this poet-singer is equally at ease in Catalan and Spanish. He has repeatedly shown that record sales are not everything to him. In 1968 he refused to represent Spain at the Eurovision song contest if he were not allowed to sing in Catalan. Accused of being anti-Spanish, he was long banned from performing in Spain.

Around the same time Nova Cançó singers were taking aim at the Franco regime, folk singers from Latin America were decrying their own corrupt military dictatorships. Songs by Victor Jara of Chile, Mercedes Sosa of Argentina and Chico Buarque of Brazil helped unite people in the fight against oppression.

Born in Mallorca, the talented singer Maria del Mar Bonet arrived in Barcelona in 1967, and embarked on a long and celebrated singing career. She sang in Catalan, and many of her searing and powerful songs were banned by the dictatorship. On concert tours abroad, she attracted worldwide attention, and she has performed with distinguished groups and soloists across the globe.

Rock Català

A specifically local strand of rock has emerged since the 1980s. Rock Català (Catalan rock) is not essentially different from rock anywhere else, except that it is sung in Catalan by local bands that appeal to local tastes. Among the most popular groups of years past include Sau, Els Pets, Lax'n Busto and the Valenciano band, Obrint Pas.

The Pinker Tones are a Barcelona duo that attained international success with an eclectic electronic mix of music, ranging from dizzy dance numbers to film soundtracks. Another Barcelona band with international ambitions and flavours is Macaco, a group that sings in different languages – Catalan, Spanish (Castilian), English and Portuguese among others – and blends Latin rhythms and electronica in their rock anthems. When people talk about 'Raval sound' (after the name of the still somewhat seedy old-city district), this is the kind of thing they mean.

RETURN OF LA RUMBA

Back in the 1950s, a new sound mixing flamenco with salsa and other Latin sounds emerged in *gitano* (Roma people) circles in the bars of Gràcia and the Barri Gòtic. One of the founders of rumba Catalana was Antonio González, known as El Pescaílla (married to the flamenco star Lola Flores). Although El Pescaílla was well known in town, the Mataró-born *gitano* Peret later took this eminently Barcelona style to a wider (eventually international) audience. By the end of the 1970s, however, rumba Catalana was running out of steam. Peret had turned to religion and El Pescaílla lived in Flores' shadow in Madrid. But Buenos Aires–born Javier Patricio 'Gato' Pérez discovered rumba in 1977 and gave it his own personal spin, bringing out several popular records, such as *Atalaya,* until the early 1980s. After Pérez, it seemed that rumba was dead. Not so fast! New rumba bands, often highly eclectic, have emerged in recent years. Ai Ai Ai, Barrio Negro, El Tío Carlos and La Pegatina are names to look out for. Others mix rumba with styles as diverse as reggae or ragga.

Far greater success across Spain has gone to Estopa, a male rock duo from Cornellà, a satellite suburb of Barcelona. The guitar-wielding brothers sing a clean Spanish rock, occasionally with a vaguely flamenco flavour. Along the same vein, the Barcelona hit trio Pastora peddles a successful brand of Spanish pop, mixing electric sounds with a strong acoustic element.

Hailing from Barcelona, Mishima is an indie pop band that has recorded a mix of albums in English and Catalan. They remained largely obscure prior to the release of their 2007 album *Set tota la vida,* which earned accolades across the music industry.

Born in El Raval, Cabo San Roque is an even more experimental group, incorporating huge soundscapes, powerful rhythms and mechanical accents often using nontraditional John Cage–style instruments in their avant-garde performances. In one show, the five-person group shared the stage with a polyphonic washing machine powered by a bicycle chain.

Another key name on El Raval's scene is 08001 (which is El Raval's postcode). This ever-evolving collective brings together musicians from all across the globe, fusing unusual sounds from hip-hop, flamenco, reggae and rock to styles from Morocco, West Africa, the Caribbean and beyond. *No Pain no Gain* (2013) is the latest album of 08001.

Classical, Opera & Baroque

Spain's contribution to the world of classical music has been modest, but Catalonia has produced a few exceptional composers. Best known is Camprodon-born Isaac Albéniz (1860–1909), a gifted pianist who later turned his hand to composition. Among his best-remembered works is the *Iberia* cycle.

Montserrat Caballé is Barcelona's most successful voice. Born in Gràcia in 1933, the soprano made her debut in 1956 in Basel (Switzerland). Her home-town launch came four years later in the Gran Teatre del Liceu. In 1965 she performed to wild acclaim at New York's Carnegie Hall and went on to become one of the world's finest 20th-century sopranos. Her daughter, Montserrat Martí, is also a singer and they occasionally appear together. Another fine Catalan soprano was Victoria de los Ángeles (1923–2005), while Catalonia's other world-class opera star is the renowned tenor Josep (José) Carreras.

Jordi Savall has assumed the task of rediscovering a European heritage in music that pre-dates the era of the classical greats. He and his late wife, soprano Montserrat Figueras, have, along with musicians from other countries, been largely responsible for resuscitating the beauties of medieval, Renaissance and baroque music. In 1987 Savall

Born in Catalonia, Pau Casals (1876–1973) was one of the greatest cellists of the 20th century. Living in exile in southern France, he declared he would not play in public as long as the Western democracies continued to tolerate Franco's regime. In 1958 he was a candidate for the Nobel Peace Prize.

founded La Capella Reial de Catalunya and two years later he formed the baroque orchestra Le Concert des Nations. You can sometimes catch their recitals in locations such as the Gran Teatre del Liceu or the Basílica de Santa Maria del Mar.

Dance

Flamenco

For those who think that the passion of flamenco is the preserve of the south, think again. The *gitanos* (Roma people) get around, and some of the big names of the genre come from Catalonia. They were already in Catalonia long before the massive migrations from the south of the 1960s, but with these waves came an exponential growth in flamenco bars as Andalucians sought to recreate a little bit of home.

First and foremost, one of the greatest *bailaoras* (flamenco dancers) of all time, Carmen Amaya (1913–63) was born in what is now Port Olímpic. She danced to her father's guitar in the streets and bars around La Rambla in pre–civil war years. Much to the bemusement of purists from the south, not a few flamenco stars today have at least trained in flamenco schools in Barcelona – dancers Antonio Canales and Joaquín Cortés are among them.

Other Catalan stars of flamenco include *cantaores* (singers) Juan Cortés Duquende and Miguel Poveda, a boy from Badalona. He took an original step in 2005 by releasing a flamenco album, *Desglaç,* in Catalan. Another interesting flamenco voice in Catalonia is Ginesa Ortega Cortés, actually born in France. She masters traditional genres ably but loves to experiment. In her 2002 album, *Por los Espejos del Agua* (Through the Water's Mirrors), she does a reggae version of flamenco and she has sung flamenco versions of songs by Joan Manuel Serrat and Billie Holiday.

An exciting combo formed in Barcelona in 1996: the seven-man, one-woman group Ojos de Brujo (Wizard's Eyes), which melded flamenco and rumba with rap, ragga and electronic music. Unfortunately, the band split up in 2013, with lead singer Marina setting off to pursue a solo career as 'Marinah'.

Sardana

The Catalan dance *par excellence* is the *sardana,* whose roots lie in the far northern Empordà region of Catalonia. Compared with flamenco, it is sober indeed but not unlike a lot of other Mediterranean folk dances.

The dancers hold hands in a circle and wait for the 10 or so musicians to begin. The performance starts with the piping of the *flabiol,* a little wooden flute. When the other musicians join in, the dancers start – a series of steps to the right, one back and then the same to the left. As the music 'heats up' the steps become more complex, the leaps are higher and the dancers lift their arms. Then they return to the initial steps and continue. If newcomers wish to join in, space is made for them as the dance continues and the whole thing proceeds in a more or less seamless fashion.

Top Albums

Techari,
Ojos de Brujo

Anells d'Aigua,
Maria del Mar Bonet

Verges 50,
Lluís Llach

Wild Animals,
Pinker Tones

Set Tota la Vida,
Mishima

Voràgine, 08001

Rey de la Rumba,
Peret

X Anniversarium,
Estopa

LONGING FOR CUBA

The oldest musical tradition to have survived to some degree in Catalonia is that of the *havaneres* (from Havana) – nostalgic songs and melancholy sea shanties brought back from Cuba by Catalans who lived, sailed and traded there in the 19th century. Even after Spain lost Cuba in 1898, the *havanera* tradition (a mix of European and Cuban rhythms) continued. A magical opportunity to enjoy these songs is the Cantada d'Havaneres (www.havanerescalella.cat, in Catalan), an evening concert held on the Costa Brava in early July. Otherwise you may stumble across performances elsewhere along the coast or even in Barcelona, but there is no set program.

Survival Guide

Transport

ARRIVING IN BARCELONA

Most travellers enter Barcelona through El Prat airport. Some budget airlines use Girona-Costa Brava airport or Reus airport.

Flights from North America take about eight hours from the east coast (typically 10 to 13 hours, including a stopover); from the west coast count on 13 or more hours including a stopover. Flights from London take around two hours; from Western Europe it's two to three hours.

Travelling by train is a pricier but perhaps more romantic way of reaching Catalonia from other European cities. The new TGV takes around seven hours from Paris to Barcelona. Long-distance trains arrive in Estació Sants, about 2.5km west of La Rambla.

Long-haul buses arrive in Estació del Nord.

Flights, cars and tours can be booked online at lonelyplanet.com/bookings.

El Prat Airport

Barcelona's **El Prat airport** (✆902 404704; www.aena.es) lies 17km southwest of Plaça de Catalunya at El Prat de Llobregat. The airport has two main terminal buildings: the new T1 terminal and the older T2, itself divided into three terminal areas (A, B and C).

In T1, the main arrivals area is on the 1st floor (with separate areas for EU Schengen Area arrivals, non-EU international arrivals and the Barcelona–Madrid corridor). Boarding gates are on the 1st and 3rd floors.

The main **tourist office** (✹8.30am-8.30pm) is on the ground floor of Terminal 2B. Others on the ground floor of Terminal 2A and in Terminal 1 operate the same hours.

Lockers come in three sizes and can be found on the 1st floor of T1.

Lost-luggage offices can be found by the arrivals belts in Terminal 1 and on the arrivals floor in Terminals 2A and 2B.

Bus

The **A1 Aerobús** (Map p286; ✆902 100104; www.aerobusbcn.com; one way/return €5.90/10.20; ✹6am-1am) runs from Terminal 1 to Plaça de Catalunya (30 to 40 minutes depending on traffic) via Plaça d'Espanya, Gran Via de les Corts Catalanes (corner of Carrer del Comte d'Urgell) and Plaça de la Universitat every five to 10 minutes from 6.10am to 1.05am. Departures from Plaça de Catalunya are from 5.30am to 12.30am and stop at the corner of Carrer de Sepúlveda and Carrer del Comte d'Urgell, and at Plaça d'Espanya.

The A2 Aerobús from Terminal 2 (stops outside terminal areas A, B and C) runs from 6am to 1am with a frequency of between 10 and 20 minutes and follows the same route as the A1 Aerobús.

Buy tickets on the bus or from agents at the bus stop. Considerably slower local buses (such as the No 46 to/from Plaça d'Espanya and a night bus, the N17, to/from Plaça de Catalunya) also serve Terminals 1 and 2.

Mon-Bus (www.monbus.cat) has regular direct buses (which originate in central Barcelona) between Terminal 1 only and Sitges (€7). In Sitges catch it at Avinguda de Vilanova 14. The trip takes about 40 minutes and runs hourly.

Alsa (✆902 422242; www.alsa.es) runs the Aerobús Ràpid service several times daily from El Prat airport to various cities including Girona, Figueres, Lleida, Reus and Tarragona. Fares range from €9/16 one way/return to Tarragona and up to €25/45 one way/return to Lleida.

Plana (✆977 553680; www.busplana.com) has services between the airport and Reus (one way/return €15/27), stopping at Tarragona, Port Aventura and other nearby southwest coastal destinations along the way.

CLIMATE CHANGE & TRAVEL

Every form of transport that relies on carbon-based fuel generates CO_2, the main cause of human-induced climate change. Modern travel is dependent on aeroplanes, which might use less fuel per kilometre per person than most cars but travel much greater distances. The altitude at which aircraft emit gases (including CO_2) and particles also contributes to their climate change impact. Many websites offer 'carbon calculators' that allow people to estimate the carbon emissions generated by their journey and, for those who wish to do so, to offset the impact of the greenhouse gases emitted with contributions to portfolios of climate-friendly initiatives throughout the world. Lonely Planet offsets the carbon footprint of all staff and author travel.

Taxi

A taxi between either terminal and the city centre – about a half-hour ride depending on traffic – costs around €25. Fares and charges are posted inside the passenger side of the taxi – make sure the meter is used.

Train

Train operator Renfe runs the R2 Nord line every half-hour from the airport (from 5.42am to 11.38pm) via several stops to Barcelona's main train station, **Estació Sants** (Plaça dels Països Catalans; MEstació Sants), and Passeig de Gràcia in central Barcelona, after which it heads northwest out of the city. The first service from Passeig de Gràcia leaves at 5.08am and the last at 11.07pm, and about five minutes later from Estació Sants. The trip between the airport and Passeig de Gràcia takes 25 minutes. A one-way ticket costs €4.50.

The airport train station is about a five-minute walk from Terminal 2. Regular shuttle buses run from the station and Terminal 2 to Terminal 1 – allow an extra 15 to 20 minutes.

Girona-Costa Brava Airport

Girona-Costa Brava airport (www.girona-airport.net) is 12km south of Girona and 92km northeast of Barcelona. You'll find a tourist of-

fice, ATMs and lost-luggage desks on the ground floor.

Bus

Sagalés (☑902 130014; www.sagales.com) runs hourly bus services from Girona-Costa Brava airport to Girona's main bus/train station (€2.75, 30 minutes) in connection with flights. The same company runs direct **Barcelona Bus** (☑902 13 00 14; www.barcelonabus.com; MGirona) services to/from **Estació del Nord bus station** (☑902 26 06 06; www.barcelonanord.cat; Carrer d'Ali Bei 80; MArc de Triomf) in Barcelona (one way/return €16/25, 75 minutes).

Taxi

A taxi ride into Girona from the airport costs €20 to €26. To Barcelona you would pay around €140.

Train

Regular **Renfe** (☑902 320320; www.renfe.es) train services run between Girona and Barcelona (€8.40 to €12.25, around 1¼ hours). Speedier Avant trains get there in 38 minutes (one way €10 to €17).

Reus Airport

Reus airport (☑902 404704; www.aena.es) is 13km west of Tarragona and 108km southwest of Barcelona. The tourist office and lost-luggage desks are in the main terminal building.

Bus

Hispano-Igualadina buses (Map p286;☑93 339 73 29; www.igualadina.com; Carrer de Viriat; MEstació Sants) run between Reus airport and **Estació d'Autobusos de Sants** (Map p286;☑93 339 73 29; Carrer de Viriat; MEstació Sants) to meet flights (one way €16, 1½ hours).

Local bus 50 (www.reus-transport.cat) serves central Reus (€3, 20 minutes), and other buses run to local coastal destinations.

GETTING AROUND BARCELONA

Metro & Train

The easy-to-use **TMB Metro** (TMB; ☑93 298 70 00; www.tmb.net) system has 11 numbered and colour-coded lines. It runs from 5am to midnight Sunday to Thursday and holidays, from 5am to 2am on Friday and days immediately preceding holidays, and 24 hours on Saturday.

Ongoing work to expand the metro continues on several lines. Líneas 9 and 10 will eventually connect with the airport (2016 at the earliest).

Suburban trains run by the **Ferrocarrils de la Generalitat de Catalunya** (FGC; ☑900 901515; www.fgc.net) include a couple of useful city lines. All lines heading north from Plaça de Catalunya stop at Carrer de

Provença and Gràcia. One of these lines (L7) goes to Tibidabo and another (L6 to Reina Elisenda) has a stop near the Monestir de Pedralbes. Most trains from Plaça de Catalunya continue beyond Barcelona to Sant Cugat, Sabadell and Terrassa. Other FGC lines head west from Plaça d'Espanya, including one for Manresa that is handy for the trip to Montserrat.

Depending on the line, these trains run from about 5am (with only one or two services before 6am) to 11pm or midnight Sunday to Thursday, and from 5am to about 1am on Friday and Saturday.

Bus

Transports Metropolitans de Barcelona (TMB; ☑93 298 70 00; www.tmb.net) buses run along most city routes every few minutes from between 5am and 6.30am to around 10pm and 11pm. Many routes pass through Plaça de Catalunya and/or Plaça de la Universitat. After 11pm a reduced network of yellow *nitbusos* (night buses) runs until 3am or 5am. All *nitbus* routes pass through Plaça de Catalunya and most run every 30 to 45 minutes.

Taxi

Taxis charge €2.10 flag fall plus meter charges of €1.03 per kilometre (€1.30 from 8pm to 8am and all day on weekends). A further €3.10 is added for all trips to/from the airport, and €1 for luggage bigger than 55cm x 35cm x 35cm. The trip from Estació Sants to Plaça de Catalunya, about 3km, costs about €11. You can flag a taxi down in the streets or call one:

Fonotaxi (☑93 300 11 00)

Radio Taxi 033 (☑93 303 30 33; http://radiotaxi033.com)

Taxi Amic (☑93 420 80 88; www.taxi-amic-adaptat.com) is a special taxi service for people with disabilities or difficult situations (such as transport of big objects). Book at least 24 hours in advance if possible.

The call-out charge is €3.40 (€4.20 at night and on weekends). In many taxis it is possible to pay with a credit card and, if you have a local telephone number, you can join the T033 Ràdio taxi service for booking taxis online (www.radiotaxi033.com, in Spanish). You can also book online at www.catalunyataxi.com.

Tram

There are a handful of **tram lines** (☑900 701 181; www.tram.cat) in the city. All standard transport passes are valid. A scenic option is the *tramvia blau* (blue tram), which runs up to the foot of Tibidabo.

T1, T2 and T3 run into the suburbs of greater Barcelona from Plaça de Francesc Macià and are of limited interest to visitors. T4 runs from behind the zoo (near the Ciutadella Vila Olímpica metro stop) to Sant Adrià via Glòries and the Fòrum. T5 runs from Glòries to Badalona (Gorg stop). T6 runs between Badalona (Gorg) and Sant Adrià.

Cable Car

Several aerial cable cars operate in Barcelona and provide excellent views over the city. The **Transbordador Aeri** (Map p270; www.telefericodebarcelona.com; Passeig Escullera; one way/return €11/16.50; ⊙11am-7pm Mar-Oct, to 5.30pm Nov-Feb; ☐17, 39, 64, Ⓜ Barceloneta) travels between the waterfront southwest of Barceloneta and Montjuïc. The two-stage **Telefèric de Montjuïc** (www.telefericdemontjuic.

TICKETS & TARGETES

The metro, FGC trains, *rodalies/cercanías* (Renfe-run local trains) and buses come under one zoned-fare regime. Single-ride tickets on all standard transport within Zone 1 cost €2.15.

Targetes are multitrip transport tickets. They are sold at all city-centre metro stations. The prices given here are for travel in Zone 1. Children under four years of age travel free. Options include the following:

➡ Targeta T-10 (€10.30) – 10 rides (each valid for 1¼ hours) on the metro, buses, FGC trains and *rodalies*. You can change between metro, FGC, *rodalies* and buses.

➡ Targeta T-DIA (€8.40) – unlimited travel on all transport for one day.

➡ Two-/three-/four-/five-day tickets (€14/21/27/32) – unlimited travel on all transport except the Aerobús; buy them at metro stations and tourist offices.

➡ T-Mes (€53) – 30 days' unlimited use of all public transport.

➡ Targeta T-50/30 (€43) – 50 trips within 30 days, valid on all transport.

➡ T-Trimestre (€142) – 90 days' unlimited use of all public transport.

cat; return adult/child €12/9; ⊙10am-9pm) runs between Estació Parc Montjuïc and the Castell de Montjuïc.

Bicycle

Over 180km of bike lanes have been laid out across the city, so it's possible to commute on two environmentally friendly wheels. A waterfront path runs northeast from Port Olímpic towards Riu Besòs. Scenic itineraries are mapped for cyclists in the Collserola parkland, and the *ronda verda* is an incomplete 75km cycling path that extends around the city's outskirts. You can cycle a well-signed 22km loop path (part of the *ronda verda*) by following the seaside bike path northeast of Barceloneta.

You can transport your bicycle on the metro on weekdays (except between 7am and 9.30am or 5pm and 8.30pm). On weekends and holidays, and during July and August, there are no restrictions. You can use FGC trains to carry your bike at any time and Renfe's *rodalies* trains from 10am to 3pm on weekdays and all day on weekends and holidays.

Countless companies around town offer bicycles (and anything remotely resembling one, from tandems to tricycle carts and more). They include the following:

BarcelonaBiking.com (Map p260; ☑656 356300; www.barcelonabiking.com; Baixada de Sant Miquel 6; bike hire per hr/24hr €5/15, tour €21; ⊙10am-8pm, tour 11am; MJaume I, Liceu)

Biciclot (Map p270;☑93 221 97 78; bikinginbarcelona.net; Passeig Marítim de la Barceloneta 33; bike hire per hr/day €5/€17; ⊙11am-6pm Mon-Fri, 10am-8pm Sat & Sun; MCiutadella Vila Olímpica)

Fat Tire Bike Tours (Map p260;☑933 42 92 75; http://barcelona.fattirebiketours.com;

Carrer de Marlet 7; bike hire per hr/half-day/day €3/8/15, tour adult/concession/child €24/22/19; ⊙10am-8pm, tour 11am; MJaume I, Liceu)

My Beautiful Parking (Map p268;☑93 186 73 65; www.mybeautifulparking.com; Carrer de la Bòria 17; bike hire per hr/24hr €5/14; ⊙10am-3pm & 4.30-8pm; MJaume I)

Rent Electric (☑902 474474; www.rentelectric.com; Plaça del Mar 1; bike hire per 2/4hr €8/12; ⊙10am-7pm; MBarceloneta)

Car & Motorcycle

With the convenience of public transport and the high price of parking in the city, it's unwise to drive in Barcelona. However, if you're planning a road trip outside the city, a car is handy.

Hire

Avis, Europcar, Natio nal/Atesa and Hertz have desks at El Prat airport, Estació Sants and Estació del Nord. Rental outlets in Barcelona include the following:

Avis (☑93 344 37 00; www.avis.com; Carrer de Còrsega 293-295; MDiagonal)

Cooltra (☑93 221 40 70; www.cooltra.com; Via Laietana 6; 10am-7pm; MBarceloneta) You can rent scooters here for around €35 (plus insurance). Cooltra also organises scooter tours.

Europcar (☑93 302 05 43; www.europcar.com; Gran Via de les Corts Catalanes 680; MGirona)

Hertz (☑902 998707; www.hertz.com; Carrer de Viriat 45; MSants Estació)

MondoRent (☑93 295 32 68; www.mondorent.com; Passeig de Joan de Borbó 80-84; 10am-7pm; MBarceloneta) Rents scooters as well as electric bikes.

National/Atesa (☑93 323 07 01; www.enterprise.es; Carrer de Muntaner 45; MUniversitat)

TOURS

There are many ways to get a more in-depth look at the city, whether on a specialised walking tour through the Ciutat Vella (Old City), on a bicycle excursion around the city centre or on a hop-on, hop-off bus tour all across town.

Walking Tours

The **Oficina d'Informació de Turisme de Barcelona** (☑93 285 38 34; www.barcelonaturisme.com; Plaça de Catalunya 17; ⊙9.30am-9.30pm; MCatalunya) organises a series of guided walking tours. One explores the Barri Gòtic (adult/child €16/free); another follows in Picasso's footsteps and winds up at the Museu Picasso, entry to which is included in the price (adult/child €22/7); and a third takes in the main jewels of Modernisme (adult/child €16/free). There's also a 'gourmet' tour of traditional purveyors of fine foodstuffs across the Ciutat Vella (adult/child €22/7). Stop by the tourist office or go online for the latest schedule. Tours typically last two hours and start at the tourist office.

More specialised tours are also bookable through the tourist office: themes include running, shopping, literary Barcelona, tapas tours, civil war tours, the Gothic quarter by night, Park Güell and half a dozen other options.

Barcelona Metro Walks Consists of seven self-guided routes across the city, combining travel on the metro and other public transport as well as stretches on foot. Tourist information points at Plaça de Catalunya and Plaça de Sant Jaume sell the €16 package, which includes a walks guide, two-day transport pass and map.

My Favourite Things (☑mob 637 265405; www.myft.net; tours from €26) Offers tours for no more than 10 participants based on numerous themes: anything from design to food. Other activities include flamenco and salsa classes, and bicycle rides in and out of Barcelona.

Runner Bean Tours (Map p264;☑636 108776; www.runnerbeantours.com; Carrer del Carme 44; ☺tours 11am year-round & 4.30pm Apr-Sep; Ⓜ Liceu) Has several daily thematic tours. It's a pay-what-you-wish tour, with a collection taken at the end for the guide. The Old City tour explores the Roman and medieval history of Barcelona, visiting highlights in the Ciutat Vella. The Gaudí tour takes in the great works of Modernista Barcelona. It involves two trips on the metro. Runner Bean Tours also has ghostly evening tours and a Kids and Family Walking Tour; check the website for departure times.

Bicycle Tours

Barcelona is awash with companies offering bicycle tours. Tours typically take two to four hours and generally stick to La Sagrada Família, the Ciutat Vella and the beaches. Operators include the following:

Bike Tours Barcelona (Map p268; www.biketoursbarcelona.com; Carrer de l'Esparteria 3; per person €23; Ⓜ Jaume I)

Barcelona By Bike (Map p272; ☑671 307325; www.barcelonabybike.com; Carrer de la Marina 13; tours €24; Ⓜ Ciutadella Vila Olímpica)

CicloTour (Map p264;☑93 317 19 70; www.barcelonaciclotour.com; Carrer dels Tallers 45; tours €22; ☺11am & 4.30pm daily mid-Apr–Oct, 11am Mon-Fri, Sat & Sun 11am & 4.30pm Nov, plus 7.30pm Thu-Sun Jun-Sep, Fri & Sat Oct; Ⓜ Universitat)

Fat Tire Bike Tours (Map p260;☑933 42 92 75; http://barcelona.fattirebiketours.com; Carrer de Marlet 7; bike hire per hr/half-day/day €3/8/15, tour adult/concession/child €24/22/19; ☺10am-8pm, tour 11am; Ⓜ Jaume I, Liceu)

BarcelonaBiking.com (Map p260;☑656 356300; www.barcelonabiking.com; Baixada de Sant Miquel 6; bike hire per hr/24hr €5/15, tour €21; ☺10am-8pm, tour 11am; Ⓜ Jaume I, Liceu)

Terra Diversions (Map p280; ☑93 416 08 05; www.terradiversions.com; Carrer de Santa Tecla 1bis; self-guided tour from €37, one-day guided tour from €75; Ⓜ Diagonal) Mostly mountain-bike tours outside the city.

Boat Tours

Several companies take passengers on short jaunts out on the water. These depart several times daily (with many departures in the summer) from Moll de las Drassanes near the southern end of La Rambla.

Las Golondrinas (Map p270; ☑93 442 31 06; www.lasgolondrinas.com; Moll de las Drassanes; 40min tour adult/child €7.40/2.80; Ⓜ Drassanes),

BC Naval Tours (Map p270; ☑93 443 60 50; www.barcelonanavaltours.com; Moll de las Drassanes; cruise 40min/2hr €7.50/20; Ⓜ Drassanes) and other companies offer scenic catamaran trips around the harbour and beyond. Avoid going on a windy day, when the seas can be rough.

Directory A–Z

Discount Cards

The ISIC (International Student Identity Card; www.isic. org) and the European Youth Card (www.euro26.org) are available from most national student organisations and allow discounted access to some sights. Students generally pay a little more than half of adult admission prices, as do children aged under 12 and senior citizens (aged 65 and over) with appropriate ID.

Possession of a **Bus Turístic** (☑93 298 70 00; www. barcelonabusturistic.cat/en; day ticket adult/child €28/16; ⊙9am-8pm) ticket entitles you to discounts at some museums.

Articket (www.articketbcn.org) gives admission to the following six sites for €30 and is valid for six months. You can pick up the ticket at the tourist offices at Plaça de Catalunya, Plaça de Sant Jaume and Estació Sants train station.

➡ Museu Picasso

➡ Museu Nacional d'Art de Catalunya (MNAC)

➡ Museu d'Art Contemporani de Barcelona (MACBA)

➡ Fundació Antoni Tàpies

➡ Centre de Cultura Contemporània de Barcelona (CCCB

➡ Fundació Joan Miró

Arqueoticket is for those with a special interest in archaeology and ancient history. The ticket (€13) is available from participating museums and tourist offices and grants free admission to the following sites:

➡ Museu d'Arqueologia de Catalunya

➡ Museu Egipci

➡ Museu d'Història de Barcelona

➡ Born Centre de Cultura i Memòria

Barcelona Card (www. barcelonacard.com) is handy if you want to see lots in a limited time. It costs €34/44/52/58 for two/ three/four/five days. You get free transport (and 20% off the Aerobús), and discounted admission prices (up to 30% off) or free entry to many museums and other sights, as well as minor discounts on purchases at a small number of shops, restaurants and bars. The card costs about 50% less for children aged four to 12. You can purchase it at tourist offices and online (buying online saves you 10%).

The **Ruta del Modernisme** (www.rutadelmodernisme.com) pack costs €12 and is well worth looking into for visiting Modernista sights at discounted rates.

Electricity

Spain uses 220V, 50Hz, like the rest of continental Europe.

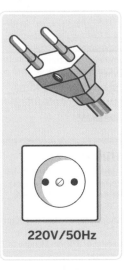

220V/50Hz

Emergency

Ambulance	☑061
Country Code	☑34
EU Standard Emergency	☑112
International Access Code	☑00
Tourist Police	☑93 256 24 30

Money

ATMs

ATMs are widely available (La Rambla has many).

Credit Cards

Major cards such as Visa, MasterCard, Maestro and Cirrus are accepted throughout the city. They can be used in many hotels, restaurants and shops, although there may be a minimum purchase requirement of €5 or €10.

When paying with a credit card, a photo ID is often required, even for chip cards where you're required to enter your PIN (for US travellers without chip cards, just indicate that you'll give a signature).

If your card is lost, stolen or swallowed by an ATM, you can telephone toll-free to immediately stop its use:

Amex (☏900 814500)

Diners Club (☏902 401112)

MasterCard (☏900 971231)

Visa (☏900 991124)

Opening Hours

Standard opening hours are as follows:

Restaurants 1pm to 4pm & 8.30pm to midnight

Shops 9am or 10am to 1.30pm or 2pm and 4pm or 4.30pm to 8pm or 8.30pm Monday to Saturday

Department stores 10am to 10pm Monday to Saturday

Bars 6pm to 2am (to 3am weekends)

Clubs Midnight to 6am Thursday to Saturday

Banks 8.30am to 2pm Monday to Friday; some also 4pm to 7pm Thursday or 9am to 1pm Saturday

Museums & art galleries Vary considerably; generally 10am to 8pm (some shut for lunch around 2pm to 4pm). Many close all day Monday and from 2pm Sunday.

Public Holidays

New Year's Day (Any Nou/Año Nuevo) 1 January

Epiphany/Three Kings' Day (Epifanía or El Dia dels Reis/Día de los Reyes Magos) 6 January

Good Friday (Divendres Sant/ Viernes Santo) March/April

Easter Monday (Dilluns de Pasqua Florida) March/April

Labour Day (Dia del Treball/ Fiesta del Trabajo) 1 May

Day after Pentecost Sunday (Dilluns de Pasqua Granda) May/June

Feast of St John the Baptist (Dia de Sant Joan/Día de San Juan Bautista) 24 June

Feast of the Assumption (L'Assumpció/La Asunción) 15 August

Catalonia's National Day (Diada Nacional de Catalunya) 11 September

Festes de la Mercè 24 September

Spanish National Day (Festa de la Hispanitat/Día de la Hispanidad) 12 October

All Saints Day (Dia de Tots Sants/Día de Todos los Santos) 1 November

Constitution Day (Día de la Constitución) 6 December

Feast of the Immaculate Conception (La Immaculada Concepció/La Inmaculada Concepción) 8 December

Christmas (Nadal/Navidad) 25 December

Boxing Day/St Stephen's Day (El Dia de Sant Esteve) 26 December

Taxes & Refunds

Value-added tax (VAT) is also known as IVA (*impuesto sobre el valor añadido;* pronounced 'EE-ba'). IVA is 10% on accommodation and restaurant prices and is usually – but not always – included in quoted prices. On most retail goods the IVA is 21%. IVA-free shopping is available in duty-free shops at all airports for people travelling between EU countries.

Non-EU residents are entitled to a refund of the 21% IVA on purchases costing more than €90 from any shop, if the goods are taken out of the EU within three months. Ask the shop for a Cashback (or similar) refund form showing the price and IVA paid for each item and identifying the vendor and purchaser. Then present the form at the customs booth for IVA refunds when you depart from Spain (or elsewhere in the EU). You will need your passport and a boarding card that shows you are leaving the EU, and your luggage (so do this before checking in bags). The officer will stamp the invoice and you hand it in at a bank at the departure point to receive a reimbursement.

PRACTICALITIES

➡ **Currency:** euro (€)

➡ **Smoking:** Banned in restaurants and bars

➡ **Newspapers:** Major Barcelona newspapers *La Vanguardia* and *El Periódico* are available in Spanish and Catalan. El País publishes an online English supplement (elpais.com/elpais/inenglish.html)

Telephone

To call Barcelona from outside Spain, dial the international access code, followed by the code for Spain (34) and the full number (including Barcelona's area code, 93, which is an integral part of the number). To make an international call, dial the international access code (00), country code, area code and number.

Mobile Phones

➡ Mobile-phone numbers start with a 6 or 7.

➡ Spain uses GSM 900/1800, compatible with the rest of Europe and Australia but not with the North American GSM 1900 or the system used in Japan. If your phone is tri- or quadriband, you will probably be fine.

➡ You can buy SIM cards and prepaid call time in Spain for your own national mobile phone (provided what you own is a GSM, dual- or tri-band cellular phone and not code-blocked).

➡ You will need your passport to open any kind of mobile-phone account, prepaid or otherwise.

Time

➡ Spain is one hour ahead of GMT/UTC during winter, and two hours ahead during daylight saving (the last Sunday in March to the last Sunday in October).

➡ Most other western European countries are on the same time as Spain year-round. The UK, Ireland and Portugal are one hour behind.

➡ Spaniards use the 24-hour clock for official business (timetables etc) but generally switch to the 12-hour version in daily conversation.

Most hotels, hostels, guesthouses and apartment rentals offer their guests wi-fi access (not always for free). A growing array of city bars and restaurants are latching on to the service – look for the black-and-white wi-fi signs.

The city also has dozens of free public wi-fi hot spots. Look for the small blue signs with the blue 'W' symbol. You can find a complete list of sites at www.bcn.cat/barcelonawifi/en.

Places in this book that offer wi-fi have the symbol 📶.

Tourist Information

Several tourist offices operate in Barcelona. A couple of general information telephone numbers worth bearing in mind are 010 and 012. The first is for Barcelona and the other is for all Catalonia (run by the Generalitat). You sometimes strike English speakers, although for the most part operators are Catalan/Spanish bilingual. In addition to tourist offices, information booths operate at Estació del Nord bus station and at Portal de la Pau, at the foot of the Mirador de Colom at the port end of La Rambla. Others set up at various points in the city centre in summer.

Plaça de Catalunya (☑93 285 38 34; www.barcelonaturisme.com; Plaça de Catalunya 17; ◷9.30am-9.30pm; ⓂCatalunya)

Plaça Sant Jaume (Map p260; ☑93 285 38 32; Carrer de la Ciutat 2; ◷8.30am-8.30pm Mon-Fri, 9am-7pm Sat, 9am-2pm Sun & holidays; ⓂJaume I)

Estació Sants (Map p286; Estació Sants; ◷8am-8pm; ⒭Estació Sants)

El Prat Airport (◷8.30am-8.30pm)

Palau Robert Regional Tourist Office (☑93 238 80 91; www.palaurobert.gencat.cat; Passeig de Gràcia 107; ◷10am-8pm Mon-Sat, to 2.30pm Sun; ⓂDiagonal) Offers a host of

material on Catalonia, audiovisual resources, a bookshop and a branch of Turisme Juvenil de Catalunya (for youth travel).

Travellers with Disabilities

➡ Some hotels and public institutions have wheelchair access. All buses in Barcelona are wheelchair accessible and a growing number of metro stations are theoretically wheelchair accessible (generally by lift, although there have been complaints that they are only good for people with prams). Líneas 2, 9, 10 and 11 are completely adapted, as are the majority of stops on Línea 1. In all, about 80% of stops have been adapted (you can check which ones by looking at a network map at: www.tmb.cat/en/transport-accessible). Ticket vending machines in metro stations are adapted for travellers with disabilities, and have Braille options for those a with visual impairment.

➡ Several taxi companies have adapted vehicles, including **Taxi Amic** (☑93 420 80 88; www.taxi-amic-adaptat.com) and **Gestverd** (☑93 303 09 09; www.gestverd.com).

➡ Most street crossings in central Barcelona are wheelchair-friendly.

For information on what the city is doing to improve

accessibility, check out the council's *Accessible Barcelona Guide* in several languages (www.barcelona-access.com).

Other services include the following:

Barcelona Turisme (☎93 285 38 34; www.barcelona-access.com) Barcelona's official tourism organisation maintains a website devoted to making the city accessible to visitors with a disability.

ONCE (Map p286;☎93 238 11 11; Carrer de Sepúlveda 1; Ⓜ Plaça d'Espanya) The national organisation for the vision-impaired can help with information, including lists of places such as restaurants where Braille menus are provided.

Download Lonely Planet's free *Accessible Travel* guide from http://lptravel.to/AccessibleTravel.

Visas

Spain is one of 26 member countries of the Schengen Convention, under which 22 EU countries (all but Bulgaria, Cyprus, Ireland, Romania and the UK) plus Iceland, Norway, Liechtenstein and Switzerland have abolished checks at common borders.

The visa situation for entering Spain is as follows:

➡ **Citizens or residents of EU & Schengen countries** No visa required.

➡ **Citizens or residents of Australia, Canada, Israel, Japan, New Zealand & the USA** No visa required for tourist visits of up to 90 days out of every 180 days.

➡ **Other countries** Check with a Spanish embassy or consulate.

➡ **To work or study in Spain** A special visa may be required – contact a Spanish embassy or consulate before travel.

Language

Catalan (català) and Spanish (español, more precisely known as castellano, or Castilian) both have official-language status in Catalonia. Aranese (aranés), which is a dialect of Gascon, is also an official language in the Val d'Aran. In Barcelona, you'll hear as much Spanish as Catalan, so we've provided some Spanish as well as Catalan basics here to get you started.

Most Spanish sounds are pronounced the same as their English counterparts. If you follow our coloured pronunciation guides, you'll be understood. Note that the kh is a throaty sound (like the 'ch' in the Scottish loch), ly is pronounced as the 'lli' in 'million', ny as the 'ni' in 'onion', th is pronounced with a lisp, and r is strongly rolled. In our pronunciation guides, the stressed syllables are in italics.

Where necessary, masculine and feminine forms are given for the words and phrases in this chapter, separated by a slash and with the masculine form first, eg perdido/a (m/f). Where both polite and informal options are given, they are indicated by the abbreviations 'pol' and 'inf' respectively.

BASICS

Hello.	Hola.	o·la
Goodbye.	Adiós.	a·dyos
How are you?	¿Qué tal?	ke tal
Fine, thanks.	Bien, gracias.	byen gra·thyas
Excuse me.	Perdón.	per·don
Sorry.	Lo siento.	lo see·en·to
Yes./No.	Sí./No.	see/no

WANT MORE?

For in-depth language information and handy phrases, check out Lonely Planet's Spanish phrasebook. You'll find it at **shop. lonelyplanet.com**, or you can buy Lonely Planet's iPhone phrasebooks at the Apple App Store.

Please.	Por favor.	por fa·vor
Thank you.	Gracias.	gra·thyas
You're welcome.	De nada.	de na·da

My name is ...
Me llamo ...   me lya·mo ...

What's your name?
¿Cómo se llama Usted?   ko·mo se lya·ma oo·ste (pol)
¿Cómo te llamas?   ko·mo te lya·mas (inf)

Do you speak (English)?
¿Habla (inglés)?   a·bla (een·gles) (pol)
¿Hablas (inglés)?   a·blas (een·gles) (inf)

I (don't) understand.
Yo (no) entiendo.   yo (no) en·tyen·do

ACCOMMODATION

I'd like to book a room.
Quisiera reservar una habitación.   kee·sye·ra re·ser·var oo·na a·bee·ta·thyon

How much is it per night/person?
¿Cuánto cuesta por noche/persona?   kwan·to kwes·ta por no·che/per·so·na

Does it include breakfast?
¿Incluye el desayuno?   een·kloo·ye el de·sa·yoo·no

hotel	hotel	o·tel
guesthouse	pensión	pen·syon
youth hostel	albergue juvenil	al·ber·ge khoo·ve·neel

I'd like a ... room.	Quisiera una habitación ...	kee·sye·ra oo·na a·bee·ta·thyon ...
single	individual	een·dee·vee·dwal
double	doble	do·ble
air-con	aire acondicionado	ai·re a·kon·dee·thyo·na·do
bathroom	baño	ba·nyo
window	ventana	ven·ta·na

KEY PATTERNS

To get by in Spanish, mix and match these simple patterns with words of your choice:

When's (the next flight)?
¿Cuándo sale — kwan·do sa·le
(el próximo vuelo)? — (el prok·see·mo vwe·lo)

Where's (the station)?
¿Dónde está — don·de es·ta
(la estación)? — (la es·ta·thyon)

Where can I (buy a ticket)?
¿Dónde puedo — don·de pwe·do
(comprar — (kom·prar
un billete)? — oon bee·lye·te)

Do you have (a map)?
¿Tiene (un mapa)? — tye·ne (oon ma·pa)

Is there (a toilet)?
¿Hay (servicios)? — ai (ser·vee·thyos)

I'd like (a coffee).
Quisiera (un café). — kee·sye·ra (oon ka·fe)

I'd like (to hire a car).
Quisiera (alquilar — kee·sye·ra (al·kee·lar
un coche). — oon ko·che)

Can I (enter)?
¿Se puede (entrar)? — se pwe·de (en·trar)

Could you please (help me)?
¿Puede (ayudarme), — pwe·de (a·yoo·dar·me)
por favor? — por fa·vor

Do I have to (get a visa)?
¿Necesito — ne·the·see·to
(obtener — (ob·te·ner
un visado)? — oon vee·sa·do)

DIRECTIONS

Where's ...?
¿Dónde está ...? — don·de es·ta ...

What's the address?
¿Cuál es la dirección? — kwal es la dee·rek·thyon

Could you please write it down?
¿Puede escribirlo, — pwe·de es·kree·beer·lo
por favor? — por fa·vor

Can you show me (on the map)?
¿Me lo puede indicar — me lo pwe·de een·dee·kar
(en el mapa)? — (en el ma·pa)

at the corner	en la esquina	en la es·kee·na
at the traffic lights	en el semáforo	en el se·ma·fo·ro
behind	detrás de	de·tras de
far (away)	lejos	le·khos
in front of	enfrente de	en·fren·te de
left	izquierda	eeth·kyer·da
near	cerca	ther·ka
next to	al lado de	al la·do de
opposite	frente a	fren·te a
right	derecha	de·re·cha
straight ahead	todo recto	to·do rek·to

EATING & DRINKING

I'd like to book a table for ...
Quisiera — kee·sye·ra
reservar una — re·ser·var oo·na
mesa para ... — me·sa pa·ra ...

(eight) o'clock — las (ocho) — las (o·cho)

(two) people — (dos) — (dos)
personas — per·so·nas

What would you recommend?
¿Qué recomienda? — ke re·ko·myen·da

What's in that dish?
¿Que lleva ese plato? — ke lye·va e·se pla·to

I don't eat ...
No como ... — no ko·mo ...

Cheers!
¡Salud! — sa·loo

That was delicious!
¡Estaba buenísimo! — es·ta·ba bwe·nee·see·mo

Please bring the bill.
Por favor nos trae — por fa·vor nos tra·e
la cuenta. — la kwen·ta

Key Words

appetisers	aperitivos	a·pe·ree·tee·vos
bar	bar	bar
bottle	botella	bo·te·lya
bowl	bol	bol
breakfast	desayuno	de·sa·yoo·no
cafe	café	ka·fe
children's menu	menú infantil	me·noo een·fan·teel
(too/very) cold	(muy) frío	(mooy) free·o
dinner	cena	the·na
food	comida	ko·mee·da
fork	tenedor	te·ne·dor
glass	vaso	va·so
highchair	trona	tro·na
hot (warm)	caliente	ka·lyen·te
knife	cuchillo	koo·chee·lyo
lunch	comida	ko·mee·da
main course	segundo plato	se·goon·do pla·to
market	mercado	mer·ka·do
menu (in English)	menú (en inglés)	oon me·noo (en een·gles)

CATALAN

The recognition of Catalan as an official language in Spain is the end result of a regional government campaign that began when the province gained autonomy at the end of the 1970s. Until the Battle of Muret in 1213, Catalan territory extended across southern France, taking in Roussillon and reaching into the Provence. Catalan was spoken, or at least understood, throughout these territories and in what is now Catalonia and Andorra. In the couple of hundred years that followed, the Catalans spread their language south into Valencia, west into Aragón and east to the Balearic Islands. The language also reached Sicily and Naples, and the Sardinian town of Alghero is still a partly Catalan-speaking outpost today. Catalan is spoken by up to 10 million people in Spain.

In Barcelona you'll hear as much Spanish as Catalan. Your chances of coming across English speakers are also good. Elsewhere in the province, don't be surprised if you get replies in Catalan to your questions in Spanish. However, you'll find that most Catalans will happily speak to you in Spanish, especially once they realise you're a foreigner. This said, the following Catalan phrases might win you a few smiles and perhaps help you make some new friends.

Hello.	*Hola.*	**Monday**	*dilluns*
Goodbye.	*Adéu.*	**Tuesday**	*dimarts*
Yes.	*Sí.*	**Wednesday**	*dimecres*
No.	*No.*	**Thursday**	*dijous*
Please.	*Sisplau./Si us plau.*	**Friday**	*divendres*
Thank you (very much).	*(Moltes) gràcies.*	**Saturday**	*dissabte*
You're welcome.	*De res.*	**Sunday**	*diumenge*
Excuse me.	*Perdoni.*		
May I?/Do you mind?	*Puc?/Em permet?*	1	*un/una* (m/f)
I'm sorry.	*Ho sento./Perdoni.*	2	*dos/dues* (m/f)
		3	*tres*
What's your name?	*Com et dius?* (inf)	4	*quatre*
	Com es diu? (pol)	5	*cinc*
My name is ...	*Em dic ...*	6	*sis*
Where are you from?	*D'on ets?*	7	*set*
Do you speak English?	*Parla anglès?*	8	*vuit*
I understand.	*Ho entenc.*	9	*nou*
I don't understand.	*No ho entenc.*	10	*deu*
Could you speak in	*Pot parlar castellà*	11	*onze*
Castilian, please?	*sisplau?*	12	*dotze*
How do you say ... in	*Com es diu ... en*	13	*tretze*
Catalan?	*català?*	14	*catorze*
		15	*quinze*
I'm looking for ...	*Estic buscant ...*	16	*setze*
How do I get to ...?	*Com puc arribar a ...?*	17	*disset*
Turn left.	*Giri a mà esquerra.*	18	*divuit*
Turn right.	*Giri a mà dreta.*	19	*dinou*
near	*a prop de*	20	*vint*
far	*a lluny de*	100	*cent*

Signs	
Abierto	Open
Cerrado	Closed
Entrada	Entrance
Hombres	Men
Mujeres	Women
Prohibido	Prohibited
Salida	Exit
Servicios/Aseos	Toilets

plate	*plato*	*pla*·to
restaurant	*restaurante*	res·tow·*ran*·te
spoon	*cuchara*	koo·*cha*·ra
supermarket	*supermercado*	soo·per·mer·*ka*·do
vegetarian food	*comida vegetariana*	ko·*mee*·da ve·khe·ta·*rya*·na
with/without	*con/sin*	kon/seen

Meat & Fish

beef	*carne de vaca*	*kar*·ne de *va*·ka
chicken	*pollo*	*po*·lyo
duck	*pato*	*pa*·to
lamb	*cordero*	kor·*de*·ro
lobster	*langosta*	lan·*gos*·ta
pork	*cerdo*	*ther*·do
prawns	*camarones*	ka·ma·*ro*·nes
tuna	*atún*	a·*toon*
turkey	*pavo*	*pa*·vo
veal	*ternera*	ter·*ne*·ra

Fruit & Vegetables

apple	*manzana*	man·*tha*·na
apricot	*albaricoque*	al·ba·ree·*ko*·ke
artichoke	*alcachofa*	al·ka·*cho*·fa
asparagus	*espárragos*	es·*pa*·ra·gos
banana	*plátano*	*pla*·ta·no
beans	*judías*	khoo·*dee*·as
beetroot	*remolacha*	re·mo·*la*·cha
cabbage	*col*	kol
carrot	*zanahoria*	tha·na·o·rya
celery	*apio*	*a*·pyo
cherry	*cereza*	the·*re*·tha
corn	*maíz*	ma·*eeth*
cucumber	*pepino*	pe·*pee*·no
fruit	*fruta*	*froo*·ta
grape	*uvas*	*oo*·vas

lemon	*limón*	lee·*mon*
lentils	*lentejas*	len·*te*·khas
lettuce	*lechuga*	le·*choo*·ga
mushroom	*champiñón*	cham·pee·*nyon*
nuts	*nueces*	*nwe*·thes
onion	*cebolla*	the·*bo*·lya
orange	*naranja*	na·*ran*·kha
peach	*melocotón*	me·lo·ko·*ton*
peas	*guisantes*	gee·*san*·tes
(red/green) pepper	*pimiento (rojo/verde)*	pee·*myen*·to (*ro*·kho/*ver*·de)
pineapple	*piña*	*pee*·nya
plum	*ciruela*	theer·*we*·la
potato	*patata*	pa·*ta*·ta
pumpkin	*calabaza*	ka·la·*ba*·tha
spinach	*espinacas*	es·pee·*na*·kas
strawberry	*fresa*	*fre*·sa
tomato	*tomate*	to·*ma*·te
vegetable	*verdura*	ver·*doo*·ra
watermelon	*sandía*	san·*dee*·a

Other

bread	*pan*	pan
butter	*mantequilla*	man·te·*kee*·lya
cheese	*queso*	*ke*·so
egg	*huevo*	*we*·vo
honey	*miel*	myel
jam	*mermelada*	mer·me·*la*·da
oil	*aceite*	a·*they*·te
pasta	*pasta*	*pas*·ta
pepper	*pimienta*	pee·*myen*·ta
rice	*arroz*	a·*roth*
salt	*sal*	sal
sugar	*azúcar*	a·*thoo*·kar
vinegar	*vinagre*	vee·*na*·gre

Drinks

beer	*cerveza*	ther·*ve*·tha
coffee	*café*	ka·*fe*
(orange) juice	*zumo (de naranja)*	*thoo*·mo (de na·*ran*·kha)
milk	*leche*	*le*·che
tea	*té*	te
(mineral) water	*agua (mineral)*	*a*·gwa (mee·ne·*ral*)
(red) wine	*vino (tinto)*	*vee*·no (*teen*·to)
(white) wine	*vino (blanco)*	*vee*·no (*blan*·ko)

EMERGENCIES

Help!	¡Socorro!	so·ko·ro
Go away!	¡Vete!	ve·te

Call ...!	¡Llame a ...!	lya·me a ...
a doctor	un médico	oon me·dee·ko
the police	la policía	la po·lee·thee·a

I'm lost.
Estoy perdido/a.   es·toy per·dee·do/a (m/f)

I had an accident.
He tenido un   e te·nee·do oon
accidente.   ak·thee·den·te

I'm ill.
Estoy enfermo/a.   es·toy en·fer·mo/a (m/f)

It hurts here.
Me duele aquí.   me dwe·le a·kee

I'm allergic to (antibiotics).
Soy alérgico/a a   soy a·ler·khee·ko/a a
(los antibióticos). (los an·tee·byo·tee·kos) (m/f)

SHOPPING & SERVICES

I'd like to buy ...
Quisiera comprar ...   kee·sye·ra kom·prar ...

I'm just looking.
Sólo estoy mirando.   so·lo es·toy mee·ran·do

Can I look at it?
¿Puedo verlo?   pwe·do ver·lo

I don't like it.
No me gusta.   no me goos·ta

How much is it?
¿Cuánto cuesta?   kwan·to kwes·ta

That's too expensive.
Es muy caro.   es mooy ka·ro

Can you lower the price?
¿Podría bajar un   po·dree·a ba·khar oon
poco el precio?   po·ko el pre·thyo

There's a mistake in the bill.
Hay un error en   ai oon e·ror en
la cuenta.   la kwen·ta

ATM	cajero automático	ka·khe·ro ow·to·ma·tee·ko
internet cafe	cibercafé	thee·ber·ka·fe
post office	correos	ko·re·os
tourist office	oficina de turismo	o·fee·thee·na de too·rees·mo

TIME & DATES

What time is it?
¿Qué hora es?   ke o·ra es

It's (10) o'clock.
Son (las diez).   son (las dyeth)

Half past (one).
Es (la una)   es (la oo·na)
y media.   ee me·dya

morning	mañana	ma·nya·na
afternoon	tarde	tar·de
evening	noche	no·che
yesterday	ayer	a·yer
today	hoy	oy
tomorrow	mañana	ma·nya·na

Monday	lunes	loo·nes
Tuesday	martes	mar·tes
Wednesday	miércoles	myer·ko·les
Thursday	jueves	khwe·bes
Friday	viernes	vyer·nes
Saturday	sábado	sa·ba·do
Sunday	domingo	do·meen·go

January	enero	e·ne·ro
February	febrero	fe·bre·ro
March	marzo	mar·tho
April	abril	a·breel
May	mayo	ma·yo
June	junio	khoo·nyo
July	julio	khoo·lyo
August	agosto	a·gos·to
September	septiembre	sep·tyem·bre
October	octubre	ok·too·bre
November	noviembre	no·vyem·bre
December	diciembre	dee·thyem·bre

TRANSPORT

boat	barco	bar·ko
bus	autobús	ow·to·boos
plane	avión	a·vyon
train	tren	tren

first	primer	pree·mer
last	último	ool·tee·mo
next	próximo	prok·see·mo

Question Words

What?	¿Qué?	ke
When?	¿Cuándo?	kwan·do
Where?	¿Dónde?	don·de
Who?	¿Quién?	kyen
Why?	¿Por qué?	por ke

I want to go to ...
Quisiera ir a ... — kee·sye·ra eer a ...

What time does it arrive/leave?
¿A qué hora llega/sale? — a ke o·ra lye·ga/sa·le

Does it stop at ...?
¿Para en ...? — pa·ra en ...

Can you tell me when we get to ...?
¿Puede avisarme — pwe·de a·vee·sar·me
cuando lleguemos a ...? — kwan·do lye·ge·mos a ...

What stop is this?
¿Cuál es esta parada? — kwal es es·ta pa·ra·da

I want to get off here.
Quiero bajarme aquí. — kye·ro ba·khar·me a·kee

a ... ticket	*un billete de ...*	oon bee·lye·te de ...
1st-class	*primera clase*	pree·me·ra kla·se
2nd-class	*segunda clase*	se·goon·da kla·se
one-way	*ida*	ee·da
return	*ida y vuelta*	ee·da ee vwel·ta
aisle seat	*asiento de pasillo*	a·syen·to de pa·see·lyo
cancelled	*cancelado*	kan·the·la·do
delayed	*retrasado*	re·tra·sa·do
platform	*plataforma*	pla·ta·for·ma
ticket office	*taquilla*	ta·kee·lya
timetable	*horario*	o·ra·ryo
train station	*estación de trenes*	es·ta·thyon de tre·nes
window seat	*asiento junto a la ventana*	a·syen·to khoon·to a la ven·ta·na
I'd like to hire a ...	*Quisiera alquilar ...*	kee·sye·ra al·kee·lar ...
bicycle	*una bicicleta*	oo·na bee·thee·kle·ta
car	*un coche*	oon ko·che
motorcycle	*una moto*	oo·na mo·to

Numbers

1	*uno*	oo·no
2	*dos*	dos
3	*tres*	tres
4	*cuatro*	kwa·tro
5	*cinco*	theen·ko
6	*seis*	seys
7	*siete*	sye·te
8	*ocho*	o·cho
9	*nueve*	nwe·ve
10	*diez*	dyeth
20	*veinte*	veyn·te
30	*treinta*	treyn·ta
40	*cuarenta*	kwa·ren·ta
50	*cincuenta*	theen·kwen·ta
60	*sesenta*	se·sen·ta
70	*setenta*	se·ten·ta
80	*ochenta*	o·chen·ta
90	*noventa*	no·ven·ta
100	*cien*	thyen
1000	*mil*	meel

diesel	*gasóleo*	ga·so·lyo
helmet	*casco*	kas·ko
mechanic	*mecánico*	me·ka·nee·ko
petrol/gas	*gasolina*	ga·so·lee·na
service station	*gasolinera*	ga·so·lee·ne·ra

(How long) Can I park here?
¿(Por cuánto tiempo) — (por kwan·to tyem·po)
Puedo aparcar aquí? — pwe·do a·par·kar a·kee

The car has broken down.
El coche se ha averiado. — el ko·che se a a·ve·rya·do

I have a flat tyre.
Tengo un pinchazo. — ten·go oon peen·cha·tho

I've run out of petrol.
Me he quedado sin gasolina. — me e ke·da·do seen ga·so·lee·na

GLOSSARY

Items listed below are in Catalan/Spanish (Castilian) where they start with the same letter. Where the two terms start with different letters, or where only the Catalan or the Spanish term is provided, they are listed separately and marked (C) for Catalan or (S) for Spanish. If an entry is not marked at all, it is because it takes the same form in both languages.

ajuntament/ayuntamiento – town hall

artesonado (S) – Mudéjar wooden ceiling with interlaced beams leaving a pattern of spaces for decoration

avinguda (C) – avenue

barcelonin (C) – inhabitant/native of Barcelona

Barcino – Roman name for Barcelona

barri/barrio – neighbourhood, quarter of Barcelona

caganer (C) – the crapper, a character appearing in Catalan nativity scenes

capella/capilla – chapel

carrer/calle – street

casa – house

castellers (C) – human-castle builders

cercanías (S) – local trains serving Barcelona's airport, suburbs and some outlying towns

comte/conde – count

correfoc (C) – appearance of firework-spouting devils at festivals; literally 'fire runs'

El Call (C) – the Jewish quarter in medieval Barcelona

església (C) – church

farmàcia/farmacia – pharmacy

festa/fiesta – festival, public holiday or party

FGC (C) – Ferrocarrils de la Generalitat de Catalunya; local trains operating alongside the Metro in Barcelona

fundació/fundación – foundation

garum – a spicy sauce made from fish entrails, found throughout the Roman Empire

gegants – huge figures paraded at *festes*

Generalitat (C) – Catalan regional government

guiri – foreigner (somewhat pejorative)

hostal – commercial establishment providing one- to three-star accommodation

iglesia (S) – church

IVA – *impost sobre el valor afegit/impuesto sobre el valor añadido*, or value-added tax

masia – Catalan country farmhouse

mercat/mercado – market

Modernisme (C) – the turn-of-the-19th-century artistic style, influenced by art nouveau, whose leading practitioner was Antoni Gaudí

Modernista – an exponent of Modernisme

Mudéjar (S) – a Muslim living under Christian rule in medieval Spain; also refers to their decorative style of architecture

palau (C) – palace

passatge (C) – laneway

pensió/pensión – commercial establishment providing one- to three-star accommodation

plaça/plaza – plaza

platja/playa – beach

Renaixença – rebirth of interest in Catalan literature, culture and language in the second half of the 19th century

rodalies (C) – see *cercanías*

saló (C) – hall

sardana – traditional Catalan folk dance

s/n (S) – *sin número* (without number)

tablao – restaurant where flamenco is performed

teatre – theatre

terrassa/terazza – terrace; often means a cafe or bar's outdoor tables

trencadís – a Modernista style of mosaic, created using broken tiles

turista – second class; economy class

Behind the Scenes

SEND US YOUR FEEDBACK

We love to hear from travellers – your comments keep us on our toes and help make our books better. Our well-travelled team reads every word on what you loved or loathed about this book. Although we cannot reply individually to your submissions, we always guarantee that your feedback goes straight to the appropriate authors, in time for the next edition. Each person who sends us information is thanked in the next edition – the most useful submissions are rewarded with a selection of digital PDF chapters.

Visit **lonelyplanet.com/contact** to submit your updates and suggestions or to ask for help. Our award-winning website also features inspirational travel stories, news and discussions.

Note: We may edit, reproduce and incorporate your comments in Lonely Planet products such as guidebooks, websites and digital products, so let us know if you don't want your comments reproduced or your name acknowledged. For a copy of our privacy policy visit lonelyplanet.com/privacy.

OUR READERS

Many thanks to the travellers who used the last edition and wrote to us with helpful hints, useful advice and interesting anecdotes: Àngels Bertran, Cristina Andreu, Deborah Galef, Lluïsa Martin and Lluna Baltasar

AUTHOR THANKS

Regis St Louis

I'm grateful to the many friends and acquaintances who provided guidance and tips along the way. Biggest thanks go to co-author Sal Davies for all her assistance, including the temporary crash pad, and to kind hosts Xabi and Lucia in El Born. Thanks also to Cristiano Nogueira for making the detour from France. Finally, big hugs to my family for all their support.

Sally Davies

Thanks chiefly go to my Barcelona support team, especially Mary-Ann Gallagher and Matthew Wrigley, but also Sarah Davison, Aurélie Herrou, Jane Darroch and John O'Donovan. Thanks to Regis St Louis for fielding questions and sharing intel, and a hat tip to foodies Buster Turner, Paul Richardson and Llibert Figueras for some excellent lunches. Extra special thanks to Tess, for putting up with it all.

ACKNOWLEDGEMENTS

Cover photograph: Palau de la Música Catalana, Hans Georg Roth/amanaimages©.

Illustration pp124-5 by Javier Zarracina.

THIS BOOK

This 10th edition of Lonely Planet's *Barcelona* guidebook was researched and written by Regis St Louis and Sally Davies. The previous edition was written by Regis, Sally and Andy Symington. The 8th edition was written by Regis, Anna Kaminski and Vesna Maric. This guidebook was produced by the following:

Destination Editors Lorna Parkes, Clifton Wilkinson
Product Editor Anne Mason
Senior Cartographer Anthony Phelan
Book Designers Mazzy Prinsep, Wendy Wright
Assisting Editors Imogen Bannister, Carolyn Boicos, Nigel Chin, Grace Dobell, Kristin Odijk, Ross Taylor
Cover Researcher Naomi Parker
Thanks to Lauren Egan, Mark Griffiths, Kate James, Kerrianne Jenkins, Andi Jones, Claire Naylor, Karyn Noble, Luna Soo, Tracy Whitmey

Index

INDEX SPORTS & ACTIVITIES

Barcelona Maps

Sights
- Beach
- Bird Sanctuary
- Buddhist
- Castle/Palace
- Christian
- Confucian
- Hindu
- Islamic
- Jain
- Jewish
- Monument
- Museum/Gallery/Historic Building
- Ruin
- Shinto
- Sikh
- Taoist
- Winery/Vineyard
- Zoo/Wildlife Sanctuary
- Other Sight

Activities, Courses & Tours
- Bodysurfing
- Diving
- Canoeing/Kayaking
- Course/Tour
- Sento Hot Baths/Onsen
- Skiing
- Snorkelling
- Surfing
- Swimming/Pool
- Walking
- Windsurfing
- Other Activity

Sleeping
- Sleeping
- Camping

Eating
- Eating

Drinking & Nightlife
- Drinking & Nightlife
- Cafe

Entertainment
- Entertainment

Shopping
- Shopping

Information
- Bank
- Embassy/Consulate
- Hospital/Medical
- Internet
- Police
- Post Office
- Telephone
- Toilet
- Tourist Information
- Other Information

Geographic
- Beach
- Gate
- Hut/Shelter
- Lighthouse
- Lookout
- Mountain/Volcano
- Oasis
- Park
- Pass
- Picnic Area
- Waterfall

Population
- Capital (National)
- Capital (State/Province)
- City/Large Town
- Town/Village

Transport
- Airport
- Border crossing
- Bus
- Cable car/Funicular
- Cycling
- Ferry
- Metro station
- Monorail
- Parking
- Petrol station
- S-Bahn/Subway station
- Taxi
- T-bane/Tunnelbana station
- Train station/Railway
- Tram
- Tube station
- U-Bahn/Underground station
- Other Transport

Note: Not all symbols displayed above appear on the maps in this book

Routes
- Tollway
- Freeway
- Primary
- Secondary
- Tertiary
- Lane
- Unsealed road
- Road under construction
- Plaza/Mall
- Steps
- Tunnel
- Pedestrian overpass
- Walking Tour
- Walking Tour detour
- Path/Walking Trail

Boundaries
- International
- State/Province
- Disputed
- Regional/Suburb
- Marine Park
- Cliff
- Wall

Hydrography
- River, Creek
- Intermittent River
- Canal
- Water
- Dry/Salt/Intermittent Lake
- Reef

Areas
- Airport/Runway
- Beach/Desert
- Cemetery (Christian)
- Cemetery (Other)
- Glacier
- Mudflat
- Park/Forest
- Sight (Building)
- Sportsground
- Swamp/Mangrove

MAP INDEX

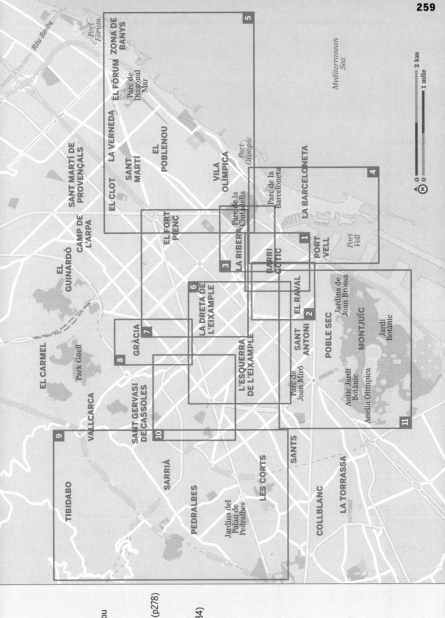

LA RAMBLA & BARRI GÒTIC

Key on p262

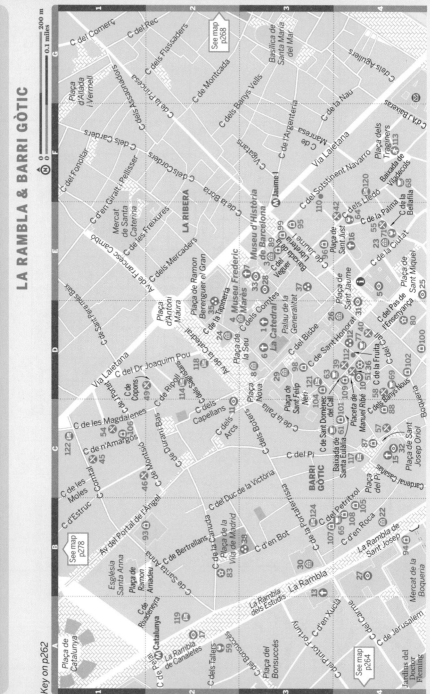

See map p268

See map p278

See map p264

200 m
0.1 miles

Plaça de Catalunya

Plaça d'Allada i Vermell

C del Comerç
C del Rec
C dels Flassaders
C de Montcada
C de la Princesa
C dels Assaonadors
C dels Carders
C del Fonollar
C d'en Giralt i Pellisser
Mercat de Santa Caterina
C de les Freixures
Av de Francesc Cambó
C dels Mercaders
C dels Corders
C de la Bòria
LA RIBERA
Basílica de Santa Maria del Mar
C dels Banys Vells
C de l'Argenteria
C dels Aguilers
Via Laietana
C de Manresa
C de la Nau
C d'Al Baixes
Plaça dels Traginers
Baixada de Viladecols
C dels Lledó
C de la Palma
C de la Bellafila
Museu d'Història de Barcelona
M Jaume I
C del Sotstinent Navarro
Plaça de Sant Just
C de la Ciutat
Plaça de Sant Miquel
Museu Frederic Marès
Plaça de Ramon Berenguer el Gran
C de la Tapineria
C dels Comtes
La Catedral
Palau de la Generalitat
Plaça de Sant Jaume
C del Pas de l'Ensenyança
Plaça de Sant Miquel
Plaça d'Antoni Maura
Av de la Catedral
Plaça de la Seu
C del Bisbe
C de Sant Honorat
C de la Fruita
C del Pi
Plaça Nova
Plaça de Sant Felip Neri
C de Sant Domènec del Call
Plaça de Manuel Ribé
C dels Banys Nous
Via Laietana
C del Dr Joaquim Pou
C de Copons
C de Ripoll
C dels Sagristans
C dels Capellans
C dels Arcs
C de les Magdalenes
C de n'Amargós
C Duran i Bas
C de Montsió
C Comtal
C de les Moles
C d'Estruc
Av del Portal de l'Àngel
C de la Canuda
C de Bertrellans
Plaça de la Vila de Madrid
C d'en Bot
C del Duc de la Victòria
C de la Portaferrissa
C del Pi
BARRI GÒTIC
Baixada de Santa Eulàlia
Plaça del Pi
Plaça de Sant Josep Oriol
Cardenal Casañas
C del Petritxol
C d'en Roca
La Rambla de Sant Josep
Mercat de la Boqueria
Església Santa Anna
Plaça de Ramon Amadeu
C de Ramon i Cajal
La Rambla de la Vila de Madrid
C de Rivadeneyra
C del Bonsuccés
La Rambla de Canaletes
M Catalunya
C del Pintor Fortuny
C d'en Xuclà
C del Carme
C de Jerusalem
La Rambla dels Estudis
La Rambla
Plaça del Bonsuccés
Jardins del Doctor Fleming
C dels Tallers

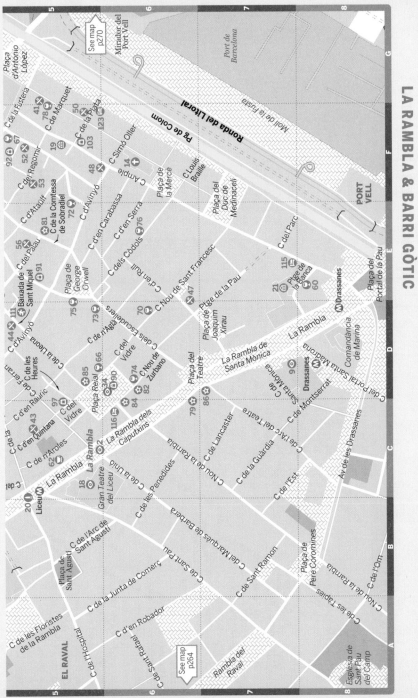

Plaça d'Antonio López

Mirador del Port Vell

See map p270

Port de Barcelona

Moll de la Fusta

Ronda del Litoral

Pg de Colom

C de la Fusteria

C de Marquet

C de la Plata

C Simó Oller

C Ample

C Louis Braille

Plaça de la Mercè

Plaça del Duc de Medinaceli

PORT VELL

C del Regomir

C d'Avinyó

C d'Ataülf

C de la Comtessa de Sobradiel

C d'en Carabassa

C d'en Serra

C del Parc

C del Palau

Baixada de Sant Miquel

Plaça de George Orwell

C dels Còdols

C d'en Rull

C Nou de Sant Francesc

Ptge de la Pau

Plaça de la Banca

Plaça del Portal de la Pau

Drassanes

C d'Avinyó

C de la Lleona

C de l'Agla

C dels Escudellers

Plaça de Joaquim Xirau

La Rambla

Comandància de Marina

C de Ferran

C de les Heures

C de Ferran

C d'en Rauric

C del Vidre

C del Vidre

C Nou de Zurbano

La Rambla de Santa Mònica

C de Santa Mònica

Drassanes

C del Portal Santa Madrona

C d'en Quintana

C de n'Aroles

C de Ferran

La Rambla

Plaça Reial

Plaça del Teatre

C de l'Arc del Teatre

C de Montserrat

Av de les Drassanes

Liceu

La Rambla

La Rambla dels Caputxins

C Nou de la Rambla

C de Lancaster

C de la Guàrdia

C de l'Est

Gran Teatre del Liceu

C de la Unió

C de les Penedides

C del Marquès de Barberà

C de Sant Ramon

Plaça de Pere Coromines

C de Sant Pau

C de l'Arc de Sant Agustí

Plaça de Sant Agustí

EL RAVAL

C de l'Hospital

C de la Junta de Comerç

C d'en Robador

C de les Floristes de la Rambla

C de Sant Rafael

See map p264

Rambla del Raval

C Nou de la Rambla

C de les Tàpies

Església de Sant Pau del Camp

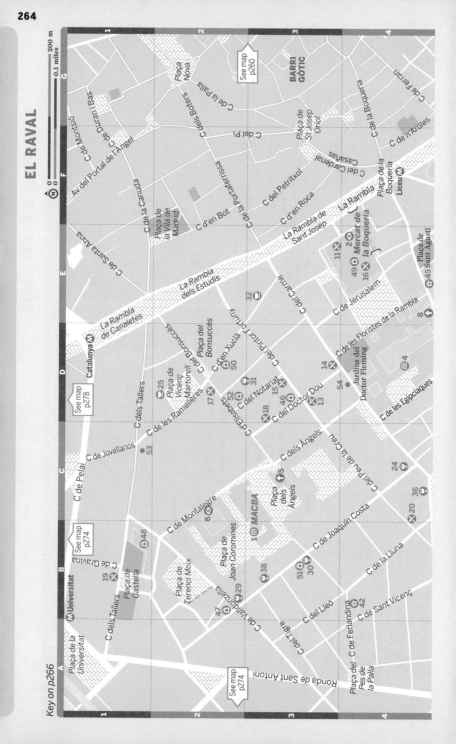

EL RAVAL

Key on p266

200 m
0.1 miles

See map p260

BARRI GÒTIC

Plaça Nova

C de la Palla

C dels Boters

C de Montsió

C de Durant i Bas

Av del Portal de l'Angel

C del Petritxol

C del Cardenal Casañas

Plaça de St Josep Oriol

C del Pi

C de n'Arolas

C de Ferran

Plaça de la Boqueria

Liceu

C de la Boqueria

C d'en Roca

C de la Portaferrissa

C d'en Bot

Plaça de la Vila de Madrid

La Rambla

La Rambla de Sant Josep

C de la Canuda

Plaça de Sant Agustí

45

C de Santa Anna

La Rambla dels Estudis

11

49 2 Mercat de la Boqueria

16

La Rambla de Canaletes

32

C del Carme

C de Jerusalem

8

Catalunya

C de les Floristes de la Rambla

C dels Tallers

Plaça de Vicenç Martorell

C del Bonsuccés

Plaça del Bonsuccés

C d'en Xuclà

50

C del Pintor Fortuny

14

Jardins del Doctor Fleming

25

17

52

C del Notariat

31

C de les Ramelleres

18

C de l'Elisabets

46

15

C del Doctor Dou

13

54

C de les Egipcíaques

53

C de Jovellanos

C dels Àngels

24

C de Pelai

5

C del Pau de la Creu

36

C de Montalegre

6

Plaça dels Àngels

20

See map p274

48

Plaça de Joan Coromines

MACBA

C de Joaquín Costa

C de la Lluna

C de Gravina

Universitat

19

Plaça de Castella

Plaça de Terenci Moix

29

38

51

30

C del Lleó

C de Sant Vicenç

47

C de Valldonzella

42

C del Tigre

C de Ferlandina

Plaça del Pes de la Palla

C dels Tallers

Plaça de la Universitat

Ronda de Sant Antoni

See map p274

See map p278

C dels Tallers

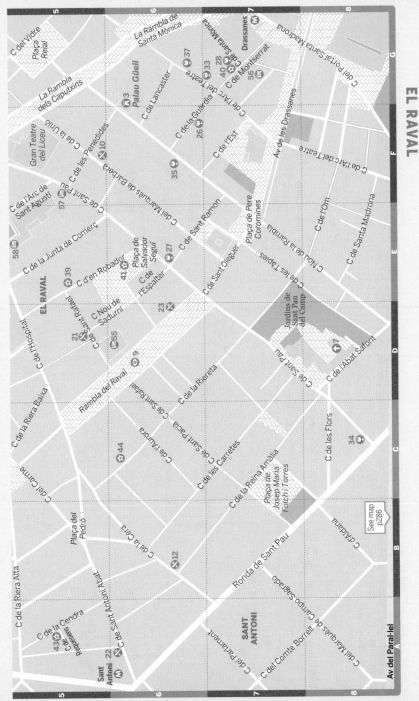

See map p286

Av del Paral·lel

EL RAVAL *Map on p264*

LA RIBERA *Map on p268*

Key on p267

LA RIBERA

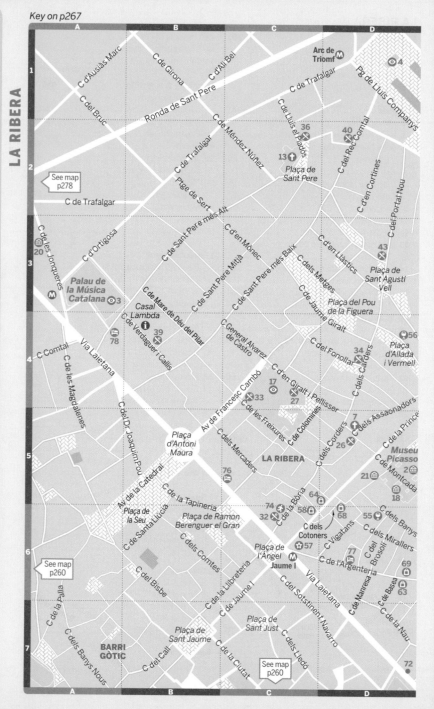

See map p278

See map p260

See map p260

BARRI GÒTIC

LA RIBERA

Museu Picasso

Palau de la Música Catalana

Casal Lambda

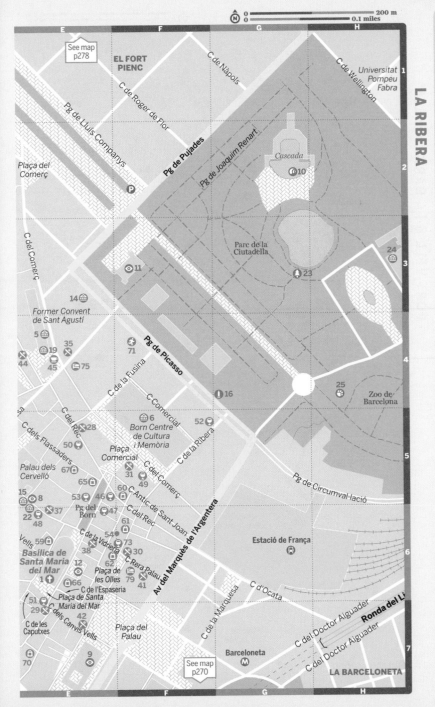

0 — 200 m
0 — 0.1 miles

N

LA RIBERA

EL FORT PIENC

See map p278

C de Nàpols

C de Roger de Flor

C de Wellington

Universitat Pompeu Fabra

Pg de Lluís Companys

Pg de Joaquim Renart

Pg de Pujades

Cascada

10

Plaça del Comerç

P

Parc de la Ciutadella

23

24

C del Comerç

11

14

Former Convent de Sant Agustí

5

35

19

71

Pg de Picasso

44

45

75

25

Zoo de Barcelona

C de la Fusina

C Comercial

16

C dels Flassaders

C del Rec

28

6

Born Centre de Cultura i Memòria

52

Plaça Comercial

50

Pg de Circumval·lació

Palau dels Cervelló

67

65

31

C del Comerç

C de la Ribera

49

15

8

53

46

60

C Antic de Sant Joan

Pg del Born

47

C del Rec

22

37

48

61

Av del Marquès de l'Argentera

Estació de França

Vells

59

54

C de la Vidriera

73

38

30

Basílica de Santa Maria del Mar

12

62

C Rera Palau

66

Plaça de les Olles

79

1

41

C de l'Espaseria

51

29

C de Santa Maria del Mar

Plaça de Santa

C dels Canvis Vells

42

C de les Caputxes

Plaça del Palau

C d'Ocata

C de la Marquesa

Ronda del Li

C del Doctor Aiguader

70

9

See map p270

Barceloneta

M

C del Doctor Aiguader

LA BARCELONETA

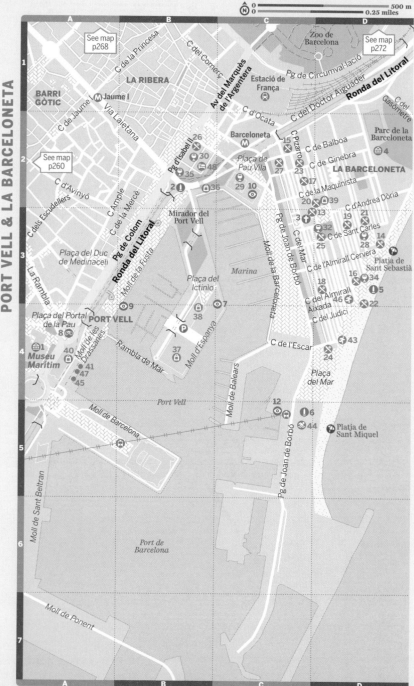

See map
p268

See map
p272

0   500 m
0   0.25 miles

Zoo de
Barcelona

Pg de Circumval·lació

Ronda del Litoral

C de la Princesa

C del Comerç

LA RIBERA

Av del Marquès
de l'Argentera

Estació de
França

C del Doctor Aiguader

C del
Gasòmetre

BARRI
GÒTIC

Jaume I

Via Laietana

C de Jaume I

C d'Ocata

Barceloneta

Parc de la
Barceloneta

4

C Pizarro

C de Balboa

15

C de Ginebra

LA BARCELONETA

See map
p260

Pg d'Isabel II

26

30

48

35

2

36

Plaça de
Pau Vila

27

29   10

23

17

C de la Maquinista

20

39

3

13

19

21

32

C de Sant Carles

14

25

28

C d'Andrea Dòria

Platja de
Sant Sebastià

C de la Mercè

C Ample

C dels Escudellers

Pg de Colom

Ronda del Litoral

Mirador del
Port Vell

Moll de la Fusta

Plaça del
Duc de
Medinaceli

La Rambla

Plaça del
Ictínio

Marina

Pg de Joan de Borbó

Moll de la Barceloneta

C del Mar

C de l'Almirall Cervera

16

34

18

5

C de l'Almirall
Aixada

46

22

9

7

C del Judici

38

PORT VELL

Plaça del Portal
de la Pau

8

Moll de les Drassanes

Rambla de Mar

37

C de l'Escar

43

24

Museu
Marítim

1

40

41

47

45

Moll d'Espanya

Moll de Balears

Plaça
del Mar

Moll de Sant Beltran

Moll de Barcelona

Port Vell

12

6

44

Platja de
Sant Miquel

Pg de Joan de Borbó

Port de
Barcelona

Moll de Ponent

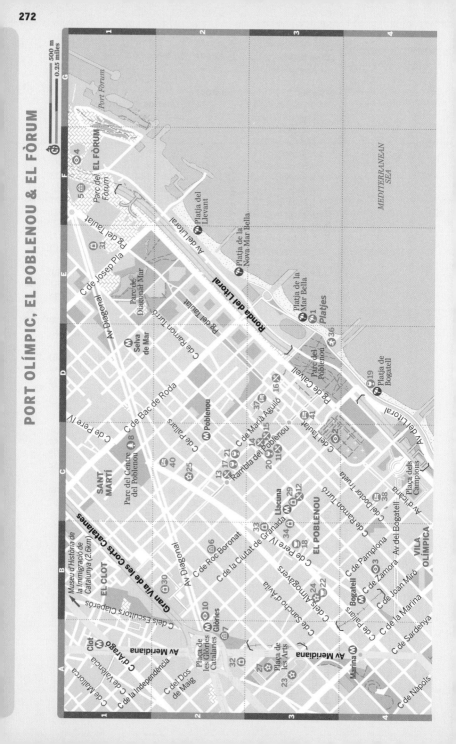

500 m
0.25 miles

Port Fòrum

Port Fòrum

EL FÒRUM

Parc del Fòrum

Platja del Llevant

Platja de la Nova Mar Bella

Platja de la Mar Bella

Platjes

Av del Litoral

Ronda del Litoral

Pg del Taulat

C de Josep Pla

Av Diagonal

Parc del Diagonal Mar

Pg del Taulat

Selva de Mar

C de Ramon Turró

Parc del Poblenou

Platja de Bogatell

MEDITERRANEAN SEA

C de Pere IV

C de Bac de Roda

C de Palaus

Poblenou

Pg de Calçell

C de Maria Aguiló

Av del Litoral

SANT MARTÍ

Parc del Centre del Poblenou

Rambla del Poblenou

C del Taulat

Museu d'Història de la Immigració de Catalunya (2.6km)

Gran Via de les Corts Catalanes

Av Diagonal

C de Roc Boronat

C de la Ciutat de Granada

Lacuna

EL POBLENOU

C de Pere IV

C de Ramon Turró

C del Doctor Trueta

Plaça dels Campions

Av d'Icària

EL CLOT

C dels Escultors Claperós

C de Sancho d'Àvila

C dels Almogàvers

C de la Marina

C de Pamplona

C de Zamora

Bogatell

C de Joan Miró

Av del Bogatell

VILA OLÍMPICA

Clot

Av Meridiana

Plaça de les Glòries Catalanes

Glòries

Plaça de les Arts

Av Meridiana

Marina

C de Sardenya

C d'Aragó

C de Mallorca

C de València

C de la Independència

C del Dos de Maig

C de Pallars

C de Nàpols

PORT OLÍMPIC, EL POBLENOU & EL FÒRUM

L'ESQUERRA DE L'EIXAMPLE

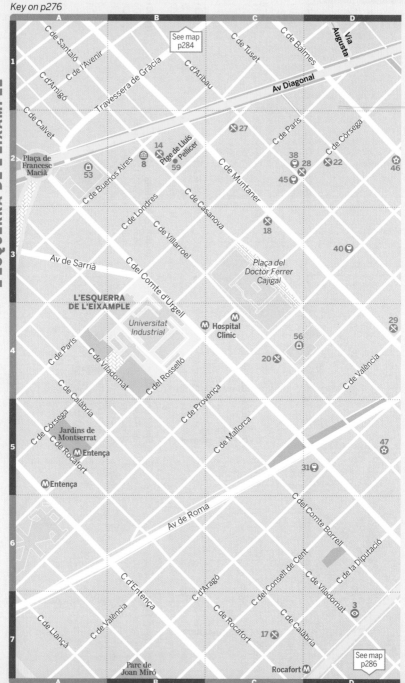

See map p284

Via Augusta

C de Santaló

C de l'Avenir

C d'Amigó

C de Calvet

Travessera de Gràcia

C d'Aribau

C de Tuset

C de Balmes

Av Diagonal

Plaça de Francesc Macià

C de Buenos Aires

53

14

8

Ptge de Lluís Pellicer

59

27

C de París

C de Còrsega

38

28

22

45

46

C de Muntaner

C de Londres

C de Villarroel

C de Casanova

18

40

Av de Sarrià

C del Comte d'Urgell

L'ESQUERRA DE L'EIXAMPLE

Plaça del Doctor Ferrer Cajigal

Universitat Industrial

Hospital Clínic

56

29

C de París

C de Viladomat

C del Rosselló

20

C de València

C de Calàbria

C de Còrsega

Jardins de Montserrat

C de Rocafort

Entença

C de Provença

C de Mallorca

47

Entença

31

Av de Roma

C del Comte Borrell

C de la Diputació

C d'Entença

C d'Aragó

C del Consell de Cent

C de Viladomat

3

C de Llança

C de València

C de Rocafort

C de Calàbria

17

Parc de Joan Miró

Rocafort

See map p286

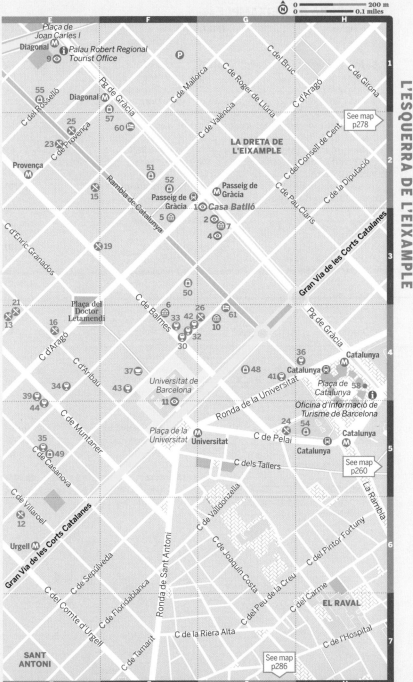

0   200 m
0   0.1 miles

Plaça de
Joan Carles I
Diagonal
9 ⊙   Palau Robert Regional
        Tourist Office

55
Diagonal

C del Rosselló

25
23
Pg de Gràcia
57
60

C de Provença
Provença

51
52
15
Rambla de Catalunya
Passeig de
Gràcia
5
19

C de Mallorca
C de Roger de Llúria
C del Bruc
C d'Aragó
C de Girona

C de València

LA DRETA DE
L'EIXAMPLE

C del Consell de Cent
C de Pau Claris
C de la Diputació

Passeig de
Gràcia
1 ⊙ Casa Batlló
2
4   7

See map
p278

50
Gran Via de les Corts Catalanes
Pg de Gràcia

21
13
16

Plaça del
Doctor
Letamendi

C de Balmes
6
33 42
32
30
26
10   61

C d'Enric Granados
C d'Aragó
C d'Aribau

34
37
43
48
41
36
Catalunya
Catalunya

Universitat de
Barcelona
11
Ronda de la Universitat
Plaça de
Catalunya
58

Oficina d'Informació de
Turisme de Barcelona

39
44
C de Muntaner
35
49
C de Casanova

Plaça de la
Universitat Universitat
C de Pelai
24
54
Catalunya
Catalunya

C dels Tallers

See map
p260

12
C de Villarroel
Urgell

La Rambla

Gran Via de les Corts Catalanes
C de Sepúlveda
C de Floridablanca
Ronda de Sant Antoni

C de Valldonzella
C de Joaquín Costa
C del Peu de la Creu
C del Pintor Fortuny
C del Carme

EL RAVAL

SANT
ANTONI
C del Comte d'Urgell
C de Tamarit
C de la Riera Alta
C de l'Hospital

See map
p286

LA DRETA DE L'EIXAMPLE *Map on p278*

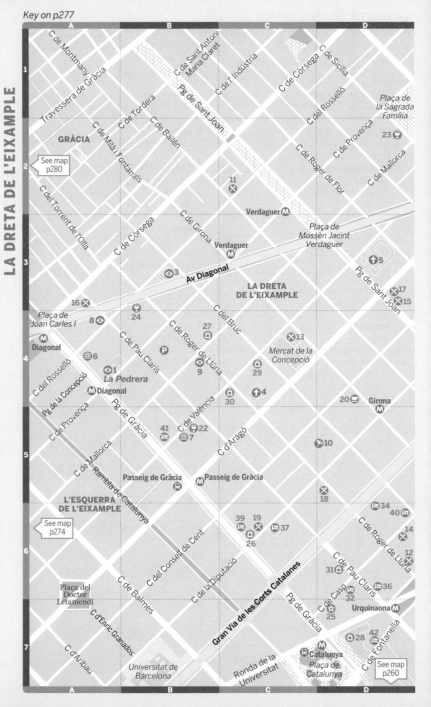

Key on p277

LA DRETA DE L'EIXAMPLE

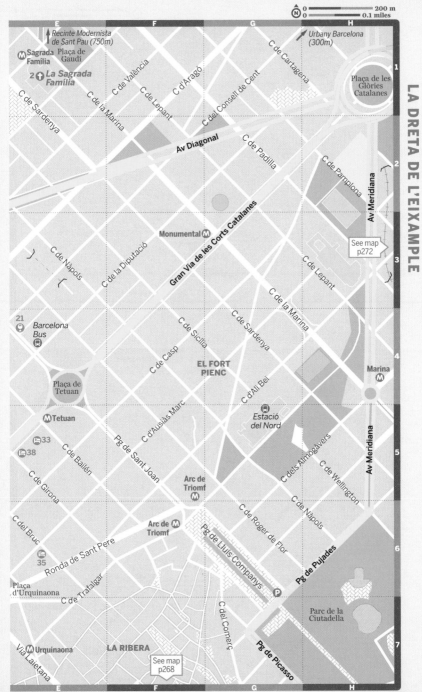

N 0 — 200 m
0 — 0.1 miles

↑ Recinte Modernista
de Sant Pau (750m)

↗ Urbany Barcelona
(300m)

Ⓜ Sagrada
Família

Plaça de
Gaudí

2 ⓘ La Sagrada
Família

C de Cartagena

Plaça de les
Glòries
Catalanes

C de València

C d'Aragó

C de la Marina

C de Lepant

C del Consell de Cent

C de Sardenya

Av Diagonal

C de Padilla

C de Pamplona

Av Meridiana

See map
p272

Monumental Ⓜ

Gran Via de les Corts Catalanes

C de Nàpols

C de la Diputació

C de Lepant

C de la Marina

C de Sardenya

21 ⓘ Barcelona
Bus

C de Sicília

C de Casp

C de Nàpols

EL FORT
PIENC

C d'Ali Bei

Marina
Ⓜ

Plaça de
Tetuan

Ⓜ Tetuan

C d'Ausiàs Marc

Estació
del Nord

🛒 33
🛒 38

C de Bailèn

Pg de Sant Joan

C de Girona

Arc de
Triomf
Ⓜ

C dels Almogàvers

C de Wellington

Av Meridiana

C de Nàpols

C del Bruc

Arc de Ⓜ
Triomf

Pg de Lluís Companys

C de Roger de Flor

Pg de Pujades

🛒 35

Ronda de Sant Pere

Plaça
d'Urquinaona

C de Trafalgar

Ⓟ

Parc de la
Ciutadella

C del Comerç

Ⓜ Urquinaona

LA RIBERA

See map
p268

Pg de Picasso

Via Laietana

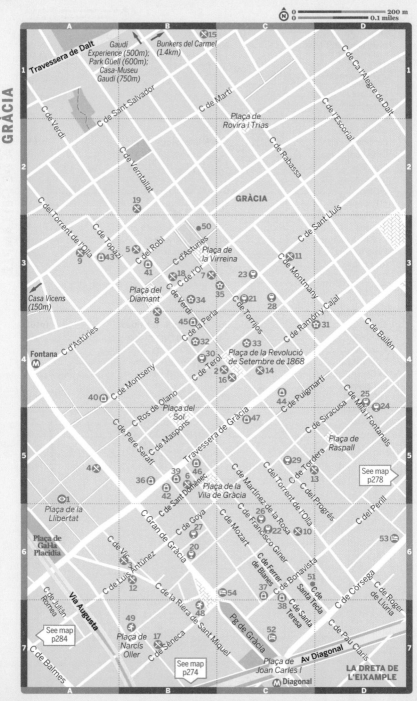

GRÀCIA

N 0 ———————— 200 m
0 ———————— 0.1 miles

Travessera de Dalt

Gaudí Experience (500m);
Park Güell (600m);
Casa-Museu Gaudí (750m)

Bunkers del Carmel (1.4km)

15

C de Verdi

C de Sant Salvador

C del Torrent de l'Olla

C de Vernallat

C de Martí

Plaça de Rovira i Trias

C de Rabassa

C de Ca l'Alegre de Dalt

C de l'Escorial

GRÀCIA

19

C de Topazi

5

C del Robí

C d'Astúries

50

Plaça de la Virreina

C de Sant Lluís

11

C de Montmany

9

43

41

18

7

23

C de l'Or

Casa Vicens (150m)

Plaça del Diamant

C de Verdi

34

35

21

28

8

45

C de la Perla

C de Torrijos

33

C de Ramón y Cajal

31

C de Ballén

Fontana

32

30

C de Terol

Plaça de la Revolució de Setembre de 1868

2

16

14

40

C de Montseny

C de Ros de Olano

Plaça del Sol

44

C de Puigmartí

C de Siracusa

25

C de Milà i Fontanals

24

Plaça de Raspall

C de Pere Serafí

C de Maspons

Travessera de Gràcia

47

See map p278

4

36

39

6

46

C de Martínez de la Rosa

29

C del Torrent de l'Olla

13

C del Progrés

C del Perill

42

C de Sant Domènec

Plaça de la Vila de Gràcia

26

C de Francisco Giner

22

10

53

Plaça de la Llibertat

1

C Gran de Gràcia

C de Goya

27

C de Mozart

C de Ferrer de Blanes

C de Bonavista

51

C de Còrsega

C de Roger de Llúria

Plaça de Gal·la Placídia

C de Vic

20

37

38

C de Santa Teresa

Santa Tecla

C de Luís Antúnez

12

C de la Riera de Sant Miquel

54

52

C de Pau Claris

Via Augusta

49

48

Pg de Gràcia

C de Julián Romea

See map p284

17

C de Sèneca

Plaça de Narcís Oller

See map p274

Plaça de Joan Carles I

Av Diagonal

LA DRETA DE L'EIXAMPLE

C de Balmes

Diagonal

GRÀCIA

LA ZONA ALTA

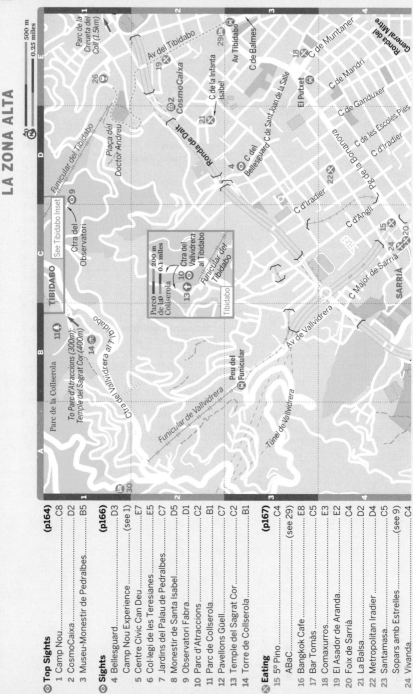

500 m
0.25 miles

200 m
0.1 miles

See Tibidabo Inset

TIBIDABO

Parc de la Creueta del Coll (1.5km)

Parc de la Collserola

To Parc d'Atraccions (300m); Temple del Sagrat Cor (400m)

Parco de la Collserola

Ctra del Vallvidrera al Tibidabo

Funicular del Tibidabo

Tibidabo

Peu del Funicular

Funicular de Vallvidrera

Túnel de Vallvidrera

Av de Vallvidrera

Plaça del Doctor Andreu

Ronda de Dalt

CosmoCaixa

Av del Tibidabo

C de la Infanta Isabel

Av Tibidabo

C de Balmes

C de Muntaner

C de Mandri

C de Ganduxer

C de les Escoles Pies

C d'Iradier

Pg de la Bonanova

C del Bellesguard

C de Sant Joan de la Salle

C d'Iradier

C d'Angli

C Major de Sarrià

SARRIÀ

Ronda del General Mitre

El Putxet

Ctra del Observatori

Ctra del Vallvidrera al Tibidabo

LA ZONA ALTA

LA ZONA ALTA EAST

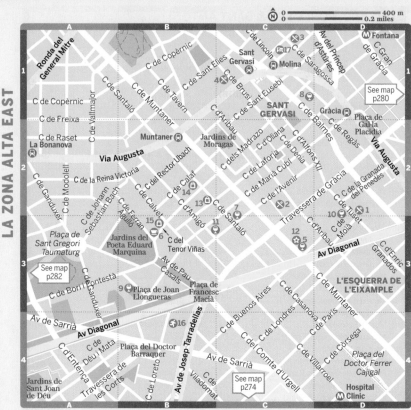

MONTJUÏC, POBLE SEC & SANT ANTONI *Map on p286*

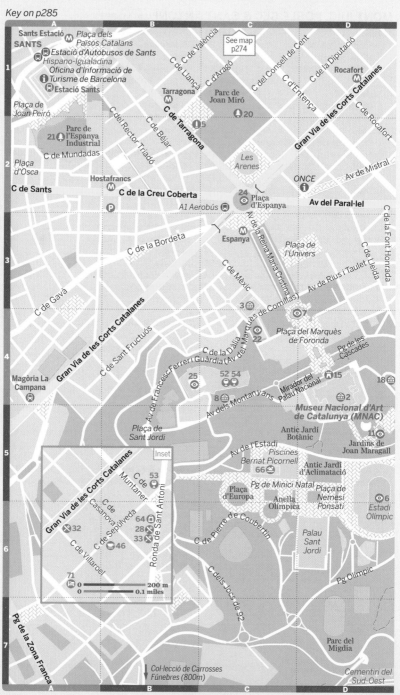

See map p274

MONTJUÏC, POBLE SEC & SANT ANTONI

Sants Estació
SANTS
Estació d'Autobusos de Sants
Hispano-Igualadina
Oficina d'Informació de
Turisme de Barcelona
Estació Sants

Plaça dels
Països Catalans

Plaça de
Joan Peiró

Parc de
l'Espanya
Industrial
C de Mundadas

Plaça
d'Osca

C de Sants

Hostafrancs

C de la Creu Coberta

A1 Aerobús

C de la Bordeta

C de Gavà

C de Sant Fructuós

Magòria La
Campana

Plaça de
Sant Jordi

C de València
C de Llançà
C d'Aragó
C del Consell de Cent
C de la Diputació
Rocafort

Tarragona
C de Tarragona
C del Rector Triadó
C de Béjar

Parc de
Joan Miró

Gran Via de les Corts Catalanes
C de Rocafort

Les
Arenes

ONCE
Av de Mistral

Plaça
d'Espanya
Av del Paral·lel

Espanya

C de Mèxic

Plaça de
l'Univers
Av de Rius i Taulet

C de Lleida
C de la Font Honrada

Av de la Reina Maria Cristina

Plaça del Marquès
de Foronda
Pg de les
Cascades

C de la Dàlia (Av del Marquès de Comillas)

Mirador del
Palau Nacional

Museu Nacional d'Art
de Catalunya (MNAC)

Antic Jardí
Botànic

Jardins de
Joan Maragall

Av de l'Estadi
Piscines
Bernat Picornell

Antic Jardí
d'Aclimatació

Pg de Minici Natal
Plaça de
Nemesí
Ponsatí

Estadi
Olímpic

Plaça
d'Europa

Anella
Olímpica

C de Pierre de Coubertin

Palau
Sant
Jordi

Pg Olímpic

C dels Jocs de 92

Parc del
Migdia

Pg de la Zona Franca

Col·lecció de Carrosses
Fúnebres (800m)

Cementiri del
Sud-Oest

Inset

Gran Via de les Corts Catalanes
C de Muntaner
C de Casanova
C de Sepúlveda
Ronda de Sant Antoni
C de Villaroel

0   200 m
0   0.1 miles

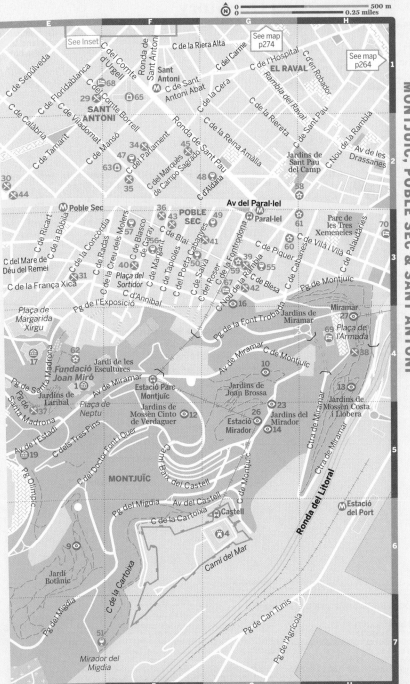

0 500 m
0 0.25 miles

See Inset

See map p274

See map p264

C de Sepúlveda
C de la Riera Alta
C del Carme
C de l'Hospital
C d'en Robador
EL RAVAL

C del Comte d'Urgell
Ronda de Sant Antoni
Sant Antoni
C de Sant Antoni Abat
C de Sant
C de la Cera
C de la Riereta
C de Sant Pau
C Nou de la Rambla
Av de les Drassanes

C de Floridablanca
68
C del Comte Borrell
65
29
SANT ANTONI
Rambla del Raval

C de Calàbria
C de Viadomar
C de la Reina Amàlia

C de Tamarit
C de Mansó
34
45
Ronda de Sant Pau
Jardins de Sant Pau del Camp
58

47
C del Parlament
C del Marquès de Campo Sagrado
48
C d'Aldana

30
63
35

44
Av del Paral·lel

Poble Sec
36
POBLE SEC
49
Paral·lel
61
Parc de les Tres Xemeneies
70

C de Ricart
C de la Bòbila
43
C de Blasco de Garay
C de Blai
41
60
C de Vilà i Vilà
C de Palaudàries

C del Mare de Déu del Remei
57
C de la Creu dels Molers
C de Margarit
C de Tapioles
50
C de la Fontrodona
39
C de Piquer
C de Cabanes
Pg de Montjuïc

31
C de la Concòrdia
C de Radas
40
Plaça del Sortidor
C del Poeta Cabanyes
C del Roser
59
C de la Rambla
55
C de Blesa

C de la França Xica
C d'Annibal
Pg de l'Exposició
67
16
42
C Nou de la Rambla

Plaça de Margarida Xirgu
Pg de la Font Trobada
Jardins de Miramar
Miramar
27
69
Plaça de l'Armada
38

17
62
Jardí de les Esculptures
Av de Miramar
C de Montjuïc
10

Fundació Joan Miró
1
Estació Parc Montjuïc
Jardins de Joan Brossa
13
Jardins de Mossèn Costa i Llobera

Jardins de Laribal
Plaça de Neptú
Jardins de Mossèn Cinto de Verdaguer
12
26
23
Jardins del Mirador
14
Ctra de Miramar

37
Pg de Santa Madrona
Pg de Santa Madrona
Estació Mirador

19
Av de l'Estadi
C dels Tres Pins
C del Doctor Font i Quer
MONTJUÏC

Pg Olímpic
Cami Baix del Castell
C de Montjuïc
Estació del Port

9
Pg del Migdia
Av del Castell
Castell
Ronda del Litoral

4
C de la Cartoixa

Jardí Botànic
Cami del Mar

C de la Cartoixa
Pg de Can Tunis
Pg de l'Agrícola

Pg del Migdia
51
Mirador del Migdia

Our Story

A beat-up old car, a few dollars in the pocket and a sense of adventure. In 1972 that's all Tony and Maureen Wheeler needed for the trip of a lifetime – across Europe and Asia over Australia. It took several months, and at the end – broke inspired – they sat at their kitchen table writing and stapling together their first travel guide, *Across Asia on the Cheap.* Within a week they'd sold 1500 copies. Lonely Planet was born.

Today, Lonely Planet has offices in Franklin, London, Melbourne, Oakland, Dublin, Beijing and Delhi, with more than 600 staff and writers. We share Tony's belief that 'a great guidebook should do three things: inform, educate and amuse'.

Our Writers

Regis St Louis

Barceloneta & the Waterfront, Gràcia & Park Güell, Camp Nou, Pedralbes & La Zona Alta, Montjuïc, Poble Sec & Sant Antoni, Day Trips

Regis fell in love with Barcelona a decade ago, after arriving in the city and being awestruck by its wild architecture, culinary creativity and warm-hearted people. Since then he has returned frequently, learning Spanish and a smattering of Catalan, and delving into the endless layers of Barcelona's deep cultural heritage. Favourite memories from his most recent trip include fêting the arrival of three bearded kings during Dia de Reis, catching a surreal circus arts show in a seaside suburb, and exploring far-flung corners of Montjuïc at sunrise. Regis is the author of the two previous editions of *Barcelona*, and he has contributed to *Spain*, *Portugal* and dozens of other Lonely Planet titles. When not on the road, he lives in New Orleans. Regis also wrote the Plan Your Trip, Drinking & Nightlife, Gay & Lesbian Barcelona, Sleeping, Understand Barcelona, Transport and Directory A–Z chapters.

Sally Davies

La Rambla & Barri Gòtic, El Raval, La Ribera, La Sagrada Família & L'Eixample

Sally landed in Seville in 1992 with a handful of pesetas and five words of Spanish, and, despite a complete inability to communicate, promptly snared a lucrative number handing out leaflets at Expo '92. In 2001 she settled in Barcelona, where she is still incredulous that her daily grind involves researching fine restaurants, wandering about museums and finding ways to convey the beauty of this spectacular city. Sally also wrote the Eating, Entertainment and Shopping chapters and co-wrote the Sleeping and Directory Directory A–Z chapters.

Published by Lonely Planet Global Limited
CRN 554153
10th edition – Nov 2016
ISBN 978 1 78657 122 9
© Lonely Planet 2016   Photographs © as indicated 2016
10 9 8 7 6 5 4 3 2 1
Printed in China